Test-Driven JavaScript Development

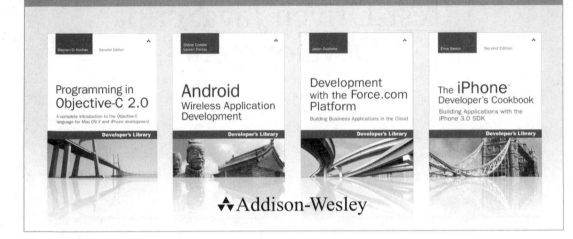

Test-Driven JavaScript Development

Christian Johansen

✦✦ Addison-Wesley

Upper Saddle River, NJ • Boston • Indianapolis • San Francisco
New York • Toronto • Montreal • London • Munich • Paris • Madrid
Capetown • Sydney • Tokyo • Singapore • Mexico City

Many of the designations used by manufacturers and sellers to distinguish their products are claimed as trademarks. Where those designations appear in this book, and the publisher was aware of a trademark claim, the designations have been printed with initial capital letters or in all capitals.

The author and publisher have taken care in the preparation of this book, but make no expressed or implied warranty of any kind and assume no responsibility for errors or omissions. No liability is assumed for incidental or consequential damages in connection with or arising out of the use of the information or programs contained herein.

The publisher offers excellent discounts on this book when ordered in quantity for bulk purchases or special sales, which may include electronic versions and/or custom covers and content particular to your business, training goals, marketing focus, and branding interests. For more information, please contact:

> U.S. Corporate and Government Sales
> (800) 382-3419
> corpsales@pearsontechgroup.com

For sales outside the United States please contact:

> International Sales
> international@pearson.com

Visit us on the Web: informit.com/aw

Library of Congress Cataloging-in-Publication Data

Johansen, Christian, 1982-
  Test-driven JavaScript development / Christian Johansen.
    p.   cm.
  Includes bibliographical references and index.
  ISBN-13: 978-0-321-68391-5 (pbk. : alk. paper)
  ISBN-10: 0-321-68391-9 (pbk. : alk. paper)
  1. JavaScript (Computer program language) I. Title.
  QA76.73.J39J64 2011
  005.13'3–dc22   2010027298

ISBN-13: 978-0-321-68391-5

ISBN-10:   0-321-68391-9

Text printed in the United States on recycled paper at RR Donnelley in Crawfordsville, Indiana.
First printing, September 2010

Acquisitions Editor
Trina MacDonald

Development Editor
Songlin Qiu

Managing Editor
John Fuller

Project Editor
Madhu Bhardwaj,
Glyph International

Project Coordinator
Elizabeth Ryan

Copy Editor
Mike Read

Indexer
Robert Swanson

Proofreader
David Daniels

Technical Reviewers
Andrea Giammarchi
Joshua Gross
Jacob Seidelin

Cover Designer
Gary Adair

Compositor
Glyph International

To Frøydis and Kristin, my special ladies.

Contents

Preface

Author's Vision for the Book

Over the recent years, JavaScript has grown up. Long gone are the glory days of "DHTML"; we are now in the age of "Ajax," possibly even "HTML5." Over the past years JavaScript gained some killer applications; it gained robust libraries to aid developers in cross-browser scripting; and it gained a host of tools such as debuggers, profilers, and unit testing frameworks. The community has worked tirelessly to bring in the tools they know and love from other languages to help give JavaScript a "real" development environment in which they can use the workflows and knowledge gained from working in other environments and focus on building quality applications.

Still, the JavaScript community at large is not particularly focused on automated testing, and test-driven development is still rare among JavaScript developers—in spite of working in the language with perhaps the widest range of target platforms. For a long time this may have been a result of lacking tool support, but new unit testing frameworks are popping up all the time, offering a myriad of ways to test your code in a manner that suits you. Even so, most web application developers skimp on testing their JavaScript. I rarely meet a web developer who has the kind of confidence to rip core functionality right out of his application and rearrange it, that a strong test suite gives you. This confidence allows you to worry less about breaking your application, and focus more on implementing new features.

With this book I hope to show you that unit testing and test-driven development in JavaScript have come a long way, and that embracing them will help you write better code and become a more productive programmer.

What This Book is About

This book is about programming JavaScript for the real world, using the techniques and workflow suggested by Test-Driven Development. It is about gaining confidence in your code through test coverage, and gaining the ability to fearlessly refactor and organically evolve your code base. It is about writing modular and testable code. It is about writing JavaScript that works in a wide variety of environments and that doesn't get in your user's way.

How This Book is Organized

This book has four parts. They may be read in any order you're comfortable with. Part II introduces a few utilities that are used throughout the book, but their usage should be clear enough, allowing you to skip that part if you already have a solid understanding of programming JavaScript, including topics such as unobtrusive JavaScript and feature detection.

Part I: Test-Driven Development

In the first part I'll introduce you to the concept of automated tests and test-driven development. We'll start by looking at what a unit test is, what it does, and what it's good for. Then we'll build our workflow around them as I introduce the test-driven development process. To round the topic off I'll show you a few available unit testing frameworks for JavaScript, discuss their pros and cons, and take a closer look at the one we'll be using the most throughout the book.

Part II: JavaScript for Programmers

In Part II we're going to get a deeper look at programming in JavaScript. This part is by no means a complete introduction to the JavaScript language. You should already either have some experience with JavaScript—perhaps by working with libraries like jQuery, Prototype, or the like—or experience from other programming languages. If you're an experienced programmer with no prior experience with JavaScript, this part should help you understand where JavaScript differs from other languages, especially less dynamic ones, and give you the foundation you'll need for the real-world scenarios in Part III.

If you're already well-versed in advanced JavaScript concepts such as closures, prototypal inheritance, the dynamic nature of this, and feature detection, you may want to skim this part for a reminder, or you may want to skip directly to Part III.

While working through some of JavaScript's finer points, I'll use unit tests to show you how the language behaves, and we'll take the opportunity to let tests drive us through the implementation of some helper utilities, which we'll use throughout Part III.

Part III: Real-World Test-Driven Development in JavaScript

In this part we'll tackle a series of small projects in varying environments. We'll see how to develop a small general purpose JavaScript API, develop a DOM dependent widget, abstract browser differences, implement a server-side JavaScript application, and more—all using test-driven development. This part focuses on how test-driven development can help in building cleaner API's, better modularized code and more robust software.

Each project introduces new test-related concepts, and shows them in practice by implementing a fully functional, yet limited piece of code. Throughout this part we will, among other things, learn how to test code that depends on browser API's, timers, event handlers, DOM manipulation, and asynchronous server requests (i.e., "Ajax"). We will also get to practice techniques such as stubbing, refactoring, and using design patterns to solve problems in elegant ways.

Throughout each chapter in this part, ideas on how to extend the functionality developed are offered, giving you the ability to practice by improving the code on your own. Extended solutions are available from the book's website.[1]

I've taken great care throughout these projects to produce runnable code that actually does things. The end result of the five chapters in Part III is a fully functional instant messaging chat client and server, written exclusively using test-driven development, in nothing but JavaScript.

Part IV: Testing Patterns

The final part of the book reviews some of the techniques used throughout Part III from a wider angle. Test doubles, such as mocks and stubs, are investigated in closer detail along with different forms of test verification. Finally, we review some guidelines to help you write good unit tests.

Conventions Used in This Book

JavaScript is the name of the language originally designed by Brendan Eich for Netscape in 1995. Since then, a number of alternative implementations have

---

1. http://tddjs.com

surfaced, and the language has been standardized by ECMA International as ECMA-262, also known as ECMAScript. Although the alternative implementations have their own names, such as Microsoft's JScript, they are generally collectively referred to as "JavaScript," and I will use JavaScript in this sense as well.

Throughout the text, monospaced font is used to refer to objects, functions, and small snippets of code.

Who Should Read This Book

This book is for programmers—especially those who write, or are interested in writing JavaScript. Whether you're a Ruby developer focusing primarily on Ruby on Rails; a Java or .Net developer working with web applications; a frontend web developer whose primary tools are JavaScript, CSS, and HTML; or even a backend developer with limited JavaScript experience, I hope and think you will find this book useful.

The book is intended for web application developers who need a firmer grasp of the finer details of the JavaScript language, as well as better understanding on how to boost their productivity and confidence while writing maintainable applications with fewer defects.

Skills Required For This Book

The reader is not required to have any previous knowledge of unit testing or test-driven development. Automated tests are present through the whole book, and reading should provide you with a strong understanding of how to successfully use them.

Equally, the reader is not required to be a JavaScript expert, or even interme-diate. My hope is that the book will be useful to programmers with very limited JavaScript experience and savvy JavaScripters alike. You are required, however, to possess some programming skills, meaning that in order to fully enjoy this book you should have experience programming in some language, and be familiar with web application development. This book is not an introductory text in any of the basic programming related topics, web application-specific topics included.

The second part of the book, which focuses on the JavaScript language, focuses solely on the qualities of JavaScript that set it apart from the pack, and as such cannot be expected to be a complete introduction to the language. It is expected that you will be able to pick up syntax and concepts not covered in this part through examples using them.

In particular, Part II focuses on JavaScript's functions and closures; JavaScript's object model, including prototypal inheritance; and models for code-reuse. Additionally, we will go through related programming practices such as unobtrusive JavaScript and feature detection, both required topics to understand for anyone targeting the general web.

About the Book's Website

The book has an accompanying website, http://tddjs.com. At this location you will find all the code listings from the book, both as zip archives and full Git repositories, which allow you to navigate the history and see how the code evolves. The Git repositories are especially useful for the Part III sample projects, where a great deal of refactoring is involved. Navigating the history of the Git repositories allows you to see each step even when they simply change existing code.

You can also find my personal website at http://cjohansen.no in which you will find additional articles, contact information, and so on. If you have any feedback regarding the book, I would love to hear back from you.

Acknowledgments

Quite a few people have made this book possible. First of all I would like to commend Trina MacDonald, my editor at Addison-Wesley, for being the one who made all of this possible. Without her, there would be no book, and I deeply appreciate her initiative as well as her ongoing help and motivation while I stumblingly worked my way through my first book.

I would also like to extend my gratitude toward the rest of the team working with me on this book; Songlin Qiu for making sure the text is comprehensible and consistent, and for keeping sane while reviewing a constantly changing manuscript. Her insights and suggestions have truly made the book better than I could ever manage on my own. The same can be said for my technical reviewers, Andrea Giammarchi, Jacob Seidelin, and Joshua Gross. Their impressive attention to detail, thoughtful feedback, and will to challenge me have helped clarify code, remove errors, and generally raise the quality of both code samples and surrounding prose, as well as the structure of the book. Last, but not least, Olivia Basego helped me cope with the administrative side of working with a publisher like Addison-Wesley and some challenges related to living in Norway while writing for an American publisher.

Closer to home, my employers and coworkers at Shortcut AS deserve an honorable mention. Their flexibility in allowing me to occasionally take time off to write and their genuine interest in the book at large have been very motivating and key to finishing the manuscript in time. In particular I would like to thank Marius Mårnes Mathiesen and August Lilleaas for frequent discussions of a truly inspiring and insightful nature, as well as feedback on early drafts.

Last, but definitely not least; Frøydis and Kristin, friends and bandmates who have given me space to complete this project and stayed patient while I've been zombie-like tired after long nights of writing, unavailable for various occasions, and generally chained to the kitchen table for months (that's right, I wrote this book in the kitchen)—thank you for your support.

Finally I would like to extend my appreciation for the open source community at large. Without it, this book would not be what it is. Open source is what ultimately got me into writing in the first place. It kept my blog alive; it crossed my path with my editor's; and now it is responsible for the book you're holding in your hands. Most of the code throughout the book would not have been possible were it not for people tirelessly putting out top-notch code for anyone to freely peruse, modify, and use.

All software involved in my part of the production of this book are open source as well. The book was written entirely in Emacs, using the document preparation system LaTeX. A host of minor open source tools have been involved in the work-flow, many of which are native citizens in my operating system of choice—GNU Linux.

When the book hits the streets, it will have brought with it at least one new open source project, and I hope I will contribute many more in the years to come.

About the Author

Christian Johansen lives in Oslo, Norway, where he currently works for Shortcut AS, a software company focusing on open source technology, web applications, and mobile applications. Originally a student in informatics, mathematics, and digital signal processing, Christian has spent his professional career specializing in web applications and frontend technologies such as JavaScript, CSS, and HTML, technologies he has been passionate about since around the time the HTML 4.01 spec was finalized.

As a consultant, Christian has worked with many high profile companies in Norway, including leading companies within the finance and telecom sector, where he has worked on small and big web applications ranging from the average CMS-backed corporate website via e-commerce to self service applications.

In later years Christian has been an avid blogger. Derived from the same desire to share and contribute to the community that gave him so much for free, Christian has involved himself in and contributed to quite a few open source projects.

After working on several projects with less than trivial amounts of JavaScript, Christian has felt the pain of developing "the cowboy style." In an attempt at improving code quality, confidence, and the ability to modify and maintain code with greater ease, he has spent a great deal of his time both at work and in his spare time over the last few years investigating unit testing and test-driven development in JavaScript. Being a sworn TDD-er while developing in traditional server-side languages, the cowboy style JavaScript approach wasn't cutting it anymore. The culmination of this passion is the book you now hold in your hands.

Part I

Test-Driven Development

Automated Testing

As web developers it is easy to find ourselves in situations where we spend unhealthy amounts of time with the refresh button in our browsers. You know the drill: type some code in your text editor, Alt+Tab to the browser, hit F5. Lather, rinse, repeat. This sort of manual testing is time-consuming, error-prone, and irreproducible. Given that our web applications are expected to run on a vast combination of browsers and platforms, testing them all manually will inevitably become an impossible task. So we focus on a few combinations and perform the occasional check-up on the broader selection. The end result is an unsatisfactory development process and possibly brittle solutions.

Over the years lots of tools have emerged to improve our lives as web developers. We now have developer tools for all the major browsers, there are several JavaScript debuggers to choose from, and even IDEs to spot typos and other mistakes. Spending some time in Firefox's Firebug plugin interacting with an application sure beats those pesky `alerts`, but we're still stuck with a manual, error-prone, and time-consuming debugging process.

Humans are lazy, programmers even more so. When manual processes slow us down, we seek to automate the manual behavior, allowing us to spend our time doing something meaningful. In fact, as web developers, our job is more often than not to automate some tedious task in order to improve business value. Online banking is a great example—instead of going to the bank, standing in line and interacting with another human to move some cash from account A to account B, we simply log in from the comfort of our couch and get the job done in a couple of minutes. Saves us time and saves the bank time.

Automated testing provides a solution to the manual testing process. Instead of filling out that form *one more time* and hitting submit to see if the client-side validations trigger as expected, we can instruct software to perform this test for us. The advantages are obvious: given a convenient way to run the automated test we can test in numerous browsers with a single effort, we can rerun the test at any later stage, and the test may even run on some schedule that requires no manual interaction whatsoever.

Automated software testing has been around for quite a while, even for JavaScript. JsUnit dates back to 2001, Selenium came along in 2004, and since then an incredible amount of tools have emerged. Still, automated testing seems to have less momentum in the JavaScript/web development community than most other programming communities. In this chapter we'll investigate one means to automate software testing, the unit test, and how it applies to the world of JavaScript.

1.1 The Unit Test

A unit test is a piece of code that tests a piece of production code. It does so by setting up one or a few more objects in a known state, exercising them (e.g., calling a method), and then inspecting the result, comparing it to the expected outcome.

Unit tests are stored on disk and should be easy and fast to run; if tests are hard or slow to run, developers are less likely to run them. Unit tests should test software components in isolation. They should also run isolated—no test should ever depend on another test, tests should be able to run simultaneously and in any order. In order to test components in isolation, it is sometimes necessary to *mock* or *stub* their dependencies. We will discuss mocking and stubbing in context in Part III, *Real-World Test-Driven Development in JavaScript* and in more detail in Chapter 16, *Mocking and Stubbing*.

Having unit tests stored on disk, and usually stored in version control along with the production code, means we can run tests at any time:

- When the implementation is complete, to verify its correct behavior
- When the implementation changes, to verify its behavior is intact
- When new units are added to the system, to verify it still fulfills its intended purpose

1.1.1 Unit Testing Frameworks

Unit tests are usually written using a unit testing framework, although that is not strictly necessary. In this chapter we'll focus on the concept of unit tests, working through the different aspects of writing and running them. We'll defer the discussion of actual testing frameworks for JavaScript to Chapter 3, *Tools of the Trade*.

It's likely that you've already written more than a few unit tests, even if you have never done any structured unit testing. Whenever you pop up a console in a browser (e.g., Firebug, Safari's Inspector or others) to debug or play live with your code, you probably issue some statements and inspect the resulting state of the involved objects. In many cases this is unit testing, only it isn't automated and it's not reproducible. We'll work through an example of this kind of testing and gradually formalize it as an *xUnit test case*.

xUnit is a common way to refer to test frameworks that are either a direct port of JUnit, or more loosely based on the ideas and concepts in it—or, more correctly, the ideas and concepts in SUnit, the Smalltalk testing framework. Kent Beck, the father of extreme programming, played an integral part in the creation of both these frameworks, and even though SUnit was the first implementation, JUnit has done the most in terms of popularizing the pattern.

1.1.2 `strftime` for JavaScript Dates

Many programming languages provide a `strftime` function or similar. It operates on a date or timestamp, accepts a format string, and produces a formatted string that represents the date. For example, in Ruby, `strftime` is available as a method on time and date objects, and Listing 1.1 shows an example of its use.

Listing 1.1 Time#strftime in Ruby

```
Time.now.strftime("Printed on %m/%d/%Y")
#=> "Printed on 09/09/2010"
```

Listing 1.2 shows an early attempt at implementing `strftime` for JavaScript. It's implemented on `Date.prototype` which makes it available as a method on all date objects. Don't despair should you find it hard to understand all the details of the code in this chapter. Concepts are more important than the actual code, and most advanced techniques will be discussed in Part II, *JavaScript for Programmers*.

Listing 1.2 Starting point for strftime for JavaScript

```
Date.prototype.strftime = (function () {
  function strftime(format) {
```

```javascript
    var date = this;

    return (format + "").replace(/%([a-zA-Z])/g,
    function (m, f) {
      var formatter = Date.formats && Date.formats[f];

      if (typeof formatter == "function") {
        return formatter.call(Date.formats, date);
      } else if (typeof formatter == "string") {
        return date.strftime(formatter);
      }

      return f;
    });
  }

  // Internal helper
  function zeroPad(num) {
    return (+num < 10 ? "0" : "") + num;
  }

  Date.formats = {
    // Formatting methods
    d: function (date) {
      return zeroPad(date.getDate());
    },

    m: function (date) {
      return zeroPad(date.getMonth() + 1);
    },

    y: function (date) {
      return date.getYear() % 100;
    },

    Y: function (date) {
      return date.getFullYear();
    },

    // Format shorthands
    F: "%Y-%m-%d",
    D: "%m/%d/%y"
  };

  return strftime;
}());
```

Date.prototype.strftime mainly consists of two parts: the replace function which takes care of replacing format specifiers with their corresponding values, and the Date.formats object which is a collection of helpers. It can be broken down as follows:

- Date.formats is an object with format specifiers as keys and methods to extract the corresponding data from a date as values
- Some format specifiers are convenient shortcuts to longer formats
- String.prototype.replace is used with a regexp that matches format specifiers
- The replacer function checks if a given specifier is available on Date.formats and uses it if it is, otherwise the specifier is left untouched (i.e., returned directly)

How would we go about testing this method? One way is to include the script in our web page and use it where we need it and then verify manually if the website displays dates correctly. If it doesn't work, we probably won't get a lot of hints as to why, and are left debugging. A slightly more sophisticated approach (although not by much) is to load it in a web page and pop open a console and play around with it. Perhaps something like the session in Listing 1.3.

Listing 1.3 Manually checking code in Firebug

```
>>> var date = new Date(2009, 11, 5);
>>> date.strftime("%Y");
"2009"
>>> date.strftime("%m");
"12"
>>> date.strftime("%d");
"05"
>>> date.strftime("%y");
"9"
```

Uh-oh. Our Firebug session indicates all is not well with our strftime. This means we'll have to investigate and rerun the test to verify that it's working. That's more manual labor. We can do better. Let's create a minimal HTML page where we load in the source script along with another script where we add some test code. This way we can inspect the result of changes without having to retype the tests. Listing 1.4 shows the HTML page that we'll use to test.

Listing 1.4 A HTML test page

```
<!DOCTYPE html PUBLIC "-//W3C//DTD HTML 4.01//EN"
           "http://www.w3.org/TR/html4/strict.dtd">
<html lang="en">
  <head>
    <title>Date.prototype.strftime test</title>
    <meta http-equiv="content-type"
          content="text/html;charset=utf-8">
  </head>
  <body>
    <script type="text/javascript" src="../src/strftime.js">
    </script>
    <script type="text/javascript" src="strftime_test.js">
    </script>
  </body>
</html>
```

We then copy our console session into a new file, shown in Listing 1.5, which will serve as the test file. To log results we'll simply use `console.log`, which is available in most modern browsers, and logs to the browser's JavaScript console.

Listing 1.5 strftime_test.js

```
var date = new Date(2009, 11, 5);
console.log(date.strftime("%Y"));
console.log(date.strftime("%m"));
console.log(date.strftime("%d"));
console.log(date.strftime("%y"));
console.log(date.strftime("%F"));
```

We now have a reproducible test case. We can then attend to the failure: `"%y"` does not zero pad the number it returns. It turns out we simply forgot to wrap the method call in a `zeroPad()` call. Listing 1.6 shows the updated `Date.formats.y` method.

Listing 1.6 Zero-pad year

```
Date.formats = {
  // ...

  y: function (date) {
    return zeroPad(date.getYear() % 100);
  }

  // ...
};
```

Now we can immediately rerun the test file in a browser and inspect the console to verify that the change fixed the "y" format specifier. In all its simplicity, we've now written a unit test. We're targeting the smallest unit possible in JavaScript—the function. You have probably done something like this many times without being aware of the fact that it is a unit test.

While automating the process of creating test objects and calling some methods on them is nice, we still need to manually check which calls are OK and which are not. For a unit test to be truly automated, it needs to be self-checking.

1.2 Assertions

At the heart of a unit test is the assertion. An assertion is a predicate that states the programmer's intended state of a system. When debugging the broken "y" format in the previous section, we carried out a manual assertion: when the strftime method is called on a date from 2009 with the format of "%y", we expect it to return the string "09". If it doesn't, our system is not working correctly. Assertions are used in unit tests to perform these checks automatically. When an assertion fails, the test is aborted and we're notified of the failure. Listing 1.7 shows a simple assert function.

Listing 1.7 A simple assert function

```
function assert(message, expr) {
  if (!expr) {
    throw new Error(message);
  }

  assert.count++;

  return true;
}

assert.count = 0;
```

The assert function simply checks that its second argument is truthy (i.e., any value except false, null, undefined, 0, "", and NaN). If it is, it increments the assertion counter, otherwise an error is thrown, using the first argument as error message. We can leverage assert in our tests from before, as seen in Listing 1.8.

Listing 1.8 Testing with assert

```
var date = new Date(2009, 9, 2);

try {
  assert("%Y should return full year",
         date.strftime("%Y") === "2009");
  assert("%m should return month",
         date.strftime("%m") === "10");
  assert("%d should return date",
         date.strftime("%d") === "02");
  assert("%y should return year as two digits",
         date.strftime("%y") === "09");
  assert("%F should act as %Y-%m-%d",
         date.strftime("%F") === "2009-10-02");

  console.log(assert.count + " tests OK");
} catch (e) {
  console.log("Test failed: " + e.message);
}
```

This requires slightly more typing, but the test now speaks for itself and is able to verify itself. The manual labor has been reduced from inspecting each and every outcome to simply inspecting the final status reported by the test.

1.2.1 Red and Green

In the world of unit testing, "red" and "green" are often used in place of "failure" and "success," respectively. Having tests go red or green makes the outcome even clearer to interpret, and demands less effort on our part. Listing 1.9 provides a simplified output function which uses the DOM to display messages in color.

Listing 1.9 Outputting messages in color

```
function output(text, color) {
  var p = document.createElement("p");
  p.innerHTML = text;
  p.style.color = color;
  document.body.appendChild(p);
}

// console.log can now be replaced with
output(assert.count + " tests OK", "#0c0");
// and, for failures:
output("Test failed: " + e.message, "#c00");
```

1.3 Test Functions, Cases, and Suites

The test we have built so far has several assertions, but because the `assert` function throws an error when a test fails, we won't know whether or not tests following a failing test fail or succeed. For more fine-grained feedback, we can organize our test into *test functions*. Each test function should exercise only one unit, but it may do so using one or more assertions. For complete control, we can also require each test to only test one specific behavior of a single unit. This means there will be many tests for each function, but they'll be short and easy to understand, and the test as a whole will provide to-the-point feedback.

A set of related test functions/methods is referred to as a test case. In the case of the `strftime` function, we can imagine a test case for the whole method, with each test testing a specific behavior of the function through one or more assertions. Test cases are usually organized in test suites in more complex systems. Listing 1.10 shows a very simple `testCase` function. It accepts a string name and an object with test methods. Every property whose name starts with the word "test" is run as a test method.

Listing 1.10 A simple `testCase` function

```
function testCase(name, tests) {
  assert.count = 0;
  var successful = 0;
  var testCount = 0;

  for (var test in tests) {
    if (!/^test/.test(test)) {
      continue;
    }

    testCount++;

    try {
      tests[test]();
      output(test, "#0c0");
      successful++;
    } catch (e) {
      output(test + " failed: " + e.message, "#c00");
    }
  }

  var color = successful == testCount ? "#0c0" : "#c00";
```

```
output("<strong>" + testCount + " tests, " +
       (testCount - successful) + " failures</strong>",
       color);
}
```

Listing 1.11 uses `testCase` to restructure the `strftime` test into a test case.

Listing 1.11 strftime test case

```
var date = new Date(2009, 9, 2);

testCase("strftime test", {
  "test format specifier %Y": function () {
    assert("%Y should return full year",
           date.strftime("%Y") === "2009");
  },

  "test format specifier %m": function () {
    assert("%m should return month",
           date.strftime("%m") === "10");
  },

  "test format specifier %d": function () {
    assert("%d should return date",
           date.strftime("%d") === "02");
  },

  "test format specifier %y": function () {
    assert("%y should return year as two digits",
           date.strftime("%y") === "09");
  },

  "test format shorthand %F": function () {
    assert("%F should act as %Y-%m-%d",
           date.strftime("%F") === "2009-10-02");
  }
});
```

The tests have so far been distinct and simple enough that we end up with one assertion in each test. The test case now groups all the tests into a single object, but the date object is still being created outside, which is unnatural as it's an integral part of the test. We could create a new object inside each test, but since we can create it the same way for all of them, that would lead to unnecessary duplication. A better option would be to gather common setup code in a single place.

1.3.1 Setup and Teardown

xUnit frameworks usually provide `setUp` and `tearDown` methods. These are called before and after each test method respectively, and allow for centralized setup of test data, also known as test fixtures. Let's add the date object as a test fixture using the `setUp` method. Listing 1.12 shows the augmented `testCase` function that checks if the test case has `setUp` and `tearDown`, and if so, runs them at the appropriate times.

Listing 1.12 Implementing `setUp` and `tearDown` in `testCase`

```
function testCase(name, tests) {
  assert.count = 0;
  var successful = 0;
  var testCount = 0;
  var hasSetup = typeof tests.setUp == "function";
  var hasTeardown = typeof tests.tearDown == "function";

  for (var test in tests) {
    if (!/^test/.test(test)) {
      continue;
    }

    testCount++;

    try {
      if (hasSetup) {
        tests.setUp();
      }

      tests[test]();
      output(test, "#0c0");

      if (hasTeardown) {
        tests.tearDown();
      }

      // If the tearDown method throws an error, it is
      // considered a test failure, so we don't count
      // success until all methods have run successfully
      successful++;
    } catch (e) {
      output(test + " failed: " + e.message, "#c00");
    }
  }
}
```

```
    var color = successful == testCount ? "#0c0" : "#c00";

    output("<strong>" + testCount + " tests, " +
           (testCount - successful) + " failures</strong>",
           color);
}
```

Using the new `setUp` method, we can add an object property to hold the test fixture, as shown in Listing 1.13

Listing 1.13 Using `setUp` in the `strftime` test case

```
testCase("strftime test", {
  setUp: function () {
    this.date = new Date(2009, 9, 2, 22, 14, 45);
  },

  "test format specifier Y": function () {
    assert("%Y should return full year",
           this.date.strftime("%Y") == 2009);
  },

  // ...
});
```

1.4 Integration Tests

Consider a car manufacturer assembly line. Unit testing corresponds to verifying each individual part of the car: the steering wheel, wheels, electric windows, and so on. Integration testing corresponds to verifying that the resulting car works as a whole, or that smaller groups of units behave as expected, e.g., making sure the wheels turn when the steering wheel is rotated. Integration tests test the sum of its parts. Ideally those parts are unit tested and known to work correctly in isolation.

Although high-level integration tests may require more capable tools, such as software to automate the browser, it is quite possible to write many kinds of integration tests using a xUnit framework. In its simplest form, an integration test is a test that exercises two or more individual components. In fact, the simplest integration tests are so close to unit tests that they are often mistaken for unit tests.

In Listing 1.6 we fixed the "y" format specifier by zero padding the result of calling `date.getYear()`. This means that we passed a unit test for `Date.prototype.strftime` by correcting `Date.formats.y`. Had the latter been a private/inner helper function, it would have been an implementation

detail of `strftime`, which would make that function the correct entry point to
test the behavior. However, because `Date.formats.y` is a publicly available
method, it should be considered a unit in its own right, which means that the aforementioned test probably should have exercised it directly. To make this distinction
clearer, Listing 1.14 adds another format method, `j`, which calculates the day of the
year for a given date.

Listing 1.14 Calculating the day of the year

```
Date.formats = {
  // ...

  j: function (date) {
    var jan1 = new Date(date.getFullYear(), 0, 1);
    var diff = date.getTime() - jan1.getTime();

    // 86400000 == 60 * 60 * 24 * 1000
    return Math.ceil(diff / 86400000);
  },

  // ...
};
```

The `Date.formats.j` method is slightly more complicated than the previous
formatting methods. How should we test it? Writing a test that asserts on the
result of `new Date().strftime("%j")` would hardly constitute a unit test
for `Date.formats.j`. In fact, following the previous definition of integration
tests, this sure looks like one: we're testing both the `strftime` method as well as
the specific formatting. A better approach is to test the format specifiers directly,
and then test the replacing logic of `strftime` in isolation.

Listing 1.15 shows the tests targeting the methods they're intended to test
directly, avoiding the "accidental integration test."

Listing 1.15 Testing format specifiers directly

```
testCase("strftime test", {
  setUp: function () {
    this.date = new Date(2009, 9, 2, 22, 14, 45);
  },

  "test format specifier %Y": function () {
    assert("%Y should return full year",
           Date.formats.Y(this.date) === 2009);
  },
```

```
  "test format specifier %m": function () {
    assert("%m should return month",
           Date.formats.m(this.date) === "10");
  },

  "test format specifier %d": function () {
    assert("%d should return date",
           Date.formats.d(this.date) === "02");
  },

  "test format specifier %y": function () {
    assert("%y should return year as two digits",
           Date.formats.y(this.date) === "09");
  },

  "test format shorthand %F": function () {
    assert("%F should be shortcut for %Y-%m-%d",
           Date.formats.F === "%Y-%m-%d");
  }
});
```

1.5 Benefits of Unit Tests

Writing tests is an investment. The most common objection to unit testing is that it takes too much time. Of course testing your application takes time. But the alternative to automated testing is usually not to avoid testing your application completely. In the absence of tests, developers are left with a manual testing process, which is highly inefficient: we write the same throwaway tests over and over again, and we rarely rigorously test our code unless it's shown to not work, or we otherwise expect it to have defects. Automated testing allows us to write a test once and run it as many times as we wish.

1.5.1 Regression Testing

Sometimes we make mistakes in our code. Those mistakes might lead to bugs that sometimes find their way into production. Even worse, sometimes we fix a bug but later have that same bug creep back out in production. Regression testing helps us avoid this. By "trapping" a bug in a test, our test suite will notify us if the bug ever makes a reappearance. Because automated tests are automated and reproducible, we can run all our tests prior to pushing code into production to make sure that past mistakes stay in the past. As a system grows in size and complexity, manual regression testing quickly turns into an impossible feat.

1.5.2 Refactoring

To refactor code is to change its implementation while leaving its behavior intact. As with unit tests, you have likely done it whether you called it refactoring or not. If you ever extracted a helper method from one method to reuse it in other methods, you have done refactoring. Renaming objects and functions is refactoring. Refactoring is vital to growing your application while preserving a good design, keeping it DRY (Don't Repeat Yourself) and being apt to adopt changing requirements.

The failure points in refactoring are many. If you're renaming a method, you need to be sure all references to that method have changed. If you're copy-pasting some code from a method into a shared helper, you need to pay attention to such details as any local variables used in the original implementation.

In his book *Refactoring: Improving the Design of Existing Code* [1], Martin Fowler describes the first step while refactoring the following way: "Build a solid set of tests for the section of code to be changed." Without tests you have no reliable metric that can tell you whether or not the refactoring was successful, and that new bugs weren't introduced. In the undying words of Hamlet D'Arcy, "don't touch anything that doesn't have coverage. Otherwise, you're not refactoring; you're just changing shit."[2]

1.5.3 Cross-Browser Testing

As web developers we develop code that is expected to run on a vast combination of platforms and user agents. Leveraging unit tests, we can greatly reduce the required effort to verify that our code works in different environments.

Take our example of the `strftime` method. Testing it the ad hoc way involves firing up a bunch of browsers, visiting a web page that uses the method and manually verifying that the dates are displayed correctly. If we want to test closer to the code in question, we might bring up the browser console as we did in Section 1.1, *The Unit Test*, and perform some tests on the fly. Testing `strftime` using unit tests simply requires us to run the unit test we already wrote in all the target environments. Given a clever *test runner* with a bunch of user agents readily awaiting our tests, this might be as simple as issuing a single command in a shell or hitting a button in our integrated development environment (IDE).

1.5.4 Other Benefits

Well-written tests serve as good documentation of the underlying interfaces. Short and focused unit tests can help new developers quickly get to know the system being developed by perusing the tests. This point is reinforced by the fact that unit tests also help us write cleaner interfaces, because the tests force us to use the interfaces as we write them, providing us with shorter feedback loops. As we'll see in Chapter 2, *The Test-Driven Development Process*, one of the strongest benefits of unit tests is their use as a design tool.

1.6 Pitfalls of Unit Testing

Writing unit tests is not always easy. In particular, writing good unit tests takes practice, and can be challenging. The benefits listed in Section 1.5, *Benefits of Unit Tests* all assume that unit tests are implemented following best practices. If you write bad unit tests, you might find that you gain none of the benefits, and instead are stuck with a bunch of tests that are time-consuming and hard to maintain.

In order to write truly great unit tests, the code you're testing needs to be *testable*. If you ever find yourself retrofitting a test suite onto an existing application that was not written with testing in mind, you'll invariably discover that parts of the application will be challenging, if not impossible, to test. As it turns out, testing units in isolation helps expose too tightly coupled code and promotes separation of concerns.

Throughout this book I will show you, through examples, characteristics of testable code and good unit tests that allow you to harness the benefits of unit testing and test-driven development.

1.7 Summary

In this chapter we have seen the similarities between some of the ad hoc testing we perform in browser consoles and structured, reproducible unit tests. We've gotten to know the most important parts of the xUnit testing frameworks: test cases, test methods, assertions, test fixtures, and how to run them through a test runner. We implemented a crude proof of concept xUnit framework to test the initial attempt at a `strftime` implementation for JavaScript.

Integration tests were also dealt with briefly in this chapter, specifically how we can realize them using said xUnit frameworks. We also looked into how integration tests and unit tests often can get mixed up, and how we usually can tell them apart by looking at whether or not they test isolated components of the application.

When looking at benefits of unit testing we see how unit testing is an investment, how tests save us time in the long run, and how they help execute regression tests. Additionally, refactoring is hard, if not impossible, to do reliably without tests.

Writing tests before refactoring greatly reduces the risk, and those same tests can make cross-browser testing considerably easier.

In Chapter 2, *The Test-Driven Development Process*, we'll continue our exploration of unit tests. We'll focus on benefits not discussed in this chapter: unit tests as a design tool, and using unit tests as the primary driver for writing new code.

The Test-Driven Development Process

In Chapter 1, *Automated Testing,* we were introduced to the unit test, and learned how it can help reduce the number of defects, catch regressions, and increase developer productivity by reducing the need to manually test and tinker with code. In this chapter we are going to turn our focus from *testing* to *specification* as we delve into test-driven development. Test-driven development (TDD) is a programming technique that moves unit tests to the front row, making them the primary entry point to production code. In test-driven development tests are written as specification before writing production code. This practice has a host of benefits, including better testability, cleaner interfaces, and improved developer confidence.

2.1 Goal and Purpose of Test-Driven Development

In his book, *Test-Driven Development By Example*[3], Kent Beck states that the goal of test-driven development is *Clean code that works.* TDD is an iterative development process in which each iteration starts by writing a test that forms a part of the specification we are implementing. The short iterations allow for more instant feedback on the code we are writing, and bad design decisions are easier to catch. By writing the tests before any production code, good unit test coverage comes with the territory, but that is merely a welcome side effect.

2.1.1 Turning Development Upside-Down

In traditional programming problems are solved by programming until a concept is fully represented in code. Ideally, the code follows some overall architectural design considerations, although in many cases, perhaps especially in the world of JavaScript, this is not the case. This style of programming solves problems by guessing at what code is required to solve them, a strategy that can easily lead to bloated and tightly coupled solutions. If there are no unit tests as well, solutions produced with this approach may even contain code that is never executed, such as error handling logic, and edge cases may not have been thoroughly tested, if tested at all.

Test-driven development turns the development cycle upside-down. Rather than focusing on what code is required to solve a problem, test-driven development starts by defining the goal. Unit tests form both the specification *and* documentation for what actions are supported and accounted for. Granted, the goal of TDD is not testing and so there is no guarantee that it handles edge cases better. However, because each line of code is tested by a representative piece of sample code, TDD is likely to produce less excessive code, and the functionality that is accounted for is likely to be more robust. Proper test-driven development ensures that a system will never contain code that is not being executed.

2.1.2 Design in Test-Driven Development

In test-driven development there is no "Big Design Up Front," but do not mistake that for "no design up front." In order to write clean code that is able to scale across the duration of a project and its lifetime beyond, we need to have a plan. TDD will not automatically make great designs appear out of nowhere, but it will help evolve designs as we go. By relying on unit tests, the TDD process focuses heavily on individual components in isolation. This focus goes a long way in helping to write decoupled code, honor the single responsibility principle, and to avoid unnecessary bloat. The tight control over the development process provided by TDD allows for many design decisions to be deferred until they are actually needed. This makes it easier to cope with changing requirements, because we rarely design features that are not needed after all, or never needed as initially expected.

Test-driven development also forces us to deal with design. Anytime a new feature is up for addition, we start by formulating a reasonable use case in the form of a unit test. Writing the unit test requires a mental exercise—we must describe the problem we are trying to solve. Only when we have done that can we actually start coding. In other words, TDD requires us to think about the results before providing the solution. We will investigate what kind of benefits we can reap from this process in Section 2.4, *Benefits of Test-Driven Development,* once we have gotten to know the process itself better.

2.2 The Process

The test-driven development process is an iterative process where each iteration consists of the following four steps:

- Write a test
- Run tests; watch the new test fail
- Make the test pass
- Refactor to remove duplication

In each iteration the test is the specification. Once enough production code has been written to make the test pass, we are done, and we may refactor the code to remove duplication and/or improve the design, as long as the tests still pass.

Even though there is no Big Design Up Front when doing TDD, we must invest time in *some* design before launching a TDD session. Design will not appear out of nowhere, and without any up front design at all, how will you even know how to write the first test? Once we have gathered enough knowledge to formulate a test, writing the test itself is an act of design. We are specifying how a certain piece of code needs to behave in certain circumstances, how responsibility is delegated between components of the system, and how they will integrate with each other. Throughout this book we will work through several examples of test-driven code in practice, seeing some examples on what kind of up front investment is required in different scenarios.

The iterations in TDD are short, typically only a few minutes, if that. It is important to stay focused and keep in mind what phase we are in. Whenever we spot something in the code that needs to change, or some feature that is missing, we make a note of it and finish the iteration before dealing with it. Many developers, including myself, keep a simple to do list for those kind of observations. Before starting a new iteration, we pick a task from the to do list. The to do list may be a simple sheet of paper, or something digital. It doesn't really matter; the important thing is that new items can be quickly and painlessly added. Personally, I use Emacs org-mode to keep to do files for all of my projects. This makes sense because I spend my entire day working in Emacs, and accessing the to do list is a simple key binding away. An entry in the to do list may be something small, such as "throw an error for missing arguments," or something more complex that can be broken down into several tests later.

2.2.1 Step 1: Write a Test

The first formal step of a test-driven development iteration is picking a feature to implement, and writing a unit test for it. As we discussed in Chapter 1, *Automated Testing*, a good unit test should be short and focus on a single behavior of a function/method. A good rule of thumb to writing single behavior tests is to add as little code as necessary to fail the test. Also, the new test should never duplicate assertions that have already been found to work. If a test is exercising two or more aspects of the system, we have either added more than the necessary amount of code to fail it, or it is testing something that has already been tested.

Beware of tests that make assumptions on, or state expectations about the implementation. Tests should describe the interface of whatever it is we are implementing, and it should not be necessary to change them unless the interface itself changes.

Assume we are implementing a `String.prototype.trim` method, i.e., a method available on string objects that remove leading and trailing white-space. A good first test for such a method could be to assert that leading white space is removed, as shown in Listing 2.1.

Listing 2.1 Initial test for `String.prototype.trim`

```
testCase("String trim test", {
  "test trim should remove leading white-space":
  function () {
    assert("should remove leading white-space",
           "a string" === "   a string".trim());
  }
});
```

Being pedantic about it, we could start even smaller by writing a test to ensure strings have a `trim` method to begin with. This may seem silly, but given that we are adding a global method (by altering a global object), there is a chance of conflicts with third party code, and starting by asserting that `typeof "".trim == "function"` will help us discover any problems when we run the test before passing it.

Unit tests test that our code behaves in expected ways by feeding them known input and asserting that the output is what we expect. "Input" in this sense is not merely function arguments. Anything the function in question relies on, including the global scope, certain state of certain objects, and so on constitute input. Likewise, output is the sum of return values and changes in the global scope or surrounding objects. Often input and output are divided into direct inputs and outputs, i.e., function arguments and return value, and indirect inputs and outputs, i.e., any object not passed as arguments or modifications to outside objects.

2.2.2 Step 2: Watch the Test Fail

As soon as the test is ready, we run it. Knowing it's going to fail may make this step feel redundant. After all, we wrote it specifically to fail, didn't we? There are a number of reasons to run the test before writing the passing code. The most important reason is that it allows us to confirm our theories about the current state of our code. While writing the test, there should be a clear expectation on *how* the test is going to fail. Unit tests are code too, and just like other code it may contain bugs. However, because unit tests should never contain branching logic, and rarely contain anything other than a few lines of simple statements, bugs are less likely, but they still occur. Running the test with an expectation on what is going to happen greatly increases the chance of catching bugs in the tests themselves.

Ideally, running the tests should be fast enough to allow us to run `all` the tests each time we add a new one. Doing this makes it easier to catch interfering tests, i.e., where one test depends on the presence of another test, or fails in the presence of another test.

Running the test before writing the passing code may also teach us something new about the code we are writing. In some cases we may experience that a test passes before we have written any code at all. Normally, this should not happen, because TDD only instructs us to add tests we expect to fail, but nevertheless, it may occur. A test may pass because we added a test for a requirement that is implicitly supported by our implementation, for instance, due to type coercion. When this happens we can remove the test, or keep it in as a stated requirement. It is also possible that a test will pass because the current environment already supports whatever it is we are trying to add. Had we run the `String.prototype.trim` method test in Firefox, we would discover that Firefox (as well as other browsers) already support this method, prompting us to implement the method in a way that preserves the native implementation when it exists.[1] Such a discovery is a good to do list candidate. Right now we are in the process of adding the `trim` method. We will make a note that a new requirement is to preserve native implementations where they exist.

---

1. In fact, ECMAScript 5, the latest edition of the specification behind JavaScript, codifies String. prototype.trim, so we can expect it to be available in all browsers in the not-so-distant future.

2.2.3 Step 3: Make the Test Pass

Once we have confirmed that the test fails, and that it fails in the expected way, we have work to do. At this point test-driven development instructs us to provide *the simplest solution that could possibly work*. In other words, our only goal is to make the tests green, by any means necessary, occasionally even by hard-coding. No matter how messy a solution we provide in this step, refactoring and subsequent steps will help us sort it out eventually. Don't fear hard-coding. There is a certain rhythm to the test-driven development process, and the power of getting through an iteration even though the provided solution is not perfect *at the moment* should not be underestimated. Usually we make a quick judgement call: is there an obvious implementation? If there is, go with it; if there isn't, fake it, and further steps will gradually make the implementation obvious. Deferring the real solution may also provide enough insight to help solve the problem in a better way at a later point.

If there is an obvious solution to a test, we can go ahead and implement it. But we must remember to only add enough code to make the test pass, even when we feel that the greater picture is just as obvious. These are the "insights" I was talking about in Section 2.2, *The Process,* and we should make a note of it and add it in another iteration. Adding more code means adding behavior, and added behavior should be represented by added requirements. If a piece of code cannot be backed up by a clear requirement, it's nothing more than bloat, bloat that will cost us by making code harder to read, harder to maintain, and harder to keep stable.

2.2.3.1 You Ain't Gonna Need It

In extreme programming, the software development methodology from which test-driven development stems, "you ain't gonna need it," or YAGNI for short, is the principle that we should not add functionality until it is necessary [4]. Adding code under the assumption that it will do us good some day is adding bloat to the code base without a clear use case demonstrating the need for it. In a dynamic language such as JavaScript, it is especially tempting to violate this principle in the face of added flexibility. One example of a YAGNI violation I personally have committed more than once is to be overly flexible on method arguments. Just because a JavaScript function can accept a variable amount of arguments of any type does not mean every function should cater for any combination of arguments possible. Until there is a test that demonstrates a reasonable use for the added code, don't add it. At best, we can write down such ideas on the to do list, and prioritize it before launching a new iteration.

2.2.3.2 Passing the Test for `String.prototype.trim`

As an example of *the simplest solution that could possibly work,* Listing 2.2 shows the sufficient amount of code to pass the test in Listing 2.1. It caters only to the case stated in that original test, leaving the rest of the requirements for following iterations.

Listing 2.2 Providing a `String.prototype.trim` method

```
String.prototype.trim = function () {
  return this.replace(/^\s+/, "");
};
```

The keen reader will probably spot several shortcomings in this method, including overwriting native implementations and only trimming left side white space. Once we are more confident in the process and the code we are writing, we can take bigger steps, but it's comforting to know that test-driven development allows for such small steps. Small steps can be an incredible boon when treading unfamiliar ground, when working with error prone methods, or when dealing with code that is highly unstable across browsers.

2.2.3.3 The Simplest Solution that Could Possibly Work

The simplest solution that could possibly work will sometimes be to hard-code values into production code. In cases where the generalized implementation is not immediately obvious, this can help move on quickly. However, for each test we should come up with some production code that signifies progress. In other words, although the simplest solution that could possibly work will sometimes be hardcoding values once, twice and maybe even three times, simply hard-coding a locked set of input/output does not signify progress. Hard-coding can form useful scaffolding to move on quickly, but the goal is to efficiently produce quality code, so generalizations are unavoidable.

The fact that TDD says it is OK to hard-code is something that worries a lot of developers unfamiliar with the technique. This should not at all be alarming so long as the technique is fully understood. TDD does not tell us to ship hard-coded solutions, but it allows them as an intermediary solution to keep the pace rather than spending too much time forcing a more generalized solution when we can see none. While reviewing the progress so far and performing refactoring, better solutions may jump out at us. When they don't, adding more use cases usually helps us pick up an underlying pattern. We will see examples of using hard coded solutions to keep up the pace in Part III, *Real-World Test-Driven Development in JavaScript.*

2.2.4 Step 4: Refactor to Remove Duplication

The last phase is the most important one in the interest of writing *clean* code. When enough code has been written to pass all the tests, it's time to review the work so far and make necessary adjustments to remove duplication and improve design. There is only one rule to obey during this phase: tests should stay green. Some good advice when refactoring code is to never perform more than one operation at a time, and make sure that the tests stay green between each operation. Remember, refactoring is changing the implementation while maintaining the same interface, so there is no need to fail tests at this point (unless we make mistakes, of course, in which case tests are especially valuable).

Duplication can occur in any number of places. The most obvious place to look is in the production code. Often, duplication is what helps us generalize from hard-coded solutions. If we start an implementation by faking it and hard-coding a response, the natural next step is to add another test, with different input, that fails in the face of the hard-coded response. If doing so does not immediately prompt us to generalize the solution, adding another hard-coded response will make the duplication obvious. The hard-coded responses may provide enough of a pattern to generalize it and extract a real solution.

Duplication can also appear inside tests, especially in the setup of the required objects to carry out the test, or faking its dependencies. Duplication is no more attractive in tests than it is in production code, and it represents a too tight coupling to the system under test. If the tests and the system are too tightly coupled, we can extract helper methods or perform other refactorings as necessary to keep duplication away. Setup and teardown methods can help centralize object creation and destruction. Tests are code, too, and need maintenance as well. Make sure maintaining them is as cheap and enjoyable as possible.

Sometimes a design can be improved by refactoring the interface itself. Doing so will often require bigger changes, both in production and test code, and running the tests between each step is of utmost importance. As long as duplication is dealt with swiftly throughout the process, changing interfaces should not cause too much of a domino effect in either your code or tests.

We should never leave the refactoring phase with failing tests. If we cannot accomplish a refactoring without adding more code to support it (i.e., we want to split a method in two, but the current solution does not completely overlap the functionality of both the two new methods), we should consider putting it off until we have run through enough iterations to support the required functionality, and then refactor.

2.2.5 Lather, Rinse, Repeat

Once refactoring is completed, and there is no more duplication to remove or improvements to be made to design, we are done. Pick a new task off the to do list and repeat the process. Repeat as many times as necessary. As you grow confident in the process and the code, you may want to start taking bigger steps, but keep in mind that you want to have short cycles in order to keep the frequent feedback. Taking too big steps lessens the value of the process because you will hit many of the problems we are trying to avoid, such as hard to trace bugs and manual debugging. When you are done for the day, leave one test failing so you know where to pick up the next day.

When there are no more tests to write, the implementation is done—it fulfills all its requirements. At this point we might want to write some more tests, this time focusing on improving test coverage. Test-driven development by nature will ensure that every line of code is tested, but it does not necessarily yield a sufficiently strong test suite. When all requirements are met, we can typically work on tests that further tests edge cases, more types of input, and most importantly, we can write integration tests between the newly written component and any dependencies that have been faked during development.

The string `trim` method has so far only been proven to remove leading white space. The next step in the test-driven development process for this method would be to test that trailing white space is being trimmed, as shown in Listing 2.3.

Listing 2.3 Second test for `String.prototype.trim`

```
"test trim should remove trailing white-space":
function () {
  assert("should remove trailing white-space",
         "a string" === "a string   ".trim());
}
```

Now it's your turn; go ahead and complete this step by running the test, making necessary changes to the code and finally looking for refactoring possibilities in either the code or the test.

2.3 Facilitating Test-Driven Development

The most crucial aspect of test-driven development is running tests. The tests need to run fast, and they need to be easy to run. If this is not the case, developers start to skip running tests every now and then, quickly adding some features not tested for, and generally making a mess of the process. This is the worst kind of situation to be in—investing extra time in test-driven development, but because it is not being done right we cannot really trust the outcome the way we are supposed to, and in the worst case we will end up spending more time writing worse code. Smoothly running tests are key.

The recommended approach is to run some form of *autotest*. Autotesting means that tests are run every single time a file is saved. A small discrete indicator light can tell us if tests are green, currently running, or red. Given that big monitors are common these days, you may even allocate some screen real-estate for a permanent test output window. This way we can speed up the process even more because we are not actively running the tests. Running the tests is more of a job for the environment; we only need to be involved when results are in. Keep in mind though that we still need to inspect the results when tests are failing. However, as long as the tests are green, we are free to hack voraciously away. Autotesting can be used this way to speed up refactoring, in which we aren't expecting tests to fail (unless mistakes are made). We'll discuss autotesting for both IDEs and the command line in Chapter 3, *Tools of the Trade.*

2.4 Benefits of Test-Driven Development

In the introduction to this chapter we touched on some of the benefits that test-driven development facilitates. In this section we will rehash some of them and touch on a few others as well.

2.4.1 Code that Works

The strongest benefit of TDD is that it produces code that works. A basic line-by-line unit test coverage goes a long way in ensuring the stability of a piece of code. Reproducible unit tests are particularly useful in JavaScript, in which we might need to test code on a wide range of browser/platform combinations. Because the tests are written to address only a single concern at a time, bugs should be easy to discover using the test suite, because the failing tests will point out which parts of the code are not working.

2.4.2 Honoring the Single Responsibility Principle

Describing and developing specialized components in isolation makes it a lot easier to write code that is loosely coupled and that honors the single responsibility principle. Unit tests written in TDD should never test a component's dependencies, which means they must be possible to replace with fakes. Additionally, the test suite serves as an additional client to any code in addition to the application as a whole. Serving two clients makes it easier to spot tight coupling than writing for only a single use case.

2.4.3 Forcing Conscious Development

Because each iteration starts by writing a test that describes a particular behavior, test-driven development forces us to *think* about our code before writing it. Thinking about a problem before trying to solve it greatly increases the chances of producing a solid solution. Starting each feature by describing it through a representative use case also tends to keep the code smaller. There is less chance of introducing features that no one needs when we start from real examples of code use. Remember, YAGNI!

2.4.4 Productivity Boost

If test-driven development is new to you, all the tests and steps may seem like they require a lot of your time. I won't pretend TDD is easy from the get go. Writing good unit tests takes practice. Throughout this book you will see enough examples to catch some patterns of good unit tests, and if you code along with them and solve the exercises given in Part III, *Real-World Test-Driven Development in JavaScript,* you will gain a good foundation to start your own TDD projects. When you are in the habit of TDD, it will improve your productivity. You will probably spend a little more time in your editor writing tests and code, but you will also spend considerably less time in a browser hammering the F5 key. On top of that, you will produce code that can be proven to work, and covered by tests, refactoring will no longer be a scary feat. You will work faster, with less stress, and with more happiness.

2.5 Summary

In this chapter we have familiarized ourselves with Test-Driven Development, the iterative programming technique borrowed from Extreme Programming. We have walked through each step of each iteration: writing tests to specify a new behavior in the system, running it to confirm that it fails in the expected way, writing just enough code to pass the test, and then finally aggressively refactoring to remove duplication and improve design. Test-driven development is a technique designed to help produce clean code we can feel more confident in, and it will very likely reduce stress levels as well help you enjoy coding a lot more. In Chapter 3, *Tools of the Trade,* we will take a closer look at some of the testing frameworks that are available for JavaScript.

Tools of the Trade

In Chapter 1, *Automated Testing,* we developed a very simple `testCase` function, capable of running basic unit tests with test case setup and teardown methods. Although rolling our own test framework is a great exercise, there are many frameworks already available for JavaScript and this chapter explores a few of them.

In this chapter we will take a look at "the tools of the trade"—essential and useful tools to support a test-driven workflow. The most important tool is of course the testing framework, and after an overview of available frameworks, we will spend some time setting up and running JsTestDriver, the testing framework used for most of this book's example code. In addition to a testing framework, this chapter looks at tools such as coverage reports and continuous integration.

3.1 xUnit Test Frameworks

In Chapter 1, *Automated Testing,* we coined *xUnit* as the term used to describe testing frameworks that lean on the design of Java's JUnit and Smalltalk's SUnit, originally designed by Kent Beck. The xUnit family of test frameworks is still the most prevalent way of writing automated tests for code, even though the past few years have seen a rise in usage for so-called *behavior-driven development* (or BDD) testing frameworks.

3.1.1 Behavior-Driven Development

Behavior-driven development, or BDD, is closely related to TDD. As discussed in Chapter 2, *The Test-Driven Development Process,* TDD is *not* about testing, but rather about design and process. However, due to the terminology used to describe the process, a lot of developers never evolve beyond the point where they simply write unit tests to verify their code, and thus never experience many of the advantages associated with using tests as a design tool. BDD seeks to ease this realization by focusing on an improved vocabulary. In fact, vocabulary is perhaps the most important aspect of BDD, because it also tries to normalize the vocabulary used by programmers, business developers, testers, and others involved in the development of a system when discussing problems, requirements, and solutions.

Another "double D" is Acceptance Test-Driven Development. In acceptance TDD, development starts by writing automated tests for high level features, based on acceptance tests defined in conjunction with the client. The goal is to pass the acceptance tests. To get there, we can identify smaller parts and proceed with "regular" TDD. In BDD this process is usually centered around *user stories*, which describe interaction with the system using a vocabulary familiar to everyone involved in the project. BDD frameworks such as Cucumber allow for user stories to be used as executable tests, meaning that acceptance tests can be written together with the client, increasing the chance of delivering the product the client had originally envisioned.

3.1.2 Continuous Integration

Continuous integration is the practice of integrating code from all developers on a regular basis, usually every time a developer pushes code to a remote version control repository. The continuous integration server typically builds all the sources and then runs tests for them. This process ensures that even when developers work on isolated units of features, the integrated whole is considered every time code is committed to the upstream repository. JavaScript does not need compiling, but running the entire test suite for the application on a regular basis can help catch errors early.

Continuous integration for JavaScript can solve tasks that are impractical for developers to perform regularly. Running the entire test suite in a wide array of browser and platform combinations is one such task. Developers working with TDD can focus their attention on a small representative selection of browsers, while the continuous integration server can test much wider, alerting the team of errors by email or RSS.

Additionally, it is common practice for JavaScript to be served minified—i.e., with unneeded white-space and comments stripped out, and optionally local identifiers munged to occupy fewer bytes—to preserve bytes over the wire. Both minifying code too aggressively or merging files incorrectly can introduce bugs. A continuous integration server can help out with these kinds of problems by running all tests on the full source as well as building concatenated and minified release files and re-running the test suite for them.

3.1.3 Asynchronous Tests

Due to the asynchronous nature of many JavaScript programming tasks such as working with XMLHttpRequest, animations and other deferred actions (i.e., any code using setTimeout or setInterval), and the fact that browsers do not offer a sleep function (because it would freeze the user interface), many testing frameworks provide a means to execute asynchronous tests. Whether or not asynchronous *unit* tests is a good idea is up for discussion. Chapter 12, *Abstracting Browser Differences: Ajax,* offers a more thorough discussion on the subject as well as an example.

3.1.4 Features of xUnit Test Frameworks

Chapter 1, *Automated Testing,* already introduced us to the basic features of the xUnit test frameworks: Given a set of test methods, the framework provides a test runner that can run them and report back the results. To ease the creation of shared test fixtures, test cases can employ the setUp and tearDown functions, which are run before and after (respectively) each individual test in a test case. Additionally, the test framework provides a set of assertions that can be used to verify the state of the system being tested. So far we have only used the assert method which accepts any value and throws an exception when the value is falsy. Most frameworks provide more assertions that help make tests more expressive. Perhaps the most common assertion is a version of assertEqual, used to compare actual results against expected values.

When evaluating test frameworks, we should assess the framework's test runner, its assertions, and its dependencies.

3.1.4.1 The Test Runner

The test runner is the most important part of the testing framework because it basically dictates the workflow. For example, most unit testing frameworks available for JavaScript today use an in-browser test runner. This means that tests must run inside a browser by loading an HTML file (often referred to as an HTML fixture) that itself loads the libraries to test, along with the unit tests and the testing framework. Other types of test runners can run in other environments, e.g., using Mozilla's Rhino implementation to run tests on the command line. What kind of test runner is suitable to test a specific application depends on whether it is a client-side application, server-side, or maybe even a browser plugin (an example of which would be FireUnit, a unit testing framework that uses Firebug and is suitable for developing Firefox plugins).

A related concern is the test report. Clear fail/success status is vital to the test-driven development process, and clear feedback with details when tests fail or have errors is needed to easily handle them as they occur. Ideally, the test runner should produce test results that are easily integrated with continuous integration software.

Additionally, some sort of plugin architecture for the test runner can enable us to gather metrics from testing, or otherwise allow us to extend the runner to improve the workflow. An example of such a plugin is the test coverage report. A coverage report shows how well the test suite covers the system by measuring how many lines in production code are executed by tests. Note that 100% coverage does not imply that every thinkable test is written, but rather that the test suite executes each and every line of production code. Even with 100% coverage, certain sets of input can still break the code—it cannot guarantee the absence of, e.g., missing error handling. Coverage reports are useful to find code that is not being exercised by tests.

3.1.5 Assertions

A rich set of assertions can really boost the expressiveness of tests. Given that a good unit test clearly states its intent, this is a massive boon. It's a lot easier to spot what a test is targeting if it compares two values with `assertEqual(expected, actual)` rather than with `assert(expected == actual)`. Although `assert` is all we really need to get the job done, more specific assertions make test code easier to read, easier to maintain, and easier to debug.

Assertions is one aspect where an exact port of the xUnit framework design from, e.g., Java leaves a little to be desired. To achieve good expressiveness in tests, it's helpful to have assertions tailored to specific language features, for instance, having assertions to handle JavaScripts special values such as `undefined`, `NaN` and `infinity`. Many other assertions can be provided to better support testing JavaScript, not just some arbitrary programming language. Luckily, specific assertions like those mentioned are easy to write piggybacking a general purpose `assert` (or, as is common, a `fail` method that can be called when the assertion does not hold).

3.1.6 Dependencies

Ideally, a testing framework should have as few dependencies as possible. More dependencies increase the chance of the mechanics of the framework not working in some browser (typically older ones). The worst kind of dependency for a testing framework is an obtrusive library that tampers with the global scope. The original version of JsUnitTest, the testing framework built for and used by the Prototype.js library, depended on Prototype.js itself, which not only adds a number of global properties but also augments a host of global constructors and objects. In practice, using it to test code that was not developed with Prototype.js would prove a futile exercise for two reasons:

- Too easy to accidentally rely on Prototype.js through the testing framework (yielding green tests for code that would fail in production, where Prototype.js would not be available)
- Too high a risk for collisions in the global scope (e.g., the MooTools library adds many of the same global properties)

3.2 In-Browser Test Frameworks

The original JavaScript port of the JUnit framework was JsUnit, first released in 2001. Not surprisingly, it has in many ways set the standard for a lot of testing frameworks following it. JsUnit runs tests in a browser: The test runner prompts for the URL to a test file to execute. The test file may be an HTML test suite which links to several test cases to execute. The tests are then run in sandboxed frames, and a green progress bar is displayed while tests are running. Obviously, the bar turns red whenever a test fails. JsUnit still sees the occasional update, but it has not been significantly updated for a long time, and it's starting to lag behind. JsUnit has served many developers well, including myself, but there are more mature and up-to-date alternatives available today.

Common for the in-browser testing frameworks is how they require an HTML fixture file to load the files to test, the testing library (usually a JavaScript and a CSS file), as well as the tests to run. Usually, the fixture can be simply copy-pasted for each new test case. The HTML fixture also serves the purpose of hosting dummy markup needed for the unit tests. If tests don't require such markup, we can lessen the burden of keeping a separate HTML file for each test case by writing a script that scans the URL for parameters naming library and test files to load, and then load them dynamically. This way we can run several test cases from the same HTML fixture simply by modifying the URL query string. The fixture could of course also be generated by a server-side application, but be careful down this route. I advise you to keep things simple—complicated test runners greatly decreases the likelihood of developers running tests.

3.2.1 YUI Test

Most of the major JavaScript libraries available today have their own unit testing framework. YUI from Yahoo! is no exception. YUI Test 3 can be safely used to test arbitrary JavaScript code (i.e., it has no obtrusive dependencies). YUI Test is, in its own words, "not a direct port from any specific xUnit framework," but it "does derive some characteristics from nUnit and JUnit," with nUnit being the .NET interpretation of the xUnit family of frameworks, written in C#. YUI Test is a mature testing framework with a rich feature set. It supports a rich set of assertions, test suites, a *mocking* library (as of YUI 3), and asynchronous tests.

3.2.1.1 Setup

Setup is very easy thanks to YUI's loader utility. To get quickly started, we can link directly to the YUI seed file on the YUI server, and use `YUI.use` to fetch the necessary dependencies. We will revisit the `strftime` example from Chapter 1, *Automated Testing,* in order to compare YUI Test to the `testCase` function introduced in that chapter. Listing 3.1 shows the HTML fixture file, which can be saved in, e.g., `strftime_yui_test.html`.

Listing 3.1 YUI Test HTML fixture file

```
<!DOCTYPE HTML PUBLIC "-//W3C//DTD HTML 4.01//EN"
  "http://www.w3.org/TR/html4/strict.dtd">
<html>
  <head>
    <title>Testing Date.prototype.strftime with YUI</title>
    <meta http-equiv="content-type"
          content="text/html; charset=UTF-8">
  </head>
  <body class="yui-skin-sam">
    <div id="yui-main"><div id="testReport"></div></div>
    <script type="text/javascript"
src="http://yui.yahooapis.com/3.0.0/build/yui/yui-min.js">
    </script>
    <script type="text/javascript" src="strftime.js">
    </script>
    <script type="text/javascript" src="strftime_test.js">
    </script>
  </body>
</html>
```

The `strftime.js` file contains the `Date.prototype.strftime` implementation presented in Listing 1.2 in Chapter 1, *Automated Testing.* Listing 3.2 shows the test script, save it in `strftime_test.js`.

Listing 3.2 `Date.prototype.strftime` YUI test case

```
YUI({
  combine: true,
  timeout: 10000
}).use("node", "console", "test", function (Y) {
  var assert = Y.Assert;

  var strftimeTestCase = new Y.Test.Case({
    // test case name - if not provided, one is generated
    name: "Date.prototype.strftime Tests",

    setUp: function () {
      this.date = new Date(2009, 9, 2, 22, 14, 45);
    },

    tearDown: function () {
      delete this.date;
    },

    "test %Y should return full year": function () {
      var year = Date.formats.Y(this.date);

      assert.isNumber(year);
      assert.areEqual(2009, year);
    },

    "test %m should return month": function () {
      var month = Date.formats.m(this.date);

      assert.isString(month);
      assert.areEqual("10", month);
    },

    "test %d should return date": function () {
      assert.areEqual("02", Date.formats.d(this.date));
    },

    "test %y should return year as two digits": function () {
      assert.areEqual("09", Date.formats.y(this.date));
    },
```

```
    "test %F should act as %Y-%m-%d": function () {
      assert.areEqual("2009-10-02", this.date.strftime("%F"));
    }
  });

  //create the console
  var r = new Y.Console({
    newestOnTop : false,
    style: 'block'
  });

  r.render("#testReport");
  Y.Test.Runner.add(strftimeTestCase);
  Y.Test.Runner.run();
});
```

When using YUI Test for production code, the required sources should be downloaded locally. Although the loader is a convenient way to get started, relying on an internet connection to run tests is bad practice because it means we cannot run tests while offline.

3.2.1.2 Running Tests

Running tests with YUI Test is as simple as loading up the HTML fixture in a browser (preferably several browsers) and watching the output in the console, as seen in Figure 3.1.

3.2.2 Other In-Browser Testing Frameworks

When choosing an in-browser testing framework, options are vast. YUI Test is among the most popular choices along with JsUnit and QUnit. As mentioned, JsUnit is long overdue for an upgrade, and I suggest you not start new projects with it at this point. QUnit is the testing framework developed and used by the jQuery team. Like YUI Test it is an in-browser test framework, but follows the traditional xUnit design less rigidly. The Dojo and Prototype.js libraries both have their test frameworks as well.

One might get the impression that there are almost as many testing frameworks out there as there are developers unit testing their scripts—there is no defacto standard way to test JavaScript. In fact, this is true for most programming tasks that are not directly related to browser scripting, because JavaScript has no general purpose standard library. CommonJS is an initiative to rectify this situation, originally motivated to standardize server-side JavaScript. CommonJS also includes a

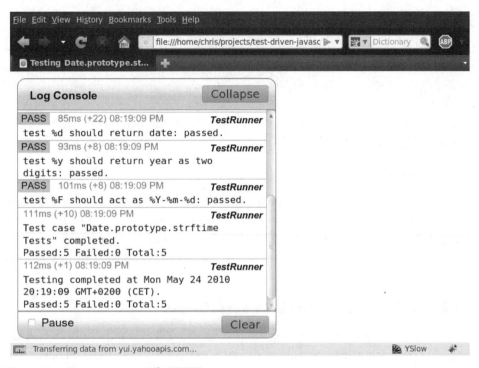

Figure 3.1 Running tests with YUI Test.

unit testing spec, which we will look into when testing a `Node.js` application in Chapter 14, *Server-Side JavaScript with Node.js.*

3.3 Headless Testing Frameworks

In-browser testing frameworks are unfit to support a test-driven development process where we need to run tests frequently and integrated into the workflow. An alternative to these frameworks is headless testing frameworks. These typically run from the command line, and can be interacted with in the same way testing frameworks for any other server-side programming language can.

There are a few solutions available for running headless JavaScript unit tests, most originating from either the Java or Ruby worlds. Both the Java and Ruby communities have strong testing cultures, and testing only half the code base (the server-side part) can only make sense for so long, probably explaining why it is these two communities in particular that have stood out in the area of headless testing solutions for JavaScript.

3.3.1 Crosscheck

Crosscheck is one of the early headless testing frameworks. It provides a Java backed emulation of Internet Explorer 6 and Firefox versions 1.0 and 1.5. Needless to say, Crosscheck is lagging behind, and its choice of browsers are unlikely to help develop applications for 2010. Crosscheck offers JavaScript unit tests much like that of YUI Test, the difference being that they can be run on the command line with the Crosscheck jar file rather than in a browser.

3.3.2 Rhino and env.js

`env.js` is a library originally developed by John Resig, creator of the jQuery JavaScript framework. It offers an implementation of the browser (i.e., BOM) and DOM APIs on top of Rhino, Mozilla's Java implementation of JavaScript. Using the env.js library together with Rhino means we can load and run in-browser tests on the command line.

3.3.3 The Issue with Headless Test Runners

Although the idea of running tests on the command line is exciting, I fail to recognize the power of running tests in an environment where production code will never run. Not only are the browser environment and DOM emulations, but the JavaScript engine (usually Rhino) is an altogether different one as well.

Relying on a testing framework that simply emulates the browser is bad for a few reasons. For one, it means tests can only be run in browsers that are emulated by the testing framework, or, as is the case for solutions using Rhino and env.js, in an alternate browser and DOM implementation altogether. Limiting the available testing targets is not an ideal feature of a testing framework and is unlikely to help write cross-browser JavaScript. Second, an emulation will never match whatever it is emulating perfectly. Microsoft probably proved this best by providing an Internet Explorer 7 emulation mode in IE8, which is in fact not an exact match of IE7. Luckily, we can get the best from both worlds, as we will see next, in Section 3.4, *One Test Runner to Rule Them All.*

3.4 One Test Runner to Rule Them All

The problem with in-browser testing frameworks is that they can be cumbersome to work with, especially in a test-driven development setting where we need to run tests continuously and integrated into the workflow. Additionally, testing on a wide array of platform/browser combinations can entail quite a bit of manual work. Headless frameworks are easier to work with, but fail at testing in the actual environment the code will be running in, reducing their usefulness as testing tools. A fairly new player on the field of xUnit testing frameworks is JsTestDriver, originating from Google. In contrast to the traditional frameworks, JsTestDriver is first and foremost a test runner, and a clever one at that. JsTestDriver solves the aforementioned problems by making it easy both to run tests and to test widely in real browsers.

3.4.1 How JsTestDriver Works

JsTestDriver uses a small server to run tests. Browsers are captured by the test runner and tests are scheduled by issuing a request to the server. As each browser runs the tests, results are sent back to the client and presented to the developer. This means that as browsers are idly awaiting tests, we can schedule runs from either the command line, the IDE, or wherever we may feel most comfortable running them from. This approach has numerous advantages:

- Tests can be run in browsers without requiring manual interaction with the browser.
- Tests can be run in browsers on multiple machines, including mobile devices, allowing for arbitrary complex testing grids.
- Tests run **fast**, due to the fact that results need not be added to the DOM and rendered, they can be run in any number of browsers simultaneously, and the browser doesn't need to reload scripts that haven't changed since the tests were last run.
- Tests can use the full DOM because no portion of the document is reserved for the test runner to display results.
- No need for an HTML fixture, simply provide one or more scripts and test scripts, an empty document is created on the fly by the test runner.

JsTestDriver tests are **fast**. The test runner can run complex test suites of several hundred tests in under a single second. Because tests are run simultaneously, tests will still run in about a second even when testing 15 browsers at the same time. Granted, some time is spent communicating with the server and optionally refreshing the browser cache, but a full run still completes in a matter of a few seconds. Single test case runs usually complete in the blink of an eye.

As if faster tests, simpler setup, and full DOM flexibility weren't enough, JsTest-Driver also offers a plugin that calculates test coverage, XML test report output compatible with JUnit's reports, meaning we can immediately use existing continuous integration servers, and it can use alternative assertion frameworks. Through plug-ins, any other JavaScript testing framework can take advantage of the JsTestDriver test runner, and at the time of writing, adapters for QUnit and YUI Test already exist. This means tests can be written using YUI Test's assertions and syntax, but run using JsTestDriver.

3.4.2 JsTestDriver Disadvantages

At the time of writing, JsTestDriver does not support any form of asynchronous testing. As we will see in Chapter 12, *Abstracting Browser Differences: Ajax,* this isn't necessarily a problem from a unit testing perspective, but it may limit the options for integration tests, in which we want to fake as little as possible. It is possible that asynchronous test support will be added to future versions of JsTestDriver.

Another disadvantage of JsTestDriver is that the JavaScript required to run tests is slightly more advanced, and may cause a problem in old browsers. For instance, by design, a browser that is to run JsTestDriver needs to support the `XMLHttpRequest` object or similar (i.e., Internet Explorer's corresponding `ActiveX` object) in order to communicate with the server. This means that browsers that don't support this object (older browsers, Internet Explorer before version 7 with ActiveX disabled) cannot be tested with the JsTestDriver test runner. This problem can be effectively circumvented, however, by using YUI Test to write tests, leaving the option of running them manually with the default test runner in any uncooperative browser.

3.4.3 Setup

Installing and setting up JsTestDriver is slightly more involved than the average in-browser testing framework; still, it will only take a few minutes. Also, the setup is only required once. Any projects started after the fact are dirt simple to get running. JsTestDriver requires Java to run both the server component and start test runs. I won't give instructions on installing Java here, but most systems have Java installed already. You can check if Java is installed by opening a shell and issue the `java -version` command. If you don't have Java installed, you will find instructions on java.com.

3.4.3.1 Download the Jar File

Once Java is set up, download the most recent JsTestDriver jar file from http://code.google.com/p/js-test-driver/downloads/list. All the examples in this book use version 1.2.1, be sure to use that version when following along with the examples. The jar file can be placed anywhere on the system, I suggest ~/bin. To make it easier to run, set up an environment variable to point to this directory, as shown in Listing 3.3.

Listing 3.3 Setting the $JSTESTDRIVER_HOME environment variable

```
export JSTESTDRIVER_HOME=~/bin
```

Set the environment variable in a login script, such as .bashrc or .zshrc (depends on the shell—most systems use Bash, i.e., ~/.bashrc, by default).

3.4.3.2 Windows Users

Windows users can set an environment variable in the cmd command line by issuing the set JSTESTDRIVER_HOME=C:\bin command. To set it permanently, right-click *My Computer* (*Computer* in Windows 7) and select *Properties.* In the *System window*, select *Advanced system properties,* then the *Advanced tab,* and then click the *Environment Variables . . .* button. Decide if you need to set the environment variable for yourself only or for all users. Click *New*, enter the name (JSTEST-DRIVER_HOME) in the top box, and then the path where you saved the jar file in the bottom one.

3.4.3.3 Start the Server

To run tests through JsTestDriver, we need a running server to capture browsers with. The server can run anywhere reachable from your machine—locally, on a machine on the local network, or a public facing machine. Beware that running the server on a public machine will make it available to anyone unless the machine restricts access by IP address or similar. To get started, I recommend running the service locally; this way you can test while being offline as well. Open a shell and issue the command in either Listing 3.4 or Listing 3.5 (current directory is not important for this command).

Listing 3.4 Starting the JsTestDriver server on Linux and OSX

```
java -jar $JSTESTDRIVER_HOME/JsTestDriver-1.2.1.jar --port
    4224
```

Listing 3.5 Starting the JsTestDriver server on Windows

```
java -jar %JSTESTDRIVER_HOME%\JsTestDriver-1.2.1.jar --port
    4224
```

Port 4224 is the defacto standard JsTestDriver port, but it is arbitrarily picked and you can run it on any port you want. Once the server is running, the shell running it must stay open for as long as you need it.

3.4.3.4 Capturing Browsers

Open any browser and point it to http://localhost:4224 (make sure you change the port number if you used another port when starting the server). The resulting page will display two links: *Capture browser* and *Capture in strict mode*. JsTestDriver runs tests inside an HTML 4.01 document, and the two links allow us to decide if we want to run tests with a transitional or strict doctype. Click the appropriate link, and leave the browser open. Repeat in as many browsers as desired. You can even try hooking up your phone or browsers on other platforms using virtual instances.

3.4.3.5 Running Tests

Tests can be run from the command line, providing feedback in much the same way a unit testing framework for any server-side language would. As tests are run, a dot will appear for every passing test, an F for a failing test, and an E for a test with errors. An error is any test error that is not a failing assertion, i.e., an unexpected exception. To run the tests, we need a small configuration file that tells JsTestDriver which source and test files to load (and in what order), and which server to run tests against. The configuration file, jsTestDriver.conf by default, uses YAML syntax, and at its simplest, it loads every source file and every test file, and runs tests at http://localhost:4224, as seen in Listing 3.6.

Listing 3.6 A barebone jsTestDriver.conf file

```
server: http://localhost:4224

load:
  - src/*.js
  - test/*.js
```

Load paths are relative to the location of the configuration file. When it's required to load certain files before others, we can specify them first and still use the `*.js` notation, JsTestDriver will only load each file once, even when it is referenced more than once. Listing 3.7 shows an example where `src/mylib.js` always need to load first.

Listing 3.7 Making sure certain files load first

```
server: http://localhost:4224

load:
  - src/mylib.js
  - src/*.js
  - test/*.js
```

In order to test the configuration we need a sample project. We will revisit the strftime example once again, so start by copying the strftime.js file into the src directory. Then add the test case from Listing 3.8 in test/strftime_test.js.

Listing 3.8 Date.prototype.strftime test with JsTestDriver

```
TestCase("strftimeTest", {
  setUp: function () {
    this.date = new Date(2009, 9, 2, 22, 14, 45);
  },

  tearDown: function () {
    delete this.date;
  },

  "test %Y should return full year": function () {
    var year = Date.formats.Y(this.date);

    assertNumber(year);
    assertEquals(2009, year);
  },

  "test %m should return month": function () {
    var month = Date.formats.m(this.date);

    assertString(month);
    assertEquals("10", month);
  },

  "test %d should return date": function () {
    assertEquals("02", Date.formats.d(this.date));
  },

  "test %y should return year as two digits": function () {
    assertEquals("09", Date.formats.y(this.date));
  },
```

```
"test %F should act as %Y-%m-%d": function () {
  assertEquals("2009-10-02", this.date.strftime("%F"));
}
});
```

The test methods are almost syntactically identical to the YUI Test example, but note how this test case has less scaffolding code to support the test runner. Now create the configuration file as shown in Listing 3.9.

Listing 3.9 JsTestDriver configuration

```
server: http://localhost:4224

load:
  - src/*.js
  - test/*.js
```

We can now schedule tests to run by issuing the command in Listing 3.10 or Listing 3.11, depending on your operating system.

Listing 3.10 Running tests with JsTestDriver on Linux and OSX

```
java -jar $JSTESTDRIVER_HOME/JsTestDriver-1.2.1.jar --tests
    all
```

Listing 3.11 Running tests with JsTestDriver on Windows

```
java -jar %JSTESTDRIVER_HOME%\JsTestDriver-1.2.1.jar--tests
    all
```

The default configuration file name is `jsTestDriver.conf`, and as long as this is used we don't need to specify it. When using another name, add the `--config path/to/file.conf` option.

When running tests, JsTestDriver forces the browser to refresh the test files. Source files, however, aren't reloaded between test runs, which may cause errors due to stale files. We can tell JsTestDriver to reload everything by adding the `--reset` option.

3.4.3.6 JsTestDriver and TDD

When TDD-ing, tests will fail frequently, and it is vital that we are able to quickly verify that we get the failures we expect in order to avoid buggy tests. A browser such as Internet Explorer is not suitable for this process for a few reasons. First, its error messages are less than helpful; you have probably seen "Object does not support this property or method" more times than you care for. The second reason is that IE, at least in older versions, handles script errors badly. Running a TDD session in IE will cause it to frequently choke, requiring you to manually refresh it. Not to mention the lack of performance in IE, which is quite noticeable compared to, e.g., Google Chrome.

Disregarding Internet Explorer, I would still advise against keeping too many browsers in your primary TDD process, because doing so clutters up the test runner's report, repeating errors and log messages once for every captured browser. My advice is to develop against one server that only captures your browser of choice, and frequently run tests against a second server that captures many browsers. You can run against this second server as often as needed—after each passed test, completed method, or if you are feeling bold, even more. Keep in mind that the more code you add between each run, the harder it will be to spot any bugs that creep up in those secondary browsers.

To ease this sort of development, it's best to remove the `server` line from the configuration file and use the `--server` command line option. Personally I do this kind of development against Firefox, which is reasonably fast, has good error messages, and always runs on my computer anyway. As soon as I pass a test, I issue a run on a remote server that captures a wider variety of browsers, new and old.

3.4.4   Using JsTestDriver From an IDE

JsTestDriver also ships plugins for popular integrated development environments (IDEs), Eclipse and IntelliJ IDEA. In this section I will walk through setting up the Eclipse plugin and using it to support a test-driven development process. If you are not interested in developing in Eclipse (or Aptana), feel free to skip to Section 3.4.5, *Improved Command Line Productivity*.

3.4.4.1   Installing JsTestDriver in Eclipse

To get started you need to have Eclipse (or Aptana Studio, an IDE based on Eclipse aimed at web developers) installed. Eclipse is a free open source IDE and can be downloaded from http://eclipse.org. Once Eclipse is running, go to the *Help* menu and select *Install new software.* In the window that opens, enter the following URL as a new *update site:* http://js-test-driver.googlecode.com/svn/update/

"JS Test Driver Eclipse Plugin" should now be displayed with a checkbox next to it. Check it and click *Next*. The next screen is a confirmation that sums up the plugins to be installed. Click *Next* once again and Eclipse asks you to accept the terms of use. Check the appropriate radio button and click *Next* if you accept. This should finish the installation.

Once the plugin is installed we need to configure it. Find the Preferences pane under the Window menu (Eclipse menu on OS X). There should be a new entry for Js Test Driver; select it. As a bare minimum we need to enter the port where Eclipse should run the server. Use 4224 to follow along with the example. You can also enter the paths to browsers installed locally to ease browser capturing, but it's not really necessary.

3.4.4.2 Running JsTestDriver in Eclipse

Next up, we need a project. Create a new project and enter the directory for the command line example as location. Now start the server. Locate the JsTestDriver panel in Eclipse and click the green play button. Once the server is running, click the browser icons to capture browsers (given that their path was configured during setup). Now right-click a file in the project, and select *Run As* and then *Run Configurations . . .* Select *Js Test Driver Test* and click the sheet of paper icon indicating "new configuration." Give the configuration a name and select the project's configuration file. Now click run and the tests run right inside Eclipse, as seen in Figure 3.2.

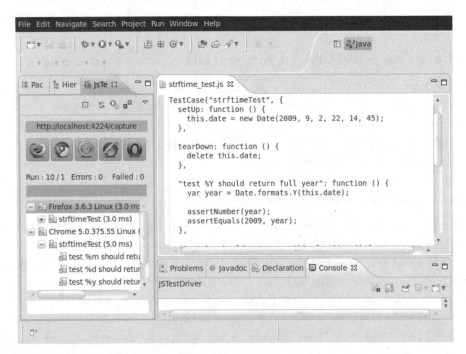

Figure 3.2 Running JsTestDriver tests inside Eclipse.

On subsequent runs, simply select *Run As* and then *Name of configuration.* Even better, check the *Run on every save* checkbox in the configuration prompt. This way, tests are run anytime a file in the project is saved, perfect for the test-driven development process.

3.4.5 Improved Command Line Productivity

If the command line is your environment of choice, the Java command to run tests quickly becomes a bit tiresome to type out. Also, it would be nice to be able to have tests run automatically whenever files in the project change, just like the Eclipse and IDEA plugins do. Jstdutil is a Ruby project that adds a thin command line interface to JsTestDriver. It provides a leaner command to run tests as well as an `jsautotest` command that runs related tests whenever files in the project change.

Jstdutil requires Ruby, which comes pre-installed on Mac OS X. For other systems, installation instructions can be found on ruby-lang.org. With Ruby installed, install Jstdutil by running `gem install jstdutil` in a shell. Jstdutil uses the previously mentioned `$JSTESTDRIVER_HOME` environment variable to locate the JsTestDriver jar file. This means that running tests is a simple matter of `jstestdriver --tests all`, or for autotest, simply `jsautotest`. If the configuration file is not automatically picked up, specify it using `jstestdriver --config path/to/file.conf --tests all`. The `jstestdriver` and `jsautotest` commands also add coloring to the test report, giving us that nice red/green visual feedback.

3.4.6 Assertions

JsTestDriver supports a rich set of assertions. These assertions allow for highly expressive tests and detailed feedback on failures, even when a custom assertion message isn't specified. The full list of supported assertions in JsTestDriver is:

- `assert(msg, value)`
- `assertTrue(msg, value)`
- `assertFalse(msg, value)`
- `assertEquals(msg, expected, actual)`
- `assertNotEquals(msg, expected, actual)`
- `assertSame(msg, expected, actual)`
- `assertNotSame(msg, expected, actual)`
- `assertNull(msg, value)`

- `assertNotNull(msg, value)`
- `assertUndefined(msg, value)`
- `assertNotUndefined(msg, value)`
- `assertNaN(msg, number)`
- `assertNotNaN(msg, number)`
- `assertException(msg, callback, type)`
- `assertNoException(msg, callback)`
- `assertArray(msg, arrayLike)`
- `assertTypeOf(msg, type, object)`
- `assertBoolean(msg, value)`
- `assertFunction(msg, value)`
- `assertNumber(msg, value)`
- `assertObject(msg, value)`
- `assertString(msg, value)`
- `assertMatch(msg, pattern, string)`
- `assertNoMatch(msg, pattern, string)`
- `assertTagName(msg, tagName, element)`
- `assertClassName(msg, className, element)`
- `assertElementId(msg, id, element)`
- `assertInstanceOf(msg, constructor, object)`
- `assertNotInstanceOf(msg, constructor, object)`

We will be using JsTestDriver for most examples throughout this book.

3.5 Summary

In this chapter we have taken a look at what tools can be helpful to support the test-driven development process, as well as a few available tools. Getting a good test-driven development rhythm requires adequate tools, and for the remaining examples of this book, JsTestDriver was selected to run tests. It offers both a highly efficient workflow as well as thorough testing on a wide array of platform and browser combinations.

This chapter also touched briefly on BDD and "specs" and how test-driven development, as practiced in this book, shares a lot in common with it.

Although we visited the topics of test coverage reports and continuous integration in this chapter, no setup or examples were given for such tools. On the book's website[1] you will find a guide to running the Coverage plugin for JsTestDriver as well as a guide on how to run JsTestDriver tests in the open source continuous integration server Hudson.

In the next chapter we will have a look at some other ways to utilize unit tests before we move on to Part II, *JavaScript for Programmers*.

---

1. http://tddjs.com

Test to Learn

In the previous three chapters we have seen how automated tests can help improve quality of code, guide design and drive development. In this chapter we will use automated tests to learn. As small executable code examples, unit tests make a perfect learning resource. Isolating a specific aspect of an interface in a unit test is a great way to learn more about how it behaves. Other types of automated tests can help our understanding of both the language and specific problems. Benchmarks are a valuable tool to measure relative performance, and can guide decisions about how to solve a specific problem.

4.1 Exploring JavaScript with Unit Tests

Quickly executing JavaScript, as in executing a few lines of script to explore the behavior of some object, is fairly simple. Most modern browsers ship with a console that serves this purpose just fine. Additionally, there are several options for JavaScript command line interfaces when the browser environment is not of particular interest. Although this sort of one-off coding session can help our understanding of an interface, it suffers from the same problems that manual application testing does. There is no way to repeat a given experiment, there is no record of previously run experiments, and there is no simple way of repeating an experiment in multiple browsers.

In Chapter 1, *Automated Testing,* we introduced unit tests as a means to solve the problems brought on by manual testing. Surely, unit tests can help us solve the same problems when we want to simply explore an interface to learn. For this purpose we can write *learning tests,* i.e., unit tests written with the goal of learning, not with the goal of testing the exercised interface per se.

As an example, let us take the built-in `Array.prototype.splice` method for a spin. This method accepts two or more arguments: an index to start with, a number of items to remove, and optional elements to insert into the array. We are curious as to whether or not this method alters the original array. We could look up the answer, or we could simply ask JavaScript to tell us, as the learning test in Listing 4.1 shows. To run the test, set up a JsTestDriver project as explained in Chapter 3, *Tools of the Trade,* with a `test` directory and save the test in a file in that directory. Add a configuration file that loads `test/*.js`.

Listing 4.1 Expecting `Array.prototype.splice` to modify the array

```
TestCase("ArrayTest", {
  "test array splice should not modify array": function () {
    var arr = [1, 2, 3, 4, 5];
    var result = arr.splice(2, 3);

    assertEquals([1, 2, 3, 4, 5], arr);
  }
});
```

Because we don't really know what the answer is, we roll with the assumption that the `splice` method is not destructive. Note how this contrasts with traditional unit testing—when testing production code we should always write assertions on firm expectation about the result. However, we are now learning by observing what the implementation can tell us, and so whatever answer we are assuming before running the test is not of grave importance. Running the test proves us wrong anyway: "expected [1, 2, 3, 4, 5] but was [1, 2]." So we have learned something new. To record our findings, Listing 4.2 updates the test to state what we now know to be true.

Listing 4.2 `Array.prototype.splice` modifies the receiving array

```
TestCase("ArrayTest", {
  "test array splice should modify array": function () {
    var arr = [1, 2, 3, 4, 5];
    var result = arr.splice(2, 3);

    assertEquals([1, 2], arr);
  }
});
```

Note how both the wording and the assertion changed. Because we have discovered that the method in question is in fact destructive, we now wonder: Does it also return the result? Listing 4.3 investigates.

Listing 4.3 Expecting `Array.prototype.splice` to return the spliced array

```
"test array splice should return modified array":
function () {
  var arr = [1, 2, 3, 4, 5];
  var result = arr.splice(2, 3);

  assertEquals(arr, result);
}
```

Running this test proves us wrong yet again: "expected [1, 2] but was [3, 4, 5]." Apparently, the `splice` method returns the removed items. Time to update the wording of our test, as seen in Listing 4.4.

Listing 4.4 Expecting `Array.prototype.splice` to return removed items

```
"test array splice should return removed items":
function () {
  var arr = [1, 2, 3, 4, 5];
  var result = arr.splice(2, 3);

  assertEquals([3, 4, 5], result);
}
```

Rather than playing with an array and the `splice` method in a browser console, we put the test in a file. With a minimum of added overhead, we now have a repeatable experiment that documents what we just learned, perfect for later review. Using the JsTestDriver test runner, we could even send this test out to an army of browsers to verify that the two tests run consistently across browsers.

Testing built-in functionality like this might seem to contradict our usual attitude toward unit testing: never to test code that we didn't write ourselves, and to mock or stub external dependencies while testing. These are still valuable pieces of advice, but they do not apply to learning tests. Learning tests aren't a part of production code; they live in a separate repository, a personal repository, and they help us document our knowledge and our learning experience.

Still, in contrast to traditional applications of unit testing, learning tests cannot be successfully collaborated on. Everyone should keep their own suite of learning tests. The reason for this advice is simply that it is not the tests themselves that provides the highest value. *Writing* the test, including all the surrounding thought process is what we primarily learn from. Keeping the tests allows us to revisit a given exercise at a later time, or run it in a newly discovered browser to see if our experience still serves us well. Browsing through a suite of learning tests written by someone else might provide a few nuggets of information, but is unlikely to embed knowledge inside our brains the same way writing learning tests does.

4.1.1 Pitfalls of Programming by Observation

When we talk about JavaScript, we are really talking about several dialects; Mozilla's JavaScript™, Microsoft's JScript and Webkit's JavaScriptCore to name a few. These all stem from the original JavaScript language invented by Netscape and have their common ground in ECMA-262, or ECMAScript, a standardization of that very language. Because we are really targeting several dialects when writing client side scripts, there is no canonical source of information of the kind we retrieved in the two learning tests from the previous section. In other words, there is no authoritative interpreter to ask for information about JavaScript—they all have their bugs and quirks, they all have their proprietary extensions, and their market share is more evenly distributed than ever (even though Microsoft still dominates with Internet Explorer versions 6-8 combined)—meaning there are no single browser that can be considered "best," our scripts will have to run in all of them anyway.

By writing the two learning tests in the previous section, we cannot blindly trust the results of some statements run in a single browser alone. And when results differ between browsers, which one do we trust? When in doubt, we need to consult the source—the ECMA-262 specification. When browsers behave differently on language features, we need to consult the spec they are trying to implement to understand properly what the correct answer is. Only when we know how something is intended to work can we get to work fixing it, either by overwriting the built-in implementation for misbehaving browsers, or by providing an abstraction.

By writing the two learning tests in the previous section, we learned a few things about the `Array.prototype.splice` method by observing the results of running our test in a browser. Drawing conclusions based on a small sample of observations can prove to be a dangerous approach, especially when dealing with browser differences.

White-space matching in regular expressions using \s is an example of how observations may lead us astray. Until recently, no implementation correctly matched all white-space characters defined by ECMA-262. Tests for certain white-space characters would fail in all browsers, possibly leading us to conclude that the \s character class isn't supposed to match the specific character being tested.

4.1.2 The Sweet Spot for Learning Tests

Even though we should exercise healthy skepticism toward "programming by observation," the learning test can be a very helpful tool aiding our understanding of the JavaScript language and the environments in which it runs. In this section we will run through a few cases where learning tests can help more efficiently accelerate and maintain learning and knowledge of the language.

4.1.2.1 Capturing Wisdom Found in the Wild

The learning test is the perfect tool to capture some wisdom picked up while reading someone else's code, an article or a book. This might not be something entirely new; it could be as simple as a clever trick. Writing it down as a test case provides several benefits. For one, it puts us through actually writing the code down, helping us remember whatever it is we are picking up. Second, having the code isolated in the test allows us to more easily play with it and run it in several browsers. It also means we can copy and modify it a few times over, bending it to learn more from it. As always, keeping the test with the rest of the learning tests provides documentation that can be reviewed at a later point.

4.1.2.2 Exploring Weird Behavior

Every now and then we stumble upon weird bugs or other unexpected behavior when developing production code. Failing to draw the necessary lessons from such experiences will set us at risk for repeating the mistake. Isolating the nature of the bug in a learning test can help us control iffy situations and become aware of them when they arise, helping us spot them as they're forming rather than when they're causing bugs in the code.

4.1.2.3 Exploring New Browsers

Keeping a suite of learning tests can kick start exploration of a newly released browser. Does the browser change any behaviors we have come to rely on? Does it fix any bugs we are currently working our way around? I'm not saying we should manually maintain comprehensive test suites for ECMA-262, the DOM, and other interfaces, but running a suite of learning tests in a newly released browser means we can check how our accumulated experience holds up, and it might immediately teach us something new.

4.1.2.4 Exploring Frameworks

Third party interfaces such as "Ajax libraries" make excellent targets for a few learning tests. The learning tests provide neutral ground to play with a library, and we get to try out the interfaces in a more free form than we probably would if we simply dropped the framework right into the application. In fact, doing a little bit of experimenting with a given framework can even influence the decision on whether or not to use it in an application. Many libraries have lots of initial appeal, but fail to live up to their expectations in practice. Exercising them in a sandboxed environment allows us to get a better feel of using them, and we are free to push them through hoops we know they will need to handle when introduced to a real production environment. Again, performing this kind of experiment in structured files rather than a console environment means we can refer to them at any point, perhaps to compare a set of libraries that was tested.

4.2 Performance Tests

Another type of automated test that can teach us a whole lot are benchmarks that test relative performance. Most problems can be solved in many ways, and sometimes it is not obvious which solution is best. For example, as we will see in Chapter 7, *Objects and Prototypal Inheritance,* there are different ways of creating JavaScript objects, mainly the pseudo-classical way, using JavaScript's constructors, and the functional approach, using closures. How do we choose which strategy to employ? Personal preference usually plays a part in such choices, as does testability, flexibility, and performance. Depending on the use case, the performance aspect can prove to be very important.

4.2.1 Benchmarks and Relative Performance

Whenever we have two or more ways to solve a given problem, a benchmark can indicate how one solution performs relative to alternatives; hence "relative performance." A benchmark is a very simple concept:

- Create a `new Date()`.
- Exercise the code alternative to measure.
- Create a `new Date()`; subtract the start date to find total time.
- Repeat for all alternatives.
- Compare results.

Exercising the code alternative to measure usually needs to be done many times in a loop to improve accuracy of the measurement. Additionally, Windows XP and

Windows Vista complicates the matter by providing browsers with timers that only update every 15ms. This means that fast-running tests can be hugely inaccurate, the best approach is to run tests for at least 500ms or so.

Listing 4.5 shows a function that we will use to run some benchmarks to measure relative performance. Save it in `lib/benchmark.js`.

Listing 4.5 A benchmark runner

```
var ol;

function runBenchmark(name, test) {
  if (!ol) {
    ol = document.createElement("ol");
    document.body.appendChild(ol);
  }

  setTimeout(function () {
    var start = new Date().getTime();
    test();
    var total = new Date().getTime() - start;

    var li = document.createElement("li");
    li.innerHTML = name + ": " + total + "ms";
    ol.appendChild(li);
  }, 15);
}
```

Listing 4.6 uses this function to measure relative performance of different looping styles. Save the file in `benchmarks/loops.js`.

Listing 4.6 Benchmarking loops

```
var loopLength = 500000;

// Populate an array to loop
var array = [];

for (var i = 0; i < loopLength; i++) {
  array[i] = "item" + i;
}

function forLoop() {
  for (var i = 0, item; i < array.length; i++) {
    item = array[i];
  }
}
```

```
function forLoopCachedLength() {
  for (var i = 0, l = array.length, item; i < l; i++) {
    item = array[i];
  }
}

function forLoopDirectAccess() {
  for (var i = 0, item; (item = array[i]); i++) {
  }
}

function whileLoop() {
  var i = 0, item;

  while (i < array.length) {
    item = array[i];
    i++;
  }
}

function whileLoopCachedLength() {
  var i = 0, l = array.length, item;

  while (i < l) {
    item = array[i];
    i++;
  }
}

function reversedWhileLoop() {
  var l = array.length, item;

  while (l--) {
    item = array[l];
  }
}

function doubleReversedWhileLoop() {
  var l = array.length, i = l, item;

  while (i--) {
    item = array[l - i - 1];
  }
}
```

```
// Run tests
runBenchmark("for-loop",
             forLoop);
runBenchmark("for-loop, cached length",
             forLoopCachedLength);
runBenchmark("for-loop, direct array access",
             forLoopDirectAccess);
runBenchmark("while-loop",
             whileLoop);
runBenchmark("while-loop, cached length property",
             whileLoopCachedLength);
runBenchmark("reversed while-loop",
             reversedWhileLoop);
runBenchmark("double reversed while-loop",
             doubleReversedWhileLoop);
```

The `setTimeout` call is important to avoid choking the browser while testing. The browser uses a single thread to run JavaScript, fire events and render web pages, and the timers allow the browser some "breathing room" to pick up on queued tasks between tests that are potentially long running. Breaking the workload up with timers also avoids browsers interrupting the tests to warn us about "slow scripts."

To run these benchmarks, all we need is a simple HTML file, like the one in Listing 4.7, that loads the script. Save the file in `benchmarks/loops.html`.

Listing 4.7 YUI Test HTML fixture file

```
<!DOCTYPE HTML PUBLIC "-//W3C//DTD HTML 4.01//EN"
  "http://www.w3.org/TR/html4/strict.dtd">
<html>
  <head>
    <title>Relative performance of loops</title>
    <meta http-equiv="content-type"
          content="text/html; charset=UTF-8">
  </head>
  <body>
    <h1>Relative performance of loops</h1>
    <script type="text/javascript" src="../lib/benchmark.js">
    </script>
    <script type="text/javascript" src="loops.js"></script>
  </body>
</html>
```

All the tests do the exact same thing: loop over all items in the array and access the current item. Accessing the current item adds to the footprint of the test, but it also allows us to compare the loop that accesses the current item in the loop conditional with the rest. This is not always a safe choice, because empty strings, `null`, 0, and other false values will terminate the loop. Also, this style of looping performs terribly on some browsers and should be avoided. Because all the tests access the current item, we can disregard the overhead as fluctuations in the test results will be the result of the different looping styles. Note that the reversed `while-loop` is not directly comparable as it loops the array backwards. However, whenever order is not important, it's commonly the fastest way to loop an array, as seen by running the above benchmark.

Benchmarks such as that in Listing 4.6 are dead easy to set up. Still, to make them easier to integrate into our workflow, we can craft a simple `benchmark` function that removes all unnecessary cruft from writing benchmarks. Listing 4.8 shows one possible such function. The function accepts a label for the series of tests and then an object where the property names are taken as test names and property values are run as tests. The last argument is optional and instructs `benchmark` as to how many times a test should be run. Results are printed in both full and average time per test.

Listing 4.8 A simple benchmarking tool

```
var benchmark = (function () {
  function init(name) {
    var heading = document.createElement("h2");
    heading.innerHTML = name;
    document.body.appendChild(heading);

    var ol = document.createElement("ol");
    document.body.appendChild(ol);

    return ol;
  }

  function runTests(tests, view, iterations) {
    for (var label in tests) {
      if (!tests.hasOwnProperty(label) ||
          typeof tests[label] != "function") {
        continue;
      }

      (function (name, test) {
        setTimeout(function () {
          var start = new Date().getTime();
          var l = iterations;

          while (l--) {
            test();
          }
```

```
      var total = new Date().getTime() - start;

      var li = document.createElement("li");
      li.innerHTML = name + ": " + total +
        "ms (total), " + (total / iterations) +
        "ms (avg)";
      view.appendChild(li);
    }, 15);
  }(label, tests[label]));
    }
  }

  function benchmark(name, tests, iterations) {
    iterations = iterations || 1000;
    var view = init(name);
    runTests(tests, view, iterations);
  }

  return benchmark;
}());
```

The benchmark function does one thing noticeably different from our previous example. It runs each iteration as a function. The test is captured as a function, which is run the specified number of times. This function call itself has a footprint, so the end result is less accurate as to how long the test took, especially for small test functions. However, in most cases the overhead is ignorable because we are testing relative performance. To avoid having the function call skew tests too much, we can write the tests so that they are sufficiently complex. An alternative way to implement this is to take advantage of the fact that functions have a length property that reveals how many formal parameters a function takes. If this number is zero, then we loop. Otherwise, we will assume that the test expects the number of iterations as an argument and simply call the function, passing the iteration count. This can be seen in Listing 4.9.

Listing 4.9 Using Function.prototype.length to loop or not

```
// Inside runTests
(function (name, test) {
  setTimeout(function () {
    var start = new Date().getTime();
    var l = iterations;

    if (!test.length) {
      while (l--) {
```

```
      test();
    }
  } else {
    test(1);
  }

  var total = new Date().getTime() - start;

  var li = document.createElement("li");
  li.innerHTML = name + ": " + total +
    "ms (total), " + (total / iterations) +
    "ms (avg)";
  view.appendChild(li);
}, 15);
}(label, tests[label]));
```

As an example of benchmark's usage, we can reformat the loop tests using it. In this example, the length of the array to loop is somewhat reduced, and the total number of iterations is increased. Listing 4.10 shows the rewritten test. Some of the tests have been removed for brevity.

Listing 4.10 Using benchmark

```
var loopLength = 100000;
var array = [];

for (var i = 0; i < loopLength; i++) {
  array[i] = "item" + i;
}

benchmark("Loop performance", {
  "for-loop": function () {
    for (var i = 0, item; i < array.length; i++) {
      item = array[i];
    }
  },

  "for-loop, cached length": function () {
    for (var i = 0, l = array.length, item; i < l; i++) {
      item = array[i];
    }
  },

  // ...

  "double reversed while-loop": function () {
```

```
    var l = array.length, i = l, item;

    while (i--) {
      item = array[l - i - 1];
    }
  }
}, 1000);
```

This sort of benchmarking utility can be extended to yield more helpful reports. Highlighting the fastest and slowest tests comes to mind as a useful extension. Listing 4.11 shows a possible solution.

Listing 4.11 Measuring and highlighting extremes

```
// Record times
var times;

function runTests (tests, view, iterations) {
  // ...
  (function (name, test) {
    // ...
    var total = new Date().getTime() - start;
    times[name] = total;
    // ...
  }(label, tests[label]));
  // ...
}

function highlightExtremes(view) {
  // The timeout is queued after all other timers, ensuring
  // that all tests are finished running and the times
  // object is populated
  setTimeout(function () {
    var min = new Date().getTime();
    var max = 0;
    var fastest, slowest;

    for (var label in times) {
      if (!times.hasOwnProperty(label)) {
        continue;
      }

      if (times[label] < min) {
        min = times[label];
        fastest = label;
      }
```

```
      if (times[label] > max) {
        max = times[label];
        slowest = label;
      }
    }

    var lis = view.getElementsByTagName("li");
    var fastRegexp = new RegExp("^" + fastest + ":");
    var slowRegexp = new RegExp("^" + slowest + ":");

    for (var i = 0, l = lis.length; i < l; i++) {
      if (slowRegexp.test(lis[i].innerHTML)) {
        lis[i].style.color = "#c00";
      }

      if (fastRegexp.test(lis[i].innerHTML)) {
        lis[i].style.color = "#0c0";
      }
    }
  }, 15);
}

// Updated benchmark function
function benchmark (name, tests, iterations) {
  iterations = iterations || 1000;
  times = {};
  var view = init(name);
  runTests(tests, view, iterations);
  highlightExtremes(view);
}
```

To further enhance benchmark we could decouple the DOM manipulation that displays results to allow for alternate report generators. This would also allow us to benchmark code in environments without a DOM, such as server-side JavaScript runtimes.

4.2.2 Profiling and Locating Bottlenecks

Firebug, the web developer add-on for Firefox, offers a profiler that can profile code as it runs. For instance, we can launch a live site, start the profiler and click a link that triggers a script. After the script finishes we stop the profiler. At this point the profile report will show us a breakdown of all functions run, along with how much time was spent on each of them. Many times the number of functions run to perform some task can in itself be valuable information that points us to overly

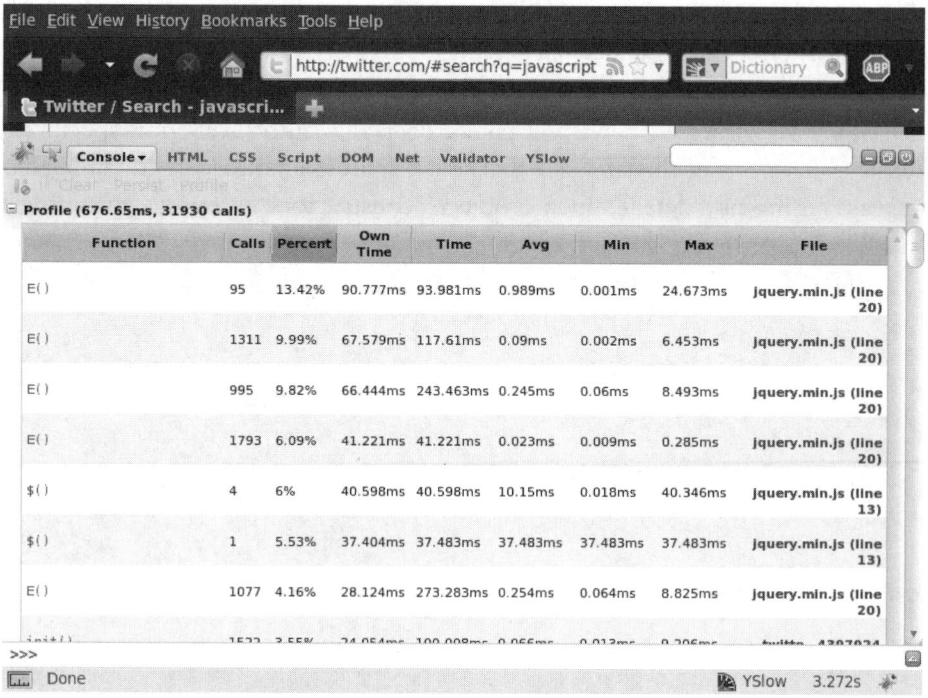

Figure 4.1 Profiling Twitter's search feature.

complex code. As an example of the Firebug profiler, Figure 4.1 shows the profile report after having used Twitter's search feature, which uses an `XMLHttpRequest` to fetch data, and manipulates the DOM to display the results. The profile report shows a lot going on inside jQuery, and a total of over 31,000 function calls.

4.3 Summary

In this chapter we have seen how unit tests can be utilized not necessarily only to support production code, but also to help us learn more about JavaScript. Keeping a suite of learning tests is a great way to document our learning, and they provide a handy reference over issues we have encountered in the past. While reading this book I encourage you to try out some of the examples and play with them to understand what is going on. If you don't already have a learning test suite, now would be a great time to start one, and you can start writing tests to further your understanding of examples from this book.

Benchmarks can help guide decisions when there are several viable ways of solving a given problem. By measuring relative performance we can learn patterns that tend to perform better, and keeping benchmarks along with learning tests makes for a powerful personal knowledge bank.

This chapter concludes the introduction to automated testing. In Part II, *JavaScript for Programmers,* we will take a deep dive into JavaScript, specifically focusing on aspects of the language that sets it apart from other programming languages. This means a detailed look at objects, constructors, and prototypes, as well as JavaScript scoping and functions.

Part II

JavaScript for Programmers

5

Functions

JavaScript functions are powerful beasts. They are first class objects, meaning they can be assigned to variables and as properties, passed as arguments to functions, have properties of their own, and more. JavaScript also supports anonymous functions, commonly used for inline callbacks to other functions and object methods.

In this chapter we will cover the somewhat theoretical side of JavaScript functions, providing us with the required background to easily dive into the more interesting uses of functions as we dig into into closures in Chapter 6, *Applied Functions and Closures,* and methods and functions as a means to implement objects in Chapter 7, *Objects and Prototypal Inheritance.*

5.1 Defining Functions

Throughout the first part of this book we have already seen several ways to define functions. In this section we will go over the different ways JavaScript allows us to do so, and investigate their pros and cons as well as some unexpected browser differences.

5.1.1 Function Declaration

The most straightforward way to define a function is by way of a function definition, seen in Listing 5.1.

Listing 5.1 A function declaration

```
function assert(message, expr) {
  if (!expr) {
    throw new Error(message);
  }

  assert.count++;

  return true;
}

assert.count = 0;
```

This is the `assert` function from Chapter 1, *Automated Testing.* The function declaration starts with the keyword `function`, followed by an identifier, `assert` in the above example. The function may define one or more *formal parameters*, i.e., named arguments. Finally, the function has a body enclosed in brackets. Functions may return a value. If no `return` statement is present, or if it's present without an expression, the function returns `undefined`. Being first class objects, functions can also have properties assigned to them, evident by the `count` property in the above example.

5.1.2 Function Expression

In addition to function declarations, JavaScript supports function expressions. A function expression results in an anonymous function that may be immediately executed, passed to another function, returned from a function, or assigned to a variable or an object property. In function expressions the identifier is optional. Listing 5.2 shows the `assert` function from before implemented as a function expression.

Listing 5.2 An anonymous function expression

```
var assert = function (message, expr) {
  if (!expr) {
    throw new Error(message);
  }

  assert.count++;

  return true;
};

assert.count = 0;
```

Note that in contrast to function declarations, function expressions—like any expression—should be terminated by a semicolon. Although not strictly necessary, automatic semicolon insertion can cause unexpected results, and best practices dictate that we always insert our own semicolons.

This alternative implementation of the `assert` function differs somewhat from the previous one. The anonymous function has no name, and so can only refer to itself by way of `arguments.callee` or through the `assert` variable, accessible through the scope chain. We will discuss both the `arguments` object and the scope chain in more detail shortly.

As noted previously, the identifier is optional in function expressions. Whether named function expressions are still anonymous functions is a matter of definition, but the functions stay anonymous to the enclosing scope. Listing 5.3 shows an example of a named function expression. We will discuss the implications and cross-browser issues surrounding named function expressions in Section 5.3.6, *Function Expressions Revisited*.

Listing 5.3 A named function expression

```
var assert = function assert(message, expr) {
  if (!expr) {
    throw new Error(message);
  }

  assert.count++;

  return true;
};

assert.count = 0;
```

5.1.3 The `Function` Constructor

JavaScript functions are first class objects, which means they can have properties, including methods, of their own. Like any other JavaScript object, functions have a prototype chain; functions inherit from `Function.prototype`, which in turn inherits from `Object.prototype`.[1] The `Function.prototype` object provides a few useful properties, such as the `call` and `apply` methods. In addition to the properties defined by their prototypes, function objects have `length` and `prototype` properties.

---

1. The details of JavaScript's prototypal inheritance are covered in Chapter 7, *Objects and Prototypal Inheritance*.

In contrast to what one might expect, the `prototype` property is *not* a reference to the function object's internal prototype (i.e., `Function.prototype`). Rather, it is an object that will serve as the prototype for any object created by using the function as a constructor. Constructors will be covered in depth in Chapter 7, *Objects and Prototypal Inheritance.*

The `length` property of a function indicates how many formal parameters it expects, sometimes referred to as the function's arity. Listing 5.4 shows an example.

Listing 5.4 Function objects `length` property

```
TestCase("FunctionTest", {
  "test function length property": function () {
    assertEquals(2, assert.length);
    assertEquals(1, document.getElementById.length);
    assertEquals(0, console.log.length); // In Firebug
  }
});
```

The test can be run with JsTestDriver by setting up a project including a configuration file as described in Chapter 3, *Tools of the Trade.*

The `benchmark` method in Listing 4.9 in Chapter 4, *Test to Learn,* used the `length` property to determine if the benchmark should be called in a loop. If the function took no formal parameters, the benchmark function looped it; otherwise the number of iterations was passed to the function to allow it to loop on its own, avoiding the overhead of the function calls.

Note in the above example how Firebug's `console.log` method does not use formal parameters at all. Still, we can pass as many arguments as we want, and they are all logged. Chrome's implementation of `document.getElementById` also has a length of 0. It turns out that formal parameters is only one of two ways to access arguments passed to a function.

The `Function` constructor can be used to create new functions as well. It can either be called as a function, i.e., `Function(p1, p2, ... , pn, body);`, or used in a new expression, as in `new Function(p1, p2, ... , pn, body);` with equal results. Both expressions create a new function object, and accept as arguments any number of formal parameters the new function should accept along with an optional function body as a string. Calling the function with no arguments results in an anonymous function that expects no formal parameters and has no function body. Listing 5.5 shows an example of defining the `assert` function via the `Function` constructor called as a function.

Listing 5.5 Creating a function via `Function`

```
var assert = Function("message", "expr",
              "if (!expr) { throw new Error(message); }" +
              "assert.count++; return true;");
assert.count = 0;
```

When creating functions this way, we can provide the formal parameters in a number of ways. The most straightforward way is to pass one string per parameter, as in the above example. However, we can also pass a single comma-separated string, or a mix of the two, i.e., `Function("p1,p2,p3", "p4", body);`.

The `Function` constructor is useful when the function body needs to be dynamically compiled, such as when creating functions tailored to the running environment or a set of input values, which can result in highly performant code.

5.2 Calling Functions

JavaScript offers two ways of calling a function—directly using parentheses or indirectly using the `call` and `apply` methods inherited from `Function. prototype`. Direct invocation works as one would expect, as seen in Listing 5.6.

Listing 5.6 Calling a function directly

```
assert("Should be true", typeof assert == "function");
```

When calling a function, JavaScript performs no check on the number of arguments. You can pass zero, one, or ten arguments to a function regardless of the number of formal parameters it specifies. Any formal parameter that does not receive an actual value will have `undefined` as its value.

5.2.1 The `arguments` Object

All of a function's arguments are available through the array-like object `arguments`. This object has a `length` property, denoting the number of received arguments, and numeric indexes from 0 to `length - 1` corresponding to the arguments passed when calling the function. Listing 5.7 shows the `assert` function using this object rather than its formal parameters.

Listing 5.7 Using `arguments`

```
function assert(message, expr) {
  if (arguments.length < 2) {
    throw new Error("Provide message and value to test");
  }

  if (!arguments[1]) {
    throw new Error(arguments[0]);
  }

  assert.count++;

  return true;
}

assert.count = 0;
```

This is not a particularly useful way to use `arguments`, but shows how it works. In general, the `arguments` object should only be used when formal parameters cannot solve the problem at hand, because using it comes with a performance price. In fact, merely referencing the object will induce some overhead, indicating that browsers optimize functions that don't use it.

The `arguments` object is array-like only through its `length` property and numeric index properties; it does not provide array methods. Still, we can use array methods on it by utilizing `Array.prototype.*` and their `call` or `apply` methods. Listing 5.8 shows an example in which we create an array consisting of all but the first argument to a function.

Listing 5.8 Using array methods with `arguments`

```
function addToArray() {
  var targetArr = arguments[0];
  var add = Array.prototype.slice.call(arguments, 1);

  return targetArr.concat(add);
}
```

As with arrays, the numerical indexes on the `arguments` object are really only properties with numbers for identifiers. Object identifiers are always converted to strings in JavaScript, which explains the code in Listing 5.9.

Listing 5.9 Accessing properties with strings

```
function addToArray() {
  var targetArr = arguments["0"];
  var add = Array.prototype.slice.call(arguments, 1);

  return targetArr.concat(add);
}
```

Some browsers like Firefox optimize arrays, indeed treating numeric property identifiers as numbers. Even so, the properties can always be accessed by string identifiers.

5.2.2 Formal Parameters and `arguments`

The `arguments` object shares a dynamic relationship with formal parameters; changing a property of the `arguments` object causes the corresponding formal parameter to change and vice versa as Listing 5.10 shows.

Listing 5.10 Modifying arguments

```
TestCase("FormalParametersArgumentsTest", {
  "test dynamic relationship": function () {
    function modify(a, b) {
      b = 42;
      arguments[0] = arguments[1];

      return a;
    }

    assertEquals(42, modify(1, 2));
  }
});
```

Setting the formal parameter b to 42 causes `arguments[1]` to update accordingly. Setting `arguments[0]` to this value in turn causes a to update as well.

This relationship only exists for formal parameters that actually receive values. Listing 5.11 shows the same example in which the second argument is left out when calling the function.

Listing 5.11 No dynamic mapping for missing parameters

```
assertUndefined(modify(1));
```

In this example, the return value is undefined because setting b does not update arguments[1] when no value was passed to b. Thus, arguments[1] is still undefined, which causes arguments[0] to be undefined. a did receive a value and is still linked to the arguments object, meaning that the returned value is undefined. Not all browsers do this by the spec, so your mileage may vary with the above examples.

This relationship may be confusing, and in some cases can be the source of mysterious bugs. A good piece of advice is to be careful when modifying function parameters, especially in functions that use both the formal parameters and the arguments object. In most cases defining a new variable is a much sounder strategy than tampering with formal parameters or arguments. For the reasons stated, ECMAScript 5, the next version of JavaScript, removes this feature in strict mode. Strict mode is discussed in detail in Chapter 8, *ECMAScript 5th Edition*.

5.3 Scope and Execution Context

JavaScript only has two kinds of scope; global scope and function scope. This might be confusing to developers used to block scope. Listing 5.12 shows an example.

Listing 5.12 Function scope

```
"test scope": function () {
  function sum() {
    assertUndefined(i);

    assertException(function () {
      assertUndefined(someVar);
    }, "ReferenceError");

    var total = arguments[0];

    if (arguments.length > 1) {
      for (var i = 1, l = arguments.length; i < l; i++) {
        total += arguments[i];
      }
    }

    assertEquals(5, i);

    return total;
  }

  sum(1, 2, 3, 4, 5);
}
```

This example shows a few interesting aspects. The `i` variable is declared even before the `var` statement inside the `for` loop. Notice how accessing some arbitrary variable will not work, and throws a `ReferenceError` (or `TypeError` in Internet Explorer). Furthermore, the `i` variable is still accessible, and has a value, after the `for` loop. A common error in methods that use more than one loop is to redeclare the `i` variable in every loop.

In addition to global scope and function scope, the `with` statement can alter the scope chain for its block, but its usage is usually discouraged and it is effectively deprecated in ECMAScript 5 strict mode. The next version of ECMAScript, currently a work-in-progress under the name of "Harmony", is slated to introduce block scope with the `let` statement. `let` has been available as a proprietary extension to Mozilla's JavaScript™ since version 1.7, first released with Firefox 2.0.

5.3.1 Execution Contexts

The ECMAScript specification describes all JavaScript code to operate in an *execution context.* Execution contexts are not accessible entities in JavaScript, but understanding them is vital to fully understand how functions and closures work. From the specification:

"Whenever control is transferred to ECMAScript executable code, control is entering an execution context. Active execution contexts logically form a stack. The top execution context on this stack is the running execution context."

5.3.2 The Variable Object

An execution context has a variable object. Any variables and functions defined inside the function are added as properties on this object. The algorithm that describes this process explain all of the examples in the previous section.

- For any formal parameters, add corresponding properties on the variable object and let their values be the values passed as arguments to the function.

- For any function declarations, add corresponding properties on the variable object whose values are the functions. If a function declaration uses the same identifier as one of the formal parameters, the property is overwritten.

- For any variable declarations, add corresponding properties on the variable object and initialize the properties to `undefined`, regardless of how the variables are initialized in source code. If a variable uses the same identifier as an already defined property (i.e., a parameter or function), do not overwrite it.

The effects of this algorithm is known as *hoisting* of functions and variable declarations. Note that although functions are hoisted in their entirety, variables only have their declaration hoisted. Initialization happens where defined in source code. This means that the code in Listing 5.12 is interpreted as Listing 5.13.

Listing 5.13 Function scope after hoisting

```
"test scope": function () {
  function sum() {
    var i;
    var l;

    assertUndefined(i);

    /* ... */
  }

  sum(1, 2, 3, 4, 5);
}
```

This explains why accessing the i variable before the var statement yields undefined whereas accessing some arbitrary variable results in a reference error. The reference error is further explained by how the scope chain works.

5.3.3 The Activation Object

The variable object does not explain why the arguments object is available inside the function. This object is a property of another object associated with execution contexts, the *activation object.* Note that both the activation object and the variable object are purely a specification mechanism, and cannot be reached by JavaScript code. For the purposes of identifier resolution, i.e., variable and function resolution, the activation object and the variable object are the same object. Because properties of the variable object are available as local variables inside an execution context, and because the variable object and the activation object is the same object, function bodies can reach the arguments object as if it was a local variable.

5.3.4 The Global Object

Before running any code, the JavaScript engine creates a global object whose initial properties are the built-ins defined by ECMAScript, such as Object, String, Array and others, in addition to host defined properties. Browser implementations of JavaScript provide a property of the global object that is itself the global object, namely window.

In addition to the `window` property (in browsers), the global object can be accessed as `this` in the global scope. Listing 5.14 shows how `window` relates to the global object in browsers.

Listing 5.14 The global object and `window`

```
var global = this;

TestCase("GlobalObjectTest", {
  "test window should be global object": function () {
    assertSame(global, window);
    assertSame(global.window, window);
    assertSame(window.window, window);
  }
});
```

In the global scope, the global object is used as the variable object, meaning that declaring variables using the `var` keyword results in corresponding properties on the global object. In other words, the two assignments in Listing 5.15 are *almost* equivalent.

Listing 5.15 Assigning properties on the global object

```
var assert = function () { /* ... */ };
this.assert = function () { /* ... */ };
```

These two statements are not fully equivalent, because the variable declaration is hoisted, whereas the property assignment is not.

5.3.5 The Scope Chain

Whenever a function is called, control enters a new execution context. This is even true for recursive calls to a function. As we've seen, the activation object is used for identifier resolution inside the function. In fact, identifier resolution occurs through the scope chain, which starts with the activation object of the current execution context. At the end of the scope chain is the global object.

Consider the simple function in Listing 5.16. Calling it with a number results in a function that, when called, adds that number to its argument.

Listing 5.16 A function that returns another function

```
function adder(base) {
  return function (num) {
```

```
    return base + num;
  };
}
```

Listing 5.17 uses `adder` to create incrementing and decrementing functions.

Listing 5.17 Incrementing and decrementing functions

```
TestCase("AdderTest", {
  "test should add or subtract one from arg": function () {
    var inc = adder(1);
    var dec = adder(-1);

    assertEquals(3, inc(2));
    assertEquals(3, dec(4));
    assertEquals(3, inc(dec(3)));
  }
});
```

The scope chain for the `inc` method contains its own activation object at the front. This object has a `num` property, corresponding to the formal parameter. The `base` variable, however, is not found on this activation object. When JavaScript does identifier resolution, it climbs the scope chain until it has no more objects. When `base` is not found, the next object in the scope chain is tried. The next object is the activation object created for `adder`, where in fact the `base` property is found. Had the property not been available here, identifier resolution would have continued on the next object in the scope chain, which in this case is the global object. If the identifier is not found on the global object, a reference error is thrown.

Inside the functions created and returned from `adder`, the `base` variable is known as a *free variable*, which may live on after the `adder` function has finished executing. This behavior is also known as a *closure*, a concept we will dig deeper into in the next chapter, Chapter 6, *Applied Functions and Closures.*

Functions created by the `Function` constructor have different scoping rules. Regardless of where they are created, these functions only have the global object in their scope chain, i.e., the containing scope is not added to their scope chain. This makes the `Function` constructor useful to avoid unintentional closures.

5.3.6 Function Expressions Revisited

With a better understanding of the scope chain we can revisit function expressions and gain a better understanding of how they work. Function expressions can be useful when we need to conditionally define a function, because function declarations are not allowed inside blocks, e.g., in an if-else statement. A common situation in which a function might be conditionally defined is when defining functions that will smooth over cross-browser differences, by employing feature detection. In Chapter 10, *Feature Detection,* we will discuss this topic in depth, and an example could be that of adding a `trim` function that trims strings. Some browsers offer the `String.prototype.trim` method, and we'd like to use this if it's available. Listing 5.18 shows a possible way to implement such a function.

Listing 5.18 Conditionally defining a function

```
var trim;

if (String.prototype.trim) {
  trim = function (str) {
    return str.trim();
  };
} else {
  trim = function (str) {
    return str.replace(/^\s+|\s+$/g, "");
  };
}
```

Using function declarations in this case would constitute a syntax error as per the ECMAScript specification. However, most browsers *will* run the example in Listing 5.19.

Listing 5.19 Conditional function declaration

```
// Danger! Don't try this at home
if (String.prototype.trim) {
  function trim(str) {
    return str.trim();
  }
} else {
  function trim(str) {
    return str.replace(/^\s+|\s+$/g, "");
  }
}
```

When this happens, we always end up with the second implementation due to function hoisting—the function declarations are hoisted before executing the conditional statement, and the second implementation always overwrites the first. An exception to this behavior is found in Firefox, which actually allows function statments as a syntax extension. Syntax extensions are legal in the spec, but not something to rely on.

The only difference between the function expressions and function declarations above is that the functions created with declarations have names. These names are useful both to call functions recursively, and even more so in debugging situations. Let's rephrase the `trim` method and rather define it directly on the `String.prototype` object for the browsers that lack it. Listing 5.20 shows an updated example.

Listing 5.20 Conditionally providing a string method

```
if (!String.prototype.trim) {
  String.prototype.trim = function () {
    return this.replace(/^\s+|\s+$/g, "");
  };
}
```

With this formulation we can always trim strings using `" string ".trim()` regardless of whether the browser supports the method natively. If we build a large application by defining methods like this, we will have trouble debugging it, because, e.g., Firebug stack traces will show a bunch of calls to anonymous functions, making it hard to navigate and use to locate the source of errors. Unit tests usually should have our backs, but readable stack traces are valuable at any rate.

Named function expressions solve this problem, as Listing 5.21 shows.

Listing 5.21 Using a named function expression

```
if (!String.prototype.trim) {
  String.prototype.trim = function trim() {
    return this.replace(/^\s+|\s+$/g, "");
  };
}
```

Named function expressions differ somewhat from function declarations; the identifier belongs to the inner scope, and should not be visible in the defining scope. Unfortunately, Internet Explorer does not respect this. In fact, Internet Explorer does not do well with named function expressions at all, as side effects of the above example show in Listing 5.22.

Listing 5.22 Named function expressions in Internet Explorer

```
// Should throw a ReferenceError, true in IE
assertFunction(trim);
```

```
if (!String.prototype.trim) {
  String.prototype.trim = function trim() {
    return this.replace(/^\s+|\s+$/g, "");
  };
}

// Should throw a ReferenceError, true in IE
assertFunction(trim);

// Even worse: IE creates two different function objects
assertNotSame(trim, String.prototype.trim);
```

This is a bleak situation; when faced with named function expressions, Internet Explorer creates two distinct function objects, leaks the identifier to the containing scope, and even hoists one of them. These discrepancies make dealing with named function expressions risky business that can easily introduce obscure bugs. By assigning the function expression to a variable with the same name, the duplicated function object can be avoided (effectively overwritten), but the scope leak and hoisting will still be there.

I tend to avoid named function expressions, favoring function declarations inside closures, utilizing different names for different branches if necessary. Of course, function declarations are hoisted and available in the containing scope as well—the difference is that this is expected behavior for function declarations, meaning no nasty surprises. The behavior of function declarations are known and predictable across browsers, and need no working around.

5.4 The this Keyword

JavaScript's this keyword throws many seasoned developers off. In most object oriented languages, this (or self) always points to the receiving object. In most object oriented languages, using this inside a method always means the object on which the method was called. This is not necessarily true in JavaScript, even though it is the default behavior in many cases. The method and method call in Listing 5.23 has this expected behavior.

Listing 5.23 Unsurprising behavior of this

```
var circle = {
  radius: 6,

  diameter: function () {
    return this.radius * 2;
```

```
  }
};

TestCase("CircleTest", {
  "test should implicitly bind to object": function () {
    assertEquals(12, circle.diameter());
  }
});
```

The fact that `this.radius` is a reference to `circle.radius` inside `circle.diameter` should not surprise you. The example in Listing 5.24 behaves differently.

Listing 5.24 The `this` value is no longer the `circle` object

```
"test implicit binding to the global object": function () {
  var myDiameter = circle.diameter;
  assertNaN(myDiameter());

  // WARNING: Never ever rely on implicit globals
  // This is just an example
  radius = 2;
  assertEquals(4, myDiameter());
}
```

This example reveals that it is the caller that decides the value of `this`. In fact, this detail was left out in the previous discussion about the execution context. In addition to creating the activation and variable objects, and appending to the scope chain, the `this` value is also decided when entering an execution context. `this` can be provided to a method either implicitly or explicitly.

5.4.1 Implicitly Setting `this`

`this` is set implicitly when calling a function using parentheses; calling it as a function causes `this` to be set to the global object; calling it as a method causes `this` to be the object through which the function is called. "Calling the function as a method" should be understood as calling the function as a property of an object. This is a highly useful feature, because it allows JavaScript objects to share function objects and still have them execute on the right object.

For instance, to borrow array methods for the `arguments` object as discussed previously, we can simply create a property on the object whose value is the method we want to execute, and execute it through `arguments`, implicitly setting `this` to `arguments`. Listing 5.25 shows such an example.

Listing 5.25 Calling a function as a method on an object

```
function addToArray() {
  var targetArr = arguments[0];
  arguments.slice = Array.prototype.slice;
  var add = arguments.slice(1);

  return targetArr.concat(add);
}
```

Calling the `addToArray` function will work exactly as the one presented in Listing 5.8. The ECMAScript specification specifically calls for many built-in methods to be generic, allowing them to be used with other objects that exhibit the right qualities. For instance, the `arguments` object has both a `length` property and numeric indexes, which satisfies `Array.prototype.slice`'s requirements.

5.4.2 Explicitly Setting `this`

When all we want is to control the value of `this` for a specific method call, it is much better to explicitly do so using the function's `call` or `apply` methods. The `Function.prototype.call` method calls a function with the first argument as `this`. Additional arguments are passed to the function when calling it. The first example of `addToArray` in Listing 5.8 used this method call `Array.prototype.slice` with `arguments` as `this`. Another example can be found in our previous `circle` example, as Listing 5.26 shows.

Listing 5.26 Using `call`

```
assertEquals(10, circle.diameter.call({ radius: 5 }));
```

Here we pass an object literal that defines a `radius` property as the `this` when calling `circle.diameter`.

5.4.3 Using Primitives As `this`

The first argument to `call` can be any object, even `null`. When passing `null`, the global object will be used as the `this` value. As we will see in Chapter 8, *ECMAScript 5th Edition,* this is about to change—in ECMAScript5 strict mode, passing `null` as the `this` value causes `this` to be `null`, not the global object.

When passing primitive types, such as a string or boolean, as the `this` value, the value is wrapped in an object. This can be troublesome, e.g., when calling methods on booleans. Listing 5.27 shows an example in which this might produce unexpected results.

Listing 5.27 Calling methods with booleans as `this`

```
Boolean.prototype.not = function () {
  return !this;
};

TestCase("BooleanTest", {
  "test should flip value of true": function () {
    assertFalse(true.not());
    assertFalse(Boolean.prototype.not.call(true));
  },

  "test should flip value of false": function () {
    // Oops! Both fail, false.not() == false
    assertTrue(false.not());
    assertTrue(Boolean.prototype.not.call(false));
  }
});
```

This method does not work as expected because the primitive booleans are converted to `Boolean` objects when used as `this`. Boolean coercion of an object always produces `true`, and using the unary logical not operator on `true` unsurprisingly results in `false`. ECMAScript 5 strict mode fixes this as well, by avoiding the object conversion before using a value as `this`.

The `apply` method is similar to `call`, except it only expects two arguments; the first argument is the `this` value as with `call` and its second argument is an array of arguments to pass to the function being called. The second argument does not need to be an actual array object; any array-like object will do, meaning that `apply` can be used to chain function calls by passing `arguments` as the second argument to `apply`.

As an example, `apply` could be used to sum all numbers in an array. First consider the function in Listing 5.28, which accepts an arbitrary amount of arguments, assumes they're numbers, and returns the sum.

Listing 5.28 Summing numbers

```
function sum() {
  var total = 0;

  for (var i = 0, l = arguments.length; i < l; i++) {
    total += arguments[i];
```

```
    }

    return total;
}
```

Listing 5.29 shows two test cases for this method. The first test sums a series of numbers by calling the function with parentheses, whereas the second test sums an array of numbers via `apply`.

Listing 5.29 Summing numbers with `apply`

```
TestCase("SumTest", {
  "test should sum numbers": function () {
    assertEquals(15, sum(1, 2, 3, 4, 5));
    assertEquals(15, sum.apply(null, [1, 2, 3, 4, 5]));
  }
});
```

Remember, passing `null` as the first argument causes `this` to implicitly bind to the global object, which is also the case when the function is called as in the first test. ECMAScript 5 does not implicitly bind the global object, causing `this` to be `undefined` in the first call and `null` in the second.

`call` and `apply` are invaluable tools when passing methods as callbacks to other functions. In the next chapter we will implement a companion method, `Function.prototype.bind`, which can bind an object as `this` to a given function without calling it immediately.

5.5 Summary

In this chapter we have covered the theoretical basics of JavaScript functions. We have seen how to create functions, how to use them as objects, how to call them, and how to manipulate arguments and the `this` value.

JavaScript functions differ from functions or methods in many other languages in that they are first class objects, and in the way the execution context and scope chain work. Also, controlling the `this` value from the caller may be an unfamiliar way to work with functions, but as we'll see throughout this book, can be very useful.

In the next chapter we will continue our look at functions and study some more interesting use cases as we dive into the concept known as closures.

Applied Functions and Closures

In the previous chapter we discussed the theoretical aspects of JavaScript functions, familiarizing ourselves with execution contexts and the scope chain. JavaScript supports nested functions, which allows for *closures* that can keep private state, and can be used for anything from ad hoc scopes to implementing memoization, function binding, modules and stateful functions, and objects.

In this chapter we will work through several examples of how to make good use of JavaScript functions and closures.

6.1 Binding Functions

When passing methods as callbacks, the implicit `this` value is lost unless the object on which it should execute is passed along with it. This can be confusing unless the semantics of `this` are familiar.

6.1.1 Losing `this`: A Lightbox Example

To illustrate the problem at hand, assume we have a "lightbox" object. A lightbox is simply an HTML element that is overlaid the page, and appears to float above the rest of the page, much like a popup, only with a web 2.0 name. In this example the lightbox pulls content from a URL and displays it in a `div` element. For convenience, an `anchorLightbox` function is provided, which turns an anchor element into a

lightbox toggler; when the anchor is clicked, the page it links to is loaded into a div
that is positioned above the current page. Listing 6.1 shows a rough outline.

Listing 6.1 Lightbox pseudo code

```
var lightbox = {
  open: function () {
    ajax.loadFragment(this.url, {
      target: this.create()
    });

    return false;
  },

  close: function () { /* ... */ },
  destroy: function () { /* ... */ },

  create: function () {
    /* Create or return container */
  }
};

function anchorLightbox(anchor, options) {
  var lb = Object.create(lightbox);
  lb.url = anchor.href;
  lb.title = anchor.title || anchor.href;
  Object.extend(lb, options);
  anchor.onclick = lb.open;

  return lb;
}
```

Note that the code will not run as provided; it's simply a conceptual example. The details of Object.create and Object.extend will be explained in
Chapter 7, *Objects and Prototypal Inheritance,* and the ajax.loadFragment
method can be assumed to load the contents of a URL into the DOM element
specified by the target option. The anchorLightbox function creates a new
object that inherits from the lightbox object, sets crucial properties, and returns
the new object. Additionally, it assigns an event handler for the click event. Using
DOM0 event properties will do for now but is generally not advisable; we'll see a
better way to add event handlers in Chapter 10, *Feature Detection.*

Unfortunately, the expected behavior fails when the link is clicked. The reason
is that when we assign the lb.open method as the event handler, we lose the
implicit binding of this to the lb object, which only occurs when the function is

called as a property of it. In the previous chapter we saw how `call` and `apply` can be used to explicitly set the `this` value when calling a function. However, those methods only help at call time.

6.1.2 Fixing `this` via an Anonymous Function

To work around the problem, we could assign an anonymous function as the event handler that when executed calls the `open` method, making sure the correct `this` value is set. Listing 6.2 shows the workaround.

Listing 6.2 Calling open through an anonymous proxy function

```
function anchorLightbox(anchor, options) {
  /* ... */

  anchor.onclick = function () {
    return lb.open();
  };

  /* ... */
}
```

Assigning the inner function as the event handler creates a *closure*. Normally, when a function exits, the execution context along with its activation and variable object are no longer referenced, and thus are available for garbage collection. However, the moment we assign the inner function as the event handler something interesting happens. Even after the `anchorLightbox` finishes, the `anchor` object, through its `onclick` property, still has access to the scope chain of the execution context created for `anchorLightbox`. The anonymous inner function uses the `lb` variable, which is neither a parameter nor a local variable; it is a *free* variable, accessible through the scope chain.

Using the closure to handle the event, effectively proxying the method call, the lightbox anchor should now work as expected. However, the manual wrapping of the method call doesn't feel quite right. If we were to define several event handlers in the same way, we would introduce duplication, which is error-prone and likely to make code harder to maintain, change, and understand. A better solution is needed.

6.1.3 `Function.prototype.bind`

ECMAScript 5 provides the `Function.prototype.bind` function, which is also found in some form in most modern JavaScript libraries. The `bind` method accepts an object as its first argument and returns a function object that, when called, calls the original function with the bound object as the `this` value. In other words, it provides the functionality we just implemented manually, and could be considered the deferred companion to `call` and `apply`. Using `bind`, we could update `anchorLightbox` as shown in Listing 6.3.

Listing 6.3 Using `bind`

```
function anchorLightbox(anchor, options) {
  /* ... */

  anchor.onclick = lb.open.bind(lb);

  /* ... */
}
```

Because not all browsers yet implement this highly useful function, we can conditionally provide our own implementation for those browsers that lack it. Listing 6.4 shows a simple implementation.

Listing 6.4 Implementation of `bind`

```
if (!Function.prototype.bind) {
  Function.prototype.bind = function (thisObj) {
    var target = this;

    return function () {
      return target.apply(thisObj, arguments);
    };
  };
}
```

The implementation returns a function—a *closure*—that maintains its reference to the `thisObj` argument and the function itself. When the returned function is executed, the original function is called with `this` explicitly set to the bound object. Any arguments passed to the returned function is passed on to the original function.

Adding the function to `Function.prototype` means it will be available as a method on all function objects, so `this` refers to the function on which the method is called. In order to access this value we need to store it in a local variable in the outer function. As we saw in the previous chapter, `this` is calculated upon entering a new execution context and is not part of the scope chain. Assigning it to a local variable makes it accessible through the scope chain in the inner function.

6.1.4 Binding with Arguments

According to the ECMAScript 5 specification (and, e.g., the Prototype.js implementation), `bind` should support binding functions to arguments as well as the `this` value. Doing so means we can "prefill" a function with arguments, bind it to an object, and pass it along to be called at some later point. This can prove extremely useful for event handlers, in cases in which the handling method needs arguments known at bind time. Another useful case for binding arguments is deferring some computation, e.g., by passing a callback to `setTimeout`.

Listing 6.5 shows an example in which `bind` is used to prefill a function with arguments to defer a benchmark with `setTimeout`. The `bench` function calls the function passed to it 10,000 times and logs the result. Rather than manually carrying out the function calls in an anonymous function passed to `setTimeout`, we use `bind` to run all the benchmarks in the `benchmarks` array by binding the `forEach` method to the array and the `bench` function as its argument.

Listing 6.5 Deferring a method call using `bind` and `setTimeout`

```
function bench(func) {
  var start = new Date().getTime();

  for (var i = 0; i < 10000; i++) {
    func();
  }

  console.log(func, new Date().getTime() - start);
}

var benchmarks = [
  function forLoop() { /* ... */ },
  function forLoopCachedLength() { /* ... */ },
  /* ... */
];

setTimeout(benchmarks.forEach.bind(benchmarks, bench), 500);
```

The above listing will cause the benchmarks to be run after 500 milliseconds. The keen reader will recognize the benchmarks from Chapter 4, *Test to Learn*.

Listing 6.6 shows one possible way of implementing `bind` such that it allows arguments bound to the function as well as the `this` value.

Listing 6.6 bind with arguments support

```
if (!Function.prototype.bind) {
  Function.prototype.bind = function (thisObj) {
    var target = this;
    var args = Array.prototype.slice.call(arguments, 1);

    return function () {
      var received = Array.prototype.slice.call(arguments);

      return target.apply(thisObj, args.concat(received));
    };
  };
}
```

This implementation is fairly straightforward. It keeps possible arguments passed to bind in an array, and when the bound function is called it concatenates this array with possible additional arguments received in the actual call.

Although simple, the above implementation is a poor performer. It is likely that bind will be used most frequently to simply bind a function to an object, i.e., no arguments. In this simple case, converting and concatenating the arguments will only slow down the call, both at bind time *and* at call time for the bound function. Fortunately, optimizing the different cases is pretty simple. The different cases are:

- Binding a function to an object, no arguments
- Binding a function to an object and one or more arguments
- Calling a bound function without arguments
- Calling a bound function with arguments

The two latter steps occur for both of the former steps, meaning that there are two cases to cater for at bind time, and four at call time. Listing 6.7 shows an optimized function.

Listing 6.7 Optimized bind

```
if (!Function.prototype.bind) {
  (function () {
    var slice = Array.prototype.slice;

    Function.prototype.bind = function (thisObj) {
      var target = this;

      if (arguments.length > 1) {
```

```
      var args = slice.call(arguments, 1);

      return function () {
        var allArgs = args;

        if (arguments.length > 0) {
          allArgs = args.concat(slice.call(arguments));
        }

        return target.apply(thisObj, allArgs);
      };
    }

    return function () {
      if (arguments.length > 0) {
        return target.apply(thisObj, arguments);
      }

      return target.call(thisObj);
    };
  };
}());
}
```

This implementation is somewhat more involved, but yields much better performance, especially for the simple case of binding a function to an object and no arguments and calling it with no arguments.

Note that the implementation given here is missing one feature from the ECMAScript 5 specification. The spec states that the resulting function should behave as the bound function when used in a new expression.

6.1.5 Currying

Currying is closely related to binding, because they both offer a way to partially apply a function. Currying differs from binding in that it only pre-fills arguments; it does not set the this value. This is useful, because it allows us to bind arguments to functions and methods while maintaining their implicit this value. The implicit this allows us to use currying to bind arguments to functions on an object's prototype, and still have the function execute with a given object as its this value. Listing 6.8 shows an example of implementing String.prototype.trim in terms of String.prototype.replace using Function.prototype.curry.

Listing 6.8 Implementing a method in terms of another one and `curry`

```
(function () {
  String.prototype.trim =
    String.prototype.replace.curry(/^\s+|\s+$/g, "");

  TestCase("CurryTest", {
    "test should trim spaces": function () {
      var str = "   some spaced string   ";

      assertEquals("some spaced string", str.trim());
    }
  });
}());
```

The implementation of `curry` in Listing 6.9 resembles the `bind` implementation from before.

Listing 6.9 Implementing `curry`

```
if (!Function.prototype.curry) {
  (function () {
    var slice = Array.prototype.slice;

    Function.prototype.curry = function () {
      var target = this;
      var args = slice.call(arguments);

      return function () {
        var allArgs = args;

        if (arguments.length > 0) {
          allArgs = args.concat(slice.call(arguments));
        }

        return target.apply(this, allArgs);
      };
    };
  }());
}
```

There's no optimization for the case in which `curry` does not receive arguments, because calling it without arguments is senseless and should be avoided.

6.2 Immediately Called Anonymous Functions

A common practice in JavaScript is to create anonymous functions that are imme-diately called. Listing 6.10 shows a typical incarnation.

Listing 6.10 An immediately called anonymous function

```
(function () {
  /* ... */
}());
```

The parentheses wrapping the entire expression serves two purposes. Leaving them out causes the function expression to be seen as a function declaration, which would constitute a syntax error without an identifier. Furthermore, expressions (as opposed to declarations) cannot start with the word "function" as it might make them ambiguous with function declarations, so giving the function a name and calling it would not work either. Thus, the parentheses are necessary to avoid syntax errors. Additionally, when assigning the return value of such a function to a variable, the leading parentheses indicates that the function expression is not what's returned from the expression.

6.2.1 Ad Hoc Scopes

JavaScript only has global scope and function scope, which may sometimes cause weird problems. The first problem we need to avoid is leaking objects into the global scope, because doing so increases our chances of naming collisions with other scripts, such as third party libraries, widgets, and web analytics scripts.

6.2.1.1 Avoiding the Global Scope

We can avoid littering the global scope with temporary variables (e.g., loop variables and other intermittent variables) by simply wrapping our code in a self-executing closure. Listing 6.11 shows an example of using the aforementioned lightbox object; every anchor element in the document with the class name `lightbox` is picked up and passed to the `anchorLightbox` function.

Listing 6.11 Creating lightboxes

```
(function () {
  var anchors = document.getElementsByTagName("a");
  var regexp = /(^|\s)lightbox(\s|$)/;

  for (var i = 0, l = anchors.length; i < l; i++) {
```

```
    if (regexp.test(anchors[i].className)) {
      anchorLightbox(anchors[i]);
    }
  }
}());
```

6.2.1.2 Simulating Block Scope

Another useful case for immediately called closures is when creating closures inside loops. Assume that we had opted for a different design of our lightbox widget, in which there was only one object, and it could be used to open any number of lightboxes. In this case we would need to add event handlers manually, as in Listing 6.12.

Listing 6.12 Adding event handlers the wrong way

```
(function () {
  var anchors = document.getElementsByTagName("a");
  var controller = Object.create(lightboxController);
  var regexp = /(^|\s)lightbox(\s|$)/;

  for (var i = 0, l = anchors.length; i < l; i++) {
    if (regexp.test(anchors[i].className)) {
      anchors[i].onclick = function () {
        controller.open(anchors[i]);
        return false;
      };
    }
  }
}());
```

This example will not work as expected. The event handler attached to the links forms a closure that can access the variables local to the outer function. However, all the closures (one for each anchor) keep a reference to the same scope; clicking any of the anchors will cause the same lightbox to open. When the event handler for an anchor is called, the outer function has changed the value of i since it was assigned, thus it will not trigger the correct lightbox to open.

To fix this we can use a closure to capture the anchor we want to associate with the event handler by storing it in a variable that is not available to the outer function, and thus cannot be changed by it. Listing 6.13 fixes the issue by passing the anchor as argument to a new closure.

Listing 6.13 Fixing scoping issues with nested closures

```
(function () {
  var anchors = document.getElementsByTagName("a");
  var controller = Object.create(lightboxController);
  var regexp = /(^|\s)lightbox(\s|$)/;

  for (var i = 0, l = anchors.length; i < l; i++) {
    if (regexp.test(anchors[i].className)) {
      (function (anchor) {
        anchor.onclick = function () {
          controller.open(anchor);
          return false;
        };
      }(anchors[i]));
    }
  }
}());
```

`anchor` is now a formal parameter to the inner closure, whose variable object cannot be accessed or tampered with by the containing scope. Thus, the event handlers will work as expected.

Examples aside, closures in loops are generally a performance issue waiting to happen. Most problems can be better solved by avoiding the nested closure, for instance, by using dedicated functions to create the closure like we did in Listing 6.11. When assigning event handlers, there is even another problem with nesting functions like this, because the circular reference between the DOM element and its event handler may cause memory leaks.

6.2.2 Namespaces

A good strategy to stay out of the global scope is to use some kind of namespacing. JavaScript does not have native namespaces, but because it offers such useful objects and functions it does not need them either. To use objects as namespaces, simply define a single object in the global scope and implement additional functions and objects as properties of it. Listing 6.14 shows how we could possibly implement the lightbox object inside our own `tddjs` namespace.

Listing 6.14 Using objects as namespaces

```
var tddjs = {
  lightbox: { /* ... */ },
```

```
anchorLightbox: function (anchor, options) {
    /* ... */
  }
};
```

In larger libraries, we might want better organization than simply defining everything inside the same object. For example, the lightbox might live in `tddjs.ui`, whereas ajax functionality could live in `tddjs.ajax`. Many libraries provide some kind of `namespace` function to help with this kind of organizing. Organizing all code inside a single file is not a sound strategy, and when splitting code inside the same object across several files, knowing if the namespace object is already created becomes an issue.

6.2.2.1 Implementing Namespaces

For this book we will use the `tddjs` object to namespace reusable code that is shared between chapters. To help with namespacing we will implement our own function that will loop each level in the namespace—provided as a string—creating objects that don't exist. Listing 6.15 shows a few test cases demonstrating its use and side-effects.

Listing 6.15 Demonstrating the `namespace` function

```
TestCase("NamespaceTest", {
  tearDown: function () {
    delete tddjs.nstest;
  },

  "test should create non-existent object":
  function () {
    tddjs.namespace("nstest");

    assertObject(tddjs.nstest);
  },

  "test should not overwrite existing objects":
  function () {
    tddjs.nstest = { nested: {} };
    var result = tddjs.namespace("nstest.nested");

    assertSame(tddjs.nstest.nested, result);
  },

  "test only create missing parts":
```

```
function () {
  var existing = {};
  tddjs.nstest = { nested: { existing: existing } };
  var result = tddjs.namespace("nstest.nested.ui");

  assertSame(existing, tddjs.nstest.nested.existing);
  assertObject(tddjs.nstest.nested.ui);
}
});
```

namespace is expected to be implemented as a method on the global tddjs object, and manages namespaces inside it. This way tddjs is completely sandboxed inside its own namespace, and using it along with immediately called closures will ensure we don't leak properties to the global object. Its implementation is found in Listing 6.16. Save it in a file called tdd.js; we will add more utilities to this file/namespace throughout the book.

Listing 6.16 The namespace function

```
var tddjs = (function () {
  function namespace(string) {
    var object = this;
    var levels = string.split(".");

    for (var i = 0, l = levels.length; i < l; i++) {
      if (typeof object[levels[i]] == "undefined") {
        object[levels[i]] = {};
      }

      object = object[levels[i]];
    }

    return object;
  }

  return {
    namespace: namespace
  };
}());
```

This implementation shows a few interesting uses of functions. It wraps the entire implementation in a closure, returning an object literal that is assigned to the global tddjs object.

Avoiding the trouble with named function expressions and taking advantage of the fact that the closure creates a local scope, we define namespace using a function declaration and then assign it to the namespace property of the returned object.

The namespace function starts resolving namespaces from this. Doing so allows the function to be easily borrowed to create namespaces in other objects than tddjs. Listing 6.17 shows an example of borrowing the method to create namespaces inside another object.

Listing 6.17 Creating custom namespaces

```
"test namespacing inside other objects":
function () {
  var custom = { namespace: tddjs.namespace };
  custom.namespace("dom.event");

  assertObject(custom.dom.event);
  assertUndefined(tddjs.dom);
}
```

As the test shows, the tddjs object is not modified when calling the method through another object, which should not be surprising.

6.2.2.2 Importing Namespaces

When organizing code in namespaces, we might tire from all the typing. Programmers are lazy creatures, and typing tddjs.ajax.request might be too much to ask. As we already saw, JavaScript does not have native namespaces, and so there is no import keyword to import a set of objects into the local scope. Luckily, closures have local scope, which means that we can simply assign nested objects to local variables to "import" them. Listing 6.18 shows an example.

Listing 6.18 Using a local variable to "import" a namespace

```
(function () {
  var request = tddjs.ajax.request;

  request(/* ... */);
  /* ... */
}());
```

Another advantage of this technique is that, unlike with global variables, local variable identifiers can safely be minified. Thus, using local aliases can help reduce the size of scripts in production as well.

Be careful when making local aliases to methods as in the above example. If the method is dependent on its this object, such local importing effectively breaks implicit binding. Because importing namespaces effectively caches the object inside the closure, it can also cause trouble when trying to mock or stub the imported object.

Using namespaces is a highly useful way to organize code in a clean way without tripping up the global namespace. You might worry that the property lookups come with a performance penalty, which they do, but compared with, e.g., DOM manipulation, the impact of these namespaces will be minute.

6.3 Stateful Functions

A closure can maintain state through its free variables. The scope chain that allows access to these free variables is only accessible from within the scope chain itself, which means that free variables by definition are private. In Chapter 7, *Objects and Prototypal Inheritance,* we will see how this can be used to create objects with private state, a feature not otherwise offered by JavaScript (i.e., no `private` keyword), in a pattern popularized as "the module pattern."

In this section we will use closures to hide implementation details for functions.

6.3.1 Generating Unique Ids

The ability to generate unique ids for any given object is useful whenever we want to use objects and functions as, e.g., property keys in objects. As we'll see in the next chapter, property identifiers in JavaScript are always coerced to strings; so even though we can set a property whose key is an object, it won't do what we expect.

Another useful application of unique ids in the case of DOM elements. Storing data as properties of DOM elements can cause memory leaks and other undesired behavior. One way to avoid these problems, currently employed by most major libraries, is to generate a unique id for an element, and keep an element storage separate from the element. This allows for an API that can get and set data on the element without actually storing data other than the unique id directly on it.

As an example of a stateful closure, we will implement a `tddjs.uid` method. The method accepts an object and returns a numeric id, which is stored in a property on the object. Listing 6.19 shows a few test cases describing its behavior.

Listing 6.19 Specification of the `uid` function

```
TestCase("UidTest", {
  "test should return numeric id":
  function () {
    var id = tddjs.uid({});
```

```
    assertNumber(id);
  },

  "test should return consistent id for object":
  function () {
    var object = {};
    var id = tddjs.uid(object);

    assertSame(id, tddjs.uid(object));
  },

  "test should return unique id":
  function () {
    var object = {};
    var object2 = {};
    var id = tddjs.uid(object);

    assertNotEquals(id, tddjs.uid(object2));
  },

  "test should return consistent id for function":
  function () {
    var func = function () {};
    var id = tddjs.uid(func);

    assertSame(id, tddjs.uid(func));
  },

  "test should return undefined for primitive":
  function () {
    var str = "my string";

    assertUndefined(tddjs.uid(str));
  }
});
```

The tests can be run with JsTestDriver, as described in Chapter 3, *Tools of the Trade.* This is not an exhaustive test suite, but it shows the basic behavior the method will support. Note that passing primitives to the function will not work as assigning properties to primitives does not actually add properties to the primitive—the primitive is wrapped in an object for the property access, which is immediately thrown away, i.e., new String("my string").__uid = 3.

The implementation is the interesting part. The uid method generates ids by looking up a counter that is incremented every time an id is requested. We could store this id as a property of the uid function object, but that would make it susceptible to outside modification, which could cause the method to return the same id twice, breaking its contract. By using a closure, we can store the counter in a free variable that is protected from outside access. Listing 6.20 shows the implementation.

Listing 6.20 Storing state in a free variable

```
(function () {
  var id = 0;

  function uid(object) {
    if (typeof object.__uid != "number") {
      object.__uid = id++;
    }

    return object.__uid;
  }

  if (typeof tddjs == "object") {
    tddjs.uid = uid;
  }
}());
```

The implementation uses an immediately called anonymous closure to create a scope in which the `id` variable can live. The `uid` function, which has access to this variable, is exposed to the world as the `tddjs.uid` method. The `typeof` check avoids a reference error if for some reason the file containing the `tddjs` object has not loaded.

6.3.2 Iterators

Iterators are objects that encapsulate the enumeration of a collection object. They provide a consistent API to traverse any kind of collection, and can provide better control over iteration than what simple `for` and `while` loops can, e.g., by ensuring that an item is never accessed more than once, that items are accessed strictly sequential and more. Closures can be used to implement iterators rather effortlessly in JavaScript. Listing 6.21 shows the basic behavior of the iterators created by `tddjs.iterator`.

Listing 6.21 Behavior of the `tddjs.iterator` method

```
TestCase("IteratorTest", {
  "test next should return first item":
  function () {
    var collection = [1, 2, 3, 4, 5];
```

```
    var iterator = tddjs.iterator(collection);

    assertSame(collection[0], iterator.next());
    assertTrue(iterator.hasNext());
  },

  "test hasNext should be false after last item":
  function () {
    var collection = [1, 2];
    var iterator = tddjs.iterator(collection);

    iterator.next();
    iterator.next();

    assertFalse(iterator.hasNext());
  },

  "test should loop collection with iterator":
  function () {
    var collection = [1, 2, 3, 4, 5];
    var it = tddjs.iterator(collection);
    var result = [];

    while (it.hasNext()) {
      result.push(it.next());
    }

    assertEquals(collection, result);
  }
});
```

A possible implementation of the iterator is shown in Listing 6.22.

Listing 6.22 Possible implementation of `tddjs.iterator`

```
(function () {
  function iterator(collection) {
    var index = 0;
    var length = collection.length;

    function next() {
      var item = collection[index++];

      return item;
    }

    function hasNext() {
```

```
      return index < length;
    }

    return {
      next: next,
      hasNext: hasNext
    };
  }

  if (typeof tddjs == "object") {
    tddjs.iterator = iterator;
  }
}());
```

The overall pattern should start to look familiar. The interesting parts are the collection, index and length free variables. The iterator function returns an object whose methods have access to the free variables, and is an implementation of the module pattern mentioned previously.

The iterator interface was purposely written to imitate that of Java's iterators. However, JavaScript's functions have more to offer, and this interface could be written in a much leaner way, as seen in Listing 6.23.

Listing 6.23 Functional iterator approach

```
(function () {
  function iterator(collection) {
    var index = 0;
    var length = collection.length;

    function next() {
      var item = collection[index++];
      next.hasNext = index < length;

      return item;
    }

    next.hasNext = index < length;

    return next;
  }

  if (typeof tddjs == "object") {
    tddjs.iterator = iterator;
  }
}());
```

This implementation simply returns the next function, and assigns hasNext as a property of it. Every call to next updates the hasNext property. Leveraging this we can update the loop test to look like Listing 6.24.

Listing 6.24 Looping with functional iterators

```
"test should loop collection with iterator":
function () {
  var collection = [1, 2, 3, 4, 5];
  var next = tddjs.iterator(collection);
  var result = [];

  while (next.hasNext) {
    result.push(next());
  }

  assertEquals(collection, result);
}
```

6.4 Memoization

Our final closure example will be provided by memoization, a caching technique at the method level and a popular example of the power of JavaScript functions.

Memoization is a technique that can be employed to avoid carrying out expensive operations repeatedly, thus speeding up programs. There are a few ways to implement memoization in JavaScript, and we'll start with the one closest to the examples we've worked with so far.

Listing 6.25 shows an implementation of the Fibonacci sequence, which uses two recursive calls to calculate the value at a given point in the sequence.

Listing 6.25 The Fibonacci sequence

```
function fibonacci(x) {
  if (x < 2) {
    return 1;
  }

  return fibonacci(x - 1) + fibonacci(x - 2);
}
```

The Fibonacci sequence is very expensive, and quickly spawns too many recursive calls for a browser to handle. By wrapping the function in a closure, we can manually memoize values to optimize this method, as seen in Listing 6.26.

Listing 6.26 Memoizing the Fibonacci sequence in a closure

```
var fibonacci = (function () {
  var cache = {};

  function fibonacci(x) {
    if (x < 2) {
      return 1;
    }

    if (!cache[x]) {
      cache[x] = fibonacci(x - 1) + fibonacci(x - 2);
    }

    return cache[x];
  }

  return fibonacci;
}());
```

This alternative version of `fibonacci` runs many orders of magnitude faster than the original one, and by extension is capable of calculating more numbers in the sequence. However, mixing computation with caching logic is a bit ugly. Again, we will add a function to `Function.prototype` to help separate concerns. The `memoize` method in Listing 6.27 is capable of wrapping a method, adding memoization without cluttering the calculation logic.

Listing 6.27 A general purpose `memoize` method

```
if (!Function.prototype.memoize) {
  Function.prototype.memoize = function () {
    var cache = {};
    var func = this;

    return function (x) {
      if (!(x in cache)) {
        cache[x] = func.call(this, x);
      }

      return cache[x];
    };
  };
}
```

This method offers a clean way to memoize functions, as seen in Listing 6.28.

Listing 6.28 Memoizing the `fibonacci` function

```
TestCase("FibonacciTest", {
  "test calculate high fib value with memoization":
  function () {
    var fibonacciFast = fibonacci.memoize();

    assertEquals(1346269, fibonacciFast(30));
  }
});
```

The `memoize` method offers a clean solution but unfortunately only deals with functions that take a single argument. Limiting its use further is the fact that it blindly coerces all arguments to strings, by nature of property assignment, which will be discussed in detail in Chapter 7, *Objects and Prototypal Inheritance*.

To improve the memoizer, we would need to serialize all arguments to use as keys. One way to do this, which is only slightly more complex than what we already have, is to simply `join` the arguments, as Listing 6.29 does.

Listing 6.29 A slightly better `memoize` method

```
if (!Function.prototype.memoize) {
  Function.prototype.memoize = function () {
    var cache = {};
    var func = this;
    var join = Array.prototype.join;

    return function () {
      var key = join.call(arguments);

      if (!(key in cache)) {
        cache[key] = func.apply(this, arguments);
      }

      return cache[key];
    };
  };
}
```

This version will not perform as well as the previous incarnation because it both calls `join` and uses `apply` rather than `call`, because we no longer can assume the number of arguments. Also, this version will coerce all arguments to strings as before, meaning it cannot differentiate between, e.g., `"12"` and `12` passed as arguments. Finally, because the cache key is generated by joining the parameters with a comma, string arguments that contain commas can cause the wrong value to be loaded, i.e., (1, "b") would generate the same cache key as ("1,b").

It is possible to implement a proper serializer that can embed type information about arguments, and possibly use `tddjs.uid` to serialize object and function arguments, but doing so would impact the performance of `memoize` in a noticeable way such that it would only help out in cases that could presumably be better optimized in other ways. Besides, serializing object arguments using `tddjs.uid`, although simple and fast, would cause the method to possibly assign new properties to arguments. That would be unexpected in most cases and should at the very least be properly documented.

6.5 Summary

In this chapter we have worked through a handful of practical function examples with a special focus on closures. With an understanding of the scope chain from Chapter 5, *Functions,* we have seen how inner functions can keep private state in free variables. Through examples we have seen how to make use of the scope and state offered by closures to solve a range of problems in an elegant way.

Some of the functions developed in this chapter will make appearances in upcoming chapters as we build on top of them and add more useful interfaces to the `tddjs` object. Throughout the book we will also meet plenty more examples of using closures.

In the next chapter we will take a look at JavaScript's objects and gain a better understanding of how property access and prototypal inheritance work, how closures can help in object oriented programming in JavaScript, as well as explore different ways to create objects and share behavior between them.

Objects and Prototypal Inheritance

JavaScript is an object oriented programming language. However, unlike most other object oriented languages, JavaScript does not have classes. Instead, JavaScript offers *prototypes* and *prototype-based inheritance* in which objects inherit from other objects. Additionally, the language offers constructors—functions that create objects, a fact that often confuses programmers and hides its nature. In this chapter we'll investigate how JavaScript objects and properties work. We'll also study the prototype chain as well as inheritance, working through several examples in a test-driven manner.

7.1 Objects and Properties

JavaScript has *object literals*, i.e., objects can be typed directly into a program using specific syntax, much like string ("a string literal") and number literals (42) can be typed directly in a program in most languages. Listing 7.1 shows an example of an object literal.

Listing 7.1 An object literal

```
var car = {
  model: {
    year: "1998",
    make: "Ford",
    model: "Mondeo"
```

```
  },

  color: "Red",
  seats: 5,
  doors: 5,
  accessories: ["Air condition", "Electric Windows"],

  drive: function () {
    console.log("Vroooom!");
  }
};
```

Incidentally, Listing 7.1 shows a few other literals available in JavaScript as well, most notably the array literal (`[]` as opposed to new `Array()`).

ECMA-262 defines a JavaScript object as an unordered collection of properties. Properties consist of a name, a value, and a set of attributes. Property names are either string literals, number literals, or identifiers. Properties may take any value, i.e., primitives (strings, numbers, booleans, `null` or `undefined`) and objects, including functions. When properties have function objects assigned to them, we usually refer to them as methods. ECMA-262 also defines a set of internal properties and methods that are not part of the language, but are used internally by the implementation. The specification encloses names of these internal properties and methods in double brackets, i.e., [[Prototype]]. I will use this notation as well.

7.1.1 Property Access

JavaScript properties can be accessed in one of two ways—using dot notation, `car.model.year`, or using a style commonly associated with dictionaries or hashes, `car["model"]["year"]`. The square bracket notation offers a great deal of flexibility when looking up properties. It can take any string or expression that returns a string. This means that you can dynamically figure out the property name at run-time and look it up on an object directly using the square brackets. Another benefit of the square bracket notation is that you can access properties whose name contain characters not allowed in identifiers such as white space. You can mix dot and bracket notation at will, making it very easy to dynamically look up properties on an object.

As you might remember, we used property names containing spaces to make our test case names more human-readable in Chapter 3, *Tools of the Trade,* as seen in Listing 7.2.

Listing 7.2 A property name with spaces

```
var testMethods = {
  "test dots and brackets should behave identically":
  function () {
    var value = "value";
    var obj = { prop: value };

    assertEquals(obj.prop, obj["prop"]);
  }
};

// Grab the test
var name = "test dots and brackets should behave identically";
var testMethod = testMethods[name];

// Mix dot and bracket notation to get number of expected
// arguments for the test method
var argc = testMethods[name].length;
```

Here we get a test method (i.e., a property) from our object using the square bracket notation, because the name of the property we are interested in contains characters that are illegal in identifiers.

It is possible to get and set properties on an object using other values than string literals, number literals, or identifiers. When you do so, the object will be converted to a string by its `toString` method if it exists (and returns a string), or its `valueOf` method. Beware that these methods may be implementation-specific (e.g., for host objects[1]), and for generic objects the `toString` method will return `"[object Object]"`. I recommend you stick to identifiers, string literals, and number literals for property names.

7.1.2 The Prototype Chain

In JavaScript every object has a prototype. The property is internal and is referred to as [[Prototype]] in the ECMA-262 specification. It is an implicit reference to the `prototype` property of the constructor that created the object. For generic objects this corresponds to `Object.prototype`. The prototype may have a prototype of its own and so on, forming a *prototype chain*. The prototype chain is used to share properties across objects in JavaScript, and forms the basis for JavaScript's inheritance model. This concept is fundamentally different from classical inheritance, in

---

1. Host objects will be discussed in Chapter 10, *Feature Detection*.

which classes inherit from other classes, and objects constitute instances of classes. We'll approach the subject by continuing our study of property access.

When you read a property on an object, JavaScript uses the object's internal [[Get]] method. This method checks if the object has a property of the given name. If it has, its value is returned. If the object does not have such a property, the interpreter checks if the object has a [[Prototype]] that is not `null` (only `Object.prototype` has a `null` [[Prototype]]). If it does, the interpreter will check whether the prototype has the property in question. If it does, its value is returned, otherwise the interpreter continues up the prototype chain until it reaches `Object.prototype`. If neither the object nor any of the objects in its prototype has a property of the given name, `undefined` is returned.

When you assign, or put, a value to an object property, the object's internal [[Put]] method is used. If the object does not already have a property of the given name, one is created and its value is set to the provided value. If the object already has a property of the same name, its value is set to the one provided.

Assignment does not affect the prototype chain. In fact, if we assign a property that already exists on the prototype chain, we are shadowing the prototype's property. Listing 7.3 shows an example of property shadowing. To run the test with JsTestDriver, set up a simple project as described in Chapter 3, *Tools of the Trade,* and add a configuration file that loads `test/*.js`.

Listing 7.3 Inheriting and shadowing properties

```
TestCase("ObjectPropertyTest", {
  "test setting property shadows property on prototype":
  function () {
    var object1 = {};
    var object2 = {};

    // Both objects inherit Object.prototype.toString
    assertEquals(object1.toString, object2.toString);

    var chris = {
      name: "Chris",

      toString: function () {
        return this.name;
      }
    };

    // chris object defines a toString property that is
    // not the same object as object1 inherits from
```

```
    // Object.prototype
    assertFalse(object1.toString === chris.toString);

    // Deleting the custom property unshadows the
    // inherited Object.prototype.toString
    delete chris.toString;
    assertEquals(object1.toString, chris.toString);
  }
});
```

As seen in Listing 7.3, `object1` and `object2` don't define a `toString` property and so they share the same object—the `Object.prototype`. `toString` method—via the prototype chain. The `chris` object, on the other hand, defines its own method, shadowing the `toString` property on the prototype chain. If we delete the custom `toString` property from the `chris` object using the `delete` operator, the property no longer exists directly on the specific object, causing the interpreter to look up the method from the prototype chain, eventually finding `Object.prototype`.

When we turn our attention to property attributes, we will discuss some additional subtleties of the [[Put]] method.

7.1.3 Extending Objects through the Prototype Chain

By manipulating the `prototype` property of JavaScript constructors we can modify the behavior of every object created by it, including objects created before the manipulation. This also holds for native objects, such as arrays. To see how this works, we're going to implement a simple `sum` method for arrays. The test in Listing 7.4 illustrates what we want to achieve.

Listing 7.4 Describing the behavior of `Array.prototype.sum`

```
TestCase("ArraySumTest", {
  "test should summarize numbers in array": function () {
    var array = [1, 2, 3, 4, 5, 6];

    assertEquals(21, array.sum());
  }
});
```

Running this test informs us that there is no `sum` method for arrays, which is not all that surprising. The implementation is a trivial summarizing loop, as seen in Listing 7.5.

Listing 7.5 Adding a method to `Array.prototype`

```
Array.prototype.sum = function () {
  var sum = 0;

  for (var i = 0, l = this.length; i < l; i++) {
    sum += this[i];
  }

  return sum;
};
```

Because all arrays inherit from `Array.prototype`, we're able to add methods to all arrays. But what happens if there already is a `sum` method for arrays? Such a method could be provided by a given browser, a library or other code running along with ours. If this is the case, we're effectively overwriting that other method. Listing 7.6 avoids this by placing our implementation inside an `if` test that verifies that the method we're adding does not already exist.

Listing 7.6 Defensively adding a method to `Array.prototype`

```
if (typeof Array.prototype.sum == "undefined") {
  Array.prototype.sum = function () {
    // ...
  };
}
```

In general, this is a good idea when extending native objects or otherwise working on global objects. This way we make sure our code doesn't trip up other code. Even so, if there already is a `sum` method available, it may not act the way we expect, causing our code that relies on our `sum` to break. We can catch these errors with a strong test suite, but this kind of problem clearly indicates that relying on extensions to global objects may not be the best approach when the focus is writing robust code.

7.1.4 Enumerable Properties

Extending native prototypes like we just did comes with a price. We already saw how this may lead to conflicts, but there is another drawback to this approach. When adding properties to an object, they are instantly enumerable on any instance that inherits it. Listing 7.7 shows an example of looping arrays.

Listing 7.7 Looping arrays with for and for-in

```
TestCase("ArrayLoopTest", {
  "test looping should iterate over all items":
  function () {
    var array = [1, 2, 3, 4, 5, 6];
    var result = [];

    // Standard for-loop
    for (var i = 0, l = array.length; i < l; i++) {
      result.push(array[i]);
    }

    assertEquals("123456", result.join(""));
  },

  "test for-in loop should iterate over all items":
  function () {
    var array = [1, 2, 3, 4, 5, 6];
    var result = [];

    for (var i in array) {
        result.push(array[i]);
    }

    assertEquals("123456", result.join(""));
  }
});
```

These two loops both attempt to copy all the elements of one array onto another, and then join both arrays into a string to verify that they do indeed contain the same elements. Running this test reveals that the second test fails with the message in Listing 7.8.

Listing 7.8 Result of running test in Listing 7.7

```
expected "123456" but was "123456function () { [... snip]"
```

To understand what's happening, we need to understand the `for-in` enumeration. `for (var property in object)` will fetch the first enumerable property of `object`. `property` is assigned the name of the property, and the body of the loop is executed. This is repeated as long as `object` has more enumerable properties, and the body of the loop does not issue `break` (or `return` if inside a function).

For an array object, the only enumerable properties are its numeric indexes. The methods and the length property provided by `Array.prototype` are not enumerable. This is why a `for-in` loop will only reveal the indexes and their associated values for array objects. However, when we add properties to an object or one of the objects in its prototype chain, they are enumerable by default. Because of this fact, these new properties will also appear in a `for-in` loop, as shown by the test failure above.

I recommend you don't use `for-in` on arrays. The problem illustrated above can be worked around, as we will see shortly, but not without trading off performance. Using `for-in` on arrays effectively means we can't normalize browser behavior by adding missing methods to `Array.prototype` without inferring a performance hit.

7.1.4.1 Object.prototype.hasOwnProperty

`Object.prototype.hasOwnProperty(name)` returns `true` if an object has a property with the given name. If the object either inherits the property from the prototype chain, *or* doesn't have such a property at all, `hasOwnProperty` returns `false`. This means that we can qualify a `for-in` loop with a call to `hasOwnProperty` to ensure we only loop the object's own properties, as seen in Listing 7.9.

Listing 7.9 Qualifying a loop with `hasOwnProperty`

```
"test looping should only iterate over own properties":
function () {
  var person = {
    name: "Christian",
    profession: "Programmer",
    location: "Norway"
  };

  var result = [];

  for (var prop in person) {
    if (person.hasOwnProperty(prop)) {
      result.push(prop);
    }
  }

  var expected = ["location", "name", "profession"];
  assertEquals(expected, result.sort());
}
```

This test passes because we now filter out properties added to the prototype chain. There are two things to keep in mind when dealing with `Object.prototype.hasOwnProperty`.

- Some browsers, such as early versions of Safari don't support it.
- Objects are frequently used as hashes; there is a risk of `hasOwnProperty` being shadowed by another property.

To guard our code against the latter case, we can implement a custom method that accepts an object and a property and returns true if the property is one of the object's own properties, even when the object's `hasOwnProperty` method is shadowed or otherwise unavailable. Listing 7.10 shows the method. Add it to the `tdd.js` file from Chapter 6, *Applied Functions and Closures.*

Listing 7.10 Sandboxed `hasOwnProperty`

```
tddjs.isOwnProperty = (function () {
  var hasOwn = Object.prototype.hasOwnProperty;

  if (typeof hasOwn == "function") {
    return function (object, property) {
      return hasOwn.call(object, property);
    };
  } else {
    // Provide an emulation if you can live with possibly
    // inaccurate results
  }
}());
```

For browsers that do not support this method we can emulate it, but it is not possible to provide a fully conforming implementation. Chances are that browsers that lack this method will present other issues as well, so failing to provide an emulation may not be your main problem. We will learn techniques to deal with such cases in Chapter 10, *Feature Detection.*

Because properties are always enumerable when added by JavaScript, and because globals make it hard for scripts to co-exist, it is widely accepted that `Object.prototype` should be left alone. `Array.prototype` should also be treated with care, especially if you are using `for-in` on arrays. Although such loops should generally be avoided for arrays, they can be useful when dealing with large, sparse arrays.

Keep in mind that although you may decide to avoid extending native objects, others may not be so nice. Filtering for-in loops with `hasOwnProperty`—even when you are not modifying `Object.prototype` and `Array.prototype` yourself—will keep your code running as expected, regardless of whether third-party code such as libraries, ad, or analytics related code decide to do so.

7.1.5 Property Attributes

ECMA-262 defines four properties that may be set for any given property. It is important to note that these attributes are set for properties by the interpreter, but JavaScript code you write has no way of setting these attributes. The `ReadOnly` and `DontDelete` attributes cannot be inspected explicitly, but we can deduce their values. ECMA-262 specifies the `Object.prototype.propertyIsEnumerable` method, which could be used to get the value of `DontEnum`; however, it does not check the prototype chain and is not reliably implemented across browsers.

7.1.5.1 ReadOnly

If a property has the `ReadOnly` attribute set, it is not possible to write to the property. Attempting to do so will pass by silently, but the property attempted to update will not change. Note that if any object on the prototype chain has a property with the attribute set, writing to the property will fail. `ReadOnly` does not imply that the value is constant and unchanging—the interpreter may change its value internally.

7.1.5.2 DontDelete

If a property has the `DontDelete` attribute set, it is not possible to delete it using the `delete` operator. Much like writing to properties with the `ReadOnly` attribute, deleting properties with the `DontDelete` attribute will fail silently. The expression will return false if the object either didn't have the given property, or if the property existed and had a `DontDelete` attribute.

7.1.5.3 DontEnum

`DontEnum` causes properties to not appear in `for-in` loops, as shown in Listing 7.9. The `DontEnum` attribute is the most important property attribute to understand because it is the one that is most likely to affect your code. In Listing 7.7 we saw an example of how enumerable properties may trip up badly written `for-in` loops. The `DontEnum` attribute is the internal mechanism that decides whether or not a property is enumerable.

Internet Explorer (including version 8) has a peculiar bug concerning the DontEnum attribute—any property on an object that has a property by the same name anywhere on its prototype chain that has DontEnum will act as though it has DontEnum as well (even though it should be impossible to have DontEnum on a user-provided object). This means that if you create an object and shadow any of the properties on Object.prototype, neither of these properties will show up in a for-in loop in Internet Explorer. If you create an object of any of the native and host types, all the properties on the respective prototype chains with DontEnum will magically disappear from a for-in loop, as seen in Listing 7.11.

Listing 7.11 Overriding properties with DontEnum

```
TestCase("PropertyEnumerationTest", {
  "test should enumerate shadowed object properties":
  function () {
    var object = {
      // Properties with DontEnum on Object.prototype
      toString: "toString",
      toLocaleString: "toLocaleString",
      valueOf: "valueOf",
      hasOwnProperty: "hasOwnProperty",
      isPrototypeOf: "isPrototypeOf",
      propertyIsEnumerable: "propertyIsEnumerable",
      constructor: "constructor"
    };

    var result = [];

    for (var property in object) {
      result.push(property);
    }

    assertEquals(7, result.length);
  },

  "test should enumerate shadowed function properties":
  function () {
    var object = function () {};

    // Additional properties with DontEnum on
    //Function.prototype
    object.prototype = "prototype";
    object.call = "call";
    object.apply = "apply";
```

```
    var result = [];

    for (var property in object) {
      result.push(property);
    }

    assertEquals(3, result.length);
  }
});
```

Both of these tests fail in all versions of Internet Explorer, including IE8; `result.length` is 0. We can solve this issue by making a special case for the non-enumerable properties on `Object.prototype` as well as `Function.prototype` if the object in question inherits from it.

The `tddjs.each` method in Listing 7.12 can be used to loop properties of an object, accounting for Internet Explorer's bug. When defined, the method attempts to loop the properties of an object that shadows all the non-enumerable properties on `Object.prototype` as well as a function that shadows non-enumerable properties on `Function.prototype`. Any property that does not show up in the loop is remembered and looped explicitly inside the `each` function.

Listing 7.12 Looping properties with a cross-browser `each` method

```
tddjs.each = (function () {
  // Returns an array of properties that are not exposed
  // in a for-in loop on the provided object
  function unEnumerated(object, properties) {
    var length = properties.length;

    for (var i = 0; i < length; i++) {
      object[properties[i]] = true;
    }

    var enumerated = length;

    for (var prop in object) {
      if (tddjs.isOwnProperty(object, prop)) {
        enumerated -= 1;
        object[prop] = false;
      }
    }

    if (!enumerated) {
      return;
```

```
    }

    var needsFix = [];

    for (i = 0; i < length; i++) {
      if (object[properties[i]]) {
        needsFix.push(properties[i]);
      }
    }

    return needsFix;
  }

  var oFixes = unEnumerated({},
    ["toString", "toLocaleString", "valueOf",
     "hasOwnProperty", "isPrototypeOf",
     "constructor", "propertyIsEnumerable"]);

  var fFixes = unEnumerated(
    function () {}, ["call", "apply", "prototype"]);

  if (fFixes && oFixes) {
    fFixes = oFixes.concat(fFixes);
  }

  var needsFix = { "object": oFixes, "function": fFixes };

  return function (object, callback) {
    if (typeof callback != "function") {
      throw new TypeError("callback is not a function");
    }

    // Normal loop, should expose all enumerable properties
    // in conforming browsers
    for (var prop in object) {
      if (tddjs.isOwnProperty(object, prop)) {
        callback(prop, object[prop]);
      }
    }

    // Loop additional properties in non-conforming browsers
    var fixes = needsFix[typeof object];

    if (fixes) {
      var property;
```

```
    for (var i = 0, l = fixes.length; i < l; i++) {
      property = fixes[i];

      if (tddjs.isOwnProperty(object, property)) {
        callback(property, object[property]);
      }
    }
  }
};
}());
```

If we change the `for-in` loops in the tests in Listing 7.11 to use the new `tddjs.each` method, the tests will run, even on Internet Explorer. Additionally, the method smoothes over a similar bug in Chrome in which function objects `prototype` property is not enumerable when shadowed.

7.2 Creating Objects with Constructors

JavaScript functions have the ability to act as constructors when invoked with the new operator, i.e., `new MyConstructor()`. There is nothing that differentiates the definition of a regular function and one that constructs objects. In fact, JavaScript provides every function with a `prototype` object in case it is used with the new operator. When the function is used as a constructor to create new objects, their internal [[Prototype]] property will be a reference to this object.

In the absence of language level checks on functions vs. constructors, constructor names are usually capitalized to indicate their intended use. Regardless of whether you use constructors or not in your own code, you should honor this idiom by not capitalizing names of functions and objects that are not constructors.

7.2.1 `prototype` and [[Prototype]]

The word "prototype" is used to describe two concepts. First, a constructor has a public `prototype` property. When the constructor is used to create new objects, those objects will have an internal [[Prototype]] property that is a reference to the constructor's `prototype` property. Second, the constructor has an internal [[Prototype]] that references the prototype of the constructor that created it, most commonly `Function.prototype`. All JavaScript objects have an internal [[Prototype]] property; only function objects have the `prototype` property.

7.2.2 Creating Objects with new

When a function is called with the new operator, a new JavaScript object is created. The function is then called using the newly created object as the this value along with any arguments that were passed in the original call.

In Listing 7.13 we see how creating objects with constructors compares with the object literal we've been using so far.

Listing 7.13 Creating objects with constructors

```
function Circle(radius) {
  this.radius = radius;
}

// Create a circle
var circ = new Circle(6);

// Create a circle-like object
var circ2 = { radius: 6 };
```

The two objects share the same properties—the radius property along with properties inherited from Object.prototype. Although both objects inherit from Object.prototype, circ2 does so directly (i.e., its [[Prototype]] property is a reference to Object.prototype), whereas circ does so indirectly through Circle.prototype. We can use the instanceof operator to determine the relationship between objects. Additionally, we can use the constructor property to inspect their origin, as seen in Listing 7.14.

Listing 7.14 Inspecting objects

```
TestCase("CircleTest", {
  "test inspect objects": function () {
    var circ = new Circle(6);
    var circ2 = { radius: 6 };

    assertTrue(circ instanceof Object);
    assertTrue(circ instanceof Circle);
    assertTrue(circ2 instanceof Object);

    assertEquals(Circle, circ.constructor);
    assertEquals(Object, circ2.constructor);
  }
});
```

The expression `a instanceof b` will return true whenever the internal [[Prototype]] property of a, or one of the objects on its prototype chain, is the same object as `b.prototype`.

7.2.3 Constructor Prototypes

Functions are always assigned a `prototype` property, which will be set as the internal [[Prototype]] property of objects created by the function when used as a constructor. The assigned prototype object's prototype is in turn `Object.prototype` and it defines a single property, `constructor`, which is a reference to the constructor itself. Because the new operator may be used with any expression that results in a constructor, we can use this property to dynamically create new objects of the same type as a known object. In Listing 7.15 we use the `constructor` property of a circle object to create a new circle object.

Listing 7.15 Creating objects of the same kind

```
"test should create another object of same kind":
function () {
  var circle = new Circle(6);
  var circle2 = new circle.constructor(9);

  assertEquals(circle.constructor, circle2.constructor);
  assertTrue(circle2 instanceof Circle);
}
```

7.2.3.1 Adding Properties to the Prototype

We can give our new circle objects new functionality by augmenting the `prototype` property of the constructor, much like we extended the behavior of native objects in Section 7.1.3, *Extending Objects through the Prototype Chain*. Listing 7.16 adds three methods for circle objects to inherit.

Listing 7.16 Adding properties to `Circle.prototype`

```
Circle.prototype.diameter = function () {
  return this.radius * 2;
};

Circle.prototype.circumference = function () {
  return this.diameter() * Math.PI;
};
```

```
Circle.prototype.area = function () {
  return this.radius * this.radius * Math.PI;
};
```

Listing 7.17 shows a simple test to verify that objects do indeed inherit the methods.

Listing 7.17 Testing `Circle.prototype.diameter`

```
"test should inherit properties from Circle.prototype":
function () {
  var circle = new Circle(6);

  assertEquals(12, circle.diameter());
}
```

Repeating `Circle.prototype` quickly becomes cumbersome and expensive (in terms of bytes to go over the wire) when adding more than a few properties to the prototype. We can improve this pattern in a number of ways. Listing 7.18 shows the shortest way—simply provide an object literal as the new prototype.

Listing 7.18 Assigning `Circle.prototype`

```
Circle.prototype = {
  diameter: function () {
    return this.radius * 2;
  },

  circumference: function () {
    return this.diameter() * Math.PI;
  },

  area: function () {
    return this.radius * this.radius * Math.PI;
  }
};
```

Unfortunately, this breaks some of our previous tests. In particular, the assertion in Listing 7.19 no longer holds.

Listing 7.19 Failing assertion on constructor equality

```
assertEquals(Circle, circle.constructor)
```

When we assign a new object to `Circle.prototype`, JavaScript no longer creates a `constructor` property for us. This means that the [[Get]] for constructor will go up the prototype chain until a value is found. In the case of our constructor, the result is `Object.prototype` whose `constructor` property is `Object`, as seen in Listing 7.20.

Listing 7.20 Broken constructor property

```
"test constructor is Object when prototype is overridden":
function () {
  function Circle() {}
  Circle.prototype = {};

  assertEquals(Object, new Circle().constructor);
}
```

Listing 7.21 solves the problem by assigning the `constructor` property manually.

Listing 7.21 Fixing the missing constructor property

```
Circle.prototype = {
  constructor: Circle,

  // ...
};
```

To avoid the problem entirely, we could also extend the given prototype property in a closure to avoid repeating `Circle.prototype` for each property. This approach is shown in Listing 7.22.

Listing 7.22 Avoiding the missing constructor problem

```
(function (p) {
  p.diameter = function () {
    return this.radius * 2;
  };

  p.circumference = function () {
    return this.diameter() * Math.PI;
  };

  p.area = function () {
    return this.radius * this.radius * Math.PI;
  };
}(Circle.prototype));
```

By not overwriting the `prototype` property, we are also avoiding its `constructor` property being enumerable. The object provided for us has the `DontEnum` attribute set, which is impossible to recreate when we assign a custom object to the `prototype` property and manually restore the `constructor` property.

7.2.4 The Problem with Constructors

There is a potential problem with constructors. Because there is nothing that separates a constructor from a function, there is no guarantee that someone won't use your constructor as a function. Listing 7.23 shows how a missing new keyword can have grave effects.

Listing 7.23 Constructor misuse

```
"test calling prototype without 'new' returns undefined":
function () {
  var circle = Circle(6);

  assertEquals("undefined", typeof circle);
  // Oops! Defined property on global object
  assertEquals(6, radius);
}
```

This example shows two rather severe consequences of calling the constructor as a function. Because the constructor does not have a return statement, the type of the `circle` ends up being `undefined`. Even worse, because we did not call the function with the new operator, JavaScript did not create a new object and set it as the function's `this` value for us. Thus, the function executes on the global object, causing `this.radius` = `radius` to set a `radius` property on the global object, as shown by the second assertion in Listing 7.23.

In Listing 7.24 the problem is mitigated by use of the `instanceof` operator.

Listing 7.24 Detecting constructor misuse

```
function Circle(radius) {
  if (!(this instanceof Circle)) {
    return new Circle(radius);
  }

  this.radius = radius;
}
```

Whenever someone forgets the new operator when calling the constructor, this will refer to the global object rather than a newly created object. By using the instanceof operator, we're able to catch this, and can explicitly call the constructor over again with the same arguments and return the new object.

ECMA-262 defines the behavior for all the native constructors when used as functions. The result of calling a constructor as a function often has the same effect as our implementation above—a new object is created as if the function was actually called with the new operator.

Assuming that calling a constructor without new is usually a typo, you may want to discourage using constructors as functions. Throwing an error rather than sweeping the error under the rug will probably ensure a more consistent code base in the long run.

7.3 Pseudo-classical Inheritance

Equipped with our understanding of constructors and their prototype properties, we can now create arbitrary hierarchies of objects, in much the same way one would create class hierarchies in a classical language. We will do this with Sphere, a constructor whose prototype property inherits from Circle.prototype rather than Object.prototype.

We need Sphere.prototype to refer to an object whose internal [[Prototype]] is Circle.prototype. In other words, we need a circle object to set up this link. Unfortunately, this process is not straightforward; In order to create a circle object we need to invoke the Circle constructor. However, the constructor may provide our prototype object with unwanted state, and it may even fail in the absence of input arguments. To circumvent this potential problem, Listing 7.25 uses an intermediate constructor that borrows Circle.prototype.

Listing 7.25 Deeper inheritance

```
function Sphere(radius) {
  this.radius = radius;
}

Sphere.prototype = (function () {
  function F() {};
  F.prototype = Circle.prototype;

  return new F();
}());
```

```
// Don't forget the constructor - else it will resolve as
// Circle through the prototype chain
Sphere.prototype.constructor = Sphere;
```

Now we can create spheres that inherit from circles, as shown by the test in Listing 7.26.

Listing 7.26 Testing the new `Sphere` constructor

```
"test spheres are circles in 3D": function () {
  var radius = 6;
  var sphere = new Sphere(radius);

  assertTrue(sphere instanceof Sphere);
  assertTrue(sphere instanceof Circle);
  assertTrue(sphere instanceof Object);
  assertEquals(12, sphere.diameter());
}
```

7.3.1 The Inherit Function

In Listing 7.25 we extended the `Sphere` constructor with the `Circle` constructor by linking their prototypes together, causing sphere objects to inherit from `Circle.prototype`. The solution is fairly obscure, especially when compared with inheritance in other languages. Unfortunately, JavaScript does not offer any abstractions over this concept, but we are free to implement our own. Listing 7.27 shows a test for what such an abstraction might look like.

Listing 7.27 Specification for `inherit`

```
TestCase("FunctionInheritTest", {
  "test should link prototypes": function () {
    var SubFn = function () {};
    var SuperFn = function () {};
    SubFn.inherit(SuperFn);

    assertTrue(new SubFn() instanceof SuperFn);
  }
});
```

We already implemented this feature in Listing 7.25, so we only need to move it into a separate function. Listing 7.28 shows the extracted function.

Listing 7.28 Implementing `inherit`

```
if (!Function.prototype.inherit) {
  (function () {
    function F() {}

    Function.prototype.inherit = function (superFn) {
      F.prototype = superFn.prototype;
      this.prototype = new F();
      this.prototype.constructor = this;
    };
  }());
}
```

This implementation uses the same intermediate constructor for all calls, only assigning the prototype for each call. Using this new function we can clean up our circles and spheres, as seen in Listing 7.29.

Listing 7.29 Making `Sphere` inherit from `Circle` with `inherit`

```
function Sphere (radius) {
  this.radius = radius;
}

Sphere.inherit(Circle);
```

More or less all the major JavaScript libraries ship with a variant of the `inherit` function, usually under the name `extend`. I've named it inherit in order to avoid confusion when we turn our attention to another `extend` method later in this chapter.

7.3.2 Accessing [[Prototype]]

The inherit function we just wrote makes it possible to easily create object hierarchies using constructors. Still, comparing the `Circle` and `Sphere` constructors tells us something isn't quite right—they both perform the same initialization of the radius property. The inheritance we've set up exists on the object level through the prototype chain, the constructors are not linked in the same way a class and a subclass are linked in a classical language. In particular, JavaScript has no `super` to directly refer to properties on objects from which an object inherits. In fact, ECMA-262 3rd edition provides no way at all to access the internal [[Prototype]] property of an object.

Even though there is no standardized way of accessing the [[Prototype]] of an object, some implementations provide a non-standard --proto-- property that exposes the internal [[Prototype]] property. ECMAScript 5 (ES5) has standardized this feature as the new method `Object.getPrototypeOf` `(object)`, giving you the ability to look up an object's [[Prototype]]. In browsers in which `__proto__` is not available, we can sometimes use the `constructor` property to get the [[Prototype]], but it requires that the object was in fact created using a constructor and that the `constructor` property is set correctly.

7.3.3 Implementing `super`

So, JavaScript has no `super`, and it is not possible to traverse the prototype chain in a standardized manner that is guaranteed to work reliably cross-browser. It's still possible to emulate the concept of `super` in JavaScript. Listing 7.30 achieves this by calling the `Circle` constructor from within the `Sphere` constructor, passing the newly created object as the `this` value.

Listing 7.30 Accessing the `Circle` constructor from within the `Sphere` constructor

```
function Sphere(radius) {
  Circle.call(this, radius);
}

Sphere.inherit(Circle);
```

Running the tests confirms that sphere objects still work as intended. We can employ the same technique to access "super methods" from other methods as well. In Listing 7.31 we call the `area` method on the prototype.

Listing 7.31 Calling a method on the prototype chain

```
Sphere.prototype.area = function () {
  return 4 * Circle.prototype.area.call(this);
};
```

Listing 7.32 shows a simple test of the new method.

Listing 7.32 Calculating surface area

```
"test should calculate sphere area": function () {
  var sphere = new Sphere(3);

  assertEquals(113, Math.round(sphere.area()));
}
```

The drawback of this solution is its verbosity; The call to `Circle.prototype.area` is long and couples `Sphere` very tightly to `Circle`. To mitigate this, Listing 7.33 makes the `inherit` function set up a "super" link for us.

Listing 7.33 Expecting the _super link to refer to the prototype

```
"test should set up link to super": function () {
  var SubFn = function () {};
  var SuperFn = function () {};
  SubFn.inherit(SuperFn);

  assertEquals(SuperFn.prototype, SubFn.prototype._super);
}
```

Note the leading underscore. ECMA-262 defines `super` as a reserved word intended for future use, so we best not use it. The implementation in Listing 7.34 is still straightforward.

Listing 7.34 Implementing a link to the prototype

```
if (!Function.prototype.inherit) {
  (function () {
    function F() {}

    Function.prototype.inherit = function (superFn) {
      F.prototype = superFn.prototype;
      this.prototype = new F();
      this.prototype.constructor = this;
      this.prototype._super = superFn.prototype;
    };
  }());
}
```

Using this new property, Listing 7.35 simplifies `Sphere.prototype.area`.

Listing 7.35 Calling a method on the prototype chain

```
Sphere.prototype.area = function () {
  return 4 * this._super.area.call(this);
};
```

7.3.3.1 The _super Method

Although I would definitely not recommend it, someone serious about emulating classical inheritance in JavaScript would probably prefer _super to be a method rather than a simple link to the prototype. Calling the method should magically call the corresponding method on the prototype chain. The concept is illustrated in Listing 7.36.

Listing 7.36 Testing the _super method

```
"test super should call method of same name on protoype":
function () {
  function Person(name) {
    this.name = name;
  }

  Person.prototype = {
    constructor: Person,

    getName: function () {
      return this.name;
    },

    speak: function () {
      return "Hello";
    }
  };

  function LoudPerson(name) {
    Person.call(this, name);
  }

  LoudPerson.inherit2(Person, {
    getName: function () {
      return this._super().toUpperCase();
    },

    speak: function () {
      return this._super() + "!!!";
    }
  });

  var np = new LoudPerson("Chris");

  assertEquals("CHRIS", np.getName());
  assertEquals("Hello!!!", np.speak());
}
```

In this example we are using `Function.prototype.inherit2` to establish the prototype chain for the `LoudPerson` objects. It accepts a second argument, which is an object that defines the methods on `LoudPerson.prototype` that need to call `_super`. Listing 7.37 shows one possible implementation.

Listing 7.37 Implementing `_super` as a method

```
if (!Function.prototype.inherit2) {
  (function () {
    function F() {}

    Function.prototype.inherit2 = function (superFn, methods) {
      F.prototype = superFn.prototype;
      this.prototype = new F();
      this.prototype.constructor = this;

      var subProto = this.prototype;

      tddjs.each(methods, function (name, method) {
        // Wrap the original method
        subProto[name] = function () {
          var returnValue;
          var oldSuper = this._super;
          this._super = superFn.prototype[name];

          try {
            returnValue = method.apply(this, arguments);
          } finally {
            this._super = oldSuper;
          }

          return returnValue;
        };
      });
    };
  }());
}
```

This implementation allows for calls to `this._super()` as if the method had special meaning. In reality, we're wrapping the original methods in a new function that takes care of setting `this._super` to the right method before calling the original method.

Using the new inherit function we could now implement `Sphere` as seen in Listing 7.38.

Listing 7.38 Implementing `Sphere` with `inherit2`

```
function Sphere(radius) {
  Circle.call(this, radius);
}

Sphere.inherit2(Circle, {
  area: function () {
    return 4 * this._super();
  }
});
```

7.3.3.2 Performance of the `super` Method

Using the `inherit2` method we can create constructors and objects that come pretty close to emulating classical inheritance. It does not, however, perform particularly well. By redefining all the methods and wrapping them in closures, `inherit2` will not only be slower than `inherit` when extending constructors, but calling `this._super()` will be slower than calling `this._super.method.call(this)` as well.

Further hits to performance are gained by the try-catch, which is used to ensure that `this._super` is restored after the method has executed. As if that wasn't enough, the method approach only allows static inheritance. Adding new methods to `Circle.prototype` will not automatically expose `_super` in same named methods on `Sphere.prototype`. To get that working we would have to implement some kind of helper function to add methods that would add the enclosing function that sets up `_super`. In any case, the result would be less than elegant and would introduce a possibly significant performance overhead.

I hope you never use this function; JavaScript has better patterns in store. If anything, I think the `_super` implementation is a testament to JavaScript's flexibility. JavaScript doesn't have classes, but it gives you the tools you need to build them, should you need to do so.

7.3.3.3 A `_super` Helper Function

A somewhat saner implementation, although not as concise, can be achieved by implementing `_super` as a helper function piggybacking the prototype link, as seen in Listing 7.39.

Listing 7.39 A simpler _super implementation

```
function _super(object, methodName) {
  var method = object._super && object._super[methodName];

  if (typeof method != "function") {
    return;
  }

  // Remove the first two arguments (object and method)
  var args = Array.prototype.slice.call(arguments, 2);

  // Pass the rest of the arguments along to the super
  return method.apply(object, args);
}
```

Listing 7.40 shows an example of using the _super function.

Listing 7.40 Using the simpler _super helper

```
function LoudPerson(name) {
  _super(this, "constructor", name);
}

LoudPerson.inherit(Person);

LoudPerson.prototype.getName = function () {
  return _super(this, "getName").toUpperCase();
};

LoudPerson.prototype.say = function (words) {
  return _super(this, "speak", words) + "!!!";
};

var np = new LoudPerson("Chris");

assertEquals("CHRIS", np.getName());
assertEquals("Hello!!!", np.say("Hello"));
```

This is unlikely to be faster to call than spelling out the method to call directly, but at least it defeats the worst performance issue brought on by implementing _super as a method. In general, we can implement sophisticated object oriented solutions without the use of the _super crutch, as we will see both throughout this chapter and the sample projects in Part III, *Real-World Test-Driven Development in JavaScript.*

7.4 Encapsulation and Information Hiding

JavaScript does not have access modifiers such as `public`, `protected`, and `private`. Additionally, the property attributes `DontDelete` and `ReadOnly` are unavailable to us. As a consequence, the objects we've created so far consist solely of public properties. In addition to being public, the objects and properties are also mutable in any context because we are unable to freeze them. This means our object's internals are open and available for modification by anyone, possibly compromising the security and integrity of our objects.

When using constructors and their prototypes, it is common to prefix properties with an underscore if they are intended to be private, i.e., `this._privateProperty`. Granted, this does not protect the properties in any way, but it may help users of your code understand which properties to stay away from. We can improve the situation by turning to closures, which are capable of producing a scope for which there is no public access.

7.4.1 Private Methods

By using closures, we can create private methods. Actually, they're more like private *functions*, as attaching them to an object effectively makes them public. These functions will be available to other functions defined in the same scope, but they will *not* be available to methods added to the object or its prototype at a later stage. Listing 7.41 shows an example.

Listing 7.41 Defining a private function

```
function Circle(radius) {
  this.radius = radius;
}

(function (circleProto) {
  // Functions declared in this scope are private, and only
  // available to other functions declared in the same scope
  function ensureValidRadius(radius) {
    return radius >= 0;
  }

  function getRadius() {
    return this.radius;
  }

  function setRadius(radius) {
    if (ensureValidRadius(radius)) {
```

```
    this.radius = radius;
    }
  }

  // Assigning the functions to properties of the prototype
  // makes them public methods
  circleProto.getRadius = getRadius;
  circleProto.setRadius = setRadius;
}(Circle.prototype));
```

In Listing 7.41 we create an anonymous closure that is immediately executed with `Circle.prototype` as the only argument. Inside we add two public methods, and keep a reference to one private function, `ensureValidRadius`.

If we need a private function to operate on the object, we can either design it to accept a circle object as first argument, or invoke it with `privFunc.call(this, /* args... */)`, thus being able to refer to the circle as `this` inside the function.

We could also have used the existing constructor as the enclosing scope to hold the private function. In that case we need to also define the public methods inside it, so they share scope with the private function, as seen in Listing 7.42.

Listing 7.42 Using a private function inside the constructor

```
function Circle(radius) {
  this.radius = radius;

  function ensureValidRadius(radius) {
    return radius >= 0;
  }

  function getRadius() {
    return this.radius;
  }

  function setRadius(radius) {
    if (ensureValidRadius(radius)) {
      this.radius = radius;
    }
  }

  // Expose public methods
  this.getRadius = getRadius;
  this.setRadius = setRadius;
}
```

This approach has a serious drawback in that it creates three function objects for every person object created. The original approach using a closure when adding properties to the prototype will only ever create three function objects that are shared between all circle objects. This means that creating n circle objects will cause the latter version to use approximately n times as much memory as the original suggestion. Additionally, object creation will be significantly slower because the constructor has to create the function objects as well. On the other hand, property resolution is quicker in the latter case because the properties are found directly on the object and no access to the prototype chain is needed.

In deep inheritance structures, looking up methods through the prototype chain *can* impact method call performance. However, in most cases inheritance structures are shallow, in which case object creation and memory consumption should be prioritized.

The latter approach also breaks our current inheritance implementation. When the `Sphere` constructor invokes the `Circle` constructor, it copies over the circle methods to the newly created sphere object, effectively shadowing the methods on `Sphere.prototype`. This means that the `Sphere` constructor needs to change as well if this is our preferred style.

7.4.2 Private Members and Privileged Methods

In the same way private functions may be created inside the constructor, we can create private members here, allowing us to protect the state of our objects. In order to make anything useful with this we'll need some public methods that can access the private properties. Methods created in the same scope—meaning the constructor—will have access to the private members, and are usually referred to as "privileged methods." Continuing our example, Listing 7.43 makes `radius` a private member of `Circle` objects.

Listing 7.43 Using private members and privileged methods

```
function Circle(radius) {
  function getSetRadius() {
    if (arguments.length > 0) {
      if (arguments[0] < 0) {
        throw new TypeError("Radius should be >= 0");
      }

      radius = arguments[0];
    }
```

```
    return radius;
  }

  function diameter() {
    return radius * 2;
  }

  function circumference() {
    return diameter() * Math.PI;
  }

  // Expose privileged methods
  this.radius = getSetRadius;
  this.diameter = diameter;
  this.circumference = circumference;

  this.radius(radius);
}
```

The new object no longer has a numeric `radius` property. Instead, it stores its state in a local variable. This means that none of the nested functions needs `this` anymore, so we can simplify the calls to them. Objects created with this constructor will be robust, because outside code cannot tamper with its internal state except through the public API.

7.4.3 Functional Inheritance

In his book, *JavaScript: The Good Parts* [5], and on his website, Douglas Crockford promotes what he calls *functional inheritance*. Functional inheritance is the next logical step from Listing 7.43, in which we've already eliminated most uses of the `this` keyword. In functional inheritance, the use of `this` is eliminated completely and the constructor is no longer needed. Instead, the constructor becomes a regular function that creates an object and returns it. The methods are defined as nested functions, which can access the free variables containing the object's state. Listing 7.44 shows an example.

Listing 7.44 Implementing `circle` using functional inheritance

```
function circle(radius) {
  // Function definitions as before

  return {
    radius: getSetRadius,
```

```
    diameter: diameter,
    area: area,
    circumference: circumference
  };
}
```

Because `circle` is no longer a constructor, its name is no longer capitalized. To use this new function we omit the `new` keyword as seen in Listing 7.45.

Listing 7.45 Using the functional inheritance pattern

```
"test should create circle object with function":
function () {
  var circ = circle(6);
  assertEquals(6, circ.radius());

  circ.radius(12);
  assertEquals(12, circ.radius());
  assertEquals(24, circ.diameter());
}
```

Crockford calls an object like the ones created by `circle` *durable* [6]. When an object is durable, its state is properly encapsulated, and it cannot be compromised by outside tampering. This is achieved by keeping state in free variables inside closures, and by never referring to the object's public interface from inside the object. Recall how we defined all the functions as inner private functions first, and *then* assigned them to properties? By always referring to the object's capability in terms of these inner functions, offending code cannot compromise our object by, e.g., injecting its own methods in place of our public methods.

7.4.3.1 Extending Objects

How can we achieve inheritance using this model? Rather than returning a new object with the public properties, we create the object we want to extend, add methods to it, and return it. You might recognize this design as the decorator pattern, and it is. The object we want to extend can be created in any way—through a constructor, from another object producing function, or even from the arguments provided to the function. Listing 7.46 shows an example using spheres and circles.

Listing 7.46 Implementing `sphere` using functional inheritance

```
function sphere(radius) {
  var sphereObj = circle(radius);
  var circleArea = sphereObj.area;

  function area() {
    return 4 * circleArea.call(this);
  }

  sphereObj.area = area;

  return sphereObj;
}
```

The inheriting function may of course provide private variables and functions of its own. It cannot, however, access the private variables and functions of the object it builds upon.

The functional style is an interesting alternative to the pseudo-classical constructors, but comes with its own limitations. The two most obvious drawbacks of this style of coding are that every object keeps its own copy of every function, increasing memory usage, and that in practice we aren't using the prototype chain, which means more cruft when we want to call the "super" function or something similar.

7.5 Object Composition and Mixins

In classical languages, class inheritance is the primary mechanism for sharing behavior and reusing code. It also serves the purpose of defining types, which is important in strongly typed languages. JavaScript is not strongly typed, and such classification is not really interesting. Even though we have the previously discussed `constructor` property and the `instanceof` operator, we're far more often concerned with what a given object can do. If it knows how to do the things we are interested in, we are happy. Which constructor created the object to begin with is of less interest.

JavaScript's dynamic object type allows for many alternatives to type inheritance in order to solve the case of shared behavior and code reuse. In this section we'll discuss how we can make new objects from old ones and how we can use mixins to share behavior.

7.5.1 The `Object.create` Method

In Section 7.3, *Pseudo-classical Inheritance,* we took a dive into JavaScript constructors and saw how they allow for a pseudo-classical inheritance model. Unfortunately,
going too far down that road leads to complex solutions that suffer on the performance side, as evidenced by our rough implementation of `super`. In this section,
as in the previous on functional inheritance, we'll focus solely on objects, bypassing
the constructors all together.

Returning to our previous example on circles and spheres, we used constructors
along with the `inherit` function to create a `sphere` object that inherited properties from `Circle.prototype`. The `Object.create` function takes an object
argument and returns a new object that inherits from it. No constructors involved,
only objects inheriting from other objects. Listing 7.47 describes the behavior with
a test.

Listing 7.47 Inheriting directly from objects

```
TestCase("ObjectCreateTest", {
  "test sphere should inherit from circle":
  function () {
    var circle = {
      radius: 6,

      area: function () {
        return this.radius * this.radius * Math.PI;
      }
    };

    var sphere = Object.create(circle);

    sphere.area = function () {
      return 4 * circle.area.call(this);
    };

    assertEquals(452, Math.round(sphere.area()));
  }
});
```

Here we expect the `circle` and `sphere` objects to behave as before, only
we use different means of creating them. We start out with a specific circle object.
Then we use `Object.create` to create a new object whose [[Prototype]] refers
to the old object, and we use this object as the sphere. The sphere object is then
modified to fit the behavior from the constructor example. Should we want new

spheres, we could simply create more objects like the one we already have, as seen in Listing 7.48.

Listing 7.48 Creating more `sphere` objects

```
"test should create more spheres based on existing":
function () {
  var circle = new Circle(6);
  var sphere = Object.create(circle);

  sphere.area = function () {
    return 4 * circle.area.call(this);
  };

  var sphere2 = Object.create(sphere);
  sphere2.radius = 10;

  assertEquals(1257, Math.round(sphere2.area()));
}
```

The `Object.create` function in Listing 7.49 is simpler than the previous `Function.prototype.inherit` method because it only needs to create a single object whose prototype is linked to the object argument.

Listing 7.49 Implementing `Object.create`

```
if (!Object.create) {
  (function () {
    function F() {}

    Object.create = function (object) {
      F.prototype = object;
      return new F();
    };
  }());
}
```

We create an intermediate constructor like before and assign the object argument to its prototype property. Finally we create a new object from the intermediate constructor and return it. The new object will have an internal [[Prototype]] property that references the original object, making it inherit directly from the object argument. We could also update our `Function.prototype.inherit` function to use this method.

ES5 codifies the `Object.create` function, which "creates a new object with a specified prototype". Our implementation does not conform, because it does not accept an optional `properties` argument. We will discuss this method further in Chapter 8, *ECMAScript 5th Edition.*

7.5.2 The `tddjs.extend` Method

Often we want to borrow behavior from one or more other objects to build the functionality we're after. We've seen this a couple of times already. Remember the `arguments` object? It acts roughly like an array, but it is not a true array, and as such, lacks certain properties we might be interested in. The `arguments` object does, however, possess the most important aspects of an array: the `length` property, and numerical indexes as property names. These two aspects are enough for most methods on `Array.prototype` to consider `arguments` an object that "walks like a duck, swims like a duck, and quacks like a duck" and therefore is a duck (or rather, an array). This means that we can borrow methods from `Array.prototype` by calling them with `arguments` as `this`, as seen in Listing 7.50.

Listing 7.50 Borrowing from `Array.prototype`

```
"test arguments should borrow from Array.prototype":
function () {
  function addToArray() {
    var args = Array.prototype.slice.call(arguments);
    var arr = args.shift();

    return arr.concat(args);
  }

  var result = addToArray([], 1, 2, 3);

  assertEquals([1, 2, 3], result);
}
```

The example borrows the `slice` function and calls it on the `arguments` object. Because we don't give it any other arguments, it will return the whole array, but the trick is now we've effectively converted `arguments` to an array, on which we can call the usual array methods.

Remember in Chapter 5, *Functions,* we illustrated implicit binding of `this` by copying a function from one object to another. Doing so causes both objects to share the same function object, so it's a memory efficient way to share behavior. Listing 7.51 shows an example.

Listing 7.51 Borrowing explicitly

```
"test arguments should borrow explicitly from Array.prototype":
function () {
  function addToArray() {
    arguments.slice = Array.prototype.slice;
    var args = arguments.slice();
    var arr = args.shift();

    return arr.concat(args);
  }

  var result = addToArray([], 1, 2, 3);

  assertEquals([1, 2, 3], result);
}
```

Using this technique, we can build objects that are collections of methods related over some topic, and then add all the properties of this object onto another object to "bless" it with the behavior. Listing 7.52 shows the initial test case for a method that will help us do exactly that.

Listing 7.52 Initial test case for `tddjs.extend`

```
TestCase("ObjectExtendTest", {
  setUp: function () {
    this.dummy = {
      setName: function (name) {
        return (this.name = name);
      },

      getName: function () {
        return this.name || null;
      }
    };
  },

  "test should copy properties": function () {
    var object = {};
    tddjs.extend(object, this.dummy);

    assertEquals("function", typeof object.getName);
    assertEquals("function", typeof object.setName);
  }
});
```

The test sets up a dummy object in the setUp method. It then asserts that when extending an object, all the properties from the source object is copied over. This method is definitely eligible for the Internet Explorer DontEnum bug, so Listing 7.53 uses the tddjs.each method to loop the properties.

Listing 7.53 Initial implementation of tddjs.extend

```
tddjs.extend = (function () {
  function extend(target, source) {
    tddjs.each(source, function (prop, val) {
      target[prop] = val;
    });
  }

  return extend;
}());
```

The next step, seen in Listing 7.54, is to ensure that the two arguments are safe to use. Any object will do on both sides; we simply need to make sure they're not null or undefined.

Listing 7.54 Extending null

```
"test should return new object when source is null":
function () {
  var object = tddjs.extend(null, this.dummy);

  assertEquals("function", typeof object.getName);
  assertEquals("function", typeof object.setName);
}
```

Note the expected return value. Listing 7.55 shows the implementation.

Listing 7.55 Allowing target to be null

```
function extend(target, source) {
  target = target || {};

  tddjs.each(source, function (prop, val) {
    target[prop] = val;
  });

  return target;
}
```

If the source is not passed in, we can simply return the target untouched, as seen in Listing 7.56.

Listing 7.56 Dealing with only one argument

```
"test should return target untouched when no source":
function () {
  var object = tddjs.extend({});
  var properties = [];

  for (var prop in object) {
    if (tddjs.isOwnProperty(object, prop)) {
      properties.push(prop);
    }
  }

  assertEquals(0, properties.length);
}
```

Now something interesting happens. This test passes in most browsers, even when `source` is `undefined`. This is because of browsers' forgiving nature, but it is violating ECMAScript 3, which states that a `TypeError` should be thrown when a `for-in` loop is trying to loop `null` or `undefined`. Interestingly, Internet Explorer 6 is one of the browsers that does behave as expected here. ECMAScript 5 changes this behavior to not throw when the object being looped is `null` or `undefined`. Listing 7.57 shows the required fix.

Listing 7.57 Aborting if there is no source

```
function extend(target, source) {
  target = target || {};

  if (!source) {
    return target;
  }

  /* ... */
}
```

Note that `tddjs.extend` always overwrites if `target` already defines a given property. We could embellish this method in several ways—adding a boolean option to allow/prevent overwrite, adding an option to allow/prevent shadowing of properties on the prototype chain, and so on. Your imagination is your limit.

7.5.3 Mixins

An object that defines a set of properties that can be used with the `tddjs.extend` method to "bless" other objects is often called a *mixin*. For instance, the Ruby standard library defines a bunch of useful methods in its `Enumerable` module, which may be *mixed in* to any object that supports the `each` method. Mixins provide an incredibly powerful mechanism for sharing behavior between objects. We could easily port the enumerable module from Ruby to a JavaScript object and mix it in with, e.g., `Array.protoype` to give all arrays additional behavior (remember to not loop arrays with `for-in`). Listing 7.58 shows an example that assumes that the enumerable object contains at least a `reject` method.

Listing 7.58 Mixing in the enumerable object to `Array.prototype`

```
TestCase("EnumerableTest", {
  "test should add enumerable methods to arrays":
  function () {
    tddjs.extend(Array.prototype, enumerable);

    var even = [1, 2, 3, 4].reject(function (i) {
      return i % 2 == 1;
    });

    assertEquals([2, 4], even);
  }
});
```

Assuming we are in a browser that supports `Array.prototype.forEach`, we could implement the `reject` method as seen in Listing 7.59.

Listing 7.59 Excerpt of JavaScript implementation of Ruby's enumerable

```
var enumerable = {
  /* ... */

  reject: function (callback) {
    var result = [];

    this.forEach(function (item) {
      if (!callback(item)) {
        result.push(item);
      }
    });
```

```
      return result;
   }
};
```

7.6 Summary

In this chapter we've seen several approaches to JavaScript object creation, and sharing of behavior between them. We started by gaining a thorough understanding of how JavaScript properties and the prototype chain work. We then moved on to constructors and used them in conjunction with their `prototype` property to implement an emulation of classical inheritance. Pseudo-classical inheritance can be tempting for developers unfamiliar with prototypes and JavaScript's native inheritance mechanism, but can lead to complex solutions that are computationally inefficient.

Dispensing the constructors, we moved on to *prototype-based inheritance* and explored how JavaScript allows us to work solely on objects by extending objects with other objects. By implementing a simple `Object.create` function, we avoided some of the confusion introduced by constructors and were able to see clearer how the prototype chain helps us extend the behavior of our objects.

Functional inheritance showed us how closures can be used to store state and achieve truly private members and methods.

To wrap it all up, we looked at object composition and mixins in JavaScript, combining all of the previously discussed patterns. Mixins are a great match for JavaScript, and often offer a great way to share behavior between objects.

Which technique to use? The answer will vary depending on whom you ask. There is no one right answer, because it depends on your situation. As we've seen, there are trade-offs when choosing between a pseudo-classical approach and a functional approach that will be affected by whether object creation, method invocation, memory usage, or security is the most crucial aspect of your application. Throughout this book we'll see how to use a few of the techniques presented in this chapter in real life examples.

ECMAScript 5th Edition

In December 2009, ECMA-262 5th Edition, commonly referred to as ECMAScript 5, or simply ES5, was finalized and published by ECMA International. This marked the first significant update to the core JavaScript language in 10 years. ECMAScript 5 is the successor to ECMAScript 3, and is a mostly backwards compatible update of the language that codifies innovation by browser vendors over the past decade and introduces a few new features.

ECMAScript 4 was never realized, and is part of the answer to why the language could go without standardized updates for 10 years. This draft was widely considered too revolutionary an update, and introduced several features that would not work well with existing browsers. To this day, Adobe's ActionScript (used in Flash) and Microsoft's JScript.Net are the only runtimes to implement a significant amount of the proposed updates from ES4.

In this chapter we will take a cursory look at the most interesting changes in ES5, and have a look at some of the programming patterns the new specification enables. Particularly interesting are new additions to objects and properties, and these will be afforded the bulk of our attention. Note that this chapter does not cover *all* changes and additions in ECMAScript 5.

8.1 The Close Future of JavaScript

Backwards compatibility has been a major concern of ES5. JavaScript is ubiquitous—every web browser released since the mid to late nineties supports it in some form or other; it's on phones and other mobile devices; it's used to develop extensions for browsers such as Mozilla Firefox and Google Chrome and has even taken the front seat in Gnome Shell, the defining technology in the Gnome 3 desktop environment for Linux. JavaScript runtimes are wild beasts. When deploying a script on the web, we can never know what kind of runtime will attempt to run our code. Couple this with the huge amount of JavaScript already deployed on the web, and you will have no problem imagining why backwards compatibility has been a key concern for ES5. The goal is not to "break the web," but rather bring it forward.

ES5 has worked hard to standardize, or *codify*, existing de facto standards—innovation in the wild adopted across browser vendors as well as common use cases found in modern JavaScript libraries. `String.prototype.trim` and `Function.prototype.bind` are good examples of the latter, whereas attribute getters and setters are good examples of the former.

Additionally, ES5 introduces *strict mode*, which points out the way moving forward. Strict mode can be enabled with a simple string literal, and makes ES5 compliant implementations, well, stricter in their parsing and execution of scripts. Strict mode sheds some of JavaScript's bad parts and is intended to serve as the starting point for future updates to the language.

The reason this section is entitled the *close* future of JavaScript is that there is reason to believe that we won't have to wait another 10 years for good browser support. This is of course speculation on my (and others) part, but as ES5 codifies some de facto standards, some of these features are already available in a good selection of browsers today. Additionally, the last couple of years have seen a somewhat revitalized "browser war," in which vendors compete harder than in a long time in creating modern standards compliant and performant browsers.

Microsoft and their Internet Explorer browser have slowed down web developers for many years, but recent development seems to suggest that they're at least back in the game *trying* to stay current. Besides, browser usage looks vastly different today compared with only 5 years ago, and fair competition regulations are already forcing Windows users in Europe to make a conscious choice of browser.

All in all, I am fairly positive to the adoption of ES5. Some of it is already supported in browsers like Chrome, Firefox, and Safari, and preview releases of all the aforementioned browsers adds more. At the time of writing, even previews of Internet Explorer 9 already implement most of ES5. I expect the situation to look even brighter once this book hits the shelves.

8.2 Updates to the Object Model

Of all the updates in ECMAScript 5, I find the updated object model to be the most exciting. As we discussed in Chapter 7, *Objects and Prototypal Inheritance,* JavaScript objects are simple mutable collections of properties, and even though ES3 defines attributes to control whether properties can be overwritten, deleted, and enumerated, they remain strictly internal, and thus cannot be harnessed by client objects. This means that objects that are dependent on their (public and mutable) properties need to employ more error checking than desired to remain reasonably robust.

8.2.1 Property Attributes

ES5 allows user-defined property descriptors to overwrite any of the following attributes for a given property.

- `enumerable` — Internal name [[Enumerable]], formerly [[DontEnum]], controls whether the property is enumerated in for-in loops
- `configurable` — Internal name [[Configurable]], formerly [[DontDelete]], controls whether the property can be deleted with `delete`
- `writable` — Internal name [[Writable]], formerly [[ReadOnly]], controls whether the property can be overwritten
- `get` — Internal name [[Get]], a function that computes the return value of property access
- `set` — Internal name [[Set]], a function that is called with the assigned value when the property is assigned to

In ES5 we can set a property in two ways. The old school way, shown in Listing 8.1, in which we simply assign a value to a property, or the new way, shown in Listing 8.2.

Listing 8.1 Simple name/value assignment

```
var circle = {};
circle.radius = 4;
```

Listing 8.2 Empowered ES5 properties

```
TestCase("ES5ObjectTest", {
  "test defineProperty": function () {
    var circle = {};

    Object.defineProperty(circle, "radius", {
      value: 4,
      writable: false,
      configurable: false
    });

    assertEquals(4, circle.radius);
  }
});
```

The `Object.defineProperty` method can be used not only to define new properties on an object, but also to update the descriptor of a property. Updating a property descriptor only works if the property's `configurable` attribute is set to `true`. Listing 8.3 shows an example of how you can use the existing descriptor to update only some attributes.

Listing 8.3 Changing a property descriptor

```
"test changing a property descriptor": function () {
  var circle = { radius: 3 };
  var descriptor =
    Object.getOwnPropertyDescriptor(circle, "radius");
  descriptor.configurable = false;
  Object.defineProperty(circle, "radius", descriptor);
  delete circle.radius;

  // Non-configurable radius cannot be deleted
  assertEquals(3, circle.radius);
}
```

In addition to controlling the property attributes, ES5 also allows control over the internal [[Extensible]] property of an object. This property controls whether or not properties can be added to the object. Calling `Object.preventExtensions(obj)` shuts the object down for further extension and cannot be undone.

Preventing object extensions and setting property attributes `writable` and `configurable` to `false` means you can now create immutable objects. This removes a lot of error checking and complexity brought on by the fact that

ES3 objects are basically mutable collections of properties. The `Object.seal` method can be used to seal an entire object; all of the object's own properties will have their `configurable` attribute set to `false`, and subsequently the object's [[Extensible]] property is set to `false`. Using a browser that supports `Object.getOwnPropertyDescriptor` and `Object.defineProperty`, the `seal` method could be implemented as in Listing 8.4.

Listing 8.4 Possible `Object.seal` implementation

```
if (!Object.seal && Object.getOwnPropertyNames &&
    Object.getOwnPropertyDescriptor &&
    Object.defineProperty && Object.preventExtensions) {
  Object.seal = function (object) {
    var properties = Object.getOwnPropertyNames(object);
    var desc, prop;

    for (var i = 0, l = properties.length; i < l; i++) {
      prop = properties[i];
      desc = Object.getOwnPropertyDescriptor(object, prop);

      if (desc.configurable) {
        desc.configurable = false;
        Object.defineProperty(object, prop, desc);
      }
    }

    Object.preventExtensions(object);

    return object;
  };
}
```

We can check whether or not an object is sealed using `Object.isSealed`. Notice how this example also uses `Object.getOwnPropertyNames`, which returns the names of all the object's own properties, including those whose `enumerable` attribute is `false`. The similar method `Object.keys` returns the property names of all enumerable properties of an object, exactly like the method in Prototype.js does today.

To easily make an entire object immutable, we can use the related, but even more restrictive function `Object.freeze`. `freeze` works like `seal`, and additionally sets all the properties `writable` attributes to false, thus completely locking the object down for modification.

8.2.2 Prototypal Inheritance

ECMAScript 5 makes prototypal inheritance in JavaScript more obvious, and avoids the clumsy constructor convention. In ES3, the only native way to create an object sphere that inherits from another object circle is by proxying via a constructor, as Listing 8.5 shows.

Listing 8.5 Create an object that inherits from another object in ES3

```
"test es3 inheritance via constructors": function () {
  var circle = { /* ... */ };

  function CircleProxy() {}
  CircleProxy.prototype = circle;

  var sphere = new CircleProxy();

  assert(circle.isPrototypeOf(sphere));
}
```

Additionally, there is no direct way of retrieving the prototype property in ES3. Mozilla added a proprietary __proto__ property that fixes both of these cases, as in Listing 8.6.

Listing 8.6 Proprietary shortcut to accessing and setting prototype

```
"test inheritance via proprietary __proto__": function () {
  var circle = { /* ... */ };
  var sphere = {};
  sphere.__proto__ = circle;

  assert(circle.isPrototypeOf(sphere));
}
```

The __proto__ property is not codified by ES5. Instead, two methods were added to work easily with prototypes. Listing 8.7 shows how we will be doing this in the future.

Listing 8.7 Creating an object that inherits from another object in ES5

```
"test inheritance, es5 style": function () {
  var circle = { /* ... */ };
  var sphere = Object.create(circle);
```

```
  assert(circle.isPrototypeOf(sphere));
  assertEquals(circle, Object.getPrototypeOf(sphere));
}
```

You might recognize `Object.create` from Section 7.5.1, *The* `Object.` `create` *Method,* in Chapter 7, *Objects and Prototypal Inheritance,* in which we did in fact implement exactly such a method. The ES5 `Object.create` does us one better—it can also add properties to the newly created object, as seen in Listing 8.8.

Listing 8.8 Create an object with properties

```
"test Object.create with properties": function () {
  var circle = { /* ... */ };

  var sphere = Object.create(circle, {
    radius: {
      value: 3,
      writable: false,
      configurable: false,
      enumerable: true
    }
  });

  assertEquals(3, sphere.radius);
}
```

As you might have guessed, `Object.create` sets the properties using `Ob-` `ject.defineProperties` (which in turn uses `Object.defineProperty`). Its implementation could possibly look like Listing 8.9.

Listing 8.9 Possible `Object.create` implementation

```
if (!Object.create && Object.defineProperties) {
  Object.create = function (object, properties) {
    function F () {}
    F.prototype = object;
    var obj = new F();

    if (typeof properties != "undefined") {
      Object.defineProperties(obj, properties);
    }

    return obj;
  };
}
```

Because `Object.defineProperties` and, by extension, `Object.defineProperty` cannot be fully simulated in ES3 environments, this is not usable, but it shows how `Object.create` works. Also note that ES5 allows the prototype to be `null`, which is not possible to emulate across browsers in ES3.

An interesting side-effect of using `Object.create` is that the `instanceof` operator may no longer provide meaningful information, as the native `Object.create` does not use a proxy constructor function to create the new object. The only function of which the newly created object will be an instance is `Object`. This may sound strange, but `instanceof` really isn't helpful in a world in which objects inherit objects. `Object.isPrototypeOf` helps determine relationships between objects, and in a language with duck typing such as JavaScript, an object's capabilities are much more interesting than its heritage.

8.2.3 Getters and Setters

As stated in the previous section, `Object.defineProperty` cannot be reliably emulated in ES3 implementations, because they do not expose property attributes. Even so, Firefox, Safari, Chrome, and Opera all implement getters and setters, which can be used to solve part of the `defineProperty` puzzle in ES3. Given that it won't work in Internet Explorer until version 9[1], getters and setters won't be applicable to the general web for still some time.

Getters and setters make it possible to add logic to getting and setting properties, without requiring change in client code. Listing 8.10 shows an example in which our `circle` uses getters and setters to add a virtual `diameter` property.

Listing 8.10 Using getters and setters

```
"test property accessors": function () {
  Object.defineProperty(circle, "diameter", {
    get: function () {
      return this.radius * 2;
    },

    set: function (diameter) {
      if (isNaN(diameter)) {
        throw new TypeError("Diameter should be a number");
      }

      this.radius = diameter / 2;
```

---

1. Internet Explorer 8 implements `Object.defineProperty`, but for some reason not for client objects.

```
    }
  });

  circle.radius = 4;

  assertEquals(8, circle.diameter);

  circle.diameter = 3;

  assertEquals(3, circle.diameter);
  assertEquals(1.5, circle.radius);

  assertException(function () {
    circle.diameter = {};
  });
}
```

8.2.4 Making Use of Property Attributes

Using the new property attributes makes it possible to create much more sophisticated programs with JavaScript. As we already saw, we can now create properly immutable objects. Additionally, we can now also emulate how the DOM works, by providing property accessors that have logic behind them.

Previously, I also argued that `Object.create` (backed by `Object.defineProperty`) will obliterate the need for object constructors along with the `instanceof` operator. In particular, the example given in Listing 8.7 creates an object with which the `instanceof` operator will only make sense with `Object`. However, using `Object.create` does not mean we cannot have a usable `instanceof` operator. Listing 8.11 shows an example in which `Object.create` is used inside a constructor to provide a meld between ES3 and ES5 style prototypal inheritance.

Listing 8.11 Constructor using `Object.create`

```
function Circle(radius) {
  var _radius;

  var circle = Object.create(Circle.prototype, {
    radius: {
      configurable: false,
      enumerable: true,

      set: function (r) {
```

```
        if (typeof r != "number" || r <= 0) {
          throw new TypeError("radius should be > 0");
        }

        _radius = r;
      },

      get: function () {
        return _radius;
      }
    }
  });

  circle.radius = radius;

  return circle;
}

Circle.prototype = Object.create(Circle.prototype, {
  diameter: {
    get: function () {
      return this.radius * 2;
    },

    configurable: false,
    enumberable: true
  },

  circumference: { /* ... */ },
  area: { /* ... */ }
});
```

This constructor can be used like any other, and even makes sense with instanceof. Listing 8.12 shows a few uses of this constructor.

Listing 8.12 Using the hybrid `Circle`

```
TestCase("CircleTest", {
  "test Object.create backed constructor": function () {
    var circle = new Circle(3);

    assert(circle instanceof Circle);
    assertEquals(6, circle.diameter);

    circle.radius = 6;
    assertEquals(12, circle.diameter);
```

```
      delete circle.radius;
      assertEquals(6, circle.radius);
  }
});
```

Defining the object and constructor this way works because of the way constructors work. If a constructor returns an object rather than a primitive value, it will not create a new object as `this`. In those cases, the new keyword is just syntactical fluff. As the example in Listing 8.13 shows, simply calling the function works just as well.

Listing 8.13 Using `Circle` without new

```
"test omitting new when creating circle": function () {
  var circle = Circle(3);

  assert(circle instanceof Circle);
  assertEquals(6, circle.diameter);
}
```

The `prototype` property is a convention used with constructors in order for the new keyword to work predictably. When we are creating our own objects and setting up the prototype chain ourselves, we don't really need it. Listing 8.14 shows an example in which we leave constructors, new and `instanceof` behind.

Listing 8.14 Using `Object.create` and a function

```
"test using a custom create method": function () {
  var circle = Object.create({}, {
    diameter: {
      get: function () {
        return this.radius * 2;
      }
    },

    circumference: { /* ... */ },
    area: { /* ... */ },

    create: {
      value: function (radius) {
        var circ = Object.create(this, {
          radius: { value: radius }
        });

        return circ;
```

```
      }
    }
  });

  var myCircle = circle.create(3);

  assertEquals(6, myCircle.diameter);
  assert(circle.isPrototypeOf(myCircle));

  // circle is not a function
  assertException(function () {
    assertFalse(myCircle instanceof circle);
  });
}
```

This example creates a single object that exposes a `create` method to construct the new object. Thus there is no need for `new` or `prototype`, and prototypal inheritance works as expected. An interesting side effect of this style is that you can call `myCircle.create(radius)` to create circles that inherit from `myCircle` and so on.

This is just one possible way to implement inheritance without constructors in JavaScript. Regardless of what you think of this particular implementation, I think the example clearly shows why constructors and the `new` keyword are unneeded in JavaScript, particularly in ES5, which provides better tools for working with objects and prototypal inheritance.

8.2.5 Reserved Keywords as Property Identifiers

In ES5, reserved keywords can be used as object property identifiers. This is particularly important in the light of the added native JSON support, because it means that JSON is not restricted in available property names. Reserved keywords as implemented in ES3 caused trouble, for instance when implementing the DOM, as Listing 8.15 shows an example of.

Listing 8.15 Reserved keywords and property identifiers

```
// ES3
element.className; // HTML attribute is "class"
element.htmlFor;   // HTML attribute is "for"

// Is valid ES5
element.class;
element.for;
```

This does not imply that the DOM API will change with ES5, but it does mean that new APIs do not need to suffer the inconsistency of the DOM API.

8.3 Strict Mode

ECMAScript 5 allows a unit—a script or a function—to operate in a strict mode syntax. This syntax does not allow some of ES3's less stellar features, is less permissive of potentially bad patterns, throws more errors, and ultimately aspires to reduce confusion and provide developers with an easier to work with environment.

Because ES5 is supposed to be backwards compatible with ES3, or at least implementations of it, strict mode is opt-in, an elegant way to deprecate features scheduled for removal in future updates.

8.3.1 Enabling Strict Mode

The example in Listing 8.16 shows how strict mode can be enabled by a single string literal directive.

Listing 8.16 Enable strict mode globally

```
"use strict";

// Following code is considered strict ES5 code
```

This simple construct may look a little silly, but it is extremely unlikely to collide with existing semantics and is completely backwards compatible—it's just a no-op string literal in ES3. Because it may not be possible to port all ES3 code to strict mode from the get-go, ES5 offers a way to enable strict mode locally. When placed inside a function, the directive will enable strict mode inside the function only. Listing 8.17 shows an example of strict and non-strict code side-by-side in the same script.

Listing 8.17 Local strict mode

```
function haphazardMethod(obj) {
  // Function is not evaluated as strict code

  with (obj) {
    // Not allowed in strict
  }
}

function es5FriendlyMethod() {
```

```
  "use strict";

  // Local scope is evaluated as strict code
}
```

Strict mode can be enabled for evaled code as well, either by making a direct call to `eval` from within other strict code, or if the code to be evaled itself begins with the strict directive. The same rules apply to a string of code passed to the `Function` constructor.

8.3.2 Strict Mode Changes

The following are changes to the language in strict mode.

8.3.2.1 No Implicit Globals

Implicit globals is likely JavaScript's least useful and certainly least appreciated feature. In ES3, assigning to an undeclared variable does not result in an error, or even a warning. Rather, it creates a property of the global object, paving the way for some truly obscure bugs. In strict mode, assigning to undeclared variables results in a `ReferenceError`. Listing 8.18 shows an example.

Listing 8.18 Implicit globals

```
function sum(numbers) {
  "use strict";
  var sum = 0;

  for (i = 0; i < numbers.length; i++) {
    sum += numbers[i];
  }

  return sum;
}

// ES3: Property i is created on global object
// ES5 strict mode: ReferenceError
```

8.3.2.2 Functions

Strict mode offers some help when dealing with functions. For instance, an error will now be thrown if two formal function parameters use the same identifier. In ES3 implementations, using the same identifier for more than one formal parameter results in only the last one to be reachable inside the function (except through `arguments`, in which all parameters are always reachable). Listing 8.19 shows the new behavior compared to the current one.

Listing 8.19 Using the same identifier for more than one formal parameter

```
"test repeated identifiers in parameters": function () {
  // Syntax error in ES5 strict mode
  function es3VsEs5(a, a, a) {
    "use strict";
    return a;
  }

  // true in ES3
  assertEquals(6, es3VsEs5(2, 3, 6));
}
```

Attempts to access the `caller` or `callee` properties of the `arguments` object will throw a `TypeError` in strict mode.

In ES3 (and non-strict ES5), the `arguments` object shares a dynamic relationship with formal parameters. Modify a formal parameter, and the value in the corresponding index of the `argument` object is modified too. Modify a value of the `arguments` object, and the corresponding parameter changes. In strict mode, this relationship goes away and `arguments` is immutable, as Listing 8.20 exemplifies.

Listing 8.20 Relationship between `arguments` and formal parameters

```
function switchArgs(a, b) {
  "use strict";
  var c = b;
  b = a;
  a = c;

  return [].slice.call(arguments);
}

TestCase("ArgumentsParametersTest", {
  "test should switch arguments": function () {
    // Passes on ES5 strict mode
    assertEquals([3, 2], switchArgs(2, 3));

    // Passes on ES3
    // assertEquals([2, 3], switchArgs(2, 3));
  }
});
```

`this` is no longer coerced to an object in strict mode. In ES3 and non-strict ES5, `this` will be coerced to an object if it is not one already. For instance, when using `call` or `apply` with function objects, passing in `null` or `undefined` will no longer cause `this` inside the called function to be coerced into the global object. Neither will primitive values used as `this` be coerced to wrapper objects.

8.3.2.3 Objects, Properties, and Variables

`eval` and `arguments` cannot be used as identifiers in ES5 strict mode. Formal parameters, variables, the exception object in a try-catch statement, and object property identifiers are all affected by this restriction.

In ES3 implementations, defining an object literal with repeated property identifiers causes the latest one to overwrite the value of previous properties sharing the identifier. In strict mode, repeating an identifier in an object literal will cause a syntax error.

As we already saw, strict mode does not allow implicit globals. Not only will implicit globals cause errors, but writing to any property of an object whose `writable` attribute is `false`, *or* writing to a non-existent property of an object whose internal `[[Extensible]]` property is `false` will throw `TypeError` as well.

The `delete` operator will no longer fail silently in strict mode. In ES3 and non-strict ES5, using the `delete` operator on a property whose `configurable` attribute is `false` will not delete the property, and the expression will return `false` to indicate that the deletion was not successful. In strict mode, such deletion causes a `TypeError`.

8.3.2.4 Additional Restrictions

The `with` statement no longer exists in strict mode. Using it will simply produce a syntax error. Some developers are less than impressed by this change, but the truth is that it is too easy to use wrong, and easily makes code unpredictable and hard to follow.

Octal number literals, such as `0377` (255 decimal), are not allowed in strict mode, this also applies to `parseInt("09")`.

8.4 Various Additions and Improvements

We have already seen most of the additions to the `Object`, but there is more to ECMAScript 5 than empowered objects.

8.4.1 Native JSON

ES5 introduces native JSON support, in form of the `JSON` object. It supports two methods, JSON.stringify and `JSON.parse` to dump and load JSON respectively. Douglas Crockford's `json2.js` provides a compatible interface for browsers that does not yet implement the new JSON interface. This means that by loading this library, we can start using this particular feature today. In fact, `json2.js` has been widely used for some time, and several browsers already support the native `JSON` object.

Both ES5 and `json2.js` also adds `Date.prototype.toJSON`, which serializes date objects as JSON by way of `Date.prototype.toISOString`, which in turn uses a simplification of the ISO 8601 Extended Format. The format is as follows: `YYYY-MM-DDTHH:mm:ss.sssZ`

8.4.2 `Function.prototype.bind`

The `bind` method, as described in Chapter 6, *Applied Functions and Closures,* is native to ES5. This should mean improved performance, and less code for libraries to maintain. The previously provided implementation is mostly equivalent to the one provided by ES5 apart from a few details. The native `bind` function returns a native object, which itself has no `prototype` property. Rather than creating a simple function that wraps the original function, a special type of internal object is created that maintains the relationship to the bound function such that, e.g., the `instanceof` operator works with the resulting function just like it would with the bound function.

8.4.3 Array Extras

Lots of new functionality is added to arrays in ES5. Most of these stem from Mozilla's JavaScript 1.6, which has been around for some time—long enough for, e.g., Safari's JavaScriptCore to implement them as well. ES5 also adds `Array.isArray`, which can determine if an object is an array by checking its internal [[Class]] property. Because `Object.prototype.toString` exposes this property, including in ES3, it can be used to provide a conforming implementation, as seen in Listing 8.21.

Listing 8.21 Implementing `Array.isArray`

```
if (!Array.isArray) {
  Array.isArray = (function () {
    function isArray(object) {
```

```
        return Object.prototype.toString.call(object) ==
               "[object Array]";
    }

    return isArray;
}());
}
```

In addition to the static `isArray` method, `Array.prototype` defines a host of new methods: `indexOf`, `lastIndexOf`, `every`, `some`, `forEach`, `map`, `filter`, `reduce`, `reduceRight`.

8.5 Summary

In this chapter we have taken a brief look at some changes in JavaScript's (hopefully) near future. ECMAScript 5 brings the spec up to speed with innovation in the wild and even brings some exciting new features to the language. Setting the course for future standards—specifically ECMAScript Harmony, the working group for the next revision to the language—ES5 introduces strict mode, opt-in deprecation of troublesome features from JavaScript's childhood.

Extensions to objects and properties open the door to interesting new ways of structuring JavaScript programs. JavaScript's prototypal nature no longer needs to be hidden behind class-like constructors, because new `Object` methods make working with prototypal inheritance easier and clearer. By finally allowing developers to both read and write property attributes, even for user-defined objects, ES5 enables better structured and more robust programs, better encapsulation, and immutable objects.

An overview of ES5, even as selective as here, can guide us in writing code that will more easily port to it once it's widely adopted. We will draw from this inspiration in the TDD examples in Part III, *Real-World Test-Driven Development in JavaScript*. Before we dive into those examples, however, we will learn about unobtrusive JavaScript and feature detection in the closing two chapters of Part II, *JavaScript for Programmers*.

Unobtrusive JavaScript

I n Chapter 2, *The Test-Driven Development Process,* we saw how test-driven development can help create "clean code that works." Unfortunately, even perceptibly clean code can cause problems, and on the web there are many degrees of "working." Unobtrusive JavaScript is a term coined to describe JavaScript applied to websites in a manner that increases user value, stays out of the user's way, and enhances pages progressively in response to detected support. Unobtrusive JavaScript guides us in our quest for truly *clean code*; code that either works, or knowingly doesn't; code that behaves in any environment for any user.

To illustrate the principles of unobtrusive JavaScript, we will review a particularly obtrusive tabbed panels implementation. Equipped with our new knowledge, we will build an improved replacement backed by unit tests.

9.1 The Goal of Unobtrusive JavaScript

Accessible websites that work for as wide an audience as possible is the ultimate goal of unobtrusive JavaScript. Its most important principles are separation of concerns and certainty over assumptions. Semantic markup is in charge of document structure, and document structure only. Semantic HTML not only enhances accessibility potential, it also provides a rich set of hooks for both CSS and JavaScript to attach to. Visual styles and layout are the responsibility of CSS; presentational attributes and elements should be avoided. Behavior is the domain of JavaScript, and it should be applied through external scripts. This means that inline scripts and intrinsic event handlers are out of the question most of the time.

The advantages of this technique are vast:

- **Accessibility**: A semantic document can make sense to a wider audience than those with visual desktop browsers. Describing content with suitable tags affords screen readers, search engine crawlers, and other user agents a better chance of making sense of content.
- **Flexibility**: The document structure can be more easily modified without requiring change to external sources. The same kind of flexibility is achieved in JavaScript and CSS. Scripts can be refactored, tuned, and modified without requiring change to the underlying document. Script features can more easily be reused for new document structures.
- **Robustness**: Building on top of a solid foundation, behavior can be added progressively. Applying feature detection, i.e., only adding features that can be inferred to work, vastly decreases the chance of scripts blowing up and ruining the user's experience. Such a defensive approach to scripting is also known as progressive enhancement.
- **Performance**: Using external scripts allows for better caching of scripts used across web pages.
- **Extensibility**: Separating scripts from the markup completely means we can more easily add more progressive enhancement for new browsers as more advanced functionality is made available.

9.2 The Rules of Unobtrusive JavaScript

Chris Heilmann is perhaps the most well-known advocate of unobtrusive JavaScript, and he has written and talked extensively on the topic. In 2007 he wrote "The Seven Rules of Unobtrusive JavaScript":

- Do not make any assumptions
- Find your hooks and relationships
- Leave traversing to the experts
- Understand browsers and users
- Understand Events
- Play well with others
- Work for the next developer

Chapter 10, *Feature Detection,* provides a solution for the script-side of "Do not make assumptions" and Chapter 6, *Applied Functions and Closures,* went over some techniques that help "Play well with others." Test-driven development, as described in Chapter 2, *The Test-Driven Development Process,* and the examples in Part III, *Real-World Test-Driven Development in JavaScript,* help us build *clean code,* which for the most part takes care of "Work for the next developer."

"Understanding Events" advises to use event handlers to decouple code. Heilmann promotes event delegation as an excellent technique to write lightweight scripts with loose coupling. Event delegation takes advantage of the fact that most user events do not only occur on target elements, but also on every containing element above it in the DOM hierarchy. For instance, given a tabbed panel, there really is no need to attach click events to all the tabs in the panel. It is sufficient to attach a single event handler to the parent element, and on each click determine which tab caused the event, and activate that tab. Implementing events this way allows for much more flexible APIs, as for instance adding new tabs will not require any event handler logic at all. Reducing the number of handlers reduces memory consumption and helps build snappier interfaces.

"Find your hooks and relationships" and "Leave traversing to the experts" both deal with separation of concerns. By describing documents using rich semantic HTML, there are lots of natural hooks inherent in the document. Again, imagine a tabbed panel; certain markup patterns can be discovered and converted to tabbed panels if necessary script support is available. CSS can keep separate styles for "enabled" and "disabled" scripted tab features.

9.2.1 An Obtrusive Tabbed Panel

In contrast to such clean separation, consider the horribly obtrusive, yet disappointingly common tabbed panel solution presented in Listing 9.1.

Listing 9.1 An obtrusive implementation of a tabbed panel

```
<div id="cont-1">
  <span class="tabs-nav tabs-selected"
        style="float: left; margin-right: 5px;">
    <span onclick="tabs = $('#cont-1 > .tabs-nav');
        tabs.removeClass('tabs-selected');
        $(this).parent().addClass('tabs-selected');
        var className = $(this).attr('class');
        var fragment_id = /fragment-\d/.exec(className);
        $('.tabs-container').addClass('tabs-hide');
```

```
        $('#'+fragment_id).removeClass('tabs-hide');"
          class="fragment-1 nav">
      Latest news
    </span>
  </span>
  <span class="tabs-nav"
        style="float: left; margin-right: 5px;">
    <span onclick="tabs = $('#cont-1 > .tabs-nav');
        tabs.removeClass('tabs-selected');
        $(this).parent().addClass('tabs-selected');
        var className = $(this).attr('class');
        var fragment_id = /fragment-\d/.exec(className);
        $('.tabs-container').addClass('tabs-hide');
        $('#'+fragment_id).removeClass('tabs-hide');"
          class="fragment-2 nav">
      Sports
    </span>
  </span>
</div>
<div class="tabs-container" id="fragment-1">
  <div class="tabbertab">
    <span style="margin: 0px 5px 0px 0px; float: left;">
      <strong>Latest news</strong>
    </span>
    <div>
      Latest news contents [...]
    </div>
  </div>
</div>
<div class="tabs-container tabs-hide" id="fragment-2">
  <div class="tabbertab">
    <span style="margin: 0px 5px 0px 0px; float: left;">
      <strong>Sports</strong>
    </span>
    <div>
      Sports contents [...]
    </div>
  </div>
</div>
<div class="tabs-container tabs-hide" id="fragment-3">
  <div class="tabbertab">
    <span style="margin: 0px 5px 0px 0px; float: left;">
      <strong>Economy</strong>
    </span>
    <div>
      Economy contents [...]
```

```
    </div>
  </div>
</div>
```

The gist of this solution is simply a list of links with inline event handlers that toggle the display of the corresponding panel of text. This solution suffers from a plethora of issues:

- All panels but the default selected one will be completely inaccessible to users without JavaScript, or with insufficient JavaScript support (i.e., some screen readers, old browsers, old and new mobile devices).
- Progressive enhancement is not possible—either it works or it doesn't.
- Markup is heavyweight and senseless, reducing accessibility and increasing complexity of associated CSS.
- Reusing scripts is practically impossible.
- Testing scripts is practically impossible.
- `span` elements are styled and scripted to act like internal anchors. `a` elements provide this functionality for free.
- Poorly written script introduces unintentional global variable `tabs`.
- Script does not make use of markup context, instead using expensive selectors on every click to access panels and other tabs.

9.2.2 Clean Tabbed Panel Markup

If "Find your hooks and relationships" can teach us anything, it is to start by writing semantic and valid markup, adding ids and classes sparingly to have enough hooks to add the scripted behavior. Analyzing the tabbed panel as implemented in Listing 9.1, we can sum up the functionality pretty simply: One or more sections of text is to be navigated by clicking "tabs"—links with the text section's heading as link text. Reasonable markup for such a requirement could be as simple as the markup in Listing 9.2. Using HTML5 could further improve its clarity.

Listing 9.2 Tabbed panels base; semantic markup

```
<div class="tabbed-panel">
  <ol id="news-tabs" class="nav">
    <li><a href="#news">Latest news</a></li>
    <li><a href="#sports">Sports</a></li>
    <li><a href="#economy">Economy</a></li>
  </ol>
```

```
<div class="section">
  <h2><a name="news">Latest news</a></h2>
  <p>Latest news contents [...]</p>
</div>
<div class="section">
  <h2><a name="sports">Sports</a></h2>
  <p>Sports contents [...]</p>
</div>
<div class="section">
  <h2><a name="economy">Economy</a></h2>
  <p>Economy contents [...]</p>
</div>
</div>
```

Note that the containing element has the class name `tabbed-panel`. This is all we need to know. The script built on top of this structure could simply look for all elements with the class name `tabs` that contain an ordered list (navigation) and sub-elements with class name `section`. Once this structure is identified, the script can convert the structure into a tabbed panels widget, so long as the required functionality can be inferred to work.

In the basic version we could possibly leave out the navigational markup, and add it in via script. However, using anchors as a "jump to" menu can easily make sense in a non-scripted version, and it frees us from too much script-based markup building.

This sort of markup also lends itself to easier styling. The default styles for `div.tabbed-panel` will target the basic solution, aimed at environments in which the panels are presented as a series of vertically stacked text boxes. The script that converts the structure into tabs and panels can add a single class name to the containing element to trigger a separate view intended for the script-driven tabs and panels look. This way the script simply enables the functionality, and CSS is still in complete control of the visual presentation.

9.2.3 TDD and Progressive Enhancement

Incidentally, the progressive enhancement style of user interface coding goes well with test-driven development. By cleanly separating structure, layout, and behavior we can keep the interface between script and markup at a minimum, enabling us to unit test most of the logic without requiring the DOM. Enabling TDD creates a positive circle as code written guided by tests tends to focus even more strongly on a clean separation of concerns. The resulting decoupling allows for better code reuse and faster tests.

9.3 Do Not Make Assumptions

"Do not make assumptions" is perhaps the most important rule of unobtrusive JavaScript. It sums up most aspects of clean JavaScript in a single phrasing. In this section we will go over the most common assumptions and why they make it challenging to write robust scripts for the web.

9.3.1 Don't Assume You Are Alone

Never assume that scripts run in isolation. This applies to application developers as much as library authors, because most websites today use code from at least one external source.

Assuming scripts run in isolation makes running them alongside scripts we don't control harder. For the last few years, all the sites I've worked on use at least one external analytics script and most of these scripts use `document.write` as a last resort. `document.write` has a nasty side-effect of wiping the entire document if used after the DOM has fully loaded. This means that asynchronously loading content invoking the offending code will cause the site's analytics script to effectively break it completely. I've seen maintenance developers break down in tears as they realize what is causing their site to fail, and it ain't a pretty sight.

9.3.1.1 How to Avoid

The less we contribute to the global environment, the less we will depend on it. Keeping our global footprint small reduces chances of conflicts with other scripts. Techniques to minimize global impact were described in Chapter 6, *Applied Functions and Closures*. Besides keeping the number of global objects low, we need to watch out for other forms of global state, such as assigning to `window.onload` or using the aforementioned `document.write`.

9.3.2 Don't Assume Markup Is Correct

When separating concerns, we should strive to keep as much markup in the document as possible. In practice this equates to using the "fallback" solution as a basis for the scripted solution as much as possible. However, this also means that scripts are no longer in complete control of markup, so we need to be careful. The original markup may be compromised in many ways; it may be compromised by other scripts, by document authors, or by invalid markup that results in a different document structure when parsed.

9.3.2.1 How to Avoid

Check the required markup using script before applying a given feature. It is particularly important to verify that the complete structure required is available when initializing widgets, so we don't accidentally start initializing a widget only to abort halfway because of unexpected changes in the document structure, effectively leaving the user with a broken page.

9.3.3 Don't Assume All Users Are Created Equal

Reaching a wide audience means meeting a lot of different needs. The web content accessibility guidelines (WCAG) instruct us not to tie functionality to a single input mechanism, such as the mouse. Triggering functionality using the `mouseover` event effectively removes the feature for users unable to handle a mouse, or handle it *well enough*. Besides, mouseover doesn't make any sense on touch devices, which are becoming increasingly popular.

9.3.3.1 How to Avoid

WCAG advices to use redundant input methods, i.e., provide keyboard alternatives for mouse-specific events. This is a good piece of advice, but there is more to keyboard accessibility than adding a `focus` event handler with every `mouseover` event handler (not even possible on some elements). Ultimately, the only way to create truly keyboard accessible websites is to test, test, and test. Ideally, those tests are carried out by actual users, both the mouse, keyboard, and possibly even the touch inclined.

9.3.4 Don't Assume Support

Never use features that may not be available; test for the existence of features before using them. This is also known as feature detection or feature testing, and we will deal with it in more detail in Chapter 10, *Feature Detection*.

9.4 When Do the Rules Apply?

Although most of the principles presented in this chapter are general characteristics of solid craftsmanship, some rules can be challenging in given cases. For instance, a JavaScript intense *application* such as Gmail could prove difficult to develop using progressive enhancement. Gmail has solved this problem by providing a scriptless environment completely detached from its main interface. This solution certainly honors accessibility by allowing clients unable to use the main application access to a less demanding one that can more easily support their needs. Additionally, a more lightweight, but still heavily scripted application, is available for mobile devices with smaller screens and less capable browsers. However, providing alternate versions is no excuse for writing sloppy code, ignoring the fact that people use different input methods or tightly coupling scripts with the document structure.

Many developers feel that unobtrusive JavaScript is too idealistic, and that it does not apply in "the real world," in which projects have budgets and deadlines. In some cases they are right, but mostly it's more about planning and attacking a problem from the right angle. Quality always takes a little more effort than spewing out anything that seems to work in whatever browser the developer keeps handy for testing. Like TDD, coding JavaScript unobtrusively will probably slow you down slightly as you start out, but you will reap the benefits over time because it makes maintenance a lot easier, causes fewer errors, and produces more accessible solutions. This translates to less time spent fixing bugs, less time spent handling complaints from users, and possibly also less serious trouble as accessibility laws get more comprehensive.

In 2006, target.com, an American online retailer, was sued for lack of accessibility after refusing to deal with accessibility complaints since early 2005. Two years later the company agreed to a $6 million settlement. I'm guessing that slightly raised development costs outrank civil action any day.

Note that a *website* is not necessarily a *web application* in terms of the user interface. Buying music, managing contacts, paying bills, and reading news rarely *need* functionality that cannot be offered in a simplified way without scripts. On the other hand, applications such as spreadsheets, real-time chat rooms, or collaborative office tools can be hard to reproduce in a meaningful way without them.

9.5 Unobtrusive Tabbed Panel Example

We have learned a few things about unobtrusive JavaScript, and we've seen the manifestation of unmaintainable obtrusive JavaScript. In this section we will walk quickly through developing an unobtrusive tabbed panel backed by tests.

To keep this example somewhat brief, we won't go into details on every step of the test-driven development process taken to develop this solution. Part III, *Real-World Test-Driven Development in JavaScript,* goes into the nitty-gritty of the process and provides several complete and narrated TDD projects. In this section we will focus on the concepts used to create an unobtrusive tabbed panel.

9.5.1 Setting Up the Test

To support the tabbed panel we will build a `tabController` interface, one test case at a time. Each test case will target a single method in this interface, which controls the state of the tabs and offers a callback that fires anytime the active tab changes.

In order for tests to share the setup code, which creates the minimum markup and keeps a reference to it available for the tests, we wrap the test cases in an anonymous closure that is immediately executed. Inside it we can add a shortcut to the namespaced object and a local `setUp` function. The setup code can be viewed in Listing 9.3.

Listing 9.3 Test setup using a shared `setUp`

```
(function () {
  var tabController = tddjs.ui.tabController;

  // All test cases can share this setUp
  function setUp() {
    /*:DOC += <ol id="tabs">
          <li><a href="#news">News</a></li>
          <li><a href="#sports">Sports</a></li>
          <li><a href="#economy">Economy</a></li>
        </ol>*/

    this.tabs = document.getElementById("tabs");
  }

  // Test cases go here
}());
```

In addition to this setup, we will use the two helpers in Listing 9.4, which simply adds and removes class names from an element's `class` attribute.

Listing 9.4 Adding and removing class names

```
(function () {
  var dom = tddjs.namespace("dom");

  function addClassName(element, cName) {
    var regexp = new RegExp("(^|\\s)" + cName + "(\\s|$)");

    if (element && !regexp.test(element.className)) {
      cName = element.className + " " + cName;
```

```
        element.className = cName.replace(/^\s+|\s+$/g, "");
    }
}

function removeClassName(element, cName) {
    var r = new RegExp("(^|\\s)" + cName + "(\\s|$)");

    if (element) {
        cName = element.className.replace(r, " ");
        element.className = cName.replace(/^\s+|\s+$/g, "");
    }
}

dom.addClassName = addClassName;
dom.removeClassName = removeClassName;
}());
```

These two methods require the `tddjs` object and its `namespace` method from Chapter 6, *Applied Functions and Closures.* To code along with this example, set up a simple JsTestDriver project as described in Chapter 3, *Tools of the Trade,* and save the `tddjs` object and its `namespace` method along with the above helpers in `lib/tdd.js`. Also save the `Object.create` implementation from Chapter 7, *Objects and Prototypal Inheritance,* in `lib/object.js`.

9.5.2 The `tabController` Object

Listing 9.5 shows the first test case, which covers the `tabController` object's create method. It accepts a container element for the tab controller. It tests its markup requirements and throws an exception if the container is not an element (determined by checking for the properties it's going to use). If the element is deemed sufficient, the `tabController` object is created and a class name is appended to the element, allowing CSS to style the tabs as, well, tabs. Note how each of the tests test a single behavior. This makes for quick feedback loops and reduces the scope we need to concentrate on at any given time.

The `create` method is going to add an event handler to the element as well, but we will cheat a little in this example. Event handlers will be discussed in Chapter 10, *Feature Detection,* and testing them will be covered through the example project in Chapter 15, *TDD and DOM Manipulation: The Chat Client.*

Listing 9.5 Test case covering the `create` method

```
TestCase("TabControllerCreateTest", {
  setUp: setUp,

  "test should fail without element": function () {
    assertException(function () {
      tabController.create();
    }, "TypeError");
  },

  "test should fail without element class": function () {
    assertException(function () {
      tabController.create({});
    }, "TypeError");
  },

  "should return object": function () {
    var controller = tabController.create(this.tabs);

    assertObject(controller);
  },

  "test should add js-tabs class name to element":
  function () {
    var tabs = tabController.create(this.tabs);

    assertClassName("js-tab-controller", this.tabs);
  },

  // Test for event handlers, explained later
});
```

The implementation shown in Listing 9.6 is fairly straightforward. Staying out of the global namespace, the `tabController` object is implemented inside the existing `tddjs` namespace.

The method makes one possibly unsafe assumption: The DOM 0 event listener (the `onclick` property). The assumption the script implicitly is making is that no other script will hijack the `ol` element's `onclick` listener. This might seem like a reasonable expectation, but using DOM 2 event listeners is a much safer choice. As mentioned previously, we will defer their use to Chapter 15, *TDD and DOM Manipulation: The Chat Client,* in which we'll also discuss how to test them.

Note that we're using event delegation here, by registering a single event handler for the whole list element and then passing along the event object to the event handler.

Listing 9.6 Implementation of `create`

```
(function () {
  var dom = tddjs.dom;

  function create(element) {
    if (!element || typeof element.className != "string") {
      throw new TypeError("element is not an element");
    }

    dom.addClassName(element, "js-tab-controller");
    var tabs = Object.create(this);

    element.onclick = function (event) {
      tabs.handleTabClick(event || window.event || {});
    };

    element = null;

    return tabs;
  }

  function handleTabClick(event) {}

  tddjs.namespace("ui").tabController = {
    create: create,
    handleTabClick: handleTabClick
  };
}());
```

The event is handled by the tab controller's `handleTabClick` method. Because we will discuss working around the cross-browser quirks of event handling in Chapter 10, *Feature Detection,* we will skip its test case for now. The `tabController` test case should concern itself with the behavior of tabs, not differing implementations of event handling. Such tests belong in a test case dedicated to an event interface whose purpose is to smooth over browser differences. In many cases this role is filled by a third party JavaScript library, but there is nothing stopping us from keeping our own set of tools for those cases in which we don't need everything that comes with a library. Listing 9.7 shows the resulting method.

Listing 9.7 Implementation of `handleTabClick`

```
function handleTabClick(event) {
  var target = event.target || event.srcElement;

  while (target && target.nodeType != 1) {
    target = target.parentNode;
  }

  this.activateTab(target);
}
```

The handler grabs the element that triggered the event. This means the `target` property of the event object in most browsers, and `srcElement` in Internet Explorer. To accommodate browsers that occasionally fire events directly on text nodes, it makes sure it got an element node. Finally, it passes the originating element to the `activateTab` method.

9.5.3 The `activateTab` Method

The `activateTab` method accepts an element as its only argument, and given that its tag name is of the expected type, it activates it by adding a class name. The method also deactivates the previously activated tab.

The reason we check the tag name is the event delegation. Any element inside the containing element will cause a click event to fire, and the `tabTagName` property allows us to configure which elements are considered "tabs." Given a selector engine, we could allow more fine-grained control of this feature by allowing arbitrary CSS selectors decide if an element is a tab. Another possibility is to expose an `isTab(element)` method that could be overridden on specific instances to provide custom behavior.

If and when the method changes the tabs state, it fires the `onTabChange` event, passing it the current and previous tabs. Listing 9.8 shows the entire test case.

Listing 9.8 Test case covering the `activateTab` method

```
TestCase("TabbedControllerActivateTabTest", {
  setUp: function () {
    setUp.call(this);
    this.controller = tabController.create(this.tabs);
    this.links = this.tabs.getElementsByTagName("a");
    this.lis = this.tabs.getElementsByTagName("li");
  },
```

```
"test should not fail without anchor": function () {
  var controller = this.controller;

  assertNoException(function () {
    controller.activateTab();
  });
},

"test should mark anchor as active": function () {
  this.controller.activateTab(this.links[0]);

  assertClassName("active-tab", this.links[0]);
},

"test should deactivate previous tab": function () {
  this.controller.activateTab(this.links[0]);
  this.controller.activateTab(this.links[1]);

  assertNoMatch(/(^|\s)active-tab(\s|$)/, this.links[0]);
  assertClassName("active-tab", this.links[1]);
},

"test should not activate unsupported element types":
function () {
  this.controller.activateTab(this.links[0]);
  this.controller.activateTab(this.lis[0]);

  assertNoMatch(/(^|\s)active-tab(\s|$)/, this.lis[0]);
  assertClassName("active-tab", this.links[0]);
},

"test should fire onTabChange": function () {
  var actualPrevious, actualCurrent;
  this.controller.activateTab(this.links[0]);
  this.controller.onTabChange = function (curr, prev) {
    actualPrevious = prev;
    actualCurrent = curr;
  };

  this.controller.activateTab(this.links[1]);

  assertSame(actualPrevious, this.links[0]);
  assertSame(actualCurrent, this.links[1]);
}
});
```

Implementation, as seen in Listing 9.9, is fairly straightforward. As the tests indicate, the method starts by checking that it actually received an element, and that its tag name matches the `tabTagName` property. It then proceeds to add and remove class names as described above, and finally calls the `onTabChange` method. Finally, we add a no-op `onTabChange`, ready for users to override.

Listing 9.9 The `activateTab` method

```
function activateTab(element) {
  if (!element || !element.tagName ||
      element.tagName.toLowerCase() != this.tabTagName) {
    return;
  }

  var className = "active-tab";
  dom.removeClassName(this.prevTab, className);
  dom.addClassName(element, className);
  var previous = this.prevTab;
  this.prevTab = element;

  this.onTabChange(element, previous);
}

tddjs.namespace("ui").tabController = {
  /* ... */
  activateTab: activateTab,
  onTabChange: function (anchor, previous) {},
  tabTagName: "a"
};
```

9.5.4 Using the Tab Controller

Using the `tabController` object we can recreate the tabbed panel in an unobtrusive way. The improved panel will be based on the markup shown in Listing 9.2. The script in Listing 9.10 grabs the `ol` element containing links to each section and creates a tab controller with it. Doing so will cause the tabs to have the `active-tab` class name toggled as we click them. We then hook into the tab controller's `onTabChange` callback and use the semantic relationship between the anchors and the sections of information to toggle active state for panels, disabling the previous panel and enabling the current selected one. Finally, the first tab anchor is fetched and activated.

Listing 9.10 Using the tab controller

```
(function () {
  if (typeof document == "undefined" ||
      !document.getElementById) {
    return;
  }

  var dom = tddjs.dom;
  var ol = document.getElementById("news-tabs");

  /* ... */

  try {
    var controller = tddjs.ui.tabController.create(ol);
    dom.addClassName(ol.parentNode, "js-tabs");

    controller.onTabChange = function (curr, prev) {
      dom.removeClassName(getPanel(prev), "active-panel");
      dom.addClassName(getPanel(curr), "active-panel");
    };

    controller.activateTab(ol.getElementsByTagName("a")[0]);
  } catch (e) {}
}());
```

The getPanel function used in the above example uses the semantic markup to find which panel an anchor should toggle. It extracts the part of the anchor's href attribute after the hash character, looks up elements with corresponding names, and finally picks the first one it finds. It then traverses the element's parent until it finds a div element. The method can be seen in Listing 9.11.

Listing 9.11 Finding the panel to toggle

```
(function () {
  /* ... */

  function getPanel(element) {
    if (!element || typeof element.href != "string") {
      return null;
    }

    var target = element.href.replace(/.*#/, "");
    var panel = document.getElementsByName(target)[0];
```

```
    while (panel && panel.tagName.toLowerCase() != "div") {
      panel = panel.parentNode;
    }

    return panel;
  }

  /* ... */
}());
```

Note that getPanel defensively checks its argument and aborts if it doesn't receive an actual element. This means that we can fearlessly call it using the curr and prev anchors in the onTabChange method, even though the prev argument will be undefined the first time it is called.

To make the tabbed panels appear as panels, we can sprinkle on some very simple CSS, as seen in Listing 9.12.

Listing 9.12 Simple tabbed panel CSS

```
.js-tabs .section {
    clear: left;
    display: none;
}

.js-tabs .active-panel {
    display: block;
}

.js-tabs .nav {
    border-bottom: 1px solid #bbb;
    margin: 0 0 6px;
    overflow: visible;
    padding: 0;
}

.js-tabs .nav li {
    display: inline;
    list-style: none;
}

.js-tabs .nav a {
    background: #eee;
    border: 1px solid #bbb;
    line-height: 1.6;
```

```
    padding: 3px 8px;
}

.js-tabs a.active-tab {
    background: #fff;
    border-bottom-color: #fff;
    color: #000;
    text-decoration: none;
}
```

All the style rules are prefixed with ".js-tabs", which means that they will only take effect if the script in Listing 9.10 completes successfully. Thus, we have a nice tabbed panel in browsers that support it and fall back to inline bookmarks and vertically presented panels of text in unsupporting browsers.

Implementation of the unobtrusive tabs might strike you as a bit verbose and it is not perfect. It is, however, a good start—something to build on. For instance, rather than coding the panel handling inline as we just did, we could create a `tabbedPanel` object to handle everything. Its `create` method could receive the outer `div` element as argument and set up a `tabController` and offer something like the `getPanel` function as a method. It could also improve the current solution in many ways, for example, by checking that the tabs do not activate panels outside the root element.

By implementing the `tabController` separately, it can easily be used for similar, yet different cases. One such example could be building a tabbed panel widget in which the links referenced external URLs. The `onTabChange` callback could in this case be used to fetch the external pages using `XMLHttpRequest`. By design, this tabbed panel would fall back to a simple list of links just like the panel we just built.

Because the original unobtrusive example used the jQuery library, we could of course have done so here as well. By using it where appropriate, we'd end up shaving off quite a few lines of code. However, although the script would end up shorter, it would come with an additional 23kB (minimum) of library code. The unobtrusive tab controller we just built weigh in at less than 2kB, have no external dependencies, and work in more browsers.

As a final note, I want to show you a compact idiomatic jQuery solution as well. Listing 9.13 shows the tabbed panel implemented in about 20 lines of (heavily wrapped) code. Note that this solution does not check markup before enabling the panel, and cannot be reused for other similar problems in a meaningful way.

Listing 9.13 Compact jQuery tabbed panels

```
jQuery.fn.tabs = function () {
  jQuery(this).
    addClass("js-tabs").
    find("> ol:first a").
    live("click", function () {
      var a = jQuery(this);
      a.parents("ol").find("a").removeClass("active-tab");
      a.addClass("active-tab");

      jQuery("[name="+this.href.replace(/^.*#/, "") + "]").
        parents("div").
        addClass("active-panel").
        siblings("div.section").
        removeClass("active-panel");
    });

  return this;
};
```

9.6 Summary

In this chapter we have discussed the principles of unobtrusive JavaScript and how they can help implement websites using progressive enhancement. A particularly obtrusive implementation of tabbed panels served to shed some light on the problems caused by making too many assumptions when coding for the client.

Unobtrusive JavaScript describes clean code the JavaScript way, including staying clean in its interaction with its surroundings, which on the web must be assumed to be highly unstable and unpredictable.

To show how unobtrusive code can be implemented to increase accessibility potential, lower error rates, and provide a more maintainable solution, we snuck a peek into a test-driven development session that culminated in an unobtrusive tabbed panel that works in browsers as old as Internet Explorer 5.0, uses no external library, and disables itself gracefully in unsupporting environments.

In Chapter 10, *Feature Detection,* we will take the concept of making no assumptions even further, and formalize some of the tests we used in this chapter as we dive into feature detection, an important part of unobtrusive JavaScript.

Feature Detection

Aspiring JavaScript developers developing for the general web are faced with a rather unique challenge, in that very little is known about the environments in which scripts will execute. Even though we can use web analytics to gather information about our visitors, and external resources such as Yahoo's graded browser support to guide us in decisions relevant to cross-browser development, we cannot fully trust these numbers; neither can they help make our scripts future proof.

Writing cross-browser JavaScript is challenging, and the number of available browsers is increasing. Old browsers see new version releases, the occasional new browser appears (the most recent noticeable one being Google Chrome), and new platforms are increasingly becoming a factor. The general web is a minefield, and our task is to avoid the mines. Surely we cannot guarantee that our scripts will run effortlessly on any unknown environment lurking around the Internet, but we should be doing our very best to avoid ruining our visitors' experience based on bad assumptions.

In this chapter we will dive into the technique known as feature detection, arguably the strongest approach to writing robust cross-browser scripts. We will see how and why browser detection fails, how feature detection can be used in its place, and how to use feature detection to allow scripts to adjust in response to collecting knowledge about the environment's capabilities.

10.1 Browser Sniffing

For as long as there has been more than one browser in popular use, developers have tried to differentiate between them to either turn down unsupported browsers, or provide individual code paths to deal with differences between them. Browser sniffing mainly comes in two flavors; user agent sniffing and object detection.

10.1.1 User Agent Sniffing

Sniffing the user agent is a primitive way of detecting browsers. By inspecting the contents of the `User-Agent` HTTP header, accessible through `navigator.userAgent`, script authors have branched their scripts to run IE specific code for IE and Netscape-specific code for Netscape, or commonly, deny access to unsupported browsers. Unwilling to have their browsers discriminated against, browser vendors adjusted the `User-Agent` header sent by the browser to include strings known to allow the browser access. This is evident to this day; Internet Explorer still includes the word "Mozilla" in its user agent string and Opera stopped identifying itself as Internet Explorer not too long ago.

As if browsers with built-in lies weren't enough, most browsers today even allow their users to manually choose how the browser should identify itself. That's about as unreliable identification as you can find.

Event handling has traditionally been rocky terrain to cover consistently across browsers. The simple event properties we used in Chapter 9, *Unobtrusive JavaScript,* is supported by just about any browser in use today, whereas the more sophisticated `EventListener` interface from the level 2 DOM specification is not. The spec calls for any `Node` to implement this interface, which among other things define the `addEventListener` method. Using this method we can add numerous event listeners to an event for a specific element, and we needn't worry about the event property accidentally being overwritten.

Most browsers available today support the `addEventListener` method, unfortunately with the exception of Internet Explorer (including version 8). IE does, however, provide the `attachEvent` method, which is similar and can be used to emulate common use cases. A naive way to work around this could involve the use of user agent sniffing, as seen in Listing 10.1.

Listing 10.1 Browser sniffing to fix event listening

```
function addEventHandler(element, type, listener) {
  // Bad example, don't try this at home
  if (/MSIE/.test(navigator.userAgent)) {
```

```
  element.attachEvent("on" + type, function () {
    // Pass event as argument to the listener and
    // correct it's this value. IE calls the listener
    // with the global object as this.
    return listener.call(element, window.event);
  });
} else {
  element.addEventListener(type, listener, false);
}
}
```

This piece of code makes many mistakes, but alas, is representative of lots of code in use even to this day. The user agent sniff is potentially dangerous in a couple of ways; it assumes that any browser that does not appear to be Internet Explorer supports `addEventListener`; it assumes that any browser appearing to be Internet Explorer supports `attachEvent`, and makes no room for a future Internet Explorer that supports the standardized API. In other words, the code will err on some browsers and definitely will need updating whenever Microsoft releases a standards-compliant browser. We will improve on the example throughout this chapter.

10.1.2 Object Detection

As sniffing the user agent string became increasingly hard due to dishonest browsers, browser detection scripts grew more sophisticated. Rather than inspecting the user agent string, developers discovered that the type of browser could very often be determined by checking for the presence of certain objects. For instance, the script in Listing 10.2 updates our previous example to avoid the user agent string and rather infer type of browser based on some objects known to exist only in Internet Explorer.

Listing 10.2 Using object detection to sniff browser

```
function addEventHandler(element, type, listener) {
  // Bad example, don't try this at home
  if (window.ActiveXObject) {
    element.attachEvent("on" + type, function () {
      return listener.call(element, window.event);
    });
  } else {
    element.addEventListener(type, listener, false);
  }
}
```

This example suffers many of the same problems as that of our user agent sniffer. Object detection is a very useful technique, but not to detect *browsers*.

Although unlikely, there is no guarantee that browsers other than Internet Explorer won't provide a global `ActiveXObject` property. For instance, older versions of Opera imitated several aspects of Internet Explorer, such as the proprietary `document.all` object, to avoid being blocked by scripts that employed bad browser detection logic.

The basic premise of browser detection relies on upfront knowledge about the environments that will run our scripts. Browser detection, in any form, does not scale, is not maintainable, and is inadequate as a cross-browser scripting strategy.

10.1.3 The State of Browser Sniffing

Unfortunately, browser detection still exists in the wild. Many of the popular libraries still to this day use browser detection, and even user agent sniffing, to solve certain cross-browser challenges. Do a search for `userAgent` or `browser` in your favorite JavaScript library, and more likely than not, you will find several decisions made based on which browser the script thinks it's faced with.

Browser sniffs cause problems even when they are used only to make certain exceptions for certain browsers, because they easily break when new browser versions are released. Additionally, even if a sniff could be shown to positively identify a certain browser, it cannot be easily shown to *not* accidentally identify other browsers that may not exhibit the same problems the sniffs were designed to smooth over.

Because browser detection frequently requires updating when new browsers are released, libraries that depend on browser sniffs put a maintenance burden on you, the application developer. To make the situation even worse, these updates are not necessarily backwards compatible, and may require you to rewrite code as well. Using JavaScript libraries can help smooth over many difficult problems, but often come at a cost that should be carefully considered.

10.2 Using Object Detection for Good

Object detection, although no good when used to detect browsers, is an excellent technique for detecting *objects*. Rather than branching on browser, a much sounder approach is branching on individual features. Before using a given feature, the script can determine whether it is available, and in cases in which the feature is known to have buggy implementations, the script can test the feature in a controlled setting to determine if it can be relied upon. This is the essence of feature detection.

10.2.1 Testing for Existence

Consider once again our event handling example. Listing 10.3 uses object detection as before, but rather than testing objects known to only exist in certain browsers, it tests the objects we're actually interested in using.

Listing 10.3 Using feature detection to branch event handling

```
function addEventHandler(element, type, listener) {
  if (element.addEventListener) {
    element.addEventListener(type, listener, false);
  } else if (element.attachEvent && listener.call) {
    element.attachEvent("on" + type, function () {
      return listener.call(element, window.event);
    });
  } else {
    // Possibly fall back to event properties or abort
  }
}
```

This example has a much better chance of surviving in the wild, and is very un-likely to need updating whenever a new browser is released. Internet Explorer 9 is scheduled to implement `addEventListener`, and even if this browser keeps `attachEvent` side by side with it to ensure backwards compatibility, our `addEventHandler` is going to do the right thing. Prodding for features rather than browser type means our script will use `addEventListener` if it's available without any manual interference. The preceding browser detection-based scripts will all have to be updated in such a scenario.

10.2.2 Type Checking

Although Listing 10.3 prods the correct objects before using them, the feature test is not completely accurate. The fact that the `addEventListener` property exists is not necessarily a guarantee that it will work as expected. The test could be made more accurate by checking that it is callable, as Listing 10.4 shows.

Listing 10.4 Type-checking features

```
function addEventHandler(element, type, listener) {
  if (typeof element.addEventListener == "function") {
    element.addEventListener(type, listener, false);
  } else if (typeof element.attachEvent == "function" &&
             typeof listener.call == "function") {
    element.attachEvent("on" + type, function () {
```

```
      return listener.call(element, window.event);
    });
  } else {
    // Possibly fall back to DOM0 event properties or abort
  }
}
```

This example employs more specific feature tests, and should ideally produce fewer false positives. Unfortunately, it does not work at all in certain browsers. To understand why, we need to familiarize ourselves with native and host objects.

10.2.3 Native and Host Objects

Any object whose semantics are described by the ECMAScript specification is known as a *native object*. By the nature of their definition, the behavior of native objects is generally predictable and, as such, using specific feature tests such as the type-check in Listing 10.4 will usually provide valuable information. However, given a buggy environment, we may encounter a browser whose typeof implementation is doing the wrong thing even if the object in question is in fact callable and works as expected. By making a feature test more specific we reduce the chances of false positives, but at the same time we demand more from the environment, possibly increasing the chances of false negatives.

Objects provided by the environment but not described by the ECMAScript specification are known as *host objects*. For example, a browser's DOM implementation consists solely of host objects. Host objects are problematic to feature test because the ECMAScript specification defines them very loosely; "implementation-defined" is commonly found in the description of host object behavior.

Host objects are, among other things, afforded the luxury of defining their own result for typeof. In fact, the third edition of the ECMAScript specification does not restrict this result in any way, and host objects may return "undefined" when used with typeof, should they so wish. Although attachEvent most definitely is callable in Internet Explorer, the browser is not cooperative in purveying this information when asked with typeof, as Listing 10.5 shows.

Listing 10.5 typeof and host objects in Internet Explorer

```
// true in Internet Explorer, including version 8
assertEquals("object", typeof document.attachEvent);
```

As if this result wasn't bad enough, other host objects such as ActiveX objects are even worse to work with. Listing 10.6 shows a few surprising results.

Listing 10.6 Unfriendly Host object behavior

```
TestCase("HostObjectTest", {
  "test IE host object behavior": function () {
    var xhr = new ActiveXObject("Microsoft.XMLHTTP");

    assertException(function () {
      if (xhr.open) {
        // Expectation: property exists
        // Reality: exception is thrown
      }
    });

    assertEquals("unknown", typeof xhr.open);

    var element = document.createElement("div");
    assertEquals("unknown", typeof element.offsetParent);

    assertException(function () {
      element.offsetParent;
    });
  }
});
```

In his article, "Feature Detection: State of the Art Browser Scripting"[1], Peter Michaux provides the isHostMethod method shown in Listing 10.7 to help with feature detection and host methods.

Listing 10.7 Checking if a host object is callable

```
tddjs.isHostMethod = (function () {
  function isHostMethod(object, property) {
    var type = typeof object[property];

    return type == "function" ||
           (type == "object" && !!object[property]) ||
           type == "unknown";
  }

  return isHostMethod;
}());
```

---

1. http://peter.michaux.ca/articles/feature-detection-state-of-the-art-browser-scripting

This method is able to recognize callable host objects based on the following observations:

- ActiveX properties always have a `typeof` result of `"unknown."`
- Non-ActiveX callable host objects in Internet Explorer usually have a `typeof` result of `"object."` The boolean coercion is required to avoid `null`, which also has a `typeof` result of `"object."`
- In other browsers, callable objects tend to have a `typeof` result of `"function,"` even host methods

Using this helper, we can improve our cross-browser event handler, as seen in Listing 10.8.

Listing 10.8 Improved feature detection for `addEventHandler`

```
function addEventHandler(element, type, listener) {
  if (tddjs.isHostMethod(element, "addEventListener")) {
    element.addEventListener(type, listener, false);
  } else if (tddjs.isHostMethod(element, "attachEvent") &&
             listener.call) {
    element.attachEvent("on" + type, function () {
      return listener.call(element, window.event);
    });
  } else {
    // Possibly fall back to DOM0 event properties or abort
  }
}
```

10.2.4 Sample Use Testing

Testing for the existence and type of an object is not always sufficient to ensure it can be used successfully. If a browser provides a buggy implementation of some feature, testing for its existence before using it will lead us straight into a trap. To avoid such buggy behavior, we can write a feature test in which we use the feature in a controlled manner before determining if the current environment supports the feature.

The `strftime` implementation provided in Chapter 1, *Automated Testing,* heavily relies on the `String.prototype.replace` method accepting a function as its second argument, a feature not available on certain older browsers. Listing 10.9 shows an implementation of `strftime` that uses `replace` in a controlled manner, and then defines the method only if the initial test passes.

Listing 10.9 Defensively defining `strftime`

```
(function () {
  if (Date.prototype.strftime ||
      !String.prototype.replace) {
    return;
  }

  var str = "%a %b";
  var regexp = /%([a-zA-Z])/g;
  var replaced = str.replace(regexp, function (m, c) {
    return "[" + m + " " + c + "]";
  });

  if (replaced != "[%a a] [%b b]") {
    return;
  }

  Date.prototype.strftime = function () {
    /* ... */
  };

  Date.formats = { /* ... */ };
}());
```

This way the `Date.prototype.strftime` method will only be provided in browsers that can support it correctly. Thus, a feature test should be employed before using it, as seen in Listing 10.10.

Listing 10.10 Using `strftime`

```
if (typeof Date.prototype.strftime == "function") {
  // Date.prototype.strftime can be relied upon
}

// ... or
if (typeof someDate.strftime == "function") {
  /* ... */
}
```

Because `strftime` is a user-defined method, the type check should be safe.

If compatibility with very old browsers was important, the `strftime` method could be implemented using `match` and a loop rather than relying on the `replace` method accepting a function argument. However, the point here is not necessarily gaining the widest possible support, i.e., supporting Internet Explorer 5.0 probably isn't your main priority. Rather, feature detection allows our scripts to know if they will succeed or not. This knowledge can be used to avoid script errors and broken web pages.

Keep in mind that not only will the feature test avoid trouble in ancient browsers, it is also a safeguard for new browsers with similar problems. This is especially interesting in light of the growing number of mobile devices with JavaScript support surfing the web. On a small device with limited resources, skipping features in either the ECMAScript, DOM, or other specifications is not unthinkable. Now I don't think `String.prototype.replace` will regress anytime soon, but the sample use technique is an interesting one.

In Chapter 7, *Objects and Prototypal Inheritance,* we already saw another example of feature testing when we defined the `Object.create` method, which is already supported by a few browsers and will appear in more browsers as support for ECMAScript 5 becomes more widespread.

10.2.5 When to Test

In the preceding sections we have seen different kinds of tests. The `addEvent-Handler` method applied feature tests at runtime, whereas the safeguard for `Date.prototype.strftime` was employed at loadtime. The runtime tests performed by `addEventHandler` generally provide the most reliable results because they test the actual objects they operate on. However, the tests may come with a performance penalty and, more importantly, at this point it may already be too late.

The overall goal of feature detection is to avoid having scripts break a website beyond repair. When building on the principles of unobtrusive JavaScript, the underlying HTML and CSS should already provide a usable experience. Applying feature tests up front can provide enough information to abort early if the environment is deemed unfit to run a given enhancement. However, in some cases, not all features can be reliably detected up front. If we have already partially applied an enhancement only to discover that the environment will not be successful in completing the enhancement, we should take steps to roll back the changes we made. This process may complicate things, and if possible should be avoided. The roll-back situation can sometimes be avoided by deferring actions that would be destructive if applied alone. For example, in the case of the tabbed panel in Chapter 9, *Unobtrusive JavaScript,* we could hold off adding the class name to the panel that triggers a design that relies on the panel being fully loaded until we know that it can do so successfully.

10.3 Feature Testing DOM Events

Events are an integral part of most client-side web page enhancements. Most events in common use today have been available for a long time, and for most simple cases, testing for them won't add much. However, as new events introduced by, e.g., the HTML5 spec start gaining ground, we can easily find ourselves in a situation in which we are unsure whether or not using a certain event is safe. If the event is fundamental to the use of the enhancement we're building, we'd better test for it before we possibly mangle the web page for unsuspecting visitors. Another case is genuinely useful proprietary events such as Internet Explorer's `mouseenter` and `mouseleave` events.

Using proprietary events, or avoiding use of buggy or non-existent events, is one of those cases in which browser sniffing still is widely used. Even though some events can be tested for by triggering them programmatically, this does not hold for all events, and doing so is often cumbersome and error-prone.

Juriy Zaytsev of perfectionkills.com has released an `isEventSupported` utility that makes feature testing events a breeze. Not only is using the utility simple, the implementation is based on two very simple facts as well:

- Most modern browsers expose a property corresponding to supported events on element objects, i.e., `"onclick" in document.documentElement` is `true` in most browsers whereas `"onjump" in document.documentElement` is not.

- Firefox does not expose same-named properties as the events an element supports. However, if an attribute named after a supported event is set on an element, methods of the same name are exposed.

In and of itself a simple concept, the hard part is discovering it. Some browsers require relevant elements to test on in order for this to work; testing for the `onchange` event on a `div` element will not necessarily uncover if the browser supports `onchange`. With this knowledge, we can peruse Juriy's implementation in Listing 10.11.

Listing 10.11 Feature detecting events

```
tddjs.isEventSupported = (function () {
  var TAGNAMES = {
    select: "input",
    change: "input",
    submit: "form",
```

```
    reset: "form",
    error: "img",
    load: "img",
    abort: "img"
  };

  function isEventSupported(eventName) {
    var tagName = TAGNAMES[eventName];
    var el = document.createElement(tagName || "div");
    eventName = "on" + eventName;
    var isSupported = (eventName in el);

    if (!isSupported) {
      el.setAttribute(eventName, "return;");
      isSupported = typeof el[eventName] == "function";
    }

    el = null;

    return isSupported;
  }

  return isEventSupported;
}());
```

The method uses an object as look-up for suitable elements to test a given event on. If no special case is needed, a `div` element is used. It then tests the two cases presented above and reports back the result. We'll see an example of using `isEventSupported` in Section 10.5, *Cross-Browser Event Handlers*.

Although the above method is good for a lot of cases, it is unfortunately not completely infallible. While working on this chapter I was informed by one of my reviewers, Andrea Giammarchi, that new versions of Chrome claim to support touch events even when the device running the browser is incapable of firing them. This means that if you need to test for touch events, you should use additional tests to verify their existence.

10.4 Feature Testing CSS Properties

If JavaScript is executing, surely CSS will work as well? This is a common assumption, and even though it is likely to be right in many cases, the two features are entirely unrelated and the assumption is dangerous to make.

In general, scripts should not be overly concerned with CSS and the visual aspects of the web page. The markup is usually the best interface between the script and CSS—add and remove class names, add, delete, or move elements and make other modifications to the DOM to trigger new CSS selectors, and by extension alternative designs. However, there are cases in which we need to adjust the presentational aspects from script, for instance when we need to modify dimensions and position in ways that CSS cannot express.

Determining basic CSS property support is easy. For each supported CSS property, an element's `style` object will provide a string property with a corresponding camel cased name. Listing 10.12 shows an example in which we check whether the current environment supports the CSS3 property `box-shadow`.

Listing 10.12   Detecting support for `box-shadow`

```
tddjs.isCSSPropertySupported = (function () {
  var element = document.createElement("div");

  function isCSSPropertySupported(property) {
    return typeof element.style[property] == "string";
  }

  return isCSSPropertySupported;
}());

// True in browsers that support box-shadow
assert(tddjs.isCSSPropertySupported("boxShadow"));
```

Because the `box-shadow` property still lives in a draft specification, most vendors that support it does so under a vendor-specific prefix, such as `-moz-` and `-webkit-`. Juriy Zaytsev, who wrote the original `isEventSupported`, also published a `getStyleProperty` method, which accepts a style property, and returns the property supported in the current environment. Listing 10.13 shows its behavior.

Listing 10.13   Get supported style properties

```
// "MozBoxShadow" in Firefox
// "WebkitBoxShadow" in Safari
// undefined in Internet Explorer
getStyleProperty("boxShadow");
```

This method can be useful in some cases, but the test is not very strong. Even though the property exists as a string on an element's `style` property, the browser may have problems with its implementation of the property. Ryan Morr has written a `isStyleSupported` method that uses `getComputedStyle` in supporting browsers, and `runtimeStyle` in Internet Explorer to check if the browser accepts specific values for various properties. The method can be found at http://ryanmorr.com/archives/detecting-browser-css-style-support.

10.5 Cross-Browser Event Handlers

As illustrated throughout this chapter, event handling is not a cross-browser picnic. To see a more complete example of how to utilize feature detection to harden scripts, we will add a cross-browser `addEventHandler` function to the `tddjs` namespace, which we will use in Part III, *Real-World Test-Driven Development in JavaScript*. The API will only be created if the current environment is deemed able to support it.

The method needs either `addEventListener` or `attachEvent` to work. Falling back to event properties is not sufficient unless we build a registry on top of them, allowing `addEventHandler` still to accept several handlers for an event on a specific element. This is possible, but considering the browser's such a solution would likely target, probably not worth the effort or the added weight. Further, we test for `Function.prototype.call`, which is needed in the `attachEvent` branch. The final method can be seen in Listing 10.14.

Listing 10.14 Feature detection based cross-browser event handling

```
(function () {
  var dom = tddjs.namespace("dom");
  var _addEventHandler;

  if (!Function.prototype.call) {
    return;
  }

  function normalizeEvent(event) {
    event.preventDefault = function () {
      event.returnValue = false;
    };

    event.target = event.srcElement;
    // More normalization

    return event;
  }
```

```
  if (tddjs.isHostMethod(document, "addEventListener")) {
    _addEventHandler = function (element, event, listener) {
      element.addEventListener(event, listener, false);
    };
  } else if (tddjs.isHostMethod(document, "attachEvent")) {
    _addEventHandler = function (element, event, listener) {
      element.attachEvent("on" + event, function () {
        var event = normalizeEvent(window.event);
        listener.call(element, event);

        return event.returnValue;
      });
    };
  } else {
    return;
  }

  dom.addEventHandler = _addEventHandler;
}());
```

This implementation is not complete; for instance, the event object is not sufficiently normalized. Because details are less important than the overall concept in this example, I leave further normalization as an exercise to the reader. Note that the event object is a host object, and so you may not be comfortable adding properties on it. An alternative approach could be to return a regular object that maps calls to the event object.

tddjs.dom.addEventHandler operates as a proxy for registering event handlers, opening the door to supporting custom events. One example of such a custom event is the proprietary mouseenter event mentioned previously, only supported by Internet Explorer. The mouseenter event only fires once as the mouse enters the bounds of an element. This is more helpful than mouseover in many cases, as event bubbling causes the latter to fire every time the user's mouse enters one of the target element's descendants, not only when the mouse enters the target element.

To allow for custom events, we can wrap the _addEventHandler function and have it first look for custom events in the dom.customEvents namespace. The mouseenter implementation is added to this namespace only if the environment does not already support it—we don't want to override a native event with an inferior version—and if the required mouseover and mouseout events are supported. Listing 10.15 shows a possible implementation.

Listing 10.15 Custom event handlers in `addEventHandler`

```
(function () {
  /* ... */

  function mouseenter(el, listener) {
    var current = null;

    _addEventHandler(el, "mouseover", function (event) {
      if (current !== el) {
        current = el;
        listener.call(el, event);
      }
    });

    _addEventHandler(el, "mouseout", function (e) {
      var target = e.relatedTarget || e.toElement;

      try {
        if (target && !target.nodeName) {
          target = target.parentNode;
        }
      } catch (exp) {
        return;
      }

      if (el !== target && !dom.contains(el, target)) {
        current = null;
      }
    });
  }

  var custom = dom.customEvents = {};

  if (!tddjs.isEventSupported("mouseenter") &&
      tddjs.isEventSupported("mouseover") &&
      tddjs.isEventSupported("mouseout")) {
    custom.mouseenter = mouseenter;
  }

  dom.supportsEvent = function (event) {
    return tddjs.isEventSupported(event) || !!custom[event];
  };

  function addEventHandler(element, event, listener) {
    if (dom.customEvents && dom.customEvents[event]) {
```

```
      return dom.customEvents[event](element, listener);
    }

    return _addEventHandler(element, event, listener);
  }

  dom.addEventHandler = addEventHandler;
}());
```

The mouseenter implementation keeps track of whether the mouse is currently hovering the target element, and fires anytime a mouseover is fired and the mouse wasn't previously hovering it. The method uses dom.contains(parent, child), which returns true if an element contains another. The try-catch protects against a bug in Firefox, which will sometimes provide an XUL element as relatedTarget. This can happen when mousing over for instance a scroll bar, and unfortunately XUL elements throw exceptions on *any* property access. Additionally, the relatedTarget may be a text node, fetching its parentNode gets us back on track.

To practice feature detection, I encourage you to take this method for a spin, find more browser quirks, and smooth them over by detecting erroneous behavior and correcting it.

10.6 Using Feature Detection

Feature detection is a powerful tool in cross-browser scripting. It can allow many features to be implemented for a very wide array of browsers; old, current, and future ones. That does not necessarily mean that employing feature detection implies that you should provide fallback solutions for any feature that may not be supported. Sometimes, dropping support for old browsers can be a statement in itself, but we should be able to do so without sniffing out the browsers we want to send down the degradation path.

10.6.1 Moving Forward

If supporting a troublesome old browser, oh say Internet Explorer 6, costs more than the benefits can defend, businesses sometimes actively decide to drop support. Doing so does not mean we should pretend "unsupported" browsers don't exist. Using unobtrusive JavaScript and feature detection can ensure that when a browser is no longer actively developed for, it will receive the usable but possibly basic fallback solution. In such cases, feature detection can be used to discriminate incapable browsers.

Going back to the `strftime` example, if we don't want to support enhanced features in browsers that cannot handle a function argument to `String.prototype.replace`, we simply abort the definition of the method in browsers in which this feature test fails. Interfaces that use this method may choose to do the same, i.e., if the `strftime` method is not available, higher level enhancements that depend on it can choose to abort as well. As long as feature detection is built into every layer of the application, avoiding some or all enhancements in inadequate browsers should not be too complicated. The upside of this approach is that it will work with *all* browsers that don't support the required functionality, old and new alike, and even those we aren't aware of.

10.6.2 Undetectable Features

Some features are hard to detect. An example can be found in how Internet Explorer 6 renders certain replaced elements, such as `select` lists. Displaying another element over such a list will cause the list to show through the overlaid element. The quirk can be fixed by layering an iframe behind the overlay. Even if we cannot detect this problem, the fix is not known to cause problems in other browsers, and so can be safely employed in all browsers. If the fix to a problem won't have ill effects in any browsers, applying the fix for everyone can often be simpler than detecting the problem. Before applying a fix preemptively, it's a good idea to consider performance implications.

Designing the problem away is another technique that is highly effective at avoiding cross-browser woes. For instance, IE's implementation of `getElement-ById` will gladly return elements whose `name` property matches the provided id. This problem is simple to detect and work around, yet it is even simpler to make sure HTML elements never use ids that match some `name` property on the page, perhaps by prefixing ids.

10.7 Summary

In this chapter we dove into feature detection, the most reliable and future proof technique available for writing cross-browser JavaScript. Browser sniffing in various forms has several pitfalls, and cannot be trusted. Not only is this technique unreliable and brittle, but it also requires knowledge about specific browsers in a way that make it a maintainability nightmare.

Feature detection—self testing code—was explored as an alternative to browser sniffing, and we have seen examples of testing both native and host objects and methods, as well prodding for supported events and CSS properties and even supported CSS values.

Feature detection is an art, and it is not an easy one to master. Fully mastering feature detection requires knowledge and experience as well as good judgment. Rarely is there a single answer, so we must apply our best sense and always be on the lookout for better ways to harden our scripts. Even though feature detection is well fit to create scripts with the widest possible support surface, it need not be used for that purpose. The main motivation when producing scripts for the general web should stay on avoiding broken web pages, and feature detection can help in this regard by aborting scripts that are unlikely to succeed.

This chapter concludes our selective tour of the JavaScript language. In Part III, *Real-World Test-Driven Development in JavaScript,* we will use test-driven development to work through five small projects that combined produce a small chat application implemented entirely in JavaScript.

Part III

Real-World Test-Driven Development in JavaScript

The Observer Pattern

The Observer pattern (also known as Publish/Subscribe, or simply pub/sub) is a design pattern that allows us to observe the state of an object and be notified when it changes. The pattern can provide objects with powerful extension points while maintaining loose coupling.

In this chapter we will let tests drive us through our first library. By focusing on a low-level library that deals with communication between JavaScript objects, we avoid the world of the DOM, staying clear of the nastiest browser inconsistencies. Working through this chapter will show you how to

- Design an API using tests.
- Continuously improve design by refactoring—both tests and production code.
- Add functionality one tiny step at a time.
- Solve simple browser inconsistencies with the help of unit tests.
- Evolve from classical language idioms to idioms that make better use of JavaScript's dynamic features.

There are two roles in The Observer—**observable** and **observer**. The observer is an object or function that will be notified when the state of the observable changes. The observable decides when to update its observers and what data to provide them with. In classical languages like Java, notification happens through a call to `observable.notifyObservers()`, which has a single optional argument (which in turn can be any object, often the observable itself). The `notifyOb-servers` method in turn calls the `update` method on each observer, allowing them to act in response.

11.1 The Observer in JavaScript

JavaScript traditionally lives in the browser, where it is used to power dynamic user interfaces. In the browser, user actions are handled asynchronously by way of DOM event handlers. In fact, the DOM event system we already know is a great example of the Observer pattern in practice. We register some function (the observer) as an event handler with a given DOM element (the observable). Whenever something interesting happens to the DOM element, i.e., someone clicks or drags it, the event handler is called, allowing us to make magic happen in response to the user's actions.

Events appear many other places in JavaScript programming as well. Consider an object that adds live search to an input field. Live search is the kind that uses the `XMLHttpRequest` object to continuously perform server-side searches as the user types, narrowing down the list of hits as the search phrase is typed out. The object would need to subscribe handlers to DOM events fired by keyboard typing in order to know when to search. It would also assign a handler to the `onreadys-tatechange` event of the `XMLHttpRequest` object to know when results are ready.

When the server comes back with some search results, the live search object may choose to update its result view by way of an animation. To allow further customization, the object may offer clients a few custom callbacks. These callbacks can be hard-coded to the object or, preferably, it can make use of a generic solution for handling observers.

11.1.1 The Observable Library

As discussed in Chapter 2, *The Test-Driven Development Process,* the test-driven development process allows us to move in very small steps when needed. In this first real-world example we will start out with the tiniest of steps. As we gain confidence in our code and the process, we will gradually increase the size of our steps when circumstances allow it (i.e., the code to implement is trivial enough). Writing code in small frequent iterations will help us design our API piece-by-piece, as well as help us make fewer mistakes. When mistakes occur, we will be able to fix them quickly as errors will be easy to track down when we run tests every time we add a handful of lines of code.

The library needs to define the role of the **observer** as well as the `observable`. However, in contrast to the Java solution mentioned earlier, JavaScript observers need not be objects that conform to a certain interface. Functions are first class objects in JavaScript, so we can simply subscribe functions directly. This means our work consists of defining the `Observable` API.

11.1.2 Setting up the Environment

For this chapter we will use `JsTestDriver` and its default assertion framework. Refer to Chapter 3, *Tools of the Trade,* if you have not yet set up JsTestDriver in your development environment.

Listing 11.1 shows the initial project layout.

Listing 11.1 Directory layout for the observable project

```
chris@laptop:~/projects/observable $ tree
.
|-- jsTestDriver.conf
|-- lib
|   `-- tdd.js
|-- src
|   `-- observable.js
`-- test
    `-- observable_test.js
```

The `lib/tdd.js` contains the `tddjs` object and the `namespace` method developed in Chapter 6, *Applied Functions and Closures.* We will use these to develop the `observable` interface namespaced inside `tddjs`.

The configuration file is just a plain default jsTestDriver configuration file that runs the server on port 4224 and includes all script files, as seen in Listing 11.2.

Listing 11.2 The jsTestDriver.conf file

```
server: http://localhost:4224

load:
  - lib/*.js
  - src/*.js
  - test/*.js
```

11.2 Adding Observers

We will kick off the project by implementing a means to add observers to an object. Doing so will take us through writing the first test, watching it fail, passing it in the dirtiest possible way, and finally refactoring it into something more sensible.

11.2.1 The First Test

To keep us going through the initial stages of developing the observable library, we will keep to the Java parallel. This means that the first test will create an observable object with the `Observable` constructor and add an observer by calling the `addObserver` method on it. To verify that this works, we will be blunt and assume that `Observable` stores its observers in an array, and check that the observer is the only item in that array. The test can be seen in Listing 11.3. Save it in `test/observable_test.js`.

Listing 11.3 Expecting `addObserver` to add observer to internal array

```
TestCase("ObservableAddObserverTest", {
  "test should store function": function () {
    var observable = new tddjs.util.Observable();
    var observer = function () {};

    observable.addObserver(observer);

    assertEquals(observer, observable.observers[0]);
  }
});
```

11.2.1.1 Running the Test and Watching it Fail

At first glance the results of running our very first test, in Listing 11.4, is devastating.

Listing 11.4 Running the test

```
chris@laptop:~/projects/observable$ jstestdriver --tests all
E
Total 1 tests (Passed: 0; Fails: 0; Errors: 1) (0.00 ms)
  Firefox 3.6.3 Linux: Run 1 tests \
  (Passed: 0; Fails: 0; Errors 1) (0.00 ms)
    Observable.addObserver.test \
    should store function error (1.00 ms): \
```

```
tddjs.util is undefined
  ()@http://localhost:4224/.../observable_test.js:5
```

11.2.1.2 Making the Test Pass

Fear not! Failure is actually a good thing: It tells us where to focus our efforts. The first serious problem is that `tddjs.util` doesn't exist. Listing 11.5 adds the object using the `tddjs.namespace` method. Save the listing in `src/observable.js`.

Listing 11.5 Creating the `util` namespace

```
tddjs.namespace("util");
```

Running the tests again yields a new error, as seen in Listing 11.6.

Listing 11.6 Tests still failing

```
chris@laptop:~/projects/observable$ jstestdriver --tests all
E
Total 1 tests (Passed: 0; Fails: 0; Errors: 1) (1.00 ms)
  Firefox 3.6.3 Linux: Run 1 tests \
  (Passed: 0; Fails: 0; Errors 1) (1.00 ms)
    Observable.addObserver.test \
    should store function error (1.00 ms): \
    tddjs.util.Observable is not a constructor
      ()@http://localhost:4224/.../observable_test.js:5
```

Listing 11.7 fixes this new issue by adding an empty `Observable` constructor.

Listing 11.7 Adding the constructor

```
(function () {
  function Observable() {
  }

  tddjs.util.Observable = Observable;
}());
```

To work around the issues with named function expressions discussed in Chapter 5, *Functions,* the constructor is defined using a function declaration inside an immediately called closure. Running the test once again brings us directly to the next problem, seen in Listing 11.8.

Listing 11.8 Missing `addObserver` method

```
chris@laptop:~/projects/observable$ jstestdriver --tests all
E
Total 1 tests (Passed: 0; Fails: 0; Errors: 1) (0.00 ms)
  Firefox 3.6.3 Linux: Run 1 tests \
  (Passed: 0; Fails: 0; Errors 1) (0.00 ms)
    Observable.addObserver.test \
    should store function error (0.00 ms): \
    observable.addObserver is not a function
      ()@http://localhost:4224/.../observable_test.js:8
```

Listing 11.9 adds the missing method.

Listing 11.9 Adding the `addObserver` method

```
function addObserver() {
}

Observable.prototype.addObserver = addObserver;
```

With the method in place, Listing 11.10 shows that the test now fails in place of a missing `observers` array.

Listing 11.10 The observers array does not exist

```
chris@laptop:~/projects/observable$ jstestdriver --tests all
E
Total 1 tests (Passed: 0; Fails: 0; Errors: 1) (1.00 ms)
  Firefox 3.6.3 Linux: Run 1 tests \
  (Passed: 0; Fails: 0; Errors 1) (1.00 ms)
    Observable.addObserver.test \
    should store function error (1.00 ms): \
    observable.observers is undefined
      ()@http://localhost:4224/.../observable_test.js:10
```

As odd as it may seem, Listing 11.11 now defines the `observers` array inside the `addObserver` method. Remember, when a test is failing, we're instructed to do *the simplest thing that could possibly work*, no matter how dirty it feels. We will get the chance to review our work once the test is passing.

Listing 11.11 Hard-coding the array

```
function addObserver(observer) {
  this.observers = [observer];
}
```

Success! As Listing 11.12 shows, the test now passes.

Listing 11.12 Test passing

```
chris@laptop:~/projects/observable$ jstestdriver --tests all
.
Total 1 tests \
(Passed: 1; Fails: 0; Errors: 0) (0.00 ms)
  Firefox 3.6.3 Linux: Run 1 tests \
  (Passed: 1; Fails: 0; Errors 0) (0.00 ms)
```

11.2.2 Refactoring

While developing the current solution, we have taken the quickest possible route
to a passing test. Now that the bar is green, we can review the solution and perform
any refactoring we deem necessary. The only rule in this last step is to keep the bar
green. This means we will have to refactor in tiny steps as well, making sure we
don't accidentally break anything.

The current implementation has two issues we should deal with. The test makes
detailed assumptions about the implementation of `Observable` and the `addOb-
server` implementation is hard-coded to our test.

We will address the hard-coding first. To expose the hard-coded solution,
Listing 11.13 augments the test to make it add two observers instead of one.

Listing 11.13 Exposing the hard-coded solution

```
"test should store function": function () {
  var observable = new tddjs.util.Observable();
  var observers = [function () {}, function () {}];

  observable.addObserver(observers[0]);
  observable.addObserver(observers[1]);

  assertEquals(observers, observable.observers);
}
```

As expected, the test now fails. The test expects that functions added as observers should stack up like any element added to an array. To achieve this, we will move the array instantiation into the constructor and simply delegate `addObserver` to the array method `push` as Listing 11.14 shows.

Listing 11.14 Adding arrays the proper way

```
function Observable() {
  this.observers = [];
}

function addObserver(observer) {
  this.observers.push(observer);
}
```

With this implementation in place, the test passes again, proving that we have taken care of the hard-coded solution. However, accessing a public property and making wild assumptions about the implementation of `Observable` is still an issue. An observable object should be observable by any number of objects, but it is of no interest to outsiders how or where the observable stores them. Ideally, we would like to be able to check with the observable if a certain observer is registered without groping around its insides. We make a note of the smell and move on. Later, we will come back to improve this test.

11.3 Checking for Observers

We will add another method to `Observable`, `hasObserver`, and use it to remove some of the clutter we added when implementing `addObserver`.

11.3.1 The Test

A new method starts with a new test. Listing 11.15 describes the desired behavior for the `hasObserver` method.

Listing 11.15 Expecting `hasObserver` to return `true` for existing observers

```
TestCase("ObservableHasObserverTest", {
  "test should return true when has observer": function () {
    var observable = new tddjs.util.Observable();
    var observer = function () {};

    observable.addObserver(observer);
```

```
    assertTrue(observable.hasObserver(observer));
  }
});
```

We expect this test to fail in the face of a missing `hasObserver`, which it does.

11.3.1.1 Making the Test Pass

Listing 11.16 shows the simplest solution that could possibly pass the current test.

Listing 11.16 Hard-coding `hasObserver`'s response

```
function hasObserver(observer) {
  return true;
}


Observable.prototype.hasObserver = hasObserver;
```

Even though we know this won't solve our problems in the long run, it keeps the tests green. Trying to review and refactor leaves us empty-handed as there are no obvious points where we can improve. The tests are our requirements, and currently they only require `hasObserver` to return `true`. Listing 11.17 introduces another test that expects `hasObserver` to return false for a non-existent observer, which can help force the real solution.

Listing 11.17 Expecting `hasObserver` to return false for non-existent observers

```
"test should return false when no observers": function () {
  var observable = new tddjs.util.Observable();

  assertFalse(observable.hasObserver(function () {}));
}
```

This test fails miserably, given that `hasObserver` always returns `true`, forcing us to produce the real implementation. Checking if an observer is registered is a simple matter of checking that the `this.observers` array contains the object originally passed to `addObserver` as Listing 11.18 does.

Listing 11.18 Actually checking for observer

```
function hasObserver(observer) {
  return this.observers.indexOf(observer) >= 0;
}
```

The `Array.prototype.indexOf` method returns a number less than 0 if the element is not present in the array, so checking that it returns a number equal to or greater than 0 will tell us if the observer exists.

11.3.1.2 Solving Browser Incompatibilities

Running the test produces somewhat surprising results as seen in the relevant excerpt in Listing 11.19.

Listing 11.19 Funky results in Internet Explorer 6

```
chris@laptop:~/projects/observable$ jstestdriver --tests all
.EE
Total 3 tests (Passed: 1; Fails: 0; Errors: 2) (11.00 ms)
  Microsoft Internet Explorer 6.0 Windows: Run 3 tests \
  (Passed: 1; Fails: 0; Errors 2) (11.00 ms)
    Observable.hasObserver.test \
      should return true when has observer error (11.00 ms): \
      Object doesn't support this property or method
    Observable.hasObserver.test \
      should return false when no observers error (0.00 ms): \
      Object doesn't support this property or method
```

Internet Explorer versions 6 and 7 failed the test with their most generic of error messages: "Object doesn't support this property or method." This can indicate any number of issues.

- We are calling a method on an object that is `null`.
- We are calling a method that does not exist.
- We are accessing a property that doesn't exist.

Luckily, TDD-ing in tiny steps, we know that the error has to relate to the recently added call to `indexOf` on our observers array. As it turns out, IE 6 and 7 does not support the JavaScript 1.6 method `Array.prototype.indexOf` (which we cannot really blame it for, it was only recently standardized with ECMAScript 5, December 2009). In other words, we are dealing with our first browser compatibility issue. At this point, we have three options:

- Circumvent the use of `Array.prototype.indexOf` in `hasObserver`, effectively duplicating native functionality in supporting browsers
- Implement `Array.prototype.indexOf` for non-supporting browsers. Alternatively implement a helper function that provides the same functionality

- Use a third-party library that provides either the missing method, or a similar method

Which one of these approaches is best suited to solve a given problem will depend on the situation; they all have their pros and cons. In the interest of keeping `Observable` self-contained, we will simply implement `hasObserver` in terms of a loop in place of the `indexOf` call, effectively working around the problem. Incidentally, that also seems to be the "simplest thing that could possibly work" at this point. Should we run into a similar situation later on, we would be advised to reconsider our decision. Listing 11.20 shows the updated `hasObserver` method.

Listing 11.20 Manually looping the array

```
function hasObserver(observer) {
  for (var i = 0, l = this.observers.length; i < l; i++) {
    if (this.observers[i] == observer) {
      return true;
    }
  }

  return false;
}
```

11.3.2 Refactoring

With the bar back to green, it's time to review our progress. We now have three tests, but two of them seem strangely similar. The first test we wrote to verify the correctness of `addObserver` basically tests for the same things as the test we wrote to verify `hasObserver`. There are two key differences between the two tests: The first test has previously been declared smelly, as it directly accesses the `observers` array inside the observable object. The first test adds two observers, ensuring they're both added. Listing 11.21 joins the tests into one that verifies that all observers added to the observable are actually added.

Listing 11.21 Removing duplicated tests

```
"test should store functions": function () {
  var observable = new tddjs.util.Observable();
  var observers = [function () {}, function () {}];

  observable.addObserver(observers[0]);
  observable.addObserver(observers[1]);
```

```
assertTrue(observable.hasObserver(observers[0]));
assertTrue(observable.hasObserver(observers[1]));
}
```

11.4 Notifying Observers

Adding observers and checking for their existence is nice, but without the ability to notify them of interesting changes, Observable isn't very useful.

In this section we will add yet another method to our library. Sticking to the Java parallel, we will call the new method notifyObservers. Because this method is slightly more complex than the previous methods, we will implement it step by step, testing a single aspect of the method at a time.

11.4.1 Ensuring That Observers Are Called

The most important task notifyObservers performs is calling all the observers. To do this, we need some way to verify that an observer has been called after the fact. To verify that a function has been called, we can set a property on the function when it is called. To verify the test we can check if the property is set. The test in Listing 11.22 uses this concept in the first test for notifyObservers.

Listing 11.22 Expecting notifyObservers to call all observers

```
TestCase("ObservableNotifyObserversTest", {
  "test should call all observers": function () {
    var observable = new tddjs.util.Observable();
    var observer1 = function () { observer1.called = true; };
    var observer2 = function () { observer2.called = true; };

    observable.addObserver(observer1);
    observable.addObserver(observer2);
    observable.notifyObservers();

    assertTrue(observer1.called);
    assertTrue(observer2.called);
  }
});
```

To pass the test we need to loop the observers array and call each function. Listing 11.23 fills in the blanks.

Listing 11.23 Calling observers

```
function notifyObservers() {
  for (var i = 0, l = this.observers.length; i < l; i++) {
    this.observers[i]();
  }
}

Observable.prototype.notifyObservers = notifyObservers;
```

11.4.2 Passing Arguments

Currently the observers are being called, but they are not being fed any data. They know something happened, but not necessarily what. Although Java's implementation defines the `update` method of observers to receive one or no arguments, JavaScript allows a more flexible solution. We will make `notifyObservers` take any number of arguments, simply passing them along to each observer. Listing 11.24 shows the requirement as a test.

Listing 11.24 Expecting arguments to `notifyObservers` to be passed to observers

```
"test should pass through arguments": function () {
  var observable = new tddjs.util.Observable();
  var actual;

  observable.addObserver(function () {
    actual = arguments;
  });

  observable.notifyObservers("String", 1, 32);

  assertEquals(["String", 1, 32], actual);
}
```

The test compares passed and received arguments by assigning the received arguments to a variable that is local to the test. Running the test confirms that it fails, which is not surprising as we are currently not touching the arguments inside `notifyObservers`.

To pass the test we can use `apply` when calling the observer, as seen in Listing 11.25.

Listing 11.25 Using `apply` to pass arguments through `notifyObservers`

```
function notifyObservers() {
  for (var i = 0, l = this.observers.length; i < l; i++) {
    this.observers[i].apply(this, arguments);
  }
}
```

With this simple fix tests go back to green. Note that we sent in `this` as the first argument to `apply`, meaning that observers will be called with the observable as `this`.

11.5 Error Handling

At this point `Observable` is functional and we have tests that verify its behavior. However, the tests only verify that the observables behave correctly in response to expected input. What happens if someone tries to register an object as an observer in place of a function? What happens if one of the observers blows up? Those are questions we need our tests to answer. Ensuring correct behavior in expected situations is important—that is what our objects will be doing most of the time. At least so we could hope. However, correct behavior even when the client is misbehaving is just as important to guarantee a stable and predictable system.

11.5.1 Adding Bogus Observers

The current implementation blindly accepts any kind of argument to `addOb-server`. This contrasts to the Java API we started out comparing to, which allows objects implementing the `Observer` interface to register as observers. Although our implementation can use any function as an observer, it cannot handle *any value*. The test in Listing 11.26 expects the observable to throw an exception when attempting to add an observer that is not callable.

Listing 11.26 Expecting non-callable arguments to cause an exception

```
"test should throw for uncallable observer": function () {
  var observable = new tddjs.util.Observable();

  assertException(function () {
    observable.addObserver({});
  }, "TypeError");
}
```

By throwing an exception already when adding the observers we don't need to worry about invalid data later when we notify observers. Had we been programming by contract, we could say that a *precondition* for the `addObserver` method is that the input must be callable. The postcondition is that the observer is added to the observable and is guaranteed to be called once the observable calls `notifyObservers`.

The test fails, so we shift our focus to getting the bar green again as quickly as possible. Unfortunately, there is no way to fake the implementation this time— throwing an exception on any call to `addObserver` will fail all the other tests. Luckily, the implementation is fairly trivial, as seen in Listing 11.27.

Listing 11.27 Throwing an exception when adding non-callable observers

```
function addObserver(observer) {
  if (typeof observer != "function") {
    throw new TypeError("observer is not function");
  }

  this.observers.push(observer);
}
```

`addObserver` now checks that the observer is in fact a function before adding it to the list. Running the tests yields that sweet feeling of success: All green.

11.5.2 Misbehaving Observers

The observable now guarantees that any observer added through `addObserver` is callable. Still, `notifyObservers` may still fail horribly if an observer throws an exception. Listing 11.28 shows a test that expects all the observers to be called even if one of them throws an exception.

Listing 11.28 Expecting `notifyObservers` to survive misbehaving observers

```
"test should notify all even when some fail": function () {
  var observable = new tddjs.util.Observable();
  var observer1 = function () { throw new Error("Oops"); };
  var observer2 = function () { observer2.called = true; };

  observable.addObserver(observer1);
  observable.addObserver(observer2);
  observable.notifyObservers();

  assertTrue(observer2.called);
}
```

Running the test reveals that the current implementation blows up along with the first observer, causing the second observer not to be called. In effect, noti-fyObservers is breaking its guarantee that it will always call all observers once they have been successfully added. To rectify the situation, the method needs to be prepared for the worst, as seen in Listing 11.29.

Listing 11.29 Catching exceptions for misbehaving observers

```
function notifyObservers() {
  for (var i = 0, l = this.observers.length; i < l; i++) {
    try {
      this.observers[i].apply(this, arguments);
    } catch (e) {}
  }
}
```

The exception is silently discarded. It is the observers responsibility to ensure that any errors are handled properly, the observable is simply fending off badly behaving observers.

11.5.3 Documenting Call Order

We have improved the robustness of the Observable module by giving it proper error handling. The module is now able to give guarantees of operation as long as it gets good input and it is able to recover should an observer fail to meet its requirements. However, the last test we added makes an assumption on undocumented features of the observable: It assumes that observers are called in the order they were added. Currently, this solution works because we used an array to implement the observers list. Should we decide to change this, however, our tests may break. So we need to decide: Do we refactor the test to *not* assume call order, or do we simply add a test that expects call order, thereby documenting call order as a feature? Call order seems like a sensible feature, so Listing 11.30 adds the test to make sure Observable keeps this behavior.

Listing 11.30 Documenting call order as a feature

```
"test should call observers in the order they were added":
function () {
  var observable = new tddjs.util.Observable();
  var calls = [];
  var observer1 = function () { calls.push(observer1); };
  var observer2 = function () { calls.push(observer2); };
  observable.addObserver(observer1);
```

```
observable.addObserver(observer2);

observable.notifyObservers();

assertEquals(observer1, calls[0]);
assertEquals(observer2, calls[1]);
}
```

Because the implementation already uses an array for the observers, this test succeeds immediately.

11.6 Observing Arbitrary Objects

In static languages with classical inheritance, arbitrary objects are made observable by subclassing the `Observable` class. The motivation for classical inheritance in these cases comes from a desire to define the mechanics of the pattern in one place and reuse the logic across vast amounts of unrelated objects. As discussed in Chapter 7, *Objects and Prototypal Inheritance,* we have several options for code reuse among JavaScript objects, so we need not confine ourselves to an emulation of the classical inheritance model.

Although the Java analogy helped us develop the basic interface, we will now break free from it by refactoring the observable interface to embrace JavaScript's object model. Assuming we have a `Newsletter` constructor that creates `newsletter` objects, there are a number of ways we can make newsletters observable, as seen in Listing 11.31.

Listing 11.31 Various ways to share observable behavior

```
var Observable = tddjs.util.Observable;

// Extending the object with an observable object
tddjs.extend(newsletter, new Observable());

// Extending all newsletters with an observable object
tddjs.extend(Newsletter.prototype, new Observable());

// Using a helper function
tddjs.util.makeObservable(newsletter);

// Calling the constructor as a function
Observable(newsletter);

// Using a "static" method:
```

```
Observable.make(newsletter);

// Telling the object to "fix itself" (requires code on
// the prototype of either Newsletter or Object)
newsletter.makeObservable();

// Classical inheritance-like
Newspaper.inherit(Observable);
```

In the interest of breaking free of the classical emulation that constructors provide, consider the examples in Listing 11.32, which assume that `tddjs. util.observable` is an object rather than a constructor.

Listing 11.32 Sharing behavior with an `observable` object

```
// Creating a single observable object
var observable = Object.create(tddjs.util.observable);

// Extending a single object
tddjs.extend(newspaper, tddjs.util.observable);

// A constructor that creates observable objects
function Newspaper() {
  /* ... */
}

Newspaper.prototype = Object.create(tddjs.util.observable);

// Extending an existing prototype
tddjs.extend(Newspaper.prototype, tddjs.util.observable);
```

Simply implementing the observable as a single object offers a great deal of flexibility. To get there we need to refactor the existing solution to get rid of the constructor.

11.6.1 Making the Constructor Obsolete

To get rid of the constructor we should first refactor `Observable` such that the constructor doesn't do any work. Luckily, the constructor only initializes the `observers` array, which shouldn't be too hard to remove. All the methods on `Observable.prototype` access the array, so we need to make sure they can all handle the case in which it hasn't been initialized. To test for this we simply need to write one test per method that calls the method in question before doing anything else.

As seen in Listing 11.33, we already have tests that call `addObserver` and `hasObserver` before doing anything else.

Listing 11.33 Tests targeting `addObserver` and `hasObserver`

```
TestCase("ObservableAddObserverTest", {
  "test should store functions": function () {
    var observable = new tddjs.util.Observable();
    var observers = [function () {}, function () {}];

    observable.addObserver(observers[0]);
    observable.addObserver(observers[1]);

    assertTrue(observable.hasObserver(observers[0]));
    assertTrue(observable.hasObserver(observers[1]));
  },

  /* ... */
});

TestCase("ObservableHasObserverTest", {
  "test should return false when no observers": function () {
    var observable = new tddjs.util.Observable();

    assertFalse(observable.hasObserver(function () {}));
  }
});
```

The `notifyObservers` method however, is only tested after `addObserver` has been called. Listing 11.34 adds a test that expects it to be possible to call this method before adding any observers.

Listing 11.34 Expecting `notifyObservers` to not fail if called before `addObserver`

```
"test should not fail if no observers": function () {
  var observable = new tddjs.util.Observable();

  assertNoException(function () {
    observable.notifyObservers();
  });
}
```

With this test in place, we can empty the constructor as seen in Listing 11.35.

Listing 11.35 Emptying the constructor

```
function Observable() {
}
```

Running the tests shows that all but one is now failing, all with the same message: "this.observers is not defined." We will deal with one method at a time. Listing 11.36 shows the updated addObserver method.

Listing 11.36 Defining the array if it does not exist in addObserver

```
function addObserver(observer) {
  if (!this.observers) {
    this.observers = [];
  }

  /* ... */
}
```

Running the tests again reveals that the updated addObserver method fixes all but the two tests that do not call it before calling other methods, such as hasObserver and notifyObservers. Next up, Listing 11.37 makes sure to return false directly from hasObserver if the array does not exist.

Listing 11.37 Aborting hasObserver when there are no observers

```
function hasObserver(observer) {
  if (!this.observers) {
    return false;
  }

  /* ... */
}
```

We can apply the exact same fix to notifyObservers, as seen in Listing 11.38.

Listing 11.38 Aborting notifyObservers when there are no observers

```
function notifyObservers(observer) {
  if (!this.observers) {
    return;
  }

  /* ... */
}
```

11.6.2 **Replacing the Constructor with an Object**

Now that the constructor doesn't do anything, it can be safely removed. We will then add all the methods directly to the `tddjs.util.observable` object, which can then be used with, e.g., `Object.create` or `tddjs.extend` to create observable objects. Note that the name is no longer capitalized as it is no longer a constructor. Listing 11.39 shows the updated implementation.

Listing 11.39 The `observable` *object*

```
(function () {
  function addObserver(observer) {
    /* ... */
  }

  function hasObserver(observer) {
    /* ... */
  }

  function notifyObservers() {
    /* ... */
  }

  tddjs.namespace("util").observable = {
    addObserver: addObserver,
    hasObserver: hasObserver,
    notifyObservers: notifyObservers
  };
}());
```

Surely, removing the constructor will cause all the tests so far to break. Fixing them is easy, however; all we need to do is to replace the new statement with a call to `Object.create`, as seen in Listing 11.40.

Listing 11.40 Using the `observable` *object* in tests

```
TestCase("ObservableAddObserverTest", {
  setUp: function () {
    this.observable = Object.create(tddjs.util.observable);
  },

  /* ... */
});

TestCase("ObservableHasObserverTest", {
  setUp: function () {
```

```
    this.observable = Object.create(tddjs.util.observable);
  },

  /* ... */
});

TestCase("ObservableNotifyObserversTest", {
  setUp: function () {
    this.observable = Object.create(tddjs.util.observable);
  },

  /* ... */
});
```

To avoid duplicating the `Object.create` call, each test case gained a `setUp` method that sets up the observable for testing. The test methods have to be updated accordingly, replacing `observable` with `this.observable`.

For the tests to run smoothly on any browser, the `Object.create` implementation from Chapter 7, *Objects and Prototypal Inheritance,* needs to be saved in `lib/object.js`.

11.6.3 Renaming Methods

While we are in the game of changing things we will take a moment to reduce the verbosity of the interface by renaming the `addObserver` and `notifyObservers` methods. We can shorten them down without sacrificing any clarity. Renaming the methods is a simple case of search-replace so we won't dwell on it too long. Listing 11.41 shows the updated interface, I'll trust you to update the test case accordingly.

Listing 11.41 The refurbished `observable` interface

```
(function () {
  function observe(observer) {
    /* ... */
  }

  /* ... */

  function notify() {
    /* ... */
  }

  tddjs.namespace("util").observable = {
```

```
    observe: observe,
    hasObserver: hasObserver,
    notify: notify
  };
}());
```

11.7 Observing Arbitrary Events

The current observable implementation is a little limited in that it only keeps a single list of observers. This means that in order to observe more than one event, observers have to determine what event occurred based on heuristics on the data they receive. We will refactor the observable to group observers by event names. Event names are arbitrary strings that the observable may use at its own discretion.

11.7.1 Supporting Events in `observe`

To support events, the `observe` method now needs to accept a string argument in addition to the function argument. The new `observe` will take the event as its first argument. As we already have several tests calling the `observe` method, we can start by updating the test case. Add a string as first argument to any call to `observe` as seen in Listing 11.42.

Listing 11.42 Updating calls to `observe`

```
TestCase("ObservableAddObserverTest", {
  /* ... */

  "test should store functions": function () {
    /* ... */
    this.observable.observe("event", observers[0]);
    this.observable.observe("event", observers[1]);
    /* ... */
  },

  /* ... *
});

TestCase("ObservableNotifyObserversTest", {
  /* ... */

  "test should call all observers": function () {
```

```
  /* ... */
  this.observable.observe("event", observer1);
  this.observable.observe("event", observer2);
  /* ... */
},

"test should pass through arguments": function () {
  /* ... */
  this.observable.observe("event", function () {
    actual = arguments;
  });
  /* ... */
},

"test should notify all even when some fail": function () {
  /* ... */
  this.observable.observe("event", observer1);
  this.observable.observe("event", observer2);
  /* ... */
},

"test should call observers in the order they were added":
  function () {
  /* ... */
  this.observable.observe("event", observer1);
  this.observable.observe("event", observer2);
  /* ... */
},

/* ... */
});
```

Unsurprisingly, this causes all the tests to fail as observe throws an exception, because the argument it thinks is the observer is not a function. To get tests back to green we simply add a formal parameter to observe, as seen in Listing 11.43.

Listing 11.43 Adding a formal event parameter to observe

```
function observe(event, observer) {
  /* ... */
}
```

We will repeat this exercise with both hasObserver and notify as well, to make room for tests that describe actual functionality. I will leave updating these other two functions (and their tests) as an exercise. When you are done you will note that one of the tests keep failing. We will deal with that last test together.

11.7.2 Supporting Events in `notify`

While updating `notify` to accept an event whose observers to notify, one of the existing tests stays in the red. The test in question is the one that compares arguments sent to `notify` against those received by the observer. The problem is that because `notify` simply passes along the arguments it receives, the observer is now receiving the event name in addition to the arguments it was supposed to receive.

To pass the test, Listing 11.44 uses `Array.prototype.slice` to pass along all but the first argument.

Listing 11.44 Passing all but the first argument to observers

```
function notify(event) {
  /* ... */

  var args = Array.prototype.slice.call(arguments, 1);

  for (var i = 0, l = this.observers.length; i < l; i++) {
    try {
      this.observers[i].apply(this, args);
    } catch (e) {}
  }
}
```

This passes the test and now `observable` has the interface to support events, even if it doesn't actually support them yet.

The test in Listing 11.45 specifies how the events are supposed to work. It registers two observers to two different events. It then calls `notify` for only one of the events and expects only the related observer to be called.

Listing 11.45 Expecting only relevant observers to be called

```
"test should notify relevant observers only": function () {
  var calls = [];

  this.observable.observe("event", function () {
    calls.push("event");
  });

  this.observable.observe("other", function () {
```

```
      calls.push("other");
    });

    this.observable.notify("other");

    assertEquals(["other"], calls);
}
```

The test obviously fails as the observable happily notifies all the observers. There is no trivial way to fix this, so we roll up our sleeves and replace the `observable` array with an object.

The new object should store observers in arrays on properties whose keys are event names. Rather than conditionally initializing the object and array in all the methods, we can add an internal helper function that retrieves the correct array for an event, creating both it and the object if necessary. Listing 11.46 shows the updated implementation.

Listing 11.46 Storing observers in an object rather than an array

```
(function () {
  function _observers(observable, event) {
    if (!observable.observers) {
      observable.observers = {};
    }

    if (!observable.observers[event]) {
      observable.observers[event] = [];
    }

    return observable.observers[event];
  }

  function observe(event, observer) {
    if (typeof observer != "function") {
      throw new TypeError("observer is not function");
    }

    _observers(this, event).push(observer);
  }

  function hasObserver(event, observer) {
    var observers = _observers(this, event);

    for (var i = 0, l = observers.length; i < l; i++) {
```

```
        if (observers[i] == observer) {
          return true;
        }
      }

      return false;
    }

  function notify(event) {
    var observers = _observers(this, event);
    var args = Array.prototype.slice.call(arguments, 1);

    for (var i = 0, l = observers.length; i < l; i++) {
      try {
        observers[i].apply(this, args);
      } catch (e) {}
    }
  }

  tddjs.namespace("util").observable = {
    observe: observe,
    hasObserver: hasObserver,
    notify: notify
  };
}());
```

Changing the entire implementation in one go is a bit of a leap, but given the small size of the interface, we took a chance, and according to the tests, we succeeded.

If you are uncomfortable making such a big change in one go, you can take smaller steps. The clue to performing structural refactorings like this in small steps is to build the new functionality side-by-side with the old and remove the old one first when the new one is complete.

To make the change we just made using smaller steps, you could introduce the object backend using another name and add observers both to this and the old array. Then, you could update notify to use the new object, passing the last test we added. From there you could write more tests, e.g., for hasObserver, and switch over from the array to the object piece by piece. When all the methods were using the object, you could remove the array and possibly rename the object. The internal helper function we added could be the result of refactoring away duplication.

As an exercise, I encourage you to improve the test case—find edge cases and weak points, document them in tests and if you find problems, update the implementation.

11.8 Summary

Through a series of small steps, we have managed to write a library that implements a design pattern, ready for use in our projects. We have seen how tests can help make design decisions, how tests form requirements, and how tests can help solve nasty bugs—even cross-browser related ones.

While developing the library we have gotten some basic practice writing tests and letting tests guide us through writing production code. We have also exercised our refactoring muscles thoroughly. By starting out with *the simplest thing that could possibly work* we have gained a good understanding of the important role of refactoring in test-driven development. It is through refactoring, both in production code and tests, that our solutions can grow refined and elegant.

In the next chapter we will deal more closely with browser inconsistencies as we dig into the mechanics of "Ajax", using test-driven development to implement a higher level interface on top of the XMLHttpRequest object.

Abstracting Browser Differences: Ajax

Ajax, (asynchronous JavaScript and XML) is a marketing term coined to describe client technologies used to create rich internet applications, with the `XMLHttpRequest` object at the center stage. It's used heavily across the web, usually through some JavaScript library.

In this chapter we will get to know `XMLHttpRequest` better by implementing our own higher level API using test-driven development. Doing so will allow us to touch ever so lightly on the inner workings of an "ajax call"; it will teach us how to use test-driven development to abstract browser inconsistencies; and most importantly, it will give us an introduction to the concept of stubbing.

The API we will build in this chapter will not be the ultimate `XMLHttp-Request` abstraction, but it will provide a bare minimum to work with asynchronous requests. Implementing just what we need is one of the guiding principles of test-driven development, and paving the road with tests will allow us to go just as far as we need, providing a solid base for future extension.

12.1 Test Driving a Request API

Before we get started, we need to plan how we will be using test-driven development to abstract browser inconsistencies. TDD can help discover inconsistencies to some degree, but the nature of some bugs are so obscure that unit tests are unlikely to discover them all by accident.

12.1.1 Discovering Browser Inconsistencies

Because unit tests are unlikely to accidentally discover all kinds of browser bugs, some amount of exploration is necessary to uncover the bugs we're abstracting. However, unit tests can help us make sure we cover the holes by triggering offending behavior from within tests and making sure that production code copes with these situations. Incidentally, this is the same way we usually use unit tests to "capture" bugs in our own logic.

12.1.2 Development Strategy

We will build the Ajax interface bottom up, starting by asserting that we can get a hold of an `XMLHttpRequest` object from the browser. From there we will focus on individual features of the object only. We will not make any server side requests from within the unit tests themselves, because doing so will make the tests harder to run (we'll need someone answering those requests) and it makes it harder to test isolated behavior. Unit tests are there to drive us through development of the higher level API. They are going to help us develop and test the logic *we* build on top of the native transport, not the logic a given browser vendor built into their `XMLHttpRequest` implementation.

Testing our own logic is all fine and dandy, but we still need to test that the implementation really works when sitting on top of an actual `XMLHttpRequest` object. To do this, we will write an integration test once the API is usable. This test will be the real deal; it will use our interface to make requests to the server. By running it from an HTML file in the browser, we can verify that it either works or fails gracefully.

12.1.3 The Goal

The decision to write an `XMLHttpRequest` wrapper without actually using it inside the tests may sound strange at first, but allow me to remind you yet again of the goal of test-driven development; TDD uses tests as a design tool whose main purpose is to guide us through development. In order to truly focus on units in isolation, we need to eliminate external dependencies as much as practically possible. For this purpose we will use stubs extensively in this chapter. Remember that our main focus is to learn test-driven development, meaning that we should concentrate on the thought process and how tests form requirements. Additionally, we will keep practicing continuous refactoring to improve the implementation, API, and tests.

Stubbing is a powerful technique that allows true isolation of the system under test. Stubs (and mocks) have not been discussed in detail thus far, so this chapter will serve as a test-driven introduction to the topic. JavaScript's dynamic nature enables us to stub manually without too much hassle. However, when we are done with this chapter we will get a better overview of patterns that would be helpful to have automated, even in the dynamic world of JavaScript. Chapter 16, *Mocking and Stubbing,* will provide a more complete background on both stubs and mocks, but you should be able to follow the examples in this and following chapters without any prior experience with them.

12.2 Implementing the Request Interface

As in Chapter 11, *The Observer Pattern,* we will use JsTestDriver to run tests for this project. Please refer to Chapter 3, *Tools of the Trade,* for an introduction and installation guide.

12.2.1 Project Layout

The project layout can be seen in Listing 12.1 and the contents of the JsTestDriver configuration file are found in Listing 12.2.

Listing 12.1 Directory layout for the ajax project

```
chris@laptop:~/projects/ajax $ tree
.
|-- jsTestDriver.conf
|-- lib
|   '-- tdd.js
|-- src
|   '-- ajax.js
|   '-- request.js
`-- test
    '-- ajax_test.js
    '-- request_test.js
```

Listing 12.2 The jsTestDriver.conf file

```
server: http://localhost:4224

load:
  - lib/*.js
  - src/*.js
  - test/*.js
```

The `tdd.js` file should contain the utilities built in Part II, *JavaScript for Programmers*. The initial project state can be downloaded off the book's website[1] for your convenience.

12.2.2 Choosing the Interface Style

The first thing we need to decide is how we want to implement the request interface. To make an informed decision, we need a quick reminder on how a basic `XML-HttpRequest` works. The following shows the bare minimum of what needs to be done (order matters).

1. Create an `XMLHttpRequest` object.
2. Call the `open` method with the desired HTTP verb, the URL, and a boolean indicating whether the request is asynchronous or not; `true` means asynchronous.
3. Set the object's `onreadystatechange` handler.
4. Call the `send` method, passing in data if any.

Users of the high-level interface shouldn't have to worry about these details. All we really need to send a request is a URL and the HTTP verb. In most cases the ability to register a response handler would be useful as well. The response handler should be available in two flavors: one to handle successful requests and one to handle failed requests.

For asynchronous requests, the `onreadystatechange` handler is called asynchronously whenever the status of the request is updated. In other words, this is where the request eventually finishes, so the handler needs some way to access the request options such as callbacks.

12.3 Creating an `XMLHttpRequest` Object

Before we can dive into the request API, we need a cross-browser way to obtain an `XMLHttpRequest` object. The most obvious "Ajax" browser inconsistencies are found in the creation of this very object.

---

1. http://tddjs.com

12.3.1 The First Test

The very first test we will write is the one that expects an XMLHttpRequest object. As outlined in Section 12.2.2, *Choosing the Interface Style,* the properties we rely on are the open and send methods. The onreadystatechange handler needs the readyState property to know when the request has finished. Last, but not least, we will eventually need the setRequestHeader method in order to, well, set request headers.

Listing 12.3 shows the test in full; save it in test/ajax_test.js.

Listing 12.3 Testing for an XMLHttpRequest object

```
TestCase("AjaxCreateTest", {
  "test should return XMLHttpRequest object": function () {
    var xhr = tddjs.ajax.create();

    assertNumber(xhr.readyState);
    assert(tddjs.isHostMethod(xhr, "open"));
    assert(tddjs.isHostMethod(xhr, "send"));
    assert(tddjs.isHostMethod(xhr, "setRequestHeader"));
  }
});
```

This test fails as expected because there is no tddjs.ajax namespace. Listing 12.4 shows the namespace declaration that goes in src/ajax.js. In order for this to run, the tddjs.namespace method from Chapter 6, *Applied Functions and Closures,* needs to be available in lib/tdd.js.

Listing 12.4 Creating the ajax namespace

```
tddjs.namespace("ajax");
```

With this in place the test fails in response to the missing create method. We will need a little background before we can implement it.

12.3.2 XMLHttpRequest **Background**

Microsoft invented XMLHttpRequest as an ActiveX object back in 1999. Competitors followed suit shortly after, and today the object is available in just about every current browser. It's even on its way to becoming a W3C standard, in Last Call Working Draft at the time of writing. Listing 12.5 shows how the object is created in the defacto standards mode versus the `ActiveXObject` in Internet Explorer.

Listing 12.5 Instantiating the `XMLHttpRequest` object

```
// Proposed standard / works in most browsers
var request = new XMLHttpRequest();

// Internet Explorer 5, 5.5 and 6 (also available in IE 7)
try {
  var request = new ActiveXObject("Microsoft.XMLHTTP");
} catch (e) {
  alert("ActiveX is disabled");
}
```

Internet Explorer 7 was the first Microsoft browser to provide a quasi-native `XMLHttpRequest` object, although it also provides the ActiveX object. Both ActiveX and IE7's native object can be disabled by users or system administrators though, so we need to be careful when creating the request. Additionally, the "native" version in IE7 is unable to make local file requests, so we will prefer the ActiveX object if it's available.

The ActiveX object identificator, "Microsoft.XMLHTTP" in Listing 12.5, is known as an ActiveX ProgId. There are several available ProgId's for the `XMLHttpRequest` object, corresponding to different versions of Msxml:

- `Microsoft.XMLHTTP`
- `Msxml2.XMLHTTP`
- `Msxml2.XMLHTTP.3.0`
- `Msxml2.XMLHTTP.4.0`
- `Msxml2.XMLHTTP.5.0`
- `Msxml2.XMLHTTP.6.0`

In short, `Microsoft.XMLHTTP` covers IE5.x on older versions of Windows, versions 4 and 5 are not intended for browser use, and the three first ProgId's will in most setups refer to the same object—`Msxml2.XMLHTTP.3.0`. Finally, some clients may have `Msxml2.XMLHTTP.6.0` installed side-by-side with `Msxml2.XMLHTTP.3.0` (which comes with IE 6). This means that either `Msxml2.XMLHTTP.6.0` or `Microsoft.XMLHTTP` is sufficient to retrieve the newest available object in Internet Explorer. Keeping things simple,

Microsoft.XMLHTTP will do, as Msxml2.XMLHTTP.3.0 (again, ships with
IE6) includes the Microsoft.XMLHTTP alias for backwards compatibility.

12.3.3 Implementing tddjs.ajax.create

With knowledge of the different objects available, we can take a shot at implementing
ajax.create, as seen in Listing 12.6.

Listing 12.6 Creating an XMLHttpRequest object

```
tddjs.namespace("ajax").create = function () {
  var options = [
    function () {
      return new ActiveXObject("Microsoft.XMLHTTP");
    },

    function () {
      return new XMLHttpRequest();
    }
  ];

  for (var i = 0, l = options.length; i < l; i++) {
    try {
      return options[i]();
    } catch (e) {}
  }

  return null;
};
```

Running the tests confirms that our implementation is sufficient. First test green!
Before we hasten on to the next test, we should look for possible duplication and
other areas that could be improved through refactoring. Although there is no obvious duplication in code, there is already duplication in execution—the try/catch to
find a suitable object is executed every time an object is created. This is wasteful,
and we can improve the method by figuring out which object is available before
defining it. This has two benefits: The call time overhead is eliminated, and feature detection becomes built-in. If there is no matching object to create, then there
will be no tddjs.ajax.create, which means that client code can simply test
for its existence to determine if XMLHttpRequest is supported by the browser.
Listing 12.7 improves the method.

Listing 12.7 Checking for support upfront

```
(function () {
  var xhr;
  var ajax = tddjs.namespace("ajax");

  var options = [/* ... */]; // Same as before

  for (var i = 0, l = options.length; i < l; i++) {
    try {
      xhr = options[i]();
      ajax.create = options[i];
      break;
    } catch (e) {}
  }
}());
```

With this implementation in place, the try/catch will only run at load time. If successfully created, `ajax.create` will call the correct function directly. The test still runs green, so we can focus on the next requirement.

12.3.4 Stronger Feature Detection

The test we just wrote is bound to work as long as it is run with the basic JsTestDriver setup (seeing as JsTestDriver requires the `XMLHttpRequest` object or equivalent). However, the checks we did in Listing 12.3 are really feature tests that verify the capabilities of the returned object. Because we have a mechanism for verifying the object only once, it would be nice to make the verification as strong as possible. For this reason, Listing 12.8 performs the same tests in the initial execution, making us more confident that a usable object is returned. It requires the `tddjs.isHostMethod` method from Chapter 10, *Feature Detection,* in `lib/tdd.js`.

Listing 12.8 Adding stronger feature detection

```
/* ... */

try {
  xhr = options[i]();

  if (typeof xhr.readyState == "number" &&
      tddjs.isHostMethod(xhr, "open") &&
      tddjs.isHostMethod(xhr, "send") &&
      tddjs.isHostMethod(xhr, "setRequestHeader")) {
    ajax.create = options[i];
    break;
  }
} catch (e) {}
```

12.4 Making Get Requests

We will start working on the request API by describing our ultimate goal: a simple interface to make requests to the server using a URL, an HTTP verb, and possibly success and failure callbacks. We'll start with the GET request, as shown in Listing 12.9; save it in `test/request-test.js`.

Listing 12.9 Test for `tddjs.ajax.get`

```
TestCase("GetRequestTest", {
  "test should define get method": function () {
    assertFunction(tddjs.ajax.get);
  }
});
```

Taking baby steps, we start by checking for the existence of the `get` method. As expected, it fails because the method does not exist. Listing 12.10 defines the method. Save it in `src/request.js`

Listing 12.10 Defining `tddjs.ajax.get`

```
tddjs.namespace("ajax").get = function () {};
```

12.4.1 Requiring a URL

The `get` method needs to accept a URL. In fact, it needs to require a URL. Listing 12.11 has the scoop.

Listing 12.11 Testing for a required URL

```
"test should throw error without url": function () {
  assertException(function () {
    tddjs.ajax.get();
  }, "TypeError");
}
```

Our code does not yet throw any exceptions at all, so we expect this method to fail because of it. Luckily it does, so we move on to Listing 12.12.

Listing 12.12 Throwing exception if URL is not a string

```
tddjs.namespace("ajax").get = function (url) {
  if (typeof url != "string") {
    throw new TypeError("URL should be string");
  }
};
```

Tests pass. Now, is there any duplication to remove? That full namespace is already starting to stick out as slightly annoying. By wrapping the test in an anonymous closure, we can "import" the ajax namespace into the local scope by assigning it to a variable. It'll save us four keystrokes for each reference, so we go for it, as seen in Listing 12.13.

Listing 12.13 "Importing" the ajax namespace in the test

```
(function () {
  var ajax = tddjs.ajax;

  TestCase("GetRequestTest", {
    "test should define get method": function () {
      assertFunction(ajax.get);
    },

    "test should throw error without url": function () {
      assertException(function () {
        ajax.get();
      }, "TypeError");
    }
  });
}());
```

We can apply the same trick to the source file as well. While we're at it, we can utilize the scope gained by the anonymous closure to use a named function as well, as seen in Listing 12.14. The function declaration avoids troublesome Internet Explorer behavior with named function expressions, as explained in Chapter 5, *Functions*.

Listing 12.14 "Importing" the ajax namespace in the source

```
(function () {
  var ajax = tddjs.namespace("ajax");

  function get(url) {
    if (typeof url != "string") {
      throw new TypeError("URL should be string");
    }
  }

  ajax.get = get;
}());
```

12.4.2 Stubbing the XMLHttpRequest Object

In order for the get method to do anything at all, it needs to create an XML-HttpRequest object. We simply expect it to create one using ajax.create. Note that this does introduce a somewhat tight coupling between the request API and the create API. A better idea would probably be to inject the transport object. However, we will keep things simple for now. Later when we see the big picture clearer, we can always refactor to improve.

In order to verify that an object is created, or rather, that a method is called, we need to somehow fake the original implementation. Stubbing and mocking are two ways to create objects that mimic real objects in tests. Along with *fakes* and *dummies*, they are often collectively referred to as *test doubles*.

12.4.2.1 Manual Stubbing

Test doubles are usually introduced in tests either when original implementations are awkward to use or when we need to isolate an interface from its dependencies. In the case of XMLHttpRequest, we want to avoid the real thing for both reasons. Rather than creating an actual object, Listing 12.15 is going to *stub* out the ajax.create method, make a call to ajax.get, and then assert that ajax.create was called.

Listing 12.15 Manually stubbing the create method

```
"test should obtain an XMLHttpRequest object": function () {
  var originalCreate = ajax.create;

  ajax.create = function () {
    ajax.create.called = true;
  };

  ajax.get("/url");

  assert(ajax.create.called);

  ajax.create = originalCreate;
}
```

The test stores a reference to the original method and overwrites it with a function that, when called, sets a flag that the test can assert on. Finally, the original method is restored. There are a couple of problems with this solution. First of all, if this test fails, the original method will *not* be restored. Asserts throw an Assert-Error exception when they fail, meaning that the last line won't be executed unless the test succeeds. To fix this we can move the reference and restoring of the original method to the `setUp` and `tearDown` methods respectively. Listing 12.16 shows the updated test case.

Listing 12.16 Stubbing and restoring `ajax.create` safely

```
TestCase("GetRequestTest", {
  setUp: function () {
    this.ajaxCreate = ajax.create;
  },

  tearDown: function () {
    ajax.create = this.ajaxCreate;
  },

  /* ... */

  "test should obtain an XMLHttpRequest object":
  function () {
    ajax.create = function () {
      ajax.create.called = true;
    };

    ajax.get("/url");

    assert(ajax.create.called);
  }
});
```

Before we fix the next problem, we need to implement the method in question. All we have to do is add a single line inside `ajax.get`, as in Listing 12.17.

Listing 12.17 Creating the object

```
function get(url) {
  /* ... */
  var transport = tddjs.ajax.create();
}
```

With this single line in place the tests go green again.

12.4.2.2 Automating Stubbing

The next issue with the stubbing solution is that it's fairly verbose. We can mitigate this by extracting a helper method that creates a function that sets a flag when called, and allows access to this flag. Listing 12.18 shows one such possible method. Save it in `lib/stub.js`.

Listing 12.18 Extracting a function stubbing helper

```
function stubFn() {
  var fn = function () {
    fn.called = true;
  };

  fn.called = false;

  return fn;
}
```

Listing 12.19 shows the updated test.

Listing 12.19 Using the stub helper

```
"test should obtain an XMLHttpRequest object": function () {
  ajax.create = stubFn();
  ajax.get("/url");

  assert(ajax.create.called);
}
```

Now that we know that `ajax.get` obtains an `XMLHttpRequest` object we need to make sure it uses it correctly. The first thing it should do is call its open method. This means that the stub helper needs to be able to return an object. Listing 12.20 shows the updated helper and the new test expecting `open` to be called with the right arguments.

Listing 12.20 Test that the open method is used correctly

```
function stubFn(returnValue) {
  var fn = function () {
    fn.called = true;
    return returnValue;
  };

  fn.called = false;

  return fn;
}
```

```
TestCase("GetRequestTest", {
  /* ... */

  "test should call open with method, url, async flag":
  function () {
    var actual;

    ajax.create = stubFn({
      open: function () {
        actual = arguments;
      }
    });

    var url = "/url";
    ajax.get(url);

    assertEquals(["GET", url, true], actual);
  }
});
```

We expect this test to fail because the open method isn't currently being called from our implementation, implying that actual should be undefined. This is exactly what happens and so we can write the implementation, as in Listing 12.21.

Listing 12.21 Calling open

```
function get(url) {
  /* ... */
  transport.open("GET", url, true);
}
```

Now a few interesting things happen. First, we hardcoded both the HTTP verb and the asynchronous flag. Remember, one step at a time; we can make those configurable later. Running the tests shows that whereas the current test succeeds, the previous test now fails. It fails because the stub in that test did not return an object, so our production code is attempting to call undefined.open, which obviously won't work.

The second test uses the stubFn function to create one stub, while manually creating a stub open method in order to inspect its received arguments. To fix these problems, we will improve stubFn and share the fake XMLHttpRequest object between tests.

12.4.2.3 Improved Stubbing

To kill the manual stub open method, Listing 12.22 improves the stubFn function by having it record the arguments it receives and making them available for verification in tests.

Listing 12.22 Improving the stub helper

```
function stubFn(returnValue) {
  var fn = function () {
    fn.called = true;
    fn.args = arguments;
    return returnValue;
  };

  fn.called = false;

  return fn;
}
```

Using the improved stubFn cleans up the second test considerably, as seen in Listing 12.23.

Listing 12.23 Using the improved stub function

```
"test should call open with method, url, async flag":
function () {
  var openStub = stubFn();
  ajax.create = stubFn({ open: openStub });
  var url = "/url";
  ajax.get(url);

  assertEquals(["GET", url, true], openStub.args);
}
```

We now generate a stub for ajax.create that is instructed to return an object with one property: a stubbed open method. To verify the test we assert that open was called with the correct arguments.

The second problem was that adding the call to transport.open caused the first test, which didn't return an object from the stubbed ajax.create method, to fail. To fix this we will extract a fake XMLHttpRequest object, which can be shared between tests by stubbing ajax.create to return it. The stub can be conveniently created in the test case's setUp. We will start with the fakeXMLHttpRequest object, which can be seen in Listing 12.24. Save it in lib/fake_xhr.js.

Listing 12.24 Extracting `fakeXMLHttpRequest`

```
var fakeXMLHttpRequest = {
  open: stubFn()
};
```

Because the fake object relies on `stubFn`, which is defined in `lib/stub.js`, we need to update `jsTestDriver.conf` to make sure the helper is loaded before the fake object. Listing 12.25 shows the updated configuration file.

Listing 12.25 Updating `jsTestDriver.conf` to load files in correct order

```
server: http://localhost:4224

load:
  - lib/stub.js
  - lib/*.js
  - src/*.js
  - test/*.js
```

Next up, we update the test case by elevating the `ajax.create` stub to `setUp`. To create the `fakeXMLHttpRequest` object we will use `Object.create` from Chapter 7, *Objects and Prototypal Inheritance,* so place this function in `lib/object.js`. Listing 12.26 shows the updated test case.

Listing 12.26 Automate stubbing of `ajax.create` and `XMLHttpRequest`

```
TestCase("GetRequestTest", {
  setUp: function () {
    this.ajaxCreate = ajax.create;
    this.xhr = Object.create(fakeXMLHttpRequest);
    ajax.create = stubFn(this.xhr);
  },

  /* ... */

  "test should obtain an XMLHttpRequest object":
  function () {
    ajax.get("/url");

    assert(ajax.create.called);
  },

  "test should call open with method, url, async flag":
  function () {
```

```
    var url = "/url";
    ajax.get(url);

    assertEquals(["GET", url, true], this.xhr.open.args);
  }
});
```

Much better. Re-running the tests confirm that they now all pass. Moving forward, we can add stubs to the `fakeXMLHttpRequest` object as we see fit, which will make testing `ajax.get` significantly simpler.

12.4.2.4 Feature Detection and `ajax.create`

`ajax.get` now relies on the `ajax.create` method, which is not available in the case that the browser does not support the `XMLHttpRequest` object. To make sure we don't provide an `ajax.get` method that has no way of retrieving a transport, we will define this method conditionally as well. Listing 12.27 shows the required test.

Listing 12.27 Bailing out if `ajax.create` is not available

```
(function () {
  var ajax = tddjs.namespace("ajax");

  if (!ajax.create) {
    return;
  }

  function get(url) {
    /* ... */
  }

  ajax.get = get;
}());
```

With this test in place, clients using the `ajax.get` method can add a similar test to check for its existence before using it. Layering feature detection this way makes it manageable to decide what features are available in a given environment.

12.4.3 Handling State Changes

Next up, the `XMLHttpRequest` object needs to have its `onreadystatechange` handler set to a function, as Listing 12.28 shows.

Listing 12.28 Verifying that the ready state handler is assigned

```
"test should add onreadystatechange handler": function () {
  ajax.get("/url");

  assertFunction(this.xhr.onreadystatechange);
}
```

As expected, the test fails because `xhr.onreadystatechange` is undefined. We can assign an empty function for now, as Listing 12.29 shows.

Listing 12.29 Assigning an empty `onreadystatechange` handler

```
function get(url) {
  /* ... */
  transport.onreadystatechange = function () {};
}
```

To kick off the request, we need to call the `send` method. This means that we need to add a stubbed `send` method to `fakeXMLHttpRequest` and assert that it was called. Listing 12.30 shows the updated object.

Listing 12.30 Adding a stub `send` method

```
var fakeXMLHttpRequest = {
  open: stubFn(),
  send: stubFn()
};
```

Listing 12.31 expects the `send` method to be called by `ajax.get`.

Listing 12.31 Expecting `get` to call `send`

```
TestCase("GetRequestTest", {
  /* ... */

  "test should call send": function () {
    ajax.get("/url");

    assert(xhr.send.called);
  }
});
```

Implementation, shown in Listing 12.32, is once again a one-liner.

Listing 12.32 Calling `send`

```
function get(url) {
  /* ... */
  transport.send();
}
```

All lights are green once again. Notice how `stubXMLHttpRequest` is already paying off. We didn't need to update any of the other stubbed tests even when we called a new method on the `XMLHttpRequest` object, seeing as they all get it from the same source.

12.4.4 Handling the State Changes

ajax.get is now complete in an extremely minimalistic way. It sure ain't done, but it could be used to send a GET request to the server. We will turn our focus to the `onreadystatechange` handler in order to allow users of the API to subscribe to the success and failure events.

The state change handler is called as the request progresses. Typically, it will be called once for each of these 4 states (from the W3C XMLHttpRequest spec draft. Note that these states have other names in some implementations):

1. **OPENED**, `open` has been called, `setRequestHeader` and `send` may be called.
2. **HEADERS_RECEIVED**, `send` has been called, and headers and status are available.
3. **LOADING**, Downloading; responseText holds partial data.
4. **DONE**, The operation is complete.

For larger responses, the handler is called with the loading state several times as chunks arrive.

12.4.4.1 Testing for Success

To reach our initial goal, we really only care about when the request is done. When it is done we check the request's HTTP status code to determine if it was successful. We can start by testing the usual case of success: ready state 4 and status 200. Listing 12.33 shows the test.

Listing 12.33 Testing ready state handler with successful request

```
TestCase("ReadyStateHandlerTest", {
  setUp: function () {
    this.ajaxCreate = ajax.create;
    this.xhr = Object.create(fakeXMLHttpRequest);
    ajax.create = stubFn(this.xhr);
  },

  tearDown: function () {
    ajax.create = this.ajaxCreate;
  },

  "test should call success handler for status 200":
  function () {
    this.xhr.readyState = 4;
    this.xhr.status = 200;
    var success = stubFn();

    ajax.get("/url", { success: success });
    this.xhr.onreadystatechange();

    assert(success.called);
  }
});
```

Because we are going to need quite a few tests targeting the `onreadystate-change` handler, we create a new test case. This way it's implicit that test names describe expectations on this particular function, allowing us to skip prefixing every test with "onreadystatechange handler should." It also allows us to run these tests alone should we run into trouble and need even tighter focus.

To pass this test we need to do a few things. First, `ajax.get` needs to accept an object of options; currently the only supported option is a success callback. Then we need to actually add a body to that ready state function we added in the previous section. The implementation can be viewed in Listing 12.34.

Listing 12.34 Accepting and calling the success callback

```
(function () {
  var ajax = tddjs.namespace("ajax");

  function requestComplete(transport, options) {
    if (transport.status == 200) {
```

```
      options.success(transport);
    }
  }

  function get(url, options) {
    if (typeof url != "string") {
      throw new TypeError("URL should be string");
    }

    var transport = ajax.create();
    transport.open("GET", url, true);

    transport.onreadystatechange = function () {
      if (transport.readyState == 4) {
        requestComplete(transport, options);
      }
    };

    transport.send();
  }

  ajax.get = get;
}());
```

In order to avoid having the `ajax.get` method encompass everything but the kitchen sink, handling the completed request was extracted into a separate function. This forced the anonymous closure around the implementation, keeping the helper function local. Finally, with an enclosing scope we could "import" the `tddjs.ajax` namespace locally here, too. Wow, that was quite a bit of work. Tests were run in between each operation, I promise. The important thing is that the tests all run with this implementation.

You may wonder why we extracted `requestComplete` and not the whole ready state handler. In order to allow the handler access to the `options` object, we would have had to either bind the handler to it or call the function from inside an anonymous function assigned to `onreadystatechange`. In either case we would have ended up with two function calls rather than one in browsers without a native `bind` implementation. For requests incurring a large response, the handler will be called many times (with `readyState` 3), and the duplicated function calls would have added unnecessary overhead.

Now then, what do you suppose would happen if the `readystatechange` handler is called and we didn't provide a success callback? Listing 12.35 intends to find out.

Listing 12.35 Coping with successful requests and no callback

```
"test should not throw error without success handler":
    function () {
  this.xhr.readyState = 4;
  this.xhr.status = 200;

  ajax.get("/url");

  assertNoException(function () {
    this.xhr.onreadystatechange();
  }.bind(this));
}
```

Because we now need to access `this.xhr` inside the callback to `assert-NoException`, we bind the callback. For this to work reliably across browsers, save the `Function.prototype.bind` implementation from Chapter 6, *Applied Functions and Closures,* in `lib/function.js`.

As expected, this test fails. `ajax.get` blindly assumes both an options object and the success callback. To pass this test we need to make the code more defensive, as in Listing 12.36.

Listing 12.36 Taking care with optional arguments

```
function requestComplete(transport, options) {
  if (transport.status == 200) {
    if (typeof options.success == "function") {
      options.success(transport);
    }
  }
}

function get(url, options) {
  /* ... */
  options = options || {};
  var transport = ajax.create();
  /* ... */
};
```

With this safety net in place, the test passes. The success handler does not need to verify the existence of the `options` argument. As an internal function we have absolute control over how it is called, and the conditional assignment in `ajax.get` guarantees it is not `null` or `undefined`.

12.5 Using the Ajax API

As crude as it is, `tddjs.ajax.get` is now complete enough that we expect it to be functional. We have built it step-by-step in small iterations from the ground up, and have covered the basic happy path. It's time to take it for a spin, to verify that it actually runs in the real world.

12.5.1 The Integration Test

To use the API we need an HTML page to host the test. The test page will make a simple request for another HTML page and add the results to the DOM. The test page can be viewed in Listing 12.37 with the test script, `successful_get_test.js`, following in Listing 12.38.

Listing 12.37 Test HTML document

```
<!DOCTYPE html PUBLIC "-//W3C//DTD HTML 4.01//EN"
          "http://www.w3.org/TR/html4/strict.dtd">
<html lang="en">
  <head>
    <meta http-equiv="content-type"
          content="text/html; charset=utf-8">
    <title>Ajax Test</title>
  </head>
  <body onload="startSuccessfulGetTest()">
    <h1>Ajax Test</h1>
    <div id="output"></div>
    <script type="text/javascript"
            src="../lib/tdd.js"></script>
    <script type="text/javascript"
            src="../src/ajax.js"></script>
    <script type="text/javascript"
            src="../src/request.js"></script>
    <script type="text/javascript"
            src="successful_get_test.js"></script>
  </body>
</html>
```

Listing 12.38 The integration test script

```
function startSuccessfulGetTest() {
  var output = document.getElementById("output");

  if (!output) {
    return;
  }
```

```
function log(text) {
  if (output && typeof output.innerHTML != "undefined") {
    output.innerHTML += text;
  } else {
    document.write(text);
  }
}

try {
  if (tddjs.ajax && tddjs.get) {
    var id = new Date().getTime();

    tddjs.ajax.get("fragment.html?id=" + id, {
      success: function (xhr) {
        log(xhr.responseText);
      }
    });
  } else {
    log("Browser does not support tddjs.ajax.get");
  }
} catch (e) {
  log("An exception occured: " + e.message);
}
}
```

As you can see from the test script's `log` function, I intend to run the tests in some ancient browsers. The fragment being requested can be seen in Listing 12.39.

Listing 12.39 HTML fragment to be loaded asynchronously

```
<h1>Remote page</h1>
<p>
  Hello, I am an HTML fragment and I  was fetched
  using <code>XMLHttpRequest</code>
</p>
```

12.5.2 Test Results

Running the tests is mostly a pleasurable experience even though it does teach us a few things about the code. Perhaps most surprisingly, the test is unsuccessful in Firefox up until version 3.0.x. Even though the Mozilla Developer Center documentation states that `send` takes an *optional* body argument, Firefox 3.0.x and previous versions will in fact throw an exception if `send` is called without an argument.

Having discovered a deficiency in the wild, our immediate reaction as TDD-ers is to capture it in a test. Capturing the bug by verifying that our code handles the exception is all fine, but does not help Firefox <= 3.0.x get the request through. A better solution is to assert that send is called with an argument. Seeing that GET requests never have a request body, we simply pass it null. The test goes in the GetRequestTest test case and can be seen in Listing 12.40.

Listing 12.40 Asserting that send is called with an argument

```
"test should pass null as argument to send": function () {
  ajax.get("/url");

  assertNull(this.xhr.send.args[0]);
}
```

The test fails, so Listing 12.41 updates ajax.get to pass null directly to send.

Listing 12.41 Passing null to send

```
function get(url, options) {
  /* ... */
  transport.send(null);
}
```

Our tests are back to a healthy green, and now the integration test runs smoothly on Firefox as well. In fact, it now runs on *all* Firefox versions, including back when it was called Firebird (0.7). Other browsers cope fine too, for instance Internet Explorer versions 5 and up run the test successfully. The code was tested on a wide variety of new and old browsers. All of them either completed the test successfully or gracefully printed that "Browser does not support tddjs.ajax.get."

12.5.3 Subtle Trouble Ahead

There is one more problem with the code as is, if not as obvious as the previous obstacle. The XMLHttpRequest object and the function assigned to its onreadystatechange property creates a circular reference that causes memory leaks in Internet Explorer. To see this in effect, create another test page like the previous one, only make 1,000 requests. Watch Internet Explorer's memory usage in the Windows task manager. It should skyrocket, and what's worse is that it will stay high even when you leave the page. This is a serious problem, but one that is luckily easy to fix; simply break the circular reference either by removing the `onreadystatechange` handler or null the request object (thus removing it from the handler's scope) once the request is finished.

We will use the test case to ensure that this issue is handled. Although nulling the transport is simple, we cannot test it, because it's a local value. We'll clear the ready state handler instead.

Clearing the handler can be done in a few ways; setting it to `null` or using the `delete` operator quickly comes to mind. Enter our old friend Internet Explorer. Using `delete` will not work in IE; it returns `false`, indicating that the property was not successfully deleted. Setting the property to `null` (or any non-function value) throws an exception. The solution is to set the property to a function that does not include the request object in its scope. We can achieve this by creating a `tddjs.noop` function that is known to have a "clean" scope chain. Using a function available outside the implementation handily lends itself to testing as well, as Listing 12.42 shows.

Listing 12.42 Asserting that the circular reference is broken

```
"test should reset onreadystatechange when complete":
function () {
  this.xhr.readyState = 4;
  ajax.get("/url");

  this.xhr.onreadystatechange();

  assertSame(tddjs.noop, this.xhr.onreadystatechange);
}
```

As expected, this test fails. Implementing it is as simple as Listing 12.43.

Listing 12.43 Breaking the circular reference

```
tddjs.noop = function () {};

(function () {
  /* ... */

  function get(url, options) {
    /* ... */

    transport.onreadystatechange = function () {
      if (transport.readyState == 4) {
```

```
        requestComplete(transport, options);
        transport.onreadystatechange = tddjs.noop;
      }
    };

    transport.send(null);
  };

  /* ... */
}());
```

Adding these two lines makes the tests pass again. Re-running the massive request integration test in Internet Explorer confirms that the memory leak is now gone.

12.5.4 Local Requests

The last issue with the current implementation is that it is unable to make local requests. Doing so results in no errors, yet "nothing happens." The reason for this is that the local file system has no concept of HTTP status codes, so the status code is 0 when `readyState` is 4. Currently our implementation only accepts status code 200, which is insufficient in any case. We will add support for local requests by checking if the script is running locally and that the status code is not set, as the test in Listing 12.44 shows.

Listing 12.44 Making sure the success handler is called for local requests

```
"test should call success handler for local requests":
function () {
  this.xhr.readyState = 4;
  this.xhr.status = 0;
  var success = stubFn();
  tddjs.isLocal = stubFn(true);

  ajax.get("file.html", { success: success });
  this.xhr.onreadystatechange();

  assert(success.called);
}
```

The test assumes a helper method `tddjs.isLocal` to check if the script is running locally. Because we are stubbing it, a reference to it is saved in the `setUp`, allowing it to be restored in `tearDown` as we did before.

To pass the test, we will call the success callback whenever the request is for a local file and the status code is not set. Listing 12.45 shows the updated ready state change handler.

Listing 12.45 Allow local requests to succeed

```
function requestComplete(transport, options) {
  var status = transport.status;

  if (status == 200 || (tddjs.isLocal() && !status)) {
    if (typeof options.success == "function") {
      options.success(transport);
    }
  }
}
```

The implementation passes the test. In order to have this working in a browser as well, we need to implement the helper that determines if the script is running locally, as seen in Listing 12.46. Add it to the `lib/tdd.js` file.

Listing 12.46 Checking current URL to decide if request is local

```
tddjs.isLocal = (function () {
  function isLocal() {
    return !!(window.location &&
             window.location.protocol.indexOf("file:") === 0);
  }

  return isLocal;
}());
```

With this helper in place we can re-run the integration test locally, and observe that it now loads the HTML fragment.

12.5.5 Testing Statuses

We finished another step—a test and a few lines of production code—it's time to review and look for duplication. Even with the stub helpers we added previously, the tests that verify behavior for different sets of `readyState` and `status` codes look awfully similar. And still we haven't tested for other 2xx status codes, or any error codes at all.

To reduce the duplication, we will add a method to the `fakeXMLHttp-Request` object that allows us to fake its ready state changing. Listing 12.47 adds a method that changes the ready state and calls the `onreadystatechange` handler.

Listing 12.47 Completing the fake request

```
var fakeXMLHttpRequest = {
  open: stubFn(),
  send: stubFn(),

  readyStateChange: function (readyState) {
    this.readyState = readyState;
    this.onreadystatechange();
  }
};
```

Using this method, we can extract a helper method that accepts as arguments a status code and a ready state, and returns an object with properties `success` and `failure`, both indicating if the corresponding callback was called. This is a bit of a leap because we haven't yet written any tests for the failure callback, but in order to move along we will make a run for it. Listing 12.48 shows the new helper function.

Listing 12.48 Request helper for tests

```
function forceStatusAndReadyState(xhr, status, rs) {
  var success = stubFn();
  var failure = stubFn();

  ajax.get("/url", {
    success: success,
    failure: failure
  });

  xhr.status = status;
  xhr.readyStateChange(rs);

  return {
    success: success.called,
    failure: failure.called
  };
}
```

Because this abstracts the whole body of a few tests, it was given a fairly verbose name so as to not take away from the clarity of the tests. You'll be the judge of whether the tests are now too abstract or still clear. Listing 12.49 shows the helper in use.

Listing 12.49 Using the request helper in tests

```
"test should call success handler for status 200":
function () {
  var request = forceStatusAndReadyState(this.xhr, 200, 4);

  assert(request.success);
},

/* ... */

"test should call success handler for local requests":
function () {
  tddjs.isLocal = stubFn(true);

  var request = forceStatusAndReadyState(this.xhr, 0, 4);

  assert(request.success);
}
```

When making big changes like this I like to introduce a few intentional bugs in the helper to make sure it's working as I expect. For instance, we could comment out the line that sets the success handler in the helper to verify that the test then fails. Also, the second test should fail if we comment out the line that stubs `tddjs.isLocal` to return `true`, which it does. Manipulating the ready state and status code is also a good way to ensure tests still behave as expected.

12.5.5.1 Further Status Code Tests

Using the new helper makes testing for new status codes a trivial task, so I will leave it as an exercise. Although testing for more status codes and making sure the failure callback is fired for status codes outside the 200 range (with the exception of 0 for local files and 304 "Not Modified") is a good exercise in test-driven development, doing so will add little new to our discussion. I urge you to run through the steps as an exercise, and when you are done you could always compare your quest to mine by downloading the sample code off the book's website[2].

---

2. http://tddjs.com

Listing 12.50 shows the resulting handler.

Listing 12.50 Dispatching success and failure callbacks

```
function isSuccess(transport) {
  var status = transport.status;

  return (status >= 200 && status < 300) ||
         status == 304 ||
         (tddjs.isLocal() && !status);
}

function requestComplete(transport, options) {
  if (isSuccess(transport)) {
    if (typeof options.success == "function") {
      options.success(transport);
    }
  } else {
    if (typeof options.failure == "function") {
      options.failure(transport);
    }
  }
}
```

12.6 Making POST Requests

With the GET requests in a fairly usable state we will move on to the subject of
POST requests. Note that there is still a lot missing from the GET implementation,
such as setting request headers and exposing the transport's `abort` method. Don't
worry, test-driven development is all about incrementally building an API, and given
a list of requirements to meet we can choose freely which ones makes sense to work
on at any given time. Implementing POST requests will bring about an interesting
refactoring, which is the motivation for doing this now.

12.6.1 Making Room for Posts

The current implementation does not lend itself easily to support new HTTP verbs.
We could pass the method as an option, but where? To the `ajax.get` method?
That wouldn't make much sense. We need to refactor the existing implementation
in three ways: First we need to extract a generic `ajax.request` method; then
we need to make the HTTP verb configurable. Last, to remove duplication we will

"nuke" the body of the `ajax.get method`, leaving it to delegate its work to `ajax.request`, forcing a GET request.

12.6.1.1 Extracting `ajax.request`

Extracting the new method isn't magic; simply copy-paste `ajax.get` and rename it, as seen in Listing 12.51.

Listing 12.51 Copy-pasting `ajax.get` to `ajax.request`

```
function request(url, options) {
  // Copy of original ajax.get function body
}

ajax.request = request;
```

Remember to run the tests after each step while refactoring. In this case, only a copy-paste mistake resulting in a syntax error could possibly break the code because the new method isn't being called yet.

12.6.1.2 Making the Method Configurable

Next up is to make the request method a configurable option on the `ajax.request` method. This is new functionality and so requires a test, as seen in Listing 12.52.

Listing 12.52 Request method should be configurable

```
function setUp() {
  this.tddjsIsLocal = tddjs.isLocal;
  this.ajaxCreate = ajax.create;
  this.xhr = Object.create(fakeXMLHttpRequest);
  ajax.create = stubFn(this.xhr);
}

function tearDown() {
  tddjs.isLocal = this.tddjsIsLocal;
  ajax.create = this.ajaxCreate;
}

TestCase("GetRequestTest", {
  setUp: setUp,
  tearDown: tearDown,
  /* ... */
});
```

```
TestCase("ReadyStateHandlerTest", {
  setUp: setUp,
  tearDown: tearDown,
  /* ... */
});

TestCase("RequestTest", {
  setUp: setUp,
  tearDown: tearDown,

  "test should use specified request method": function () {
    ajax.request("/uri", { method: "POST" });

    assertEquals("POST", this.xhr.open.args[0]);
  }
});
```

We add a new test case for the `ajax.request` method. This makes three test cases using the same setup and teardown methods, so we extract them as functions inside the anonymous closure to share them across test cases.

The test asserts that the request method uses POST as the request method when specified to do so. The choice of method is not coincidental. When TDD-ing, we should always add tests that we expect to fail somehow, tests that signify progress. Using POST also forces us to produce a real solution, as hard-coding POST would make one of the other tests fail. This is another quality mark of a unit test suite; breaking fundamental behavior in production code only results in one (or a few) breaking tests. This indicates tests are distinct and don't retest already tested behavior.

Onwards to a solution. Listing 12.53 shows how `ajax.request` could make the request method a configuration option.

Listing 12.53 Making the method configurable

```
function request(url, options) {
  /* ... */
  transport.open(options.method || "GET", url, true);
  /* ... */
}
```

That's really all there is to it. Tests are passing.

12.6.1.3 Updating `ajax.get`

Now to the actual refactoring. `ajax.request` now does the same job as `ajax.get`, only slightly more flexible. This means that all `ajax.get` really needs to do is to make sure the method used is GET and let `ajax.request` do all the work. Listing 12.54 shows the spiffy new `ajax.get`.

Listing 12.54 Cropping `ajax.get`'s body

```
function get(url, options) {
  options = tddjs.extend({}, options);
  options.method = "GET";
  ajax.request(url, options);
}
```

As we are now overriding the `method` option, we use the `tddjs.extend` method from Chapter 7, *Objects and Prototypal Inheritance,* to make a copy of the `options` object before making changes to it. Running the tests confirms that this works as expected, and voila, we have a foundation for the post method.

Now that the interface changed, our tests are in need of some maintenance. Most tests now target `ajax.get` while actually testing the internals of `ajax.request`. As we discussed as early as in Chapter 1, *Automated Testing,* voila, this kind of indirection in tests is generally not appreciated. Unit tests need maintenance as much as production code, and the key to avoiding that becoming a problem is dealing with these cases as they arise. In other words, we should update our test cases immediately.

Fortunately, housekeeping is simple at this point. All the tests except "should define get method" can be moved from GetRequestTest to RequestTest. The only modification we need to make is to change all calls to `get` to `request` directly. The tests for the ready state change handler already have their own test case, Ready-StateHandlerTest. In this case we only need to update the method calls from `get` to `request`. This includes the call inside the `forceStatusAndReadyState` helper.

Moving tests, changing method calls, and re-running the tests takes about half a minute, no big deal. In more complex situations, such changes may be more involved, and in those cases some folks feel it's a good idea to employ more test helpers to avoid coupling the tests too tightly to the interface being tested. I think this practice takes away some of the value of tests as documentation, and I use it sparingly.

12.6.1.4 Introducing `ajax.post`

With `ajax.request` in place, implementing POST requests should be a breeze. Feeling brave, we skip the simple test to prove the method's existence this time around. Instead, the test in Listing 12.55 shows how we expect the method to behave.

Listing 12.55 Expecting `ajax.post` to delegate to `ajax.request`

```
TestCase("PostRequestTest", {
  setUp: function () {
    this.ajaxRequest = ajax.request;
  },

  tearDown: function () {
    ajax.request = this.ajaxRequest;
  },

  "test should call request with POST method": function () {
    ajax.request = stubFn();

    ajax.post("/url");

    assertEquals("POST", ajax.request.args[1].method);
  }
});
```

Implementation is trivial, as seen in Listing 12.56.

Listing 12.56 Delegating `ajax.post` to `ajax.request` with POST as method

```
function post(url, options) {
  options = tddjs.extend({}, options);
  options.method = "POST";
  ajax.request(url, options);
}

ajax.post = post;
```

Running the tests confirms that this implementation solves the newly added requirement. As always, we look for duplication before moving on. Obviously, the `get` and `post` methods are very similar. We *could* extract a helper method, but saving only two lines in two methods at the expense of another function call and another level of indirection doesn't seem worthwhile at this point. You may feel differently.

12.6.2 Sending Data

In order for the POST request to make any sense, we need to send data with it. To send data to the server the same way a browser posts a form we need to do two things: encode the data using either `encodeURI` or `encodeURIComponent` (depending on how we receive the data) and set the Content-Type header. We will start with the data.

Before we head into the request test case to formulate a test that expects encoded data, let's take a step back and consider what we are doing. Encoding strings isn't a task unique to server requests; it could be useful in other cases as well. This insight points in the direction of separating string encoding into its own interface. I won't go through the steps required to build such an interface here; instead Listing 12.57 shows a very simple implementation.

Listing 12.57 Simplified url parameter encoder

```
(function () {
  if (typeof encodeURIComponent == "undefined") {
    return;
  }

  function urlParams(object) {
    if (!object) {
      return "";
    }

    if (typeof object == "string") {
      return encodeURI(object);
    }

    var pieces = [];

    tddjs.each(object, function (prop, val) {
      pieces.push(encodeURIComponent(prop) + "=" +
                  encodeURIComponent(val));
    });

    return pieces.join("&");
  }

  tddjs.namespace("util").urlParams = urlParams;
}());
```

Obviously, this method could be extended to properly encode arrays and other kinds of data as well. Because the `encodeURIComponent` function isn't guaranteed to be available, feature detection is used to conditionally define the method.

12.6.2.1 Encoding Data in `ajax.request`

For post requests, data should be encoded and passed as an argument to the `send` method. Let's start by writing a test that ensures data is encoded, as in Listing 12.58.

Listing 12.58 Asserting data sent to post

```
function setUp() {
  this.tddjsUrlParams = tddjs.util.urlParams;
  /* ... */
}

function tearDown() {
  tddjs.util.urlParams = this.tddjsUrlParams;
  /* ... */
}

TestCase("RequestTest", {
  /* ... */

  "test should encode data": function () {
    tddjs.util.urlParams = stubFn();
    var object = { field1: "13", field2: "Lots of data!" };

    ajax.request("/url", { data: object, method: "POST" });

    assertSame(object, tddjs.util.urlParams.args[0]);
  }
});
```

Making this test pass isn't so hard, as Listing 12.59 shows.

Listing 12.59 Encoding data if any is available

```
function request(url, options) {
  /* ... */
  options = tddjs.extend({}, options);
  options.data = tddjs.util.urlParams(options.data);
  /* ... */
}
```

We don't need to check if `data` exists because `urlParams` was designed to handle a missing argument. Note that because the encoding interface was separated from the ajax interface, it would probably be a good idea to add a feature test for it. We could force such a feature test by writing a test that removed the method locally for the duration of the test and assert that the method did not throw an exception. I'll leave that as an exercise.

12.6.2.2 Sending Encoded Data

Next up is sending the data. For POST requests we want the data sent to `send`, as Listing 12.60 specifies.

Listing 12.60 Expecting data to be sent for POST requests

```
"test should send data with send() for POST": function () {
  var object = { field1: "$13", field2: "Lots of data!" };
  var expected = tddjs.util.urlParams(object);

  ajax.request("/url", { data: object, method: "POST" });

  assertEquals(expected, this.xhr.send.args[0]);
}
```

This test fails because we are force-feeding the `send` method `null`. Also note how we now trust `tddjs.util.urlParams` to provide the expected value. It should have its own set of tests, which should guarantee as much. If we are reluctant to trust it, we could stub it out to avoid it cluttering up the test. Some developers always stub or mock out dependencies such as this, and theoretically, not doing so makes the unit test slightly bend toward an integration test. We will discuss pros and cons of different levels of stubbing and mocking more extensively in Chapter 16, *Mocking and Stubbing.* For now, we will leave `tddjs.util.urlParams` live in our tests.

To make the test pass we need to add data handling to `ajax.request`, as Listing 12.61 does.

Listing 12.61 Initial attempt at handling data

```
function request(url, options) {
  /* ... */
  options = tddjs.extend({}, options);
  options.data = tddjs.util.urlParams(options.data);
  var data = null;
```

```
  if (options.method == "POST") {
    data = options.data;
  }

  /* ... */

  transport.send(data);
};
```

This is not optimal, but passes the test without failing the previous one that expects send to receive null. One way to clean up the ajax.request method is to refactor to extract the data handling, as Listing 12.62 shows.

Listing 12.62 Extracting a data handling function

```
function setData(options) {
  if (options.method == "POST") {
    options.data = tddjs.util.urlParams(options.data);
  } else {
    options.data = null;
  }
}

function request(url, options) {
  /* ... */
  options = tddjs.extend({}, options);
  setData(options);

  /* ... */

  transport.send(options.data);
};
```

This somewhat obtrusively blanks data for GET requests, so we will deal with that immediately.

12.6.2.3 Sending Data with GET Requests

Before we can move on to setting request headers we must make sure that it is possible to send data with GET requests as well. With GET, data is not passed to the send method, but rather encoded on the URL. Listing 12.63 shows a test specifying the behavior.

Listing 12.63 Testing that GET requests can send data

```
"test should send data on URL for GET": function () {
  var url = "/url";
  var object = { field1: "$13", field2: "Lots of data!" };
  var expected = url + "?" + tddjs.util.urlParams(object);

  ajax.request(url, { data: object, method: "GET" });

  assertEquals(expected, this.xhr.open.args[1]);
}
```

With this test in place we need to modify the data processing. For both GET and POST requests we need to encode data, but for GET requests the data goes on the URL, and we must remember to still pass `null` to the `send` method.

At this point we have enough requirements to make keeping them all in our heads a confusing affair. Tests are slowly becoming a fantastic asset; because we don't need to worry about requirements we have already met, we can code along without being weighed down by ever-growing amounts of requirements. The implementation can be seen in Listing 12.64.

Listing 12.64 Adding data to get requests

```
function setData(options) {
  if (options.data) {
    options.data = tddjs.util.urlParams(options.data);

    if (options.method == "GET") {
      options.url += "?" + options.data;
      options.data = null;
    }
  } else {
    options.data = null;
  }
}

function request(url, options) {
  /* ... */
  options = tddjs.extend({}, options);
  options.url = url;
  setData(options);
  /* ... */

  transport.open(options.method || "GET", options.url, true);
```

```
/* ... */
  transport.send(options.data);
};
```

Because the data handling might include modifying the URL to embed data onto it, we added it to the `options` object and passed that to `setData`, as before. Obviously, the above solution will break down if the URL already has query parameters on it. As an exercise, I urge you to test for such a URL and update `setData` as necessary.

12.6.3 Setting Request Headers

The last thing we need to do in order to pass data is setting request headers. Headers can be set using the `setRequestHeader(name, value)` method. At this point adding in header handling is pretty straightforward, so I will leave doing that as an exercise. To test this you will need to augment the `fakeXMLHttp-Request` object to record headers set on it so you can inspect them from your tests. Listing 12.65 shows an updated version of the object you can use for this purpose.

Listing 12.65 Adding a fake `setRequestHeader` method

```
var fakeXMLHttpRequest = {
  open: stubFn(),
  send: stubFn(),

  setRequestHeader: function (header, value) {
    if (!this.headers) {
      this.headers = {};
    }

    this.headers[header] = value;
  },

  readyStateChange: function (readyState) {
    this.readyState = readyState;
    this.onreadystatechange();
  }
};
```

12.7 Reviewing the Request API

Even though we didn't walk through setting request headers, I want to show you
the resulting ajax.request after implementing header handling (this is but one
possible solution). The full implementation can be seen in Listing 12.66.

Listing 12.66 The "final" version of tddjs.ajax.request

```
tddjs.noop = function () {};

(function () {
  var ajax = tddjs.namespace("ajax");

  if (!ajax.create) {
    return;
  }

  function isSuccess(transport) {
    var status = transport.status;

    return (status >= 200 && status < 300) ||
      status == 304 ||
      (tddjs.isLocal() && !status);
  }

  function requestComplete(options) {
    var transport = options.transport;

    if (isSuccess(transport)) {
      if (typeof options.success == "function") {
        options.success(transport);
      }
    } else {
      if (typeof options.failure == "function") {
        options.failure(transport);
      }
    }
  }

  function setData(options) {
    if (options.data) {
      options.data = tddjs.util.urlParams(options.data);

      if (options.method == "GET") {
        var hasParams = options.url.indexOf("?") >= 0;
        options.url += hasParams ? "&" : "?";
```

```
        options.url += options.data;
        options.data = null;
      }
    } else {
      options.data = null;
    }
  }

  function defaultHeader(transport, headers, header, val) {
    if (!headers[header]) {
      transport.setRequestHeader(header, val);
    }
  }

  function setHeaders(options) {
    var headers = options.headers || {};
    var transport = options.transport;

    tddjs.each(headers, function (header, value) {
      transport.setRequestHeader(header, value);
    });

    if (options.method == "POST" && options.data) {
      defaultHeader(transport, headers,
                    "Content-Type",
                    "application/x-www-form-urlencoded");

      defaultHeader(transport, headers,
                    "Content-Length", options.data.length);
    }

    defaultHeader(transport, headers,
                  "X-Requested-With", "XMLHttpRequest");
  }

  // Public methods

  function request(url, options) {
    if (typeof url != "string") {
      throw new TypeError("URL should be string");
    }

    options = tddjs.extend({}, options);
    options.url = url;
    setData(options);
```

```
    var transport = tddjs.ajax.create();
    options.transport = transport;
    transport.open(options.method || "GET", options.url, true);
    setHeaders(options);

    transport.onreadystatechange = function () {
      if (transport.readyState == 4) {
        requestComplete(options);
        transport.onreadystatechange = tddjs.noop;
      }
    };

    transport.send(options.data);
  }

  ajax.request = request;

  function get(url, options) {
    options = tddjs.extend({}, options);
    options.method = "GET";
    ajax.request(url, options);
  }

  ajax.get = get;

  function post(url, options) {
    options = tddjs.extend({}, options);
    options.method = "POST";
    ajax.request(url, options);
  }

  ajax.post = post;
}());
```

The ajax namespace now contains enough functionality to serve most uses of asynchronous communication, although it is far from complete. Reviewing the implementation so far seems to suggest that refactoring to extract a request object as the baseline interface would be a good idea. Peeking through the code in Listing 12.66, we can spot several helpers that accept an options object. I'd suggest that this object in fact represents the state of the request, and might as well have been dubbed request at this point. In doing so, we could move the logic around, making the helpers methods of the request object instead. Following this train of thought possibly could lead our ajax.get and ajax.post implementations to look something like Listing 12.67.

Listing 12.67 Possible direction of the request API

```
(function () {
  /* ... */

  function setRequestOptions(request, options) {
    options = tddjs.extend({}, options);
    request.success = options.success;
    request.failure = options.failure;
    request.headers(options.headers || {});
    request.data(options.data);
  }

  function get(url, options) {
    var request = ajax.request.create(ajax.create());
    setRequestOptions(request, options);
    request.method("GET");

    request.send(url);
  };

  ajax.get = get;

  function post(url, options) {
    var request = ajax.request.create(ajax.create());
    setRequestOptions(request, options);
    request.method("POST");

    request.send(url);
  };

  ajax.post = post;
}());
```

Here the `request.create` takes a transport as its only argument, meaning
that we provide it with its main dependency rather than having it retrieve the object
itself. Furthermore, the method now returns a request object that can be sent when
configured. This brings the base API closer to the `XMLHttpRequest` object it's
wrapping, but still contains logic to set default headers, pre-process data, even out
browser inconsistencies, and so on. Such an object could easily be extended in order
to create more specific requesters as well, such as a `JSONRequest`. That object
could pre-process the response as well, by for instance passing readily parsed JSON
to callbacks.

The test cases (or *test suite* if you will) built in this chapter provide some insight into the kind of tests TDD leaves you with. Even with close to 100% code coverage (every line of code is executed by the tests), we have several holes in tests; more tests for cases when things go wrong—methods receive the wrong kind of arguments, and other edge cases are needed. Even so, the tests document our entire API, provides decent coverage, and makes for an excellent start in regards to a more solid test suite.

12.8 Summary

In this chapter we have used tests as our driver in developing a higher level API for the XMLHttpRequest object. The API deals with certain cross-browser issues, such as differing object creation, memory leaks, and buggy send methods. Whenever a bug was uncovered, tests were written to ensure that the API deals with the issue at hand.

This chapter also introduced extensive use of stubbing. Even though we saw how stubbing functions and objects could easily be done manually, we quickly realized that doing so leads to too much duplication. The duplication prompted us to write a simple function that helps with stubbing. We will pick up on this idea in Chapter 16, *Mocking and Stubbing,* and solve the case we didn't solve in this chapter; stubbing functions that will be called multiple times.

Coding through tddjs.ajax.request and friends, we have refactored both production code and tests aggressively. Refactoring is perhaps the most valuable tool when it comes to producing clean code and removing duplication. By frequently refactoring the implementation, we avoid getting stuck trying to come up with the greatest design at any given time—we can always improve it later, when we understand the problem better. As food for thought, we rounded off by discussing a refactoring idea to further improve the API.

The end result of the coding exercise in this chapter is a usable, yet hardly complete, "ajax" API. We will use this in the next chapter, when we build an interface to poll the server and stream data.

Streaming Data with Ajax and Comet

In Chapter 12, *Abstracting Browser Differences: Ajax,* we saw how the XML-HttpRequest object enables web pages to take the role of interactive applications that can both update data on the back-end server by issuing POST requests, as well as incrementally update the page without reloading it using GET requests.

In this chapter we will take a look at technologies used to implement live data streaming between the server and client. This concept was first enabled by Netscape's Server Push in 1995, and is possible to implement in a variety of ways in today's browsers under umbrella terms such as *Comet, Reverse Ajax,* and *Ajax Push.* We will look into two implementations in this chapter; regular polling and so-called long polling.

This chapter will add some features to the tddjs.ajax.request interface developed in the previous chapter, add a new interface, and finally integrate with tddjs.util.observable, developed in Chapter 11, *The Observer Pattern,* enabling us to create a streaming data client that allows JavaScript objects to observe server-side events.

The goal of this exercise is twofold: learning more about models for client-server interaction, and of course test-driven development. Important TDD lessons in this chapter includes delving deeper into testing asynchronous interfaces and testing timers. We will continue our discussion of stubbing, and get a glimpse of the workflow and choices presented to us as we develop more than a single interface.

13.1 Polling for Data

Although one-off requests to the server can enable highly dynamic and interesting applications, it doesn't open up for real live applications. Applications such as Facebook's and GTalk's in-browser chats are examples of applications that cannot make sense without a constant data stream. Other features, such as stock tickers, auctions, and Twitter's web interface become significantly more useful with a live data stream.

The simplest way to keep a constant data stream to the client is to *poll* the server on some fixed interval. Polling is as simple as issuing a new request every so many milliseconds. The shorter delay between requests, the more live the application. We will discuss some ups and downs with polling later, but in order for that discussion to be code-driven we will jump right into test driving development of a poller.

13.1.1 Project Layout

As usual we will use JsTestDriver to run tests. The initial project layout can be seen in Listing 13.1 and is available for download from the book's website.[1]

Listing 13.1 Directory layout for the poller project

```
chris@laptop:~/projects/poller $ tree
.
|-- jsTestDriver.conf
|-- lib
|    `-- ajax.js
|    `-- fake_xhr.js
|    `-- function.js
|    `-- object.js
|    `-- stub.js
|    `-- tdd.js
|    `-- url_params.js
|-- src
|    `-- poller.js
|    `-- request.js
`-- test
     `-- poller_test.js
     `-- request_test.js
```

---

1. http://tddjs.com

In many ways this project is a continuation of the previous one. Most files can be recognized from the previous chapter. The `request.js` file, and its test case are brought along for further development, and we will add some functionality to them. Note that the final refactoring discussed in Chapter 12, *Abstracting Browser Differences: Ajax,* in which `tdd.ajax.request` returns an object representing the request, is not implemented. Doing so would probably be a good idea, but we'll try not to tie the two interfaces too tightly together, allowing the refactoring to be performed at some later time. Sticking with the code exactly as we developed it in the previous chapter will avoid any surprises, allowing us to focus entirely on new features.

The `jsTestDriver.conf` configuration file needs a slight tweak for this project. The `lib` directory now contains an `ajax.js` file that depends on the `tddjs` object defined in `tdd.js`; however, it will be loaded before the file it depends on. The solution is to manually specify the `tdd.js` file first, then load the remaining lib files, as seen in Listing 13.2.

Listing 13.2 Ensuring correct load order of test files

```
server: http://localhost:4224

load:
  - lib/tdd.js
  - lib/stub.js
  - lib/*.js
  - src/*.js
  - test/*.js
```

13.1.2 The Poller: `tddjs.ajax.poller`

In Chapter 12, *Abstracting Browser Differences: Ajax,* we built the request interface by focusing heavily on the simplest use case, calling `tddjs.ajax.get` or `tddjs.ajax.post` to make one-off GET or POST requests. In this chapter we are going to flip things around and focus our efforts on building a stateful object, such as the one we realized could be refactored from `tddjs.ajax.request`. This will show us a different way to work, and, because test-driven development really is about design and specification, a slightly different result. Once the object is useful we will implement a cute one-liner interface on top of it to go along with the `get` and `post` methods.

13.1.2.1 Defining the Object

The first thing we expect from the interface is simply that it exists, as Listing 13.3 shows.

Listing 13.3 Expecting `tddjs.ajax.poller` to be an object

```
(function () {
  var ajax = tddjs.ajax;

  TestCase("PollerTest", {
    "test should be object": function () {
      assertObject(ajax.poller);
    }
  });
}());
```

This test jumps the gun on a few details; we know that we are going to want to shorten the full namespace, and doing so requires the anonymous closure to avoid leaking the shortcut into the global namespace. Implementation is a simple matter of defining an object, as seen in Listing 13.4.

Listing 13.4 Defining `tddjs.ajax.poller`

```
(function () {
  var ajax = tddjs.namespace("ajax");

  ajax.poller = {};
}());
```

The same initial setup (anonymous closure, local alias for namespace) is done here as well. Our first test passes.

13.1.2.2 Start Polling

The bulk of the poller's work is already covered by the request object, so it is simply going to organize issuing requests periodically. The only extra option the poller needs is the interval length in milliseconds.

To start polling, the object should offer a `start` method. In order to make any requests at all we will need a URL to poll, so the test in Listing 13.5 specifies that the method should throw an exception if no `url` property is set.

Listing 13.5 Expecting `start` to throw an exception on missing URL

```
"test start should throw exception for missing URL":
function () {
  var poller = Object.create(ajax.poller);

  assertException(function () {
    poller.start();
  }, "TypeError");
}
```

As usual, we run the test before implementing it. The first run coughs up an error stating that there is no `Object.create` method. To fix this we fetch it from Chapter 7, *Objects and Prototypal Inheritance,* and stick it in `tdd.js`. What happens next is interesting; the test passes. Somehow a `TypeError` is thrown, yet we haven't done anything other than defining the object. To see what's happening, we edit the test and remove the `assertException` call, simply calling `poller.start()` directly in the test. JsTestDriver should pick up the exception and tell us what's going on.

As you might have guessed, the missing `start` method triggers a `TypeError` of its own. This indicates that the test isn't good enough. To improve the situation we add another test stating that there should be a `start` method, as seen in Listing 13.6.

Listing 13.6 Expecting the poller to define a `start` method

```
"test should define a start method":
function () {
  assertFunction(ajax.poller.start);
}
```

With this test in place, we now get a failure stating that `start` was expected to be a function, but rather was `undefined`. The previous test still passes. We will fix the newly added test by simply adding a `start` method, as in Listing 13.7.

Listing 13.7 Adding the `start` method

```
(function () {
  var ajax = tddjs.namespace("ajax");

  function start() {
  }

  ajax.poller = {
    start: start
  };
}());
```

Running the tests again confirms that the existence test passes, but the original test expecting an exception now fails. This is all good and leads us to the next step, seen in Listing 13.8; throwing an exception for the missing URL.

Listing 13.8 Throwing an exception for missing URL

```
function start() {
  if (!this.url) {
    throw new TypeError("Must specify URL to poll");
  }
}
```

Running the tests over confirms that they are successful.

13.1.2.3 Deciding the Stubbing Strategy

Once a URL is set, the `start` method should make its first request. At this point we have a choice to make. We still don't want to make actual requests to the server in the tests, so we will continue stubbing like we did in the previous chapter. However, at this point we have a choice of where to stub. We could keep stubbing `ajax.create` and have it return a fake request object, or we could hook in higher up, stubbing the `ajax.request` method. Both approaches have their pros and cons.

Some developers will always prefer stubbing and mocking as many of an interface's dependencies as possible (you might even see the term *mockists* used about these developers). This approach is common in behavior-driven development. Following the mockist way means stubbing (or mocking, but we'll deal with that in Chapter 16, *Mocking and Stubbing*) `ajax.request` and possibly other non-trivial dependencies. The advantage of the mockist approach is that it allows us to freely decide development strategy. For instance, by stubbing all of the poller's dependencies, we could easily have built this object first and then used the stubbed calls as starting points for tests for the request interface when we were done. This strategy is known as top-down—in contrast to the current bottom-up strategy—and it even allows a team to work in parallel on dependent interfaces.

The opposite approach is to stub and mock as little as possible; only fake those dependencies that are truly inconvenient, slow, or complicated to setup and/or run through in tests. In a dynamically typed language such as JavaScript, stubs and mocks come with a price; because the interface of a test double cannot be enforced (e.g., by an "implements" keyword or similar) in a practical way, there is a real possibility of using fakes in tests that are incompatible with their production counterparts. Making tests succeed with such fakes will guarantee the resulting code will break when faced with the real implementation in an integration test, or worse, in production.

Whereas we had no choice of where to stub while developing `ajax.request` (it only depended on the `XMLHttpRequest` object via the `ajax.create` method), we now have the opportunity to choose if we want to stub `ajax.request`
or `ajax.create`. We will try a slightly different approach in this chapter by stubbing "lower." This makes our tests mini integration tests, as discussed in Chapter 1, *Automated Testing,* with the pros and cons that follow. However, as we have just developed a reasonable test suite for `ajax.request`, we should be able to trust it for the cases we covered in Chapter 12, *Abstracting Browser Differences: Ajax.*

While developing the poller we will strive to fake as little as possible, but we need to cut off the actual server requests. To do this we will simply keep using the `fakeXMLHttpRequest` object from Chapter 12, *Abstracting Browser Differences: Ajax.*

13.1.2.4   The First Request

To specify that the `start` method should start polling, we need to assert somehow that a URL made it across to the `XMLHttpRequest` object. To do this we assert that its `open` method was called with the expected URL, as seen in Listing 13.9.

Listing 13.9 Expecting the poller to issue a request

```
setUp: function () {
  this.ajaxCreate = ajax.create;
  this.xhr = Object.create(fakeXMLHttpRequest);
  ajax.create = stubFn(this.xhr);
},

tearDown: function () {
  ajax.create = this.ajaxCreate;
},

/* ... */

"test start should make XHR request with URL": function () {
  var poller = Object.create(ajax.poller);
  poller.url = "/url";

  poller.start();

  assert(this.xhr.open.called);
  assertEquals(poller.url, this.xhr.open.args[1]);
}
```

Again, we use `Object.create` to create a new fake object, assign it to a property of the test case, and then stub `ajax.create` to return it. The implementation should be straightforward, as seen in Listing 13.10.

Listing 13.10 Making a request

```
function start() {
  if (!this.url) {
    throw new TypeError("Must provide URL property");
  }

  ajax.request(this.url);
}
```

Note that the test did not specify specifically to use `ajax.request`. We could have made the request any way we wanted, so long as we used the transport provided by `ajax.create`. This means, for instance, that we could carry out the aforementioned refactoring on the request interface without touching the poller tests.

Running the tests confirms that they all pass. However, the test is not quite as concise as it could be. Knowing that the `open` method was called on the transport doesn't necessarily mean that the request was sent. We'd better add an assertion that checks that `send` was called as well, as Listing 13.11 shows.

Listing 13.11 Expecting request to be sent

```
"test start should make XHR request with URL": function () {
  var poller = Object.create(ajax.poller);
  poller.url = "/url";

  poller.start();

  var expectedArgs = ["GET", poller.url, true];
  var actualArgs = [].slice.call(this.xhr.open.args);
  assert(this.xhr.open.called);
  assertEquals(expectedArgs, actualArgs);
  assert(this.xhr.send.called);
}
```

13.1.2.5 The `complete` Callback

How will we issue the requests periodically? A simple solution is to make the request through `setInterval`. However, doing so may cause severe problems. Issuing new requests without knowing whether or not previous requests completed could lead to multiple simultaneous connections, which is not desired. A better solution is to trigger a delayed request once the previous one finishes. This means that we have to wrap the success and failure callbacks.

Rather than adding identical success and failure callbacks (save for which user defined callback they delegate to), we are going to make a small addition to `tddjs.ajax.request`; the `complete` callback will be called when a request is complete, regardless of success. Listing 13.12 shows the update needed in the `requestWithReadyStateAndStatus` helper, as well as three new tests, asserting that the `complete` callback is called for successful, failed, and local requests.

Listing 13.12 Specifying the `complete` callback

```
function forceStatusAndReadyState(xhr, status, rs) {
  var success = stubFn();
  var failure = stubFn();
  var complete = stubFn();

  ajax.get("/url", {
    success: success,
    failure: failure,
    complete: complete
  });

  xhr.complete(status, rs);

  return {
    success: success.called,
    failure: failure.called,
    complete: complete.called
  };
}

TestCase("ReadyStateHandlerTest", {
  /* ... */

  "test should call complete handler for status 200":
  function () {
    var request = forceStatusAndReadyState(this.xhr, 200, 4);

    assert(request.complete);
  },

  "test should call complete handler for status 400":
```

```
function () {
  var request = forceStatusAndReadyState(this.xhr, 400, 4);

  assert(request.complete);
},

"test should call complete handler for status 0":
function () {
  var request = forceStatusAndReadyState(this.xhr, 0, 4);

  assert(request.complete);
}
});
```

As expected, all three tests fail given that no `complete` callback is called anywhere. Adding it in is straightforward, as Listing 13.13 illustrates.

Listing 13.13 Calling the `complete` callback

```
function requestComplete(options) {
  var transport = options.transport;

  if (isSuccess(transport)) {
    if (typeof options.success == "function") {
      options.success(transport);
    }
  } else {
    if (typeof options.failure == "function") {
      options.failure(transport);
    }
  }

  if (typeof options.complete == "function") {
    options.complete(transport);
  }
}
```

When a request is completed, the poller should schedule another request. Scheduling ahead of time is done with timers, typically `setTimeout` for a single execution such as this. Because the new request will end up calling the same callback that scheduled it, another one will be scheduled, and we have a continuous polling scheme, even without `setInterval`. Before we can implement this feature we need to understand how we can test timers.

13.1.3 Testing Timers

JsTestDriver does not do asynchronous tests, so we need some other way of testing use of timers. There is basically two ways of working with timers. The obvious approach is stubbing them as we have done with `ajax.request` and `ajax.create` (or in a similar fashion). To stub them easily within tests, stub the `window` object's `setTimeout` property, as seen in Listing 13.14.

Listing 13.14 Stubbing `setTimeout`

```
(function () {
  TestCase("ExampleTestCase", {
    setUp: function () {
      this.setTimeout = window.setTimeout;
    },

    tearDown: function () {
      window.setTimeout = this.setTimeout;
    },

    "test timer example": function () {
      window.setTimeout = stubFn();
      // Setup test

      assert(window.setTimeout.called);
    }
  });
}());
```

JsUnit, although not the most modern testing solution around (as discussed in Chapter 3, *Tools of the Trade*), does bring with it a few gems. One of these is `jsUnitMockTimeout.js`, a simple library to aid testing of timers. Note that although the file is named "mock," the helpers it defines are more in line with what we have been calling stubs.

jsUnitMockTimeout provides a `Clock` object and overrides the native `setTimeout`, `setInterval`, `clearTimeout`, and `clearInterval` functions. When `Clock.tick(ms)` is called, any function scheduled to run sometime within the next ms number of milliseconds will be called. This allows the test to effectively fast-forward time and verify that certain functions were called when scheduled to.

The nice thing about the JsUnit clock implementation is that it makes tests focus more clearly on the expected behavior rather than the actual implementation—do some work, pass some time, and assert that some functions were called. Contrast this to the usual stubbing approach in which we stub the timer, do some work and then assert that the stub was used as expected. Stubbing yields shorter tests, but using the clock yields more communicative tests. We will use the clock to test the poller to get a feel of the difference.

The jsUnitMockTimeout.js can be downloaded off the book's website.[2] Copy it into the project's lib directory.

13.1.3.1 Scheduling New Requests

In order to test that the poller schedules new requests we need to:

- Create a poller with a URL
- Start the poller
- Simulate the first request completing
- Stub the send method over again
- Fast-forward time the desired amount of milliseconds
- Assert that the send method is called a second time (this would have been called while the clock passed time)

To complete the request we will add yet another helper to the fakeXML-HttpRequest object, which sets the HTTP status code to 200 and calls the onreadystatechange handler with ready state 4. Listing 13.15 shows the new method.

Listing 13.15 Adding a helper method to complete request

```
var fakeXMLHttpRequest = {
  /* ... */

  complete: function () {
    this.status = 200;
    this.readyStateChange(4);
  }
};
```

Using this method, Listing 13.16 shows the test following the above requirements.

---

2. http://tddjs.com

Listing 13.16 Expecting a new request to be scheduled upon completion

```
"test should schedule new request when complete":
function () {
  var poller = Object.create(ajax.poller);
  poller.url = "/url";

  poller.start();
  this.xhr.complete();
  this.xhr.send = stubFn();
  Clock.tick(1000);

  assert(this.xhr.send.called);
}
```

The second stub deserves a little explanation. The `ajax.request` method used by the poller creates a new `XMLHttpRequest` object on each request. How can we expect that simply redefining the `send` method on the fake instance will be sufficient? The trick is the `ajax.create` stub—it will be called once for each request, but it always returns the same instance within a single test, which is why this works. In order for the final assert in the above test to succeed, the poller needs to fire a new request asynchronously after the original request finished.

To implement this we need to schedule a new request from within the `complete` callback, as seen in Listing 13.17.

Listing 13.17 Scheduling a new request

```
function start() {
  if (!this.url) {
    throw new TypeError("Must specify URL to poll");
  }

  var poller = this;

  ajax.request(this.url, {
    complete: function () {
      setTimeout(function () {
        poller.start();
      }, 1000);
    }
  });
}
```

Running the tests verifies that this works. Note that the way the test was written will allow it to succeed for any interval smaller than 1,000 milliseconds. If we wanted to ensure that the delay is exactly 1,000, not any value below it, we can write another test that ticks the clock 999 milliseconds and asserts that the callback was not called.

Before we move on we need to inspect the code so far for duplication and other possible refactorings. All the tests are going to need a poller object, and seeing as there is more than one line involved in creating one, we will extract setting up the object to the setUp method, as seen in Listing 13.18.

Listing 13.18 Extracting poller setup

```
setUp: function () {
  /* ... */
  this.poller = Object.create(ajax.poller);
  this.poller.url = "/url";
}
```

Moving common setup to the right place enables us to write simpler tests while still doing the same amount of work. This makes tests easier to read, better at communicating their intent, and less prone to errors—so long as we don't extract too much.

Listing 13.19 shows the test that makes sure we wait the full interval.

Listing 13.19 Making sure the full 1,000ms wait is required

```
"test should not make new request until 1000ms passed":
function () {
  this.poller.start();
  this.xhr.complete();
  this.xhr.send = stubFn();
  Clock.tick(999);

  assertFalse(this.xhr.send.called);
}
```

This test passes immediately, as we already implemented the setTimeout call correctly.

13.1.3.2 Configurable Intervals

The next step is to make the polling interval configurable. Listing 13.20 shows how we expect the poller interface to accept interval configuration.

Listing 13.20 Expecting the request interval to be configurable

```
TestCase("PollerTest", {
  /* ... */

  tearDown: function () {
    ajax.create = this.ajaxCreate;
    Clock.reset();
  },

  /* ... */

  "test should configure request interval":
  function () {
    this.poller.interval = 350;
    this.poller.start();
    this.xhr.complete();
    this.xhr.send = stubFn();

    Clock.tick(349);
    assertFalse(this.xhr.send.called);

    Clock.tick(1);
    assert(this.xhr.send.called);
  }
});
```

This test does a few things different from the previous two tests. First of all, we add the call to `Clock.reset` in the `tearDown` method to avoid tests interfering with each other. Second, this test first skips ahead 349ms, asserts that the new request was *not* issued, then leaps the last millisecond and expects the request to have been made.

We usually try hard to keep each test focused on a single behavior, which is why we rarely make an assertion, exercise the code more, and then make another assertion the way this test does. Normally, I advise against it, but in this case both of the asserts contribute to testing the same behavior—that the new request is issued exactly 350ms after the first request finishes; no less and no more.

Implementing the test is a simple matter of using `poller.interval` if it is a number, falling back to the default 1,000ms, as Listing 13.21 shows.

Listing 13.21 Configurable interval

```
function start() {
  /* ... */
  var interval = 1000;
```

```
  if (typeof this.interval == "number") {
    interval = this.interval;
  }

  ajax.request(this.url, {
    complete: function () {
      setTimeout(function () {
        poller.start();
      }, interval);
    }
  });
}
```

Running the tests once more yields that wonderful green confirmation of success.

13.1.4 Configurable Headers and Callbacks

Before we can consider the poller somewhat complete we need to allow users of the object to set request headers and add callbacks. Let's deal with the headers first. The test in Listing 13.22 inspects the headers passed to the fake XMLHttpRequest object.

Listing 13.22 Expecting headers to be passed to request

```
"test should pass headers to request": function () {
  this.poller.headers = {
    "Header-One": "1",
    "Header-Two": "2"
  };

  this.poller.start();

  var actual = this.xhr.headers;
  var expected = this.poller.headers;
  assertEquals(expected["Header-One"],
               actual["Header-One"]);
  assertEquals(expected["Header-Two"],
               actual["Header-Two"]);
}
```

This test sets two bogus headers, and simply asserts that they were set on the transport (and thus can safely be expected to be sent with the request).

You may sometimes be tempted to skip running the tests before writing the implementation—after all, we *know* they're going to fail, right? While writing this test, I made a typo, accidentally writing `var expected = this.xhr.headers`. It's an easy mistake to make. Running the test right away made me aware that something was amiss as the test was passing. Inspecting it one more time alerted me to the typo. Not running the test before writing the implementation would have made it impossible to discover the error. No matter how we had eventually implemented the headers, as long as it didn't result in an exception or a syntax error, the test would have passed, lulling us into the false illusion that everything is fine. Always run tests after updating either the tests or the implementation!

The implementation in Listing 13.23 is fairly mundane.

Listing 13.23 Passing on the headers

```
function start() {
  /* ... */

  ajax.request(this.url, {
    complete: function () {
      setTimeout(function () {
        poller.start();
      }, interval);
    },

    headers: poller.headers
  });
}
```

Next up, we want to ensure all the callbacks are passed along as well. We'll start with the success callback. To test that it is passed we can use the `complete` method we added to the fake `XMLHttpRequest` object previously. This simulates a successful request, and thus should call the success callback. Listing 13.24 shows the test.

Listing 13.24 Expecting the success callback to be called

```
"test should pass success callback": function () {
  this.poller.success = stubFn();

  this.poller.start();
  this.xhr.complete();

  assert(this.poller.success.called);
}
```

Implementing this is a simple matter of adding another line like the one that passed headers, as seen in Listing 13.25.

Listing 13.25 Passing the success callback

```
ajax.request(this.url, {
  /* ... */

  headers: poller.headers,
  success: poller.success
});
```

In order to check the failure callback the same way, we need to extend the fake `XMLHttpRequest` object. Specifically, we now need to simulate completing a request that failed in addition to the already implemented successful request. To do this we can make `complete` accept an optional HTTP status code argument, as Listing 13.26 shows.

Listing 13.26 Completing requests with any status

```
complete: function (status) {
  this.status = status || 200;
  this.readyStateChange(4);
}
```

Keeping 200 as the default status allows us to make this change without updating or breaking any of the other tests. Now we can write a similar test and implementation to require the failure callback to be passed. The test is listed in Listing 13.27 and implementation in Listing 13.28

Listing 13.27 Expecting the failure callback to be passed

```
"test should pass failure callback": function () {
  this.poller.failure = stubFn();

  this.poller.start();
  this.xhr.complete(400);

  assert(this.poller.failure.called);
}
```

Listing 13.28 Passing the failure callback

```
ajax.request(this.url, {
  /* ... */

  headers: poller.headers,
  success: poller.success,
  failure: poller.failure
});
```

The last thing to check is that the `complete` callback can be used by clients as well. Testing that it is called when the request completes is no different than the previous two tests, so I'll leave doing so as an exercise. The implementation, however, is slightly different, as can be seen in Listing 13.29.

Listing 13.29 Calling the `complete` callback if available

```
ajax.request(this.url, {
  complete: function () {
    setTimeout(function () {
      poller.start();
    }, interval);

    if (typeof poller.complete == "function") {
      poller.complete();
    }
  },

  /* ... */
});
```

13.1.5 The One-Liner

At this point the poller interface is in a usable state. It's very basic, and lacks several aspects before it would be safe for production use. A glaring omission is the lack of request timeouts and a `stop` method, partly because timeouts and `abort` were also missing from the `ajax.request` implementation. Using what you have now learned you should be able to add these, guided by tests, and I urge you to give it a shot. Using these methods the poller could be improved to properly handle problems such as network issues.

As promised in the introduction to this chapter, we will add a simple one-liner interface to go along with `ajax.request`, `ajax.get` and `ajax.post`. It will use the `ajax.poller` object we just built, which means that we can specify its behavior mostly in terms of a stubbed implementation of it.

The first test will assert that an object inheriting from `ajax.poller` is created using `Object.create` and that its `start` method is called, as Listing 13.30 shows.

Listing 13.30 Expecting the `start` method to be called

```
TestCase("PollTest", {
  setUp: function () {
    this.request = ajax.request;
    this.create = Object.create;
    ajax.request = stubFn();
  },

  tearDown: function () {
    ajax.request = this.request;
    Object.create = this.create;
  },

  "test should call start on poller object": function () {
    var poller = { start: stubFn() };
    Object.create = stubFn(poller);

    ajax.poll("/url");

    assert(poller.start.called);
  }
});
```

This test case does the usual setup to stub and recover a few methods. By now, this wasteful duplication should definitely be rubbing you the wrong way. As mentioned in the previous chapter, we will have to live with it for now, as we will introduce better stubbing tools in Chapter 16, *Mocking and Stubbing*.

Apart from the setup, the first test makes sure a new object is created and that its `start` method is called, and the implementation can be seen in Listing 13.31.

Listing 13.31 Creating and starting a poller

```
function poll(url, options) {
  var poller = Object.create(ajax.poller);
  poller.start();
}

ajax.poll = poll;
```

Next up, Listing 13.32 makes sure the url property is set on the poller. In order to make this assertion we need a reference to the poller object, so the method will need to return it.

Listing 13.32 Expecting the url property to be set

```
"test should set url property on poller object":
function () {
  var poller = ajax.poll("/url");

  assertSame("/url", poller.url);
}
```

Implementing this test requires two additional lines, as in Listing 13.33.

Listing 13.33 Setting the URL

```
function poll(url, options) {
  var poller = Object.create(ajax.poller);
  poller.url = url;
  poller.start();

  return poller;
}
```

The remaining tests will simply check that the headers, callbacks, and interval are set properly on the poller. Doing so closely resembles what we just did with the underlying poller interface, so I'll leave writing the tests as an exercise.

Listing 13.34 shows the final version of ajax.poll.

Listing 13.34 Final version of ajax.poll

```
function poll(url, options) {
  var poller = Object.create(ajax.poller);
  poller.url = url;
  options = options || {};
  poller.headers = options.headers;
  poller.success = options.success;
  poller.failure = options.failure;
  poller.complete = options.complete;
  poller.interval = options.interval;
  poller.start();

  return poller;
}

ajax.poll = poll;
```

13.2 Comet

Polling will definitely help move an application in the general direction of "live" by making a more continuous data stream from the server to the client possible. However, this simple model has two major drawbacks:

- Polling too infrequently yields high latency.
- Polling too frequently yields too much server load, which may be unnecessary if few requests actually bring back data.

In systems requiring very low latency, such as instant messaging, polling to keep a constant data flow could easily mean hammering servers frequently enough to make the constant requests a scalability issue. When the traditional polling strategy becomes a problem, we need to consider alternative options.

Comet, Ajax Push, and *Reverse Ajax* are all umbrella terms for various ways to implement web applications such that the server is effectively able to push data to the client at any given time. The straightforward polling mechanism we just built is possibly the simplest way to do this—if it can be defined as a Comet implementation—but as we have just seen, it yields high latency or poor scalability.

There are a multitude of ways to implement live data streams, and shortly we will take a shot at one of them. Before we dive back into code, I want to quickly discuss a few of the options.

13.2.1 Forever Frames

One technique that works without even requiring the `XMLHttpRequest` object is so-called "forever frames." A hidden iframe is used to request a resource from the server. This request never finishes, and the server uses it to push script tags to the page whenever new events occur. Because HTML documents are loaded and parsed incrementally, new script blocks will be executed when the browser receives them, even if the whole page hasn't loaded yet. Usually the script tag ends with a call to a globally defined function that will receive data, possibly implemented as JSON-P ("JSON with padding").

The iframe solution has a few problems. The biggest one is lack of error handling. Because the connection is not controlled by code, there is little we can do if something goes wrong. Another issue that can be worked around is browser loading indicators. Because the frame never finishes loading, some browsers will (rightfully so) indicate to the user that the page is still loading. This is usually not a desirable feature, seeing as the data stream should be a background progress the user doesn't need to consider.

The forever frame approach effectively allows for true streaming of data and only uses a single connection.

13.2.2 Streaming XMLHttpRequest

Similar streaming to that of the forever frames is possible using the XMLHttp-Request object. By keeping the connection open and flushing whenever new data is available, the server can push a multipart response to the client, which enables it to receive chunks of data several times over the same connection. Not all browsers support the required multipart responses, meaning that this approach cannot be easily implemented in a cross-browser manner.

13.2.3 HTML5

HTML5 provides a couple of new ways to improve server-client communication. One alternative is the new element, eventsource, which can be used to listen to server-side events rather effortlessly. The element is provided with a src attribute and an onmessage event handler. Browser support is still scarce.

Another important API in the HTML5 specification is the WebSocket API. Once widely supported, any solution using separate connections to fetch and update data will be mostly superfluous. Web sockets offer a full-duplex communications channel, which can be held open for as long as required and allows true streaming of data between client and server with proper error handling.

13.3 Long Polling XMLHttpRequest

Our Comet implementation will use XMLHttpRequest long polling. Long polling is an improved polling mechanism not very different from the one we have already implemented. In long polling the client makes a request and the server keeps the connection open until it has new data, at which point it returns the data and closes the connection. The client then immediately opens a new connection and waits for more data. This model vastly improves communication in those cases in which the client needs data as soon as they're available, yet data does not appear too often. If new data appear very often, the long polling method performs like regular polling, and could possibly be subject to the same failing, in which clients poll too intensively.

Implementing the client side of long polling is easy. Whether or not we are using regular or long polling is decided by the behavior of the server, wherein implementation is less trivial, at least with traditional threaded servers. For these, such as Apache, long polling does not work well. The one thread-per-connection model does not scale with long polling, because every client keeps a near-consistent connection. Evented server architecture is much more apt to deal with these situations, and allows minimal overhead. We'll take a closer look at the server-side in Chapter 14, *Server-Side JavaScript with Node.js.*

13.3.1 Implementing Long Polling Support

We will use what we have learned to add long polling support to our poller without requiring a long timeout between requests. The goal of long polling is low latency, and as such we would like to eliminate the timeout, at least in its current state. However, because frequent events may cause the client to make too frequent requests, we need a way to throttle requests in the extreme cases.

The solution is to modify the way we use the timeout. Rather than timing out the desired amount of milliseconds between requests, we will count elapsed time from each started request and make sure requests are never fired too close to each other.

13.3.1.1 Stubbing `Date`

To test this feature we will need to fake the `Date` constructor. As with measuring performance, we're going to use a `new Date()` to keep track of elapsed time. To fake this in tests, we will use a simple helper. The helper accepts a single date object, and overrides the `Date` constructor. The next time the constructor is used, the fake object is returned and the native constructor is restored. The helper lives in `lib/stub.js` and can be seen in Listing 13.35.

Listing 13.35 Stubbing the `Date` constructor for fixed output

```
(function (global) {
  var NativeDate = global.Date;

  global.stubDateConstructor = function (fakeDate) {
    global.Date = function () {
      global.Date = NativeDate;
      return fakeDate;
    };
  };
}(this));
```

This helper contains enough logic that it should not be simply dropped into the project without tests. Testing the helper is left as an exercise.

13.3.1.2 Testing with Stubbed Dates

Now that we have a way of faking time, we can formulate the test that expects new requests to be made immediately if the minimum interval has passed since the last request was issued. Listing 13.36 shows the test.

Listing 13.36 Expecting long-running request to immediately re-connect upon completion

```
TestCase("PollerTest", {
  setUp: function () {
    /* ... */
    this.ajaxRequest = ajax.request;
    /* ... */
  },

  tearDown: function () {
    ajax.request = this.ajaxRequest;
    /* ... */
  },

  /* ... */

  "test should re-request immediately after long request":
  function () {
    this.poller.interval = 500;
    this.poller.start();
    var ahead = new Date().getTime() + 600;
    stubDateConstructor(new Date(ahead));
    ajax.request = stubFn();

    this.xhr.complete();

    assert(ajax.request.called);
  }
});
```

The test sets up the poller interval to 500ms, and proceeds to simulate a request lasting for 600ms. It does this by making `new Date` return an object 600ms into the future, and then uses `this.xhr.complete()` to complete the fake request. Once this happens, the minimum interval has elapsed since the previous request started and so we expect a new request to have fired immediately. The test fails and Listing 13.37 shows how to pass it.

Listing 13.37 Using the interval as minimum interval between started requests

```
function start() {
  /* ... */
  var requestStart = new Date().getTime();

  ajax.request(this.url, {
    complete: function () {
      var elapsed = new Date().getTime() - requestStart;
      var remaining = interval - elapsed;

      setTimeout(function () {
        poller.start();
      }, Math.max(0, remaining));
      /* ... */
    },

    /* ... */
  });
}
```

Running the tests, somewhat surprisingly, reveals that the test still fails. The clue is the setTimeout call. Note that even if the required interval is 0, we make the next request through setTimeout, which never executes synchronously.

One benefit of this approach is that we avoid deep call stacks. Using an asynchronous call to schedule the next request means that the current request call exits immediately, and we avoid making new requests recursively. However, this cleverness is also what is causing us trouble. The test assumes that the new request is scheduled immediately, which it isn't. We need to "touch" the clock inside the test in order to have it fire queued timers that are ready to run. Listing 13.38 shows the updated test.

Listing 13.38 Touching the clock to fire ready timers

```
"test should re-request immediately after long request":
function () {
  this.poller.interval = 500;
  this.poller.start();
  var ahead = new Date().getTime() + 600;
  stubDateConstructor(new Date(ahead));
```

```
  ajax.request = stubFn();

  this.xhr.complete();
  Clock.tick(0);

  assert(ajax.request.called);
}
```

And that's it. The poller now supports long polling with an optional minimal interval between new requests to the server. The poller could be further extended to support another option to set minimum grace period between requests, regardless of the time any given request takes. This would increase latency, but could help a stressed system.

13.3.2 Avoiding Cache Issues

One possible challenge with the current implementation of the poller is that of caching. Polling is typically used when we need to stream fresh data off the server, and having the browser cache responses is likely to cause trouble. Caching can be controlled from the server via response headers, but sometimes we don't control the server implementation. In the interest of making the poller as generally useful as possible, we will extend it to add some random fuzz to the URL, which effectively avoids caching.

To test the cache buster, we simply expect the open method of the transport to be called with the URL including a timestamp, as seen in Listing 13.39.

Listing 13.39 Expecting poller to add cache buster to URL

```
"test should add cache buster to URL": function () {
  var date = new Date();
  var ts = date.getTime();
  stubDateConstructor(date);
  this.poller.url = "/url";

  this.poller.start();

  assertEquals("/url?" + ts, this.xhr.open.args[1]);
}
```

To pass this test, Listing 13.40 simply adds the date it is already recording to the URL when making a request.

Listing 13.40 Adding a cache buster

```
function start() {
  /* ... */

  var requestStart = new Date().getTime();

  /* ... */

  ajax.request(this.url + "?" + requestStart, {
    /* ... */
  });
}
```

Although the cache buster test passes, the test from Listing 13.11 now fails because it is expecting the unmodified URL to be used. The URL is now being tested in a dedicated test, and the URL comparison in the original test can be removed.

As we discussed in the previous chapter, adding query parameters to arbitrary URLs such as here will break if the URL already includes query parameters. Testing for such a URL and updating the implementation is left as an exercise.

13.3.3 Feature Tests

As we did with the `request` interface, we will guard the poller with feature detection, making sure we don't define the interface if it cannot be successfully used. Listing 13.41 shows the required tests.

Listing 13.41 Poller feature tests

```
(function () {
  if (typeof tddjs == "undefined") {
    return;
  }

  var ajax = tddjs.namespace("ajax");

  if (!ajax.request || !Object.create) {
    return;
  }

  /* ... */
}());
```

13.4 The Comet Client

Although long polling offers good latency and near-constant connections, it also comes with limitations. The most serious limitation is that of number of concurrent http connections to any given host in most browsers. Older browsers ship with a maximum of 2 concurrent connections by default (even though it can be changed by the user), whereas newer browsers can default to as many as 8. In any case, the connection limit is important. If you deploy an interface that uses long polling and a user opens the interface in two tabs, he will wait indefinitely for the third tab—no HTML, images, or CSS can be downloaded at all, because the poller is currently using the 2 available connections. Add the fact that XMLHttpRequest cannot be used for cross-domain requests, and you have a potential problem on your hands.

This means that long polling should be used consciously. It also means that keeping more than a single long polling connection in a single page is not a viable approach. To reliably handle data from multiple sources, we need to pipe all messages from the server through the same connection, and use a client that can help delegate the data.

In this section we will implement a client that acts as a proxy for the server. It will poll a given URL for data and allow JavaScript objects to observe different topics. Whenever data arrive from the server, the client extracts messages by topic and notifies respective observers. This way, we can limit ourselves to a single connection, yet still receive messages relating to a wide range of topics.

The client will use the observable object developed in Chapter 11, *The Observer Pattern,* to handle observers and the ajax.poll interface we just implemented to handle the server connection. In other words, the client is a thin piece of glue to simplify working with server-side events.

13.4.1 Messaging Format

For this example we will keep the messaging format used between the server and the client very simple. We want client-side objects to be able to observe a single topic, much like the observable objects did, and be called with a single object as argument every time new data is available. The simplest solution to this problem seems to be to send JSON data from the server. Each response sends back an object whose property names are topics, and their values are arrays of data related to that topic. Listing 13.42 shows an example response from the server.

Listing 13.42 Typical JSON response from server

```
{
  "chatMessage": [{
    "id": "38912",
    "from": "chris",
    "to": "",
    "body": "Some text ...",
    "sent_at": "2010-02-21T21:23:43.687Z"
  }, {
    "id": "38913",
    "from": "lebowski",
    "to": "",
    "body": "More text ...",
    "sent_at": "2010-02-21T21:23:47.970Z"
  }],

  "stock": { /* ... */ },
  /* ... */
}
```

Observers could possibly be interested in new stock prices, so they would show their interest through `client.observe("stock", fn);` Others may be more interested in the chat messages coming through. I'm not sure what kind of site would provide both stock tickers and real-time chat on the same page, but surely in this crazy Web 2.0 day and age, such a site exists. The point being, the data from the server may be of a diverse nature because a single connection is used for all streaming needs.

The client will provide a consistent interface by doing two things. First, it allows observers to observe a single topic rather than the entire feed. Second, it will call each observer once per message on that topic. This means that in the above example, observers to the "chatMessage" topic will be called twice, once for each chat message.

The client interface will look and behave exactly like the observables developed in Chapter 11, *The Observer Pattern*. This way code using the client does not need to be aware of the fact that data is fetched from and sent to a server. Furthermore, having two identical interfaces means that we can use a regular `observable` in tests for code using the client without having to stub `XMLHttpRequest` to avoid going to the server in tests.

13.4.2 Introducing `ajax.cometClient`

As usual we'll start out real simple, asserting that the object in question exists. `ajax.cometClient` seems like a reasonable name, and Listing 13.43 tests for its existence. The test lives in the new file `test/comet-client-test.js`.

Listing 13.43 Expecting `ajax.cometClient` to exist

```
(function () {
  var ajax = tddjs.ajax;

  TestCase("CometClientTest", {
    "test should be object": function () {
      assertObject(ajax.cometClient);
    }
  });
}());
```

Implementation is a matter of initial file setup as per usual, seen in Listing 13.44.

Listing 13.44 Setting up the `comet-client.js` file

```
(function () {
  var ajax = tddjs.namespace("ajax");

  ajax.cometClient = {};
}());
```

13.4.3 Dispatching Data

When an observer is added, we expect it to be called when data is dispatched from the client. Although we could write tests to dictate the internals of the `observe` method, those would be needlessly implementation specific, without describing the expected behavior very well. Besides, we are going to use the `observable` object to handle observers and we don't want to replicate the entire `observable` test case for the client's `observe` method.

We will start by implementing `dispatch`, which later can help us verify the behavior of `observe`. Dispatching is the act of breaking up data received from the server and sending it out to observers.

13.4.3.1 Adding `ajax.cometClient.dispatch`

The first test for dispatching data is simply asserting that a method exists, as Listing 13.45 shows.

Listing 13.45 Expecting `dispatch` to exist

```
"test should have dispatch method": function () {
  var client = Object.create(ajax.cometClient);

  assertFunction(client.dispatch);
}
```

This test fails, so Listing 13.46 adds it in.

Listing 13.46 Adding the `dispatch` method

```
function dispatch() {
}

ajax.cometClient = {
  dispatch: dispatch
};
```

13.4.3.2 Delegating Data

Next, we're going to feed `dispatch` an object, and make sure it pushes data out to observers. However, we haven't written `observe` yet, which means that if we now write a test that requires both methods to work correctly, we're in trouble if either fail. Failing unit tests should give a clear indication of where a problem occurred, and using two methods to verify each other's behavior is not a good idea when none of them exist. Instead, we will leverage the fact that we're going to use `observable` to implement both of these. Listing 13.47 expects `dispatch` to call `notify` on the observable `observers` object.

Listing 13.47 Expecting `dispatch` to `notify`

```
"test dispatch should notify observers": function () {
  var client = Object.create(ajax.cometClient);
  client.observers = { notify: stubFn() };

  client.dispatch({ someEvent: [{ id: 1234 }] });

  var args = client.observers.notify.args;
```

```
    assert(client.observers.notify.called);
    assertEquals("someEvent", args[0]);
    assertEquals({ id: 1234 }, args[1]);
}
```

The simple data object in this test conforms to the format we specified in the introduction. To pass this test we need to loop the properties of the data object, and then loop each topic's events and pass them to the observers, one by one. Listing 13.48 takes the job.

Listing 13.48 Dispatching data

```
function dispatch(data) {
  var observers = this.observers;

  tddjs.each(data, function (topic, events) {
    for (var i = 0, l = events.length; i < l; i++) {
      observers.notify(topic, events[i]);
    }
  });
}
```

The test passes, but this method clearly makes a fair share of assumptions; thus, it can easily break in lots of situations. We'll harden the implementation through a series of small tests for discrepancies.

13.4.3.3 Improved Error Handling

Listing 13.49 asserts that it doesn't break if there are no observers.

Listing 13.49 What happens if there are no observers?

```
TestCase("CometClientDispatchTest", {
  setUp: function () {
    this.client = Object.create(ajax.cometClient);
  },

  /* ... */

  "test should not throw if no observers": function () {
    this.client.observers = null;

    assertNoException(function () {
      this.client.dispatch({ someEvent: [{}] });
    }.bind(this));
  },
```

```
"test should not throw if notify undefined": function () {
  this.client.observers = {};

  assertNoException(function () {
    this.client.dispatch({ someEvent: [{}] });
  }.bind(this));
}
});
```

All the dispatch tests are now grouped inside their own test case. The test case adds two new tests: one that checks that `dispatch` can deal with the case in which there is no `observers` object, and another in which the `observers` object has been tampered with. The latter test is there simply because the object is public and could possibly be mangled. Both tests fail, so Listing 13.50 hardens the implementation.

Listing 13.50 Being careful with observers

```
function dispatch(data) {
  var observers = this.observers;

  if (!observers || typeof observers.notify != "function") {
    return;
  }

  /* ... */
}
```

Next up, we go a little easier on the assumptions on the data structure the method receives. Listing 13.51 adds two tests that tries (successfully, for now) to overthrow `dispatch` by feeding it bad data.

Listing 13.51 Testing `dispatch` with bad data

```
TestCase("CometClientDispatchTest", {
  setUp: function () {
    this.client = Object.create(ajax.cometClient);
    this.client.observers = { notify: stubFn() };
  },

  /* ... */

  "test should not throw if data is not provided":
  function () {
```

```
  assertNoException(function () {
    this.client.dispatch();
  }.bind(this));
},

"test should not throw if event is null": function () {
  assertNoException(function () {
    this.client.dispatch({ myEvent: null });
  }.bind(this));
  }
});
```

Running the tests somewhat surprisingly reveals that only the last test fails. The tddjs.each method that is used for looping was built to handle input not suitable for looping, so dispatch can already handle null and a missing data argument. To pass the last test, we need to be a little more careful in the loop over event objects, as seen in Listing 13.52.

Listing 13.52 Carefully looping event data

```
function dispatch(data) {
  /* ... */

  tddjs.each(data, function (topic, events) {
    var length = events && events.length;

    for (var i = 0; i < length; i++) {
      observers.notify(topic, events[i]);
    }
  });
}
```

In order to make the dispatch test case complete, we should add some tests that make sure that notify is really called for all topics in data, and that all events are passed to observers of a topic. I'll leave doing so as an exercise.

13.4.4 Adding Observers

With a functional dispatch we have what we need to test the observe method. Listing 13.53 shows a simple test that expects that observers to be called when data is available.

Listing 13.53 Testing observers

```
TestCase("CometClientObserveTest", {
  setUp: function () {
    this.client = Object.create(ajax.cometClient);
  },

  "test should remember observers": function () {
    var observers = [stubFn(), stubFn()];
    this.client.observe("myEvent", observers[0]);
    this.client.observe("myEvent", observers[1]);
    var data = { myEvent: [{}] };

    this.client.dispatch(data);

    assert(observers[0].called);
    assertSame(data.myEvent[0], observers[0].args[0]);
    assert(observers[1].called);
    assertSame(data.myEvent[0], observers[1].args[0]);
  }
});
```

observe is still an empty method, so this test fails. Listing 13.54 pieces in the missing link. For this to work you need to save the observable implementation from Chapter 11, *The Observer Pattern,* in lib/observable.js.

Listing 13.54 Remembering observers

```
(function () {
  var ajax = tddjs.ajax;
  var util = tddjs.util;

  /* ... */

  function observe(topic, observer) {
    if (!this.observers) {
      this.observers = Object.create(util.observable);
    }

    this.observers.observe(topic, observer);
  }

  ajax.cometClient = {
    dispatch: dispatch,
    observe: observe
  };
});
```

The tests now all pass. The observe method could probably benefit from type checking this.observers.observe like we did with notify in dispatch. You might also have noticed that there are no tests asserting what happens if either topic or events is not what we expect it to be. I urge you to cover those paths as an exercise.

Both topic and observer are actually checked for us by observable. observe, but relying on it ties the client more tightly to its dependencies. Besides, it's generally not considered best practice to allow exceptions to bubble a long way through a library, because it yields stack traces that are hard to debug for a developer using our code.

13.4.5 Server Connection

So far, all we have really done is to wrap an observable for a given data format. It's time to move on to connecting to the server and making it pass response data to the dispatch method. The first thing we need to do is to obtain a connection, as Listing 13.55 specifies.

Listing 13.55 Expecting connect to obtain a connection

```
TestCase("CometClientConnectTest", {
  setUp: function () {
    this.client = Object.create(ajax.cometClient);
    this.ajaxPoll = ajax.poll;
  },

  tearDown: function () {
    ajax.poll = this.ajaxPoll;
  },

  "test connect should start polling": function () {
    this.client.url = "/my/url";
    ajax.poll = stubFn({});

    this.client.connect();

    assert(ajax.poll.called);
    assertEquals("/my/url", ajax.poll.args[0]);
  }
});
```

In this test we no longer use the fake XMLHttpRequest object, because the semantics of ajax.poll better describes the expected behavior. Asserting that the method started polling in terms of fakeXMLHttpRequest would basically mean duplicating ajax.poll's test case.

The test fails because connect is not a method. We will add it along with the call to ajax.poll in one go, as seen in Listing 13.56.

Listing 13.56 Connecting by calling ajax.poll

```
(function () {
  /* ... */

  function connect() {
    ajax.poll(this.url);
  }

  ajax.cometClient = {
    connect: connect,
    dispatch: dispatch,
    observe: observe
  }
});
```

What happens if we call connect when the client is already connected? From the looks of things, more polling. Listing 13.57 asserts that only one connection is made.

Listing 13.57 Verifying that ajax.poll is only called once

```
"test should not connect if connected": function () {
  this.client.url = "/my/url";
  ajax.poll = stubFn({});
  this.client.connect();
  ajax.poll = stubFn({});

  this.client.connect();

  assertFalse(ajax.poll.called);
}
```

To pass this test we need to keep a reference to the poller, and only connect if this reference does not exist, as Listing 13.58 shows.

Listing 13.58 Only connect once

```
function connect() {
  if (!this.poller) {
    this.poller = ajax.poll(this.url);
  }
}
```

Listing 13.59 tests for a missing `url` property.

Listing 13.59 Expecting missing URL to cause an exception

```
"test connect should throw error if no url exists":
function () {
  var client = Object.create(ajax.cometClient);
  ajax.poll = stubFn({});

  assertException(function () {
    client.connect();
  }, "TypeError");
}
```

Passing this test is three lines of code away, as seen in Listing 13.60.

Listing 13.60 Throwing an exception if there is no URL

```
function connect() {
  if (!this.url) {
    throw new TypeError("client url is null");
  }

  if (!this.poller) {
    this.poller = ajax.poll(this.url);
  }
}
```

The final missing piece is the success handler that should call `dispatch` with the returned data. The resulting data will be a string of JSON data, which needs to be passed to `dispatch` as an object. To test this we will use the `fakeXML-HttpRequest` object once again, to simulate a completed request that returns with some JSON data. Listing 13.61 updates the `fakeXMLHttpRequest.complete` method to accept an optional response text argument.

Listing 13.61 Accepting response data in `complete`

```
var fakeXMLHttpRequest = {
  /* ... */

  complete: function (status, responseText) {
    this.status = status || 200;
    this.responseText = responseText;
    this.readyStateChange(4);
  }
}
```

Listing 13.62 shows the test, which uses the updated `complete` method.

Listing 13.62 Expecting client to dispatch data

```
TestCase("CometClientConnectTest", {
  setUp: function () {
    /* ... */
    this.ajaxCreate = ajax.create;
    this.xhr = Object.create(fakeXMLHttpRequest);
    ajax.create = stubFn(this.xhr);
  },

  tearDown: function () {
    /* ... */
    ajax.create = this.ajaxCreate;
  },

  /* ... */

  "test should dispatch data from request": function () {
    var data = { topic: [{ id: "1234" }],
                 otherTopic: [{ name: "Me" }] };
    this.client.url = "/my/url";
    this.client.dispatch = stubFn();

    this.client.connect();
    this.xhr.complete(200, JSON.stringify(data));

    assert(this.client.dispatch.called);
    assertEquals(data, this.client.dispatch.args[0]);
  }
});
```

The test fails as `dispatch` was not called. To fix this we need to parse the `responseText` as JSON and call the method from within the success callback of the request. A very naive implementation can be seen in Listing 13.63.

Listing 13.63 Naive success callback to the poller

```
function connect() {
  if (!this.url) {
    throw new TypeError("Provide client URL");
  }

  if (!this.poller) {
    this.poller = ajax.poll(this.url, {
      success: function (xhr) {
        this.dispatch(JSON.parse(xhr.responseText));
      }.bind(this)
    });
  }
}
```

At this point I am expecting this test to still fail in at least a few browsers. As we discussed in Chapter 8, *ECMAScript 5th Edition,* EcmaScript5 specifies a `JSON` object. However, it is not yet widely implemented, least of all in older browsers such as Internet Explorer 6. Still, the tests pass. What's happening is that JsTestDriver is already using Douglas Crockford's JSON parser internally, and because it does not namespace its dependencies in the test runner, our test accidentally works because the environment loads our dependencies for us. Hopefully, this issue with JsTest-Driver will be worked out, but until then, we need to keep this in the back of our heads. The proper solution is of course to add, e.g., `json2.js` from json.org in `lib/`.

I mentioned that the above implementation was naive. A successful response from the server does not imply valid JSON. What do you suppose happens when the test in Listing 13.64 runs?

Listing 13.64 Expecting badly formed data not to be dispatched

```
"test should not dispatch badly formed data": function () {
  this.client.url = "/my/url";
  this.client.dispatch = stubFn();

  this.client.connect();
```

```
this.xhr.complete(200, "OK");

assertFalse(this.client.dispatch.called);
}
```

Furthermore, if we expect the server to return JSON data, it would probably be a good idea to indicate as much by sending the right `Accept` header with the request.

13.4.5.1 Separating Concerns

The current implementation has a code smell—something that doesn't feel quite right. JSON parsing doesn't really belong inside a Comet client; its responsibilities are delegating server-side events to client-side observers and publishing client-side events to the server. Ideally the transport would handle correct encoding of data. As I've mentioned more than a few times already, the `ajax.request` should be refactored such that it provides an object that can be extended. This would have allowed us to extend it to provide a custom request object specifically for JSON requests, seeing as that is quite a common case. Using such an API, the `connect` method could look something like Listing 13.65, which is a lot leaner.

Listing 13.65 Using tailored JSON requests

```
function connect() {
  if (!this.url) {
    throw new TypeError("Provide client URL");
  }

  if (!this.poller) {
    this.poller = ajax.json.poll(this.url, {
      success: function (jsonData) {
        this.dispatch(jsonData);
      }.bind(this)
    });
  }
}
```

Granted, such a poller could be provided with the current implementation of `ajax.request` and `ajax.poll`, but parsing JSON belongs in `ajax.poll` as little as it does in `ajax.cometClient`.

13.4.6 Tracking Requests and Received Data

When polling, we need to know what data to retrieve on each request. With long polling, the client polls the server; the server keeps the connection until new data is available, passes it, and closes. Even if the client immediately makes another request, there is a risk of loosing data between requests. This situation gets even worse with normal polling. How will the server know what data to send back on a given request?

To be sure all the data makes it to the client, we need a token to track requests. Ideally, the server should not need to keep track of its clients. When polling a single source of data, such as "tweets" on Twitter, a reasonable token could be the unique id of the last tweet received by the client. The client sends the id with each request, instructing the server to respond with any newer tweets.

In the case of the Comet client, we expect it to handle all kinds of data streams, and unless the server uses some kind of universally unique id, we cannot rely on the id token. Another possibility is to have the client pass along a timestamp indicating when the previous request finished. In other words, the client asks the server to respond with all data that was created since the last request finished. This approach has a major disadvantage; it assumes that the client and server are in sync, possibly down to millisecond granularity and beyond. Such an approach is so fragile it cannot even be expected to work reliably with clients in the same time zone.

An alternative solution is to have the server return a token with each response. The kind of token can be decided by the server, all the client needs to do is to include it in the following request. This model works well with both the id and timestamp approaches as well as others. The client doesn't even know what the token represents.

To include the token in the request, a custom request header or a URL parameter are both good choices. We will make the Comet client pass it along as a request header, called `X-Access-Token`. The server will respond with data guaranteed to be newer than data represented by the token.

Listing 13.66 expects the custom header to be provided.

Listing 13.66 Expecting the custom header to be set

```
"test should provide custom header": function () {
  this.client.connect();

  assertNotUndefined(this.xhr.headers["X-Access-Token"]);
}
```

This test fails as expected, and the implementation can be seen in Listing 13.67.

Listing 13.67 Adding a custom header

```
function connect() {
  /* ... */

  if (!this.poller) {
    this.poller = ajax.poll(this.url, {
      /* ... */

      headers: {
        "Content-Type": "application/json",
        "X-Access-Token": ""
      }
    });
  }
}
```

For the first request the token will be blank. In a more sophisticated implementation the initial token could possibly be set manually, e.g., by reading it from a cookie or local database to allow a user to pick up where she left off.

Sending blank tokens on every request doesn't really help us track requests. The next test, shown in Listing 13.68, expects that the token returned from the server is sent on the following request.

Listing 13.68 Expecting the received token to be passed on second request

```
tearDown: function () {
  /* ... */
  Clock.reset();
},

/* ... */

"test should pass token on following request":
function () {
  this.client.connect();
  var data = { token: 1267482145219 };

  this.xhr.complete(200, JSON.stringify(data));
  Clock.tick(1000);

  var headers = this.xhr.headers;
  assertEquals(data.token, headers["X-Access-Token"]);
}
```

This test simulates a successful request with a JSON response that includes only the token. After completing the request, the clock is ticked 1,000 milliseconds ahead to trigger a new request, and for this request we expect the token header to be sent with the received token. The test fails as expected; the token is still the blank string.

Note that because we didn't make it possible to configure the polling interval through the client, we cannot set the polling interval explicitly in the test. This makes the `Clock.tick(1000)` something of a magical incantation, as it is not obvious why it is ticked exactly 1,000 milliseconds ahead. The client should have a way to set the poller interval, and when it does, this test should be updated for clarity.

To pass this test we need a reference to the `headers` object so we can change it after each request. Listing 13.69 shows the implementation.

Listing 13.69 Updating the request header upon request completion

```
function connect() {
  /* ... */

  var headers = {
    "Content-Type": "application/json",
    "X-Access-Token": ""
  };

  if (!this.poller) {
    this.poller = ajax.poll(this.url, {
      success: function (xhr) {
        try {
          var data = JSON.parse(xhr.responseText);
          headers["X-Access-Token"] = data.token;
          this.dispatch(data);
        } catch (e) {}
      }.bind(this),

      headers: headers
    });
  }
}
```

With this implementation in place the test passes, yet we are not done. If, for some reason, the server fails to deliver a token in response to a request, we should not blatantly overwrite the token we already have with a blank one, losing track of our progress. Also, we do not need to send the token to the `dispatch` method.

Are there other cases related to the request token that should be tested? Think it over, write tests, and update the implementation to fit.

13.4.7 Publishing Data

The Comet client also needs a `notify` method. As an exercise, try to use TDD to implement this method according to these requirements:

- The signature should be `client.notify(topic, data)`
- The method should POST to `client.url`
- The data should be sent as an object with properties `topic` and `data`

What `Content-Type` will you send the request with? Will the choice of `Content-Type` affect the body of the request?

13.4.8 Feature Tests

The `cometClient` object only depends directly on `observable` and the poller, so adding feature tests to allow it to fail gracefully is fairly simple, as seen in Listing 13.70.

Listing 13.70 Comet client feature tests

```
(function () {
  if (typeof tddjs == "undefined") {
    return;
  }

  var ajax = tddjs.namespace("ajax");
  var util = tddjs.namespace("util");

  if (!ajax.poll || !util.observable) {
    return;
  }

  /* ... */
}());
```

13.5 Summary

In this chapter we have built on top of the ajax methods developed in Chapter 12, *Abstracting Browser Differences: Ajax,* and implemented polling, the client side of long polling and finally a simple Comet client that leveraged the `observable` object developed in Chapter 11, *The Observer Pattern.* The main focus has, as usual, been on the testing and how to properly use the tests to instruct us as we dig deeper and deeper. Still, we have been able to get a cursory look at technologies collectively referred to as Comet, Reverse Ajax, and others.

In the previous chapter we introduced and worked closely with stubs. In this chapter we developed the poller slightly differently by not stubbing its immediate dependency. The result yields less implementation specific tests at the cost of making them mini integration tests.

This chapter also gave an example on how to stub and test timers and the `Date` constructor. Having used the `Clock` object to fake time, we have seen how it would be useful if the `Date` constructor could somehow be synced with it to more effectively fake time in tests.

This chapter concludes our client-side library development for now. The next chapter will use test-driven development to implement the server-side of a long polling application using the `node.js` framework.

Server-Side JavaScript
with Node.js

Netscape pushed JavaScript on the server way back in 1996. Since then, several others have tried to do the same, yet none of these projects have made a big impact on the developer community. That is, until 2009, when Ryan Dahl released the Node.js runtime. At the same time, CommonJS, an attempt at a standard library specification for JavaScript, is rapidly gaining attention and involvement from several server-side JavaScript library authors and users alike. Server-side JavaScript is happening, and it's going to be big.

In this chapter we will use test-driven development to develop a small server-side application using Node. Through this exercise we'll get to know Node and its conventions, work with JavaScript in a more predictable environment than browsers, and draw from our experience with TDD and evented programming from previous chapters to produce the backend of an in-browser chat application that we will finish in the next chapter.

14.1 The Node.js Runtime

Node.js—"Evented I/O for V8 JavaScript"—is an evented server-side JavaScript runtime implemented on top of Google's V8 engine, the same engine that powers Google Chrome. Node uses an event loop and consists almost entirely of asynchronous non-blocking API's, making it a good fit for streaming applications such as those built using Comet or WebSockets.

As we discussed in Chapter 13, *Streaming Data with Ajax and Comet,* web servers that allocate one thread per connection, such as Apache httpd, do not scale well in terms of concurrency. Even more so when concurrent connections are long lived.

When Node receives a request, it will start listening for certain events, such as data ready from a database, the file system, or a network service. It then goes to sleep. Once the data is ready, events notify the request, which then finishes the connection. This is all seamlessly handled by Node's event loop.

JavaScript developers should feel right at home in Node's evented world. After all, the browser is evented too, and most JavaScript code is triggered by events. Just take a look at the code we've developed throughout this book. In Chapter 10, *Feature Detection,* we wrote a cross browser way to assign event handlers to DOM elements; in Chapter 11, *The Observer Pattern,* we wrote a library to observe events on any JavaScript object; and in Chapter 12, *Abstracting Browser Differences: Ajax* and Chapter 13, *Streaming Data with Ajax and Comet,* we used callbacks to asynchronously fetch data from the server.

14.1.1 Setting up the Environment

Setting up Node is pretty straightforward, unless you're on Windows. Unfortunately, at the time of writing, Node does not run on Windows. It is possible to get it running in Cygwin with some effort, but I think the easiest approach for Windows users is to download and install the free virtualization software VirtualBox[1] and run, e.g., Ubuntu Linux[2] inside it. To install Node, download the source from http://nodejs.org and follow instructions.

14.1.1.1 Directory Structure

The project directory structure can be seen in Listing 14.1.

Listing 14.1 Initial directory structure

```
chris@laptop:~/projects/chapp$ tree
.
|-- deps
|-- lib
|   '-- chapp
'-- test
    '-- chapp
```

---

1. http://www.virtualbox.org/
2. http://www.ubuntu.com/

I named the project "chapp," as in "chat app." The `deps` directory is for third party dependencies; the other two should be self-explanatory.

14.1.1.2   Testing Framework

Node has a CommonJS compliant Assert module, but in line with the low-level focus of Node, it only provides a few assertions. No test runner, no test cases, and no high-level testing utilities; just the bare knuckles assertions, enabling framework authors to build their own.

For this chapter we will be using a version of a small testing framework called Nodeunit. Nodeunit was originally designed to look like QUnit, jQuery's unit testing framework. I have added some bells and whistles to it to bring it slightly closer to JsTestDriver in style, so testing with it should look familiar.

The version of Nodeunit used for this chapter can be downloaded from the book's website,[3] and should live in `deps/nodeunit`. Listing 14.2 shows a small script to help run tests. Save it in `./run_tests` and make it executable with `chmod +x run_tests`.

Listing 14.2 Script to run tests

```
#!/usr/local/bin/node

require.paths.push(__dirname);
require.paths.push(__dirname + "/deps");
require.paths.push(__dirname + "/lib");

require("nodeunit").testrunner.run(["test/chapp"]);
```

14.1.2   Starting Point

There's a lot of code ahead of us, and to get us started I will provide a basic starting point, consisting of a small HTTP server and a convenient script to start it. We will then proceed top-down, actually taking the server for a spin halfway.

14.1.2.1   The Server

To create an HTTP server in Node we need the `http` module and its `create-Server` method. This method accepts a function, which will be attached as a request *listener*. CommonJS modules will be properly introduced in a moment,

---

as will Node's event module. Listing 14.3 shows the server, which should live in `lib/chapp/server.js`.

Listing 14.3 A Node.js HTTP server

```
var http = require("http");
var url = require("url");
var crController = require("chapp/chat_room_controller");

module.exports = http.createServer(function (req, res) {
  if (url.parse(req.url).pathname == "/comet") {
    var controller = crController.create(req, res);
    controller[req.method.toLowerCase()]();
  }
});
```

The server requires the first module that we are going to write—the `chat-RoomController`, which deals with the request/response logic. The server currently only responds to requests to the `/comet` URL.

14.1.2.2 The Startup Script

To start the server we need a script similar to the `run_tests` script, which sets up the load path, requires the server file, and starts the server. Listing 14.4 shows the script, which should be saved in `./run_server`, and should be made executable with `chmod +x run_server`.

Listing 14.4 Startup script

```
#!/usr/local/bin/node

require.paths.push(__dirname);
require.paths.push(__dirname + "/deps");
require.paths.push(__dirname + "/lib");

require("chapp/server").listen(process.argv[2] || 8000);
```

The `listen` call starts the server. `process.argv` contains all the command line arguments, i.e., the interpreter, the file being run, and any additional arguments given when running the script. The script is run with `./run_server 8080`. Leaving out the port number starts the server on the default port 8000.

14.2 The Controller

For any request to the `/comet` URL, the server will call the controller's `create` method, passing it request and response objects. It then proceeds to call a method on the resulting controller corresponding to the HTTP method used. In this chapter we will only implement the `get` and `post` methods.

14.2.1 CommonJS Modules

Node implements CommonJS modules, a structured way to manage reusable JavaScript components. Unlike script files loaded in browsers, the implicit scope in modules is not the global scope. This means that we don't need to wrap everything in anonymous closures to avoid leaking identifiers. To add a function or object to the module, we assign properties on the special `exports` object. Alternatively, we can specify the entire module as a single object, and assign this to `module.exports = myModule`.

Modules are loaded with `require("my_module")`. This function uses the paths specified in the `require.paths` array, which can be modified as we see fit, just like we did in Listing 14.2. We can also load modules not on the load path by prefixing the module name with `"./"`, which causes Node to look for the module relative to the current module file.

14.2.2 Defining the Module: The First Test

With a basic overview of CommonJS modules, we can write our very first test, as seen in Listing 14.5. It asserts that the controller object exists, and that it has a `create` method.

Listing 14.5 Expecting the controller to exist

```
var testCase = require("nodeunit").testCase;
var chatRoomController = require("chapp/chat_room_controller");

testCase(exports, "chatRoomController", {
  "should be object": function (test) {
    test.isNotNull(chatRoomController);
    test.isFunction(chatRoomController.create);
    test.done();
  }
});
```

Save the test in `test/chapp/chat-room-controller-test.js` and run it with `./run-tests`. It fails horribly with an exception stating that Node "Can't find module chapp/chat-room-controller." Save the contents of Listing 14.6 in `lib/chapp/chat-room-controller.js` to resolve the issue.

Listing 14.6 Creating the controller module

```
var chatRoomController = {
  create: function () {}
};

module.exports = chatRoomController;
```

Running the tests again should produce more uplifting output along the lines of Listing 14.7.

Listing 14.7 First successful test

```
chris@laptop:~/projects/chapp$ ./run_tests
test/chapp/chat_room_controller_test.js
chatRoomController should be object

OK: 2 assertions (2ms)
```

Note how the test case receives a `test` object and calls its `done` method. Nodeunit runs tests asynchronously, so we need to let it know explicitly when a test is done. In Part I, *Test-Driven Development,* I argued that unit tests rarely need to be asynchronous. For Node the situation is a little bit different, because not allowing asynchronous tests would basically mean having to stub or mock *every* system call, which simply is not a viable option. Doing so would make testing challenging, and without proper interface enforcement, error-prone.

14.2.3 Creating a Controller

Listing 14.8 creates a controller and asserts that it has `request` and `response` properties corresponding to the arguments we pass the `create` method.

Listing 14.8 Test creating new controllers

```
testCase(exports, "chatRoomController.create", {
  "should return object with request and response":
  function (test) {
    var req = {};
    var res = {};
```

```
    var controller = chatRoomController.create(req, res);

    test.inherits(controller, chatRoomController);
    test.strictEqual(controller.request, req);
    test.strictEqual(controller.response, res);
    test.done();
  }
});
```

Notice that Node's assertions flip the order of the arguments compared with what we're used to with JsTestDriver. Here, the order is `actual, expected` rather than the usual `expected, actual`. This is an important detail to get right, as failure messages will suffer if we don't.

As V8 implements parts of ECMAScript5, we can pass this test by using `Object.create`, as Listing 14.9 shows.

Listing 14.9 Creating controllers

```
var chatRoomController = {
  create: function (request, response) {
    return Object.create(this, {
      request: { value: request },
      response: { value: response }
    });
  }
};
```

The test passes. Defining `request` and `response` this way means that their `enumerable`, `configurable` and `writable` attributes are set to the default value, which in all cases is `false`. But you don't need to trust me, you can test it using `test.isWritable`, `test.isConfigurable` and `test.isEnumerable`, or their counterparts, `test.isNot*`.

14.2.4 Adding Messages on POST

The `post` action accepts JSON in the format sent by `cometClient` from Chapter 13, *Streaming Data with Ajax and Comet,* and creates messages. If your memory's a bit rusty on the JSON format, a sample request to create a message can be seen in Listing 14.10.

Listing 14.10 JSON request to create message

```
{ "topic": "message",
  "data": {
    "user": "cjno",
    "message": "Listening to the new 1349 album"
  }
}
```

The outer "topic" property describes what kind of event to create, in this example a new message, whereas the outer "data" property holds the actual data. The client was made this way so it could post different types of client-side events to the same server resource. For instance, when someone joins the chat, the client might send JSON like Listing 14.11.

Listing 14.11 JSON request to join the chat room

```
{ "topic": "userEnter",
  "data": {
    "user": "cjno"
  }
}
```

If the backend is ever extended to support several chat rooms, the message might also include which room the user entered.

14.2.4.1 Reading the Request Body

The first thing `post` needs to do is retrieve the request body, which contains the URL encoded JSON string. As a request comes in, the `request` object will emit "data" events, passing chunks of the request body. When all chunks have arrived, the `request` object emits a "end" event. The equivalent of our `observable` from Chapter 11, *The Observer Pattern,* that powers Node's events is the `events.EventEmitter` interface.

In tests, we will stub the `request` object, which needs to be an `EventEmitter` so we can trigger the "data" and "end" events we are interested in testing. We can then emit a couple of chunks from the test, and assert that the joined string is passed to `JSON.parse`. To verify that the entire body is passed to `JSON.parse`, we can stub it using the stub function from Chapter 12, *Abstracting Browser Differences: Ajax.* Save Listing 14.12 in `deps/stub.js`.

Listing 14.12 Using `stubFn` with Node

```
module.exports = function (returnValue) {
  function stub() {
    stub.called = true;
    stub.args = arguments;
    stub.thisArg = this;
    return returnValue;
  }

  stub.called = false;

  return stub;
};
```

Listing 14.13 shows the test. It includes quite a bit of setup code, which we will move around in a moment.

Listing 14.13 Expecting the request body to be parsed as JSON

```
var EventEmitter = require("events").EventEmitter;
var stub = require("stub");

/* ... */

testCase(exports, "chatRoomController.post", {
  setUp: function () {
    this.jsonParse = JSON.parse;
  },

  tearDown: function () {
    JSON.parse = this.jsonParse;
  },

  "should parse request body as JSON": function (test) {
    var req = new EventEmitter();
    var controller = chatRoomController.create(req, {});
    var data = { data: { user: "cjno", message: "hi" } };
    var stringData = JSON.stringify(data);
    var str = encodeURI(stringData);

    JSON.parse = stub(data);
    controller.post();
    req.emit("data", str.substring(0, str.length / 2));
    req.emit("data", str.substring(str.length / 2));
    req.emit("end");
```

```
      test.equals(JSON.parse.args[0], stringData);
      test.done();
    }
});
```

setUp and tearDown take care of restoring JSON.parse after the test has stubbed it out. We then create a controller object using fake request and response objects along with some test data to POST. Because the tddjs.ajax tools built in the two previous chapters currently only support URL encoded data, we must encode the test data to fit.

The test then emits a simple URL encoded JSON string in two chunks, the "end" event, and finally expects the JSON.parse method to have been called. Phew! Listing 14.14 shows one way to pass the test.

Listing 14.14 Reading the request body and parsing it as JSON

```
var chatRoomController = {
  /* ... */

  post: function () {
    var body = "";

    this.request.addListener("data", function (chunk) {
      body += chunk;
    });

    this.request.addListener("end", function () {
      JSON.parse(decodeURI(body));
    });
  }
};
```

As the test passes it is time to remove duplication. Aggressively removing duplication is the key to a flexible code base that is easy to change and mold any way we see fit. The tests are part of code base, and need constant refactoring and improvement too. Both the test cases for create and post create a controller instance using stub request and response objects, and sure enough, the get test case will do just the same. We can extract this into a function that can be used as a shared setup method. Listing 14.15 has the lowdown.

Listing 14.15 Sharing setup

```
function controllerSetUp() {
  var req = this.req = new EventEmitter();
  var res = this.res = {};
  this.controller = chatRoomController.create(req, res);
  this.jsonParse = JSON.parse;
}

function controllerTearDown() {
  JSON.parse = this.jsonParse;
}

/* ... */

testCase(exports, "chatRoomController.create", {
  setUp: controllerSetUp,
  /* ... */
});

testCase(exports, "chatRoomController.post", {
  setUp: controllerSetUp,
  tearDown: controllerTearDown,
  /* ... */
});
```

With this change the tests should refer to `controller`, `req` and `res` as properties of `this`.

14.2.4.2 Extracting the Message

With the request body readily parsed as JSON, we need to extract the message from the resulting object and pass it somewhere it will be kept safe. As we're going through this exercise top-down, we don't have a data model yet. We will have to decide roughly what it's going to look like, and stub it while we finish the `post` method.

Messages should belong to a chat room. As the chat room needs to persist between requests, the controller will depend on the server assigning it a `chatRoom` object, on which it can call `addMessage(user, message)`.

The test in Listing 14.16 verifies that `post` passes data to `addMessage` according to this interface.

Listing 14.16 Expecting `post` to add message

```
"should add message from request body": function (test) {
  var data = { data: { user: "cjno", message: "hi" } };

  this.controller.chatRoom = { addMessage: stub() };
  this.controller.post();
  this.req.emit("data", encodeURI(JSON.stringify(data)));
  this.req.emit("end");

  test.ok(this.controller.chatRoom.addMessage.called);
  var args = this.controller.chatRoom.addMessage.args;
  test.equals(args[0], data.data.user);
  test.equals(args[1], data.data.message);
  test.done();
}
```

As before, we call the `post` method to have it add its request body listeners, then we emit some fake request data. Finally we expect the controller to have called `chatRoom.addMessage` with the correct arguments.

To pass this test we need to access `this.chatRoom` from inside the anonymous "end" event handler. To achieve this we can bind it to avoid having to manually keep local references to `this`. At the time of writing, V8 does not yet support `Function.prototype.bind`, but we can use the custom implementation from Listing 6.7 in Chapter 6, *Applied Functions and Closures*. Save the implementation in `deps/function-bind.js` and Listing 14.17 should run as expected.

Listing 14.17 Adding messages on POST

```
require("function-bind");

var chatRoomController = {
  /* ... */

  post: function () {
    /* ... */

    this.request.addListener("end", function () {
      var data = JSON.parse(decodeURI(body)).data;
      this.chatRoom.addMessage(data.user, data.message);
    }.bind(this));
  }
};
```

Unfortunately, this doesn't play out exactly as planned. The previous test, which also calls `post`, is now attempting to call `addMessage` on `chatRoom`, which is `undefined` in that test. We can fix the issue by moving the `chatRoom` stub into `setUp` as Listing 14.18 does.

Listing 14.18 Sharing the `chatRoom` stub

```
function controllerSetUp() {
  /* ... */
  this.controller.chatRoom = { addMessage: stub() };
}
```

All the tests go back to a soothing green, and we can turn our attention to the duplicated logic we just introduced in the second test. In particular, both tests simulates sending a request with a body. We can simplify the tests considerably by extracting this logic into the setup. Listing 14.19 shows the updated tests.

Listing 14.19 Cleaning up `post` tests

```
function controllerSetUp() {
  /* ... */

  this.sendRequest = function (data) {
    var str = encodeURI(JSON.stringify(data));
    this.req.emit("data", str.substring(0, str.length / 2));
    this.req.emit("data", str.substring(str.length / 2));
    this.req.emit("end");
  };
}

testCase(exports, "chatRoomController.post", {
  /* ... */

  "should parse request body as JSON": function (test) {
    var data = { data: { user: "cjno", message: "hi" } };
    JSON.parse = stub(data);

    this.controller.post();
    this.sendRequest(data);

    test.equals(JSON.parse.args[0], JSON.stringify(data));
    test.done();
  },

  /* ... */
});
```

The cleaned up tests certainly are a lot easier to follow, and with the send-Request helper method, writing new tests that make requests will be easier as well. All tests pass and we can move on.

14.2.4.3 Malicious Data

Notice that we are currently accepting messages completely unfiltered. This can lead to all kinds of scary situations, for instance consider the effects of the request in Listing 14.20

Listing 14.20 Malicious request

```
{ "topic": "message",
  "data": {
    "user": "cjno",
    "message":
      "<script>window.location = 'http://hacked';</script>"
  }
}
```

Before deploying an application like the one we are currently building we should take care to not blindly accept any end user data unfiltered.

14.2.5 Responding to Requests

When the controller has added the message, it should respond and close the connection. In most web frameworks, output buffering and closing the connection happen automatically behind the scenes. The HTTP server support in Node, however, was consciously designed with data streaming and long polling in mind. For this reason, data is never buffered, and connections are never closed until told to do so.

http.ServerResponse objects offer a few methods useful to output a response, namely writeHead, which writes the status code and response headers; write, which writes a chunk to the response body; and finally end.

14.2.5.1 Status Code

As there really isn't much feedback to give the user when a message is added, Listing 14.21 simply expects post to respond with an empty "201 Created."

Listing 14.21 Expecting status code 201

```
function controllerSetUp() {
  /* ... */
  var res = this.res = { writeHead: stub() };
```

```
    /* ... */
}

testCase(exports, "chatRoomController.post", {
    /* ... */
    "should write status header": function (test) {
        var data = { data: { user: "cjno", message: "hi" } };

        this.controller.post();
        this.sendRequest(data);

        test.ok(this.res.writeHead.called);
        test.equals(this.res.writeHead.args[0], 201);
        test.done();
    }
});
```

Listing 14.22 faces the challenge and makes the actual call to writeHead.

Listing 14.22 Setting the response code

```
post: function () {
    /* ... */

    this.request.addListener("end", function () {
        var data = JSON.parse(decodeURI(body)).data;
        this.chatRoom.addMessage(data.user, data.message);
        this.response.writeHead(201);
    }.bind(this));
}
```

14.2.5.2 Closing the Connection

Once the headers have been written, we should make sure the connection is closed. Listing 14.23 shows the test.

Listing 14.23 Expecting the response to be closed

```
function controllerSetUp() {
    /* ... */
    var res = this.res = {
        writeHead: stub(),
        end: stub()
    };

    /* ... */
};
```

```
testCase(exports, "chatRoomController.post", {
  /* ... */
  "should close connection": function (test) {
    var data = { data: { user: "cjno", message: "hi" } };

    this.controller.post();
    this.sendRequest(data);

    test.ok(this.res.end.called);
    test.done();
  }
});
```

The test fails, and Listing 14.24 shows the updated post method, which passes all the tests.

Listing 14.24 Closing the response

```
post: function () {
  /* ... */

  this.request.addListener("end", function () {
    /* ... */
    this.response.end();
  }.bind(this));
}
```

That's it for the post method. It is now functional enough to properly handle well-formed requests. In a real-world setting, however, I encourage more rigid input verification and error handling. Making the method more resilient is left as an exercise.

14.2.6 Taking the Application for a Spin

If we make a small adjustment to the server, we can now take the application for a spin. In the original listing, the server did not set up a chatRoom for the controller. To successfully run the application, update the server to match Listing 14.25.

Listing 14.25 The final server

```
var http = require("http");
var url = require("url");
var crController = require("chapp/chat_room_controller");
var chatRoom = require("chapp/chat_room");
```

```
var room = Object.create(chatRoom);

module.exports = http.createServer(function (req, res) {
  if (url.parse(req.url).pathname == "/comet") {
    var controller = crController.create(req, res);
    controller.chatRoom = room;
    controller[req.method.toLowerCase()]();
  }
});
```

For this to work, we need to add a fake chatRoom module. Save the contents of Listing 14.26 to lib/chapp/chat_room.js.

Listing 14.26 A fake chat room

```
var sys = require("sys");

var chatRoom = {
  addMessage: function (user, message) {
    sys.puts(user + ": " + message);
  }
};

module.exports = chatRoom;
```

Listing 14.27 shows how to use node-repl, an interactive Node shell, to encode some POST data and post it to the application using curl, the command line HTTP client. Run it in another shell, and watch the output from the shell that is running the application.

Listing 14.27 Manually testing the app from the command line

```
$ node-repl
node> var msg = { user:"cjno", message:"Enjoying Node.js" };
node> var data = { topic: "message", data: msg };
node> var encoded = encodeURI(JSON.stringify(data));
node> require("fs").writeFileSync("chapp.txt", encoded);
node> Ctrl-d
$ curl -d `cat chapp.txt` http://localhost:8000/comet
```

When you enter that last command, you should get an immediate response (i.e., it simply returns to your prompt) and the shell that is running the server should output "cjno: Enjoying Node.js." In Chapter 15, *TDD and DOM Manipulation: The Chat Client,* we will build a proper frontend for the application.

14.3 Domain Model and Storage

The domain model of the chat application will consist of a single `chatRoom` object for the duration of our exercise. `chatRoom` will simply store messages in memory, but we will design it following Node's I/O conventions.

14.3.1 Creating a Chat Room

As with the controller, we will rely on `Object.create` to create new objects inheriting from `chatRoom`. However, until proved otherwise, `chatRoom` does not need an initializer, so we can simply create objects with `Object.create` directly. Should we decide to add an initializer at a later point, we must update the places that create chat room objects in the tests, which should be a good motivator to keep from duplicating the call.

14.3.2 I/O in Node

Because the `chatRoom` interface will take the role as the storage backend, we classify it as an I/O interface. This means it should follow Node's carefully thought out conventions for asynchronous I/O, even if it's just an in-memory store for now. Doing so allows us to very easily refactor to use a persistence mechanism, such as a database or web service, at a later point.

In Node, asynchronous interfaces accept an optional callback as their last argument. The first argument passed to the callback is always either `null` or an error object. This removes the need for a dedicated "errback" function. Listing 14.28 shows an example using the file system module.

Listing 14.28 Callback and errback convention in Node

```
var fs = require("fs");

fs.rename("./tetx.txt", "./text.txt", function (err) {
  if (err) {
    throw err;
  }

  // Renamed successfully, carry on
});
```

This convention is used for all low-level system interfaces, and it will be our starting point as well.

14.3.3 Adding Messages

As dictated by the controller using it, the `chatRoom` object should have an `addMessage` method that accepts a username and a message.

14.3.3.1 Dealing with Bad Data

For basic data consistency, the `addMessage` method should err if either the username or message is missing. However, as an asynchronous I/O interface, it cannot simply throw exceptions. Rather, we will expect errors to be passed as the first argument to the callback registered with `addMessage`, as is the Node way. Listing 14.29 shows the test for missing username. Save it in `test/chapp/chat_room_test.js`.

Listing 14.29 `addMessage` should require username

```
var testCase = require("nodeunit").testCase;
var chatRoom = require("chapp/chat_room");

testCase(exports, "chatRoom.addMessage", {
  "should require username": function (test) {
    var room = Object.create(chatRoom);

    room.addMessage(null, "a message", function (err) {
      test.isNotNull(err);
      test.inherits(err, TypeError);
      test.done();
    });
  }
});
```

The test fails as expected, and so we add a check on the `user` parameter, as Listing 14.30 shows.

Listing 14.30 Checking the username

```
var chatRoom = {
  addMessage: function (user, message, callback) {
    if (!user) {
      callback(new TypeError("user is null"));
    }
  }
};
```

The test passes, and we can move on to checking the message. The test in Listing 14.31 expects `addMessage` to require a message.

Listing 14.31 `addMessage` should require message

```
"should require message": function (test) {
  var room = Object.create(chatRoom);

  room.addMessage("cjno", null, function (err) {
    test.isNotNull(err);
    test.inherits(err, TypeError);
    test.done();
  });
}
```

The test introduces some duplication that we'll deal with shortly. First, Listing 14.32 makes the check that passes it.

Listing 14.32 Checking the message

```
addMessage: function (user, message, callback) {
  /* ... */

  if (!message) {
    callback(new TypeError("message is null"));
  }
}
```

All the tests pass. Listing 14.33 adds a `setUp` method to remove the duplicated creation of the `chatRoom` object.

Listing 14.33 Adding a `setUp` method

```
testCase(exports, "chatRoom.addMessage", {
  setUp: function () {
    this.room = Object.create(chatRoom);
  },

  /* ... */
});
```

As we decided previously, the callback should be optional, so Listing 14.34 adds a test that expects the method *not* to fail when the callback is missing.

Listing 14.34 Expecting `addMessage` not to require a callback

```
/* ... */
require("function-bind");

/* ... */

testCase(exports, "chatRoom.addMessage", {
  /* ... */

  "should not require a callback": function (test) {
    test.noException(function () {
      this.room.addMessage();
      test.done();
    }.bind(this));
  }
}
```

Once again we load the custom `bind` implementation to bind the anonymous callback to `test.noException`. To pass the test we need to check that the callback is callable before calling it, as Listing 14.35 shows.

Listing 14.35 Verifying that callback is callable before calling it

```
addMessage: function (user, message, callback) {
  var err = null;

  if (!user) { err = new TypeError("user is null"); }
  if (!message) { err = new TypeError("message is null"); }

  if (typeof callback == "function") {
    callback(err);
  }
}
```

14.3.3.2 Successfully Adding Messages

We won't be able to verify that messages are actually stored until we have a way to retrieve them, but we should get some indication on whether or not adding the message was successful. To do this we'll expect the method to call the callback with a message object. The object should contain the data we passed in along with an id. The test can be seen in Listing 14.36.

Listing 14.36 Expecting `addMessage` to pass the created message

```
"should call callback with new object": function (test) {
  var txt = "Some message";

  this.room.addMessage("cjno", txt, function (err, msg) {
    test.isObject(msg);
    test.isNumber(msg.id);
    test.equals(msg.message, txt);
    test.equals(msg.user, "cjno");
    test.done();
  });
}
```

Listing 14.37 shows an attempt at passing the test. It calls the callback with an object and cheats the id by hard-coding it to 1.

Listing 14.37 Passing the object to the callback

```
addMessage: function (user, message, callback) {
  /* ... */
  var data;

  if (!err) {
    data = { id: 1, user: user, message: message };
  }

  if (typeof callback == "function") {
    callback(err, data);
  }
}
```

With this in place, the tests are back to green. Next up, the id should be unique for every message. Listing 14.38 shows the test.

Listing 14.38 Expecting unique message ids

```
"should assign unique ids to messages": function (test) {
  var user = "cjno";

  this.room.addMessage(user, "a", function (err, msg1) {
    this.room.addMessage(user, "b", function (err, msg2) {
      test.notEquals(msg1.id, msg2.id);
      test.done();
    });
  }.bind(this));
}
```

The test exposes our cheat, so we need to find a better way to generate ids. Listing 14.39 uses a simple variable that is incremented each time a message is added.

Listing 14.39 Assigning unique integer ids

```
var id = 0;

var chatRoom = {
  addMessage: function (user, message, callback) {
    /* ... */

    if (!err) {
      data = { id: id++, user: user, message: message };
    }

    /* ... */
  }
};
```

Tests are passing again. You might worry that we're not actually storing the message anywhere. That *is* a problem, but it's not currently being addressed by the test case. To do so we must start testing message retrieval.

14.3.4 Fetching Messages

In the next chapter we will interface with the chat backend using the comet-Client from Chapter 13, *Streaming Data with Ajax and Comet.* This means that chatRoom needs some way to retrieve all messages since some token. We'll add a getMessagesSince method that accepts an id and yields an array of messages to the callback.

14.3.4.1 The getMessagesSince Method

The initial test for this method in Listing 14.40 adds two messages, then tries to retrieve all messages since the id of the first. This way we don't program any assumptions about how the ids are generated into the tests.

Listing 14.40 Testing message retrieval

```
testCase(exports, "chatRoom.getMessagesSince", {
  "should get messages since given id": function (test) {
    var room = Object.create(chatRoom);
    var user = "cjno";
```

```
    room.addMessage(user, "msg", function (e, first) {
      room.addMessage(user, "msg2", function (e, second) {
        room.getMessagesSince(first.id, function (e, msgs) {
          test.isArray(msgs);
          test.same(msgs, [second]);
          test.done();
        });
      });
    });
  }
});
```

The test fails in the face of a missing `getMessagesSince`. Listing 14.41 adds an empty method that simply calls the callback without arguments.

Listing 14.41 Adding `getMessagesSince`

```
var chatRoom = {
  addMessage: function (user, message, callback) { /* ... */ },

  getMessagesSince: function (id, callback) {
    callback();
  }
};
```

Because `addMessage` isn't really storing the messages anywhere, there's no way for `getMessagesSince` to retrieve it. In other words, to pass this test we need to fix `addMessage`, like Listing 14.42 shows.

Listing 14.42 Actually adding messages

```
addMessage: function (user, message, callback) {
  /* ... */

  if (!err) {
    if (!this.messages) {
      this.messages = [];
    }

    var id = this.messages.length + 1;
    data = { id: id, user: user, message: message };
    this.messages.push(data);
  }

  /* ... */
}
```

Now that we have an array to store messages in, we can retrieve ids from the array's length instead of keeping a dedicated counter around. The id adds one to the length to make it 1-based rather than 0-based. The reason for this is that `getMessagesSince` is supposed to retrieve all messages added *after* some id. Using 0-based ids we'd have to call this method with -1 to get all messages, rather than the slightly more natural looking 0. It's just a matter of preference, you may disagree with me.

Running the tests confirms that all the previous tests are still passing. As ids are now directly related to the length of the `messages` array, retrieval is trivial as Listing 14.43 shows.

Listing 14.43   Fetching messages

```
getMessagesSince: function (id, callback) {
  callback(null, this.messages.slice(id));
}
```

And just like that, all the tests, including the one test for `getMessagesSince`, pass. `getMessagesSince` helped us properly implement `addMessage`, and the best case situation is now covered. However, there are a few more cases to fix for it to work reliably.

- It should yield an empty array if the `messages` array does not exist.
- It should yield an empty array if no relevant messages exist.
- It could possibly not throw exceptions if no callback is provided.
- The test cases for `addMessage` and `getMessagesSince` should be refactored to share setup methods.

Testing and implementing these additional cases is left as an exercise.

14.3.4.2 Making `addMessage` Asynchronous

The `addMessage` method, although callback-based, is still a synchronous interface. This is not necessarily a problem, but there is a possibility that someone using the interface spins off some heavy lifting in the callback, inadvertently causing `addMessage` to block. To alleviate the problem we can utilize Node's `process.nextTick(callback)` method, which calls its callback on the next pass of the event loop. First, Listing 14.44 tests for the desired behavior.

Listing 14.44 Expecting `addMessage` to be asynchronous

```
"should be asynchronous": function (test) {
  var id;

  this.room.addMessage("cjno", "Hey", function (err, msg) {
    id = msg.id;
  });

  this.room.getMessagesSince(id - 1, function (err, msgs) {
    test.equals(msgs.length, 0);
    test.done();
  });
}
```

This test fails because the method indeed is synchronous at this point. Listing 14.45 updates `addMessage` to utilize the `nextTick` method.

Listing 14.45 Making `addMessage` asynchronous

```
require("function-bind");
var id = 0;

var chatRoom = {
  addMessage: function (user, message, callback) {
    process.nextTick(function () {
      /* ... */
    }.bind(this));
  },

  /* ... */
}
```

The test now passes. However, it only passes because `getMessagesSince` is still synchronous. The moment we make this method asynchronous as well (as we should), the test will not pass. That leaves us with checking the `messages` array directly. Testing implementation details is usually frowned upon, as it ties the tests too hard to the implementation. I think the test for the asynchronous behavior falls under the same category; thus, I'd rather remove that test than to add yet another one that digs inside the implementation.

14.4 Promises

One of the biggest challenges of working exclusively with asynchronous interfaces lies in deeply nested callbacks; any task that requires the result of asynchronous calls to be processed in order must be nested to ensure ordered execution. Not only is deeply nested code ugly and cumbersome to work with, it also presents a more grave problem; nested calls cannot benefit from the possibility of parallel execution, a bad trade-off to enable ordered processing.

We can untangle nested callbacks using *promises*. A promise is a representation of an *eventual value* and it offers an elegant way of working with asynchronous code. When an asynchronous method uses promises, it does not accept a callback, but rather returns a promise, an object representing the eventual fulfillment of that call. The returned object is observable, allowing calling code to subscribe to success and error events on it.

When the original call that spawned the promise finishes, it calls the promise's `resolve` method, which causes its success callback to fire. Similarly, in the event that a call failed, the promise offers the `reject` method, which can be passed an exception.

Using promises means that we don't have to nest callbacks unless we truly depend on calls to occur in succession; thus, we gain more flexibility. For example, we can issue a host of asynchronous calls and have them execute in parallel, but use promises to group and process the results in any order we wish.

Node no longer comes with a promise API, but Kris Zyp has a nice implementation[4] that implements his proposal for a CommonJS Promise specification. The version used in this book is available from the book's website.[5] Download it to `deps/node-promise`.

14.4.1 Refactoring `addMessage` to Use Promises

We will refactor the `addMessage` method to use promises. As we refactor, it is vital that we run the tests between each step, and always keep them passing, to be sure we didn't break anything. Changing the way a method works can be done by keeping the old behavior until the new behavior is in place and all tests have been updated.

The fact that we can carry out a refactoring like this—changing fundamental behavior—without worrying about breaking the application, is one of the true benefits of a good test suite.

---

4. http://github.com/kriszyp/node-promise
5. http://tddjs.com

14.4.1.1 Returning a Promise

We will start refactoring by introducing a new test, one that expects `addMessage` to return a promise object, seen in Listing 14.46.

Listing 14.46 Expecting `addMessage` to return a promise

```
testCase(exports, "chatRoom.addMessage", {
  /* ... */

  "should return a promise": function (test) {
    var result = this.room.addMessage("cjno", "message");

    test.isObject(result);
    test.isFunction(result.then);
    test.done();
  }
});
```

Notice that I assume you've solved the exercise from before; the test case should now be using a setup method to create a `chatRoom` object, available in `this.room`.

The test fails as the method is currently not returning an object. We'll fix that by returning an empty promise object, as in Listing 14.47.

Listing 14.47 Returning an empty promise object

```
require("function-bind");
var Promise = require("node-promise/promise").Promise;
var id = 0;

var chatRoom = {
  addMessage: function (user, message, callback) {
    process.nextTick(function () {
      /* ... */
    }.bind(this));

    return new Promise();
  },

  /* ... */
};
```

14.4.1.2 Rejecting the Promise

Next up, we'll start changing the original tests to work with promises. The first test we wrote expects addMessage to call the callback, passing an error if no username is passed to it. The updated test can be seen in Listing 14.48.

Listing 14.48 Using the returned promise

```
"should require username": function (test) {
  var promise = this.room.addMessage(null, "message");

  promise.then(function () {}, function (err) {
    test.isNotNull(err);
    test.inherits(err, TypeError);
    test.done();
  });
}
```

The promise has a then method, which allows consumers to add callbacks to be called when it is fulfilled. It accepts one or two functions; the first function is the success callback and the second is the error callback. Another way of doing this is to use the addCallback and addErrback methods, but I like the way "then" reads: addMessage(user, msg).then(callback).

To pass this test, we need to duplicate some efforts in addMessage, as we're not yet ready to drop the old implementation. Listing 14.49 shows the updated method.

Listing 14.49 Updating addMessage

```
addMessage: function (user, message, callback) {
  var promise = new Promise();

  process.nextTick(function () {
    /* ... */

    if (err) {
      promise.reject(err, true);
    }
  }.bind(this));

  return promise;
}
```

Here we call the promise's reject method, passing it an error. Normally, the promise will throw an exception if reject is called and no error handler is registered. Because the remaining tests have not yet been updated to use the promise, and because we previously decided that not handling the error was permissible, we pass in `true` as the second argument to suppress this behavior. The test passes.

The next test is similar to the one we just fixed, only it verifies that leaving out the message causes an error. Passing this test using a promise does not require further modification of `addMessage`, so I will leave updating the test as an exercise.

14.4.1.3 Resolving the Promise

The next significant test to update is the one that asserts that the newly added message object is passed to the callback. This test only requires a small change. Because the promise has separate success and failure handlers, we can remove the error parameter to the callback. The test can be seen in Listing 14.50.

Listing 14.50 Expecting the promise to emit success

```
"should call callback with new object": function (test) {
  var txt = "Some message";

  this.room.addMessage("cjno", txt).then(function (msg) {
    test.isObject(msg);
    test.isNumber(msg.id);
    test.equals(msg.message, txt);
    test.equals(msg.user, "cjno");
    test.done();
  });
}
```

Updating the implementation is a matter of calling the promise's `resolve` method, as seen in Listing 14.51.

Listing 14.51 Resolving with the message

```
addMessage: function (user, message, callback) {
  var promise = new Promise()

  process.nextTick(function () {
    /* ... */

    if (!err) {
      /* ... */
      this.messages.push(data);
      promise.resolve(data);
    }
```

```
    /* ... */
  }.bind(this));

  return promise;
}
```

Yet another converted test passes. Converting the remaining tests should be fairly straightforward, so I will leave doing so as an exercise. Once all the tests have been updated, we need to decide whether or not we should remove the callback. Keeping it will allow users to decide which pattern they prefer to use, but it also means more code to maintain on our part. Because the promise handles all the callbacks for us, removing the manual callback means we don't need to concern ourselves with whether or not it was passed, if it's callable, and so on. I recommend relying solely on the promises.

14.4.2 Consuming Promises

Now that the `addMessage` method uses promises we can simplify code that needs to add more than one message. For instance, the test that asserts that each message is given its own unique id originally used nested callbacks to add two messages and then compare them. `Node-promise` offers an `all` function, which accepts any number of promises and returns a new promise. This new promise emits success once all the promises are fulfilled. We can use this to write the unique id test in another way, as seen in Listing 14.52.

Listing 14.52 Grouping promises with `all`

```
/* ... */
var all = require("node-promise/promise").all;

/* ... */

testCase(exports, "chatRoom.addMessage", {
  /* ... */

  "should assign unique ids to messages": function (test) {
    var room = this.room;
    var messages = [];
    var collect = function (msg) { messages.push(msg); };

    var add = all(room.addMessage("u", "a").then(collect),
                  room.addMessage("u", "b").then(collect));
```

```
    add.then(function () {
      test.notEquals(messages[0].id, messages[1].id);
      test.done();
    });
  },

  /* ... */
});
```

For consistency, the `getMessagesSince` method should be updated to use promises as well. I will leave doing so as yet another exercise. Try to make sure you never fail more than one test at a time while refactoring. When you're done you should end up with something like Listing 14.53.

Listing 14.53 `getMessagesSince` using promises

```
getMessagesSince: function (id) {
  var promise = new Promise();

  process.nextTick(function () {
    promise.resolve((this.messages || []).slice(id));
  }.bind(this));

  return promise;
}
```

14.5 Event Emitters

When the client polls the server for new messages, one of two things can happen. Either new messages are available, in which case the request is responded to and ended immediately, or the server should hold the request until messages are ready. So far we've covered the first case, but the second case, the one that enables long polling, is not yet covered.

`chatRoom` will provide a `waitForMessagesSince` method, which works just like the `getMessagesSince` method; except if no messages are available, it will idly wait for some to become available. In order to implement this, we need `chatRoom` to emit an event when new messages are added.

14.5.1 Making `chatRoom` an Event Emitter

The first test to verify that `chatRoom` is an event emitter is to test that it has the `addListener` and `emit` methods, as Listing 14.54 shows.

Listing 14.54 Expecting `chatRoom` to be event emitter

```
testCase(exports, "chatRoom", {
  "should be event emitter": function (test) {
    test.isFunction(chatRoom.addListener);
    test.isFunction(chatRoom.emit);
    test.done();
  }
});
```

We can pass this test by popping `EventEmitter.prototype` in as chat-Room's prototype, as seen in Listing 14.55.

Listing 14.55 `chatRoom` inheriting from `EventEmitter.prototype`

```
/* ... */
var EventEmitter = require("events").EventEmitter;
/* ... */

var chatRoom = Object.create(EventEmitter.prototype);

chatRoom.addMessage = function (user, message) {/* ... */};
chatRoom.getMessagesSince = function (id) {/* ... */};
```

Note that because V8 fully supports ECMAScript 5's `Object.create`, we could have used property descriptors to add the methods as well, as seen in Listing 14.56.

Listing 14.56 `chatRoom` defined with property descriptors

```
var chatRoom = Object.create(EventEmitter.prototype, {
  addMessage: {
    value: function (user, message) {
      /* ... */
    }
  },

  getMessagesSince: {
    value: function (id) {
      /* ... */
    }
  }
});
```

At this point the property descriptors don't provide anything we have a documented need for (i.e., the ability to override default property attribute values), so we'll avoid the added indentation and stick with the simple assignments in Listing 14.55.

Next up, we make sure that `addMessage` emits an event. Listing 14.57 shows the test.

Listing 14.57 Expecting `addMessage` to emit a "message" event

```
testCase(exports, "chatRoom.addMessage", {
  /* ... */

  "should emit 'message' event": function (test) {
    var message;

    this.room.addListener("message", function (m) {
      message = m;
    });

    this.room.addMessage("cjno", "msg").then(function (m) {
      test.same(m, message);
      test.done();
    });
  }
});
```

To pass this test we need to place a call to `emit` right before we resolve the promise, as seen in Listing 14.58.

Listing 14.58 Emitting a message event

```
chatRoom.addMessage= function (user, message, callback) {
  var promise = new Promise()

  process.nextTick(function () {
    /* ... */

    if (!err) {
      /* ... */
      this.emit("message", data);
      promise.resolve(data);
    } else {
      promise.reject(err, true);
    }
```

```
  }.bind(this));

  return promise;
};
```

With the event in place, we can build the `waitForMessagesSince` method.

14.5.2 Waiting for Messages

The `waitForMessagesSince` method will do one of two things; if messages are available since the provided id, the returned promise will resolve immediately. If no messages are currently available, the method will add a listener for the "message" event, and the returned promise will resolve once a new message is added.

The test in Listing 14.59 expects that the promise is immediately resolved if messages are available.

Listing 14.59 Expecting available messages to resolve immediately

```
/* ... */
var Promise = require("node-promise/promise").Promise;
var stub = require("stub");
/* ... */

testCase(exports, "chatRoom.waitForMessagesSince", {
  setUp: chatRoomSetup,

  "should yield existing messages": function (test) {
    var promise = new Promise();
    promise.resolve([{ id: 43 }]);
    this.room.getMessagesSince = stub(promise);

    this.room.waitForMessagesSince(42).then(function (m) {
      test.same([{ id: 43 }], m);
      test.done();
    });
  }
});
```

This test stubs the `getMessagesSince` method to verify that its results are used if there are any. To pass this test we can simply return the promise returned from `getMessagesSince`, as seen in Listing 14.60.

Listing 14.60 Proxying `getMessagesSince`

```
chatRoom.waitForMessagesSince = function (id) {
  return this.getMessagesSince(id);
};
```

Now to the interesting part. If the attempt to fetch existing methods does not succeed, the method should add a listener for the "message" event and go to sleep. Listing 14.61 tests this by stubbing `addListener`.

Listing 14.61 Expecting the wait method to add a listener

```
"should add listener when no messages": function (test) {
  this.room.addListener = stub();
  var promise = new Promise();
  promise.resolve([]);
  this.room.getMessagesSince = stub(promise);

  this.room.waitForMessagesSince(0);

  process.nextTick(function () {
    test.equals(this.room.addListener.args[0], "message");
    test.isFunction(this.room.addListener.args[1]);
    test.done();
  }.bind(this));
}
```

Again we stub the `getMessagesSince` method to control its output. We then resolve the promise it's stubbed to return, passing an empty array. This should cause the `waitForMessagesSince` method to register a listener for the "message" event. Seeing as `waitForMessagesSince` does not add a listener, the test fails. To pass it, we need to change the implementation as seen in Listing 14.62.

Listing 14.62 Adding a listener if no messages are available

```
chatRoom.waitForMessagesSince = function (id) {
  var promise = new Promise();

  this.getMessagesSince(id).then(function (messages) {
    if (messages.length > 0) {
      promise.resolve(messages);
    } else {
      this.addListener("message", function () {});
    }
```

```
  }.bind(this));

  return promise;
};
```

The listener we just added is empty, as we don't yet have a test that tells us what it needs to do. That seems like a suitable topic for the next test, which will assert that adding a message causes `waitForMessagesSince` to resolve with the new message. For symmetry with `getMessagesSince`, we expect the single message to arrive as an array. Listing 14.63 shows the test.

Listing 14.63 Adding a message should resolve waiting requests

```
"new message should resolve waiting": function (test) {
  var user = "cjno";
  var msg = "Are you waiting for this?";

  this.room.waitForMessagesSince(0).then(function (msgs) {
    test.isArray(msgs);
    test.equals(msgs.length, 1);
    test.equals(msgs[0].user, user);
    test.equals(msgs[0].message, msg);
    test.done();
  });

  process.nextTick(function () {
    this.room.addMessage(user, msg);
  }.bind(this));
}
```

Unsurprisingly, the test does not pass, prompting us to fill in the "message" listener we just added. Listing 14.64 shows the working listener.

Listing 14.64 Implementing the message listener

```
/* ... */

this.addListener("message", function (message) {
  promise.resolve([message]);
});

/* ... */
```

And that's all it takes, the tests all pass, and our very rudimentary data layer is complete enough to serve its purpose in the application. Still, there is one very important task to complete, and one that I will leave as an exercise. Once the promise returned from waitForMessagesSince is resolved, the listener added to the "message" event needs to be cleared. Otherwise, the original call to waitForMessagesSince will have its callback called every time a message is added, even after the current request has ended.

To do this you will need a reference to the function added as a handler, and use this.removeListener. To test it, it will be helpful to know that room.listeners() returns the array of listeners, for your inspection pleasure.

14.6 Returning to the Controller

With a functional data layer we can get back to finishing the controller. We're going to give post the final polish and implement get.

14.6.1 Finishing the post Method

The post method currently responds with the 201 status code, regardless of whether the message was added or not, which is in violation with the semantics of a 201 response; the HTTP spec states that "The origin server MUST create the resource before returning the 201 status code." Having implemented the addMessage method we know that this is not necessarily the case in our current implementation. Let's get right on fixing that.

The test that expects post to call writeHead needs updating. We now expect the headers to be written once the addMessage method resolves. Listing 14.65 shows the updated test.

Listing 14.65 Expecting post to respond immediately when addMessage resolves

```
/* ... */
var Promise = require("node-promise/promise").Promise;
/* ... */

function controllerSetUp() {
  /* ... */
  var promise = this.addMessagePromise = new Promise();
  this.controller.chatRoom = { addMessage: stub(promise) };
  /* ... */
}

/* ... */

testCase(exports, "chatRoomController.post", {
```

```
/* ... */

"should write status header when addMessage resolves":
function (test) {
  var data = { data: { user: "cjno", message: "hi" } };

  this.controller.post();
  this.sendRequest(data);
  this.addMessagePromise.resolve({});

  process.nextTick(function () {
    test.ok(this.res.writeHead.called);
    test.equals(this.res.writeHead.args[0], 201);
    test.done();
  }.bind(this));
},

/* ... */
});
```

Delaying the verification doesn't affect the test very much, so the fact that it still passes only tells us none of the new setup code is broken. We can apply the same update to the following test, which expects the connection to be closed. Listing 14.66 shows the updated test.

Listing 14.66 Expecting post not to close connection immediately

```
"should close connection when addMessage resolves":
function (test) {
  var data = { data: { user: "cjno", message: "hi" } };
  this.controller.post();
  this.sendRequest(data);
  this.addMessagePromise.resolve({});

  process.nextTick(function () {
    test.ok(this.res.end.called);
    test.done();
  }.bind(this));
}
```

Listing 14.67 shows a new test, which contradicts the two tests the way they were previously written. This test specifically expects the action *not* to respond before addMessage has resolved.

Listing 14.67 Expecting `post` not to respond immediately

```
"should not respond immediately": function (test) {
  this.controller.post();
  this.sendRequest({ data: {} });

  test.ok(!this.res.end.called);
  test.done();
}
```

This test does not run as smoothly as the previous two. Passing it is a matter of deferring the closing calls until the promise returned by `addMessage` resolves. Listing 14.68 has the lowdown.

Listing 14.68 `post` responds when `addMessage` resolves

```
post: function () {
  /* ... */

  this.request.addListener("end", function () {
    var data = JSON.parse(decodeURI(body)).data;

    this.chatRoom.addMessage(
      data.user, data.message
    ).then(function () {
      this.response.writeHead(201);
      this.response.end();
    }.bind(this));
  }.bind(this));
}
```

That's about it for the `post` method. Note that the method does not handle errors in any way; in fact it will respond with a 201 status even if the message was not added successfully. I'll leave fixing it as an exercise.

14.6.2 Streaming Messages with GET

GET requests should either be immediately responded to with messages, or held open until messages are available. Luckily, we did most of the heavy lifting while implementing `chatRoom.waitForMessagesSince`, so the `get` method of the controller will simply glue together the request and the data.

14.6.2.1 Filtering Messages with Access Tokens

Remember how the `cometClient` from Chapter 13, *Streaming Data with Ajax and Comet,* informs the server of what data to retrieve? We set it up to use the `X-Access-Token` header, which can contain any value and is controlled by the server. Because we built `waitForMessagesSince` to use ids, it should not come as a surprise that we are going to track progress using them.

When a client connects for the first time, it's going to send an empty `X-Access-Token`, so handling that case seems like a good start. Listing 14.69 shows the test for the initial attempt. We expect the controller to simply return all available messages on first attempt, meaning that empty access token should imply waiting for messages since 0.

Listing 14.69 Expecting the client to grab all messages

```
testCase(exports, "chatRoomController.get", {
  setUp: controllerSetUp,
  tearDown: controllerTearDown,

  "should wait for any message": function (test) {
    this.req.headers = { "x-access-token": "" };
    var chatRoom = this.controller.chatRoom;
    chatRoom.waitForMessagesSince = stub();

    this.controller.get();

    test.ok(chatRoom.waitForMessagesSince.called);
    test.equals(chatRoom.waitForMessagesSince.args[0], 0);
    test.done();
  }
});
```

Notice that Node downcases the headers. Failing to recognize this may take away some precious minutes from your life. Or so I've heard. To pass this test we can cheat by passing the expected id directly to the method, as Listing 14.70 does.

Listing 14.70 Cheating to pass tests

```
var chatRoomController = {
  /* ... */

  get: function () {
    this.chatRoom.waitForMessagesSince(0);
  }
};
```

The test passes. Onward to the subsequent requests, which should be coming in with an access token. Listing 14.71 stubs the access token with an actual value, and expects this to be passed to `waitForMessagesSince`.

Listing 14.71 Expecting `get` to pass the access token

```
"should wait for messages since X-Access-Token":
function (test) {
  this.req.headers = { "x-access-token": "2" };
  var chatRoom = this.controller.chatRoom;
  chatRoom.waitForMessagesSince = stub();

  this.controller.get();

  test.ok(chatRoom.waitForMessagesSince.called);
  test.equals(chatRoom.waitForMessagesSince.args[0], 2);
  test.done();
}
```

This test looks a lot like the previous one, only it expects the passed id to be the same as provided with the `X-Access-Token` header. These tests could need some cleaning up, and I encourage you to give them a spin. Passing the test is simple, as Listing 14.72 shows.

Listing 14.72 Passing the access token header

```
get: function () {
  var id = this.request.headers["x-access-token"] || 0;
  this.chatRoom.waitForMessagesSince(id);
}
```

14.6.2.2 The `respond` Method

Along with the response body, which should be a JSON response of some kind, the `get` method should also send status code and possibly some response headers, and finally close the connection. This sounds awfully similar to what `post` is currently doing. We'll extract the response into a new method in order to reuse it with the `get` request. Listing 14.73 shows two test cases for it, copied from the `post` test case.

Listing 14.73 Initial tests for `respond`

```
testCase(exports, "chatRoomController.respond", {
  setUp: controllerSetUp,

  "should write status code": function (test) {
    this.controller.respond(201);
```

```
      test.ok(this.res.writeHead.called);
      test.equals(this.res.writeHead.args[0], 201);
      test.done();
    },

  "should close connection": function (test) {
    this.controller.respond(201);

    test.ok(this.res.end.called);
    test.done();
  }
});
```

We can pass these tests by copying the two lines we last added to `post` into the new `respond` method, as Listing 14.74 shows.

Listing 14.74 A dedicated `respond` method

```
var chatRoomController = {
  /* ... */

  respond: function (status) {
    this.response.writeHead(status);
    this.response.end();
  }
};
```

Now we can simplify the `post` method by calling this method instead. Doing so also allows us to merge the original tests for status code and connection closing, by stubbing `respond` and asserting that it was called.

14.6.2.3 Formatting Messages

Next up for the `get` method is properly formatting messages. Again we'll need to lean on the `cometClient`, which defines the data format. The method should respond with a JSON object whose properties name the topic and values are arrays of objects. Additionally, the JSON object should include a `token` property. The JSON string should be written to the response body.

We can formulate this as a test by stubbing `respond` as we did before, this time expecting an object passed as the second argument. Thus, we will need to embellish `respond` later, having it write its second argument to the response body as a JSON string. Listing 14.75 shows the test.

Listing 14.75 Expecting an object passed to `respond`

```
function controllerSetUp() {
  var req = this.req = new EventEmitter();
  req.headers = { "x-access-token": "" };

  /* ... */

  var add = this.addMessagePromise = new Promise();
  var wait = this.waitForMessagesPromise = new Promise();

  this.controller.chatRoom = {
    addMessage: stub(add),
    waitForMessagesSince: stub(wait)
  };

  /* ... */
}

/* ... */

testCase(exports, "chatRoomController.respond", {
  /* ... */

  "should respond with formatted data": function (test) {
    this.controller.respond = stub();
    var messages = [{ user: "cjno", message: "hi" }];
    this.waitForMessagesPromise.resolve(messages);

    this.controller.get();

    process.nextTick(function () {
      test.ok(this.controller.respond.called);
      var args = this.controller.respond.args;
      test.same(args[0], 201);
      test.same(args[1].message, messages);
      test.done();
    }.bind(this));
  }
});
```

This test is a bit of a mouthful, and to make it slightly easier to digest, the `setUp` method was augmented. All the tests so far have stubbed `waitForMessagesSince`, and all of them require the headers to be set. Pulling these out makes it easier to focus on what the test in question is trying to achieve.

The test resolves the promise returned by `waitForMessagesSince`, and expects the resolving data to be wrapped in a `cometClient` friendly object and passed to the `resolve` method along with a 200 status. Listing 14.76 shows the required code to pass the test.

Listing 14.76 Responding from `get`

```
get: function () {
  var id = this.request.headers["x-access-token"] || 0;
  var wait = this.chatRoom.waitForMessagesSince(id);

  wait.then(function (msgs) {
    this.respond(200, { message: msgs });
  }.bind(this));
}
```

14.6.2.4 Updating the Token

Along with the messages, the `get` method needs to embed a token in its response. The token will automatically be picked up by `cometClient` and sent with the `X-Access-Token` header on subsequent requests. Listing 14.77 expects the token to be passed along with the message.

Listing 14.77 Expecting a token embedded in the response

```
"should include token in response": function (test) {
  this.controller.respond = stub();
  this.waitForMessagesPromise.resolve([{id:24}, {id:25}]);

  this.controller.get();

  process.nextTick(function () {
    test.same(this.controller.respond.args[1].token, 25);
    test.done();
  }.bind(this));
}
```

Passing the test involves passing the id of the last message as the token as seen in Listing 14.78.

Listing 14.78 Embedding the token

```
get: function () {
  /* ... */

  wait.then(function (messages) {
```

```
    this.respond(200, {
      message: messages,
      token: messages[messages.length - 1].id
    });
  }.bind(this));
}
```

14.6.3 Response Headers and Body

The final missing piece of the puzzle is encoding the response data as JSON and writing the response body. I will leave TDD-ing these features into the respond method as a last exercise for this chapter. For completeness, Listing 14.79 shows one possible outcome of the respond method.

Listing 14.79 The respond method

```
respond: function (status, data) {
  var strData = JSON.stringify(data) || "{}";

  this.response.writeHead(status, {
    "Content-Type": "application/json",
    "Content-Length": strData.length
  });

  this.response.write(strData);
  this.response.end();
}
```

And that's it! To take the application for a spin, we can launch another command line session, as Listing 14.80 shows.

Listing 14.80 Manually testing the finished app from the command line

```
$ node-repl
node> var msg = { user:"cjno", message:"Enjoying Node.js" };
node> var data = { topic: "message", data: msg };
node> var encoded = encodeURI(JSON.stringify(data));
node> require("fs").writeFileSync("chapp.txt", encoded);
node> Ctrl-d
$ curl -d `cat chapp.txt` http://localhost:8000/comet
$ curl http://localhost:8000/comet
{"message":[{"id":1,"user":"cjno",\
"message":"Enjoying Node.js"}],"token":1}
```

14.7 Summary

In this chapter we have gotten to know Node.js, asynchronous I/O for V8 JavaScript, and we have practiced JavaScript TDD outside the browser to see how the experience from previous exercises fares in a completely different environment than we're used to. By building a small web server to power a chat application we have gotten to know Node's HTTP, Assert, and Event APIs in addition to the third party node-promise library.

To provide the application with data, we also built an I/O interface that first mimicked Node's conventional use of callbacks and later went through a detailed refactoring exercise to convert it to use promises. Promises offer an elegant way of working with asynchronous interfaces, and makes concurrency a lot easier, even when we need to work with results in a predictable order. Promises are usable in any JavaScript setting, and the Ajax tools seems particularly fit for this style of interface.

In the next chapter we will use the tools built in Chapter 12, *Abstracting Browser Differences: Ajax,* and Chapter 13, *Streaming Data with Ajax and Comet,* to build a client for the Node backend, resulting in a completely usable in-browser instant chat application.

TDD and DOM Manipulation: The Chat Client

Developing client-side JavaScript includes a fair amount of DOM manipulation. In this chapter we will use test-driven development to implement a client for the chat backend we developed in Chapter 14, *Server-Side JavaScript with Node.js.* By doing so we will see how to apply the techniques we have learned so far to test DOM manipulation and event handling.

The DOM is an API just like any other, which means that testing it should be fairly straightforward so long as we adhere to the single responsibility principle and keep components loosely coupled. The DOM does potentially present a challenge in that it consists entirely of host objects, but as we will see, we can work around the potential problems.

15.1 Planning the Client

The task at hand is building a simple chat GUI. The resulting application will have two views: when the user enters the application she will be presented with a form in which to enter the desired username. Submitting the form will remove it and display a list of messages and a form to enter new ones in its place. As usual, we will keep the scope at a minimum to get through the entire exercise, so for example, there will be no cookie management to remember the user. Throughout the chapter ideas on how to add more features to the client will be suggested as exercises.

15.1.1 Directory Structure

Again, we will use JsTestDriver to run the tests. The client will eventually use all the code developed throughout Part III, *Real-World Test-Driven Development in JavaScript,* but we will start with a bare minimum and add in dependencies as they are required. For the TDD session, some of the dependencies will always be stubbed, meaning we won't need them to develop the client. Listing 15.1 shows the initial directory structure.

Listing 15.1 Initial directory structure

```
chris@laptop:~/projects/chat_client$ tree
.
|-- jsTestDriver.conf
|-- lib
|   |-- stub.js
|   `-- tdd.js
|-- src
`-- test
```

stub.js contains the stubFn function from Chapter 13, *Streaming Data with Ajax and Comet,* and tdd.js contains the tddjs object along with the various tools built in Part II, *JavaScript for Programmers,* Listing 15.2 shows the contents of the jsTestDriver.conf configuration file. As usual, you can download the initial project state from the book's website.[1]

Listing 15.2 The initial JsTestDriver configuration

```
server: http://localhost:4224

load:
  - lib/*.js
  - src/*.js
  - test/*.js
```

15.1.2 Choosing the Approach

Prior to launching the TDD session we need a general idea on how we're going to build the client. Our main priorities are to keep a clear separation between the DOM and the data (provided by cometClient from Chapter 13, *Streaming Data*

---

1. http://tddjs.com

with Ajax and Comet) and to control all dependencies from the outside, i.e., using dependency injection. To achieve this we will employ a derivative of the Model-View-Controller (MVC) design pattern frequently referred to as Model-View-Presenter (MVP), which is very well suited to facilitate unit testing and fits well with test-driven development.

15.1.2.1 Passive View

MVP is practiced in a variety of ways and we will apply it in a manner that leans toward what Martin Fowler, renowned programmer, author, and thinker, calls Passive View. In this model, the view notifies the presenter—*controller* in Passive View—of user input, and the controller completely controls the state of the view. The controller responds to events in the view and manipulates the underlying model.

In a browser setting, the DOM is the view. For the chat application the model will be provided by the `cometClient` object, and our main task is to develop the controllers. Note the plural form; there are many controllers, each discrete widget or even widget component can be represented by its own view and controller, sometimes referred to as an *MVP axis*. This makes it easy to adhere to the single responsibility principle, in which each object has one well-defined task. Throughout this chapter we will refer to a controller/view duo as a *component*.

We will divide the chat client into three distinct components: the user form, the message list, and the message form. The message list and form will not be displayed until the user form is successfully completed. However, this flow will be controlled from the outside, as controllers will not be aware of other controllers. Keeping them completely decoupled means we can more easily manipulate the client by adding or removing components, and it makes them easier to test.

15.1.2.2 Displaying the Client

We need some DOM elements to display the components. To keep the scope manageable within the confines of a single chapter, we're going to manually write the required markup in the HTML file that serves the application.

The client is not going to make any sense to users without JavaScript, or without a sufficiently capable JavaScript engine. To avoid presenting the user with controls they cannot meaningfully use, we will initially hide all the chat related markup, and have the individual controllers append the "js-chat" class name to the various elements used by the client. This way we can use CSS to display elements as JavaScript enhances them.

15.2 The User Form

The user form is in charge of collecting the user's desired chat name. As the server currently has no concept of connected users, it does not need to validate the user name in any way, i.e., two users may be online at the same time using the same name. The controller requires a DOM form element as its view, and expects this to contain at least one text input, from which it will read the username when the form is submitted.

When the form is submitted, the controller will assign the user to a property of the model object, to make it available to the rest of the application. Then it will emit an event, allowing other parts of the application to act on the newly arrived user.

15.2.1 Setting the View

The first task is to set the view, i.e., assign the DOM element that is the visual representation of the component.

15.2.1.1 Setting Up the Test Case

We start by setting up the test case and adding the first test, which expects user-FormController to be an object. Listing 15.3 shows the initial test case. Save it in test/user-form-controller-test.js.

Listing 15.3 Expecting the object to exist

```
(function () {
  var userController = tddjs.chat.userFormController;

  TestCase("UserFormControllerTest", {
    "test should be object": function () {
      assertObject(userController);
    }
  });
}());
```

Listing 15.4 passes the test by setting up the userFormController object. Save the listing in src/user-form-controller.js.

Listing 15.4 Defining the controller

```
tddjs.namespace("chat").userFormController = {};
```

The next test, shown in Listing 15.5, expects setView to be a function.

Listing 15.5 Expecting setView to be a function

```
"test should have setView method": function () {
  assertFunction(userController.setView);
}
```

Listing 15.6 adds an empty method to pass the test.

Listing 15.6 Adding an empty setView method

```
(function () {
  function setView(element) {}

  tddjs.namespace("chat").userFormController = {
    setView: setView
  };
}());
```

15.2.1.2 Adding a Class

The first actual behavior we'll test for is that the "js-chat" class name is added to the DOM element, as seen in Listing 15.7. Note that the test requires the Object.create implementation from Chapter 7, *Objects and Prototypal Inheritance,* in lib/object.js to run smoothly across browsers.

Listing 15.7 Expecting the view to have its class name set

```
TestCase("UserFormControllerSetViewTest", {
  "test should add js-chat class": function () {
    var controller = Object.create(userController);
    var element = {};

    controller.setView(element);

    assertClassName("js-chat", element);
  }
});
```

The first thing that sticks out about this test is that it contains no DOM elements. It does, however, use the assertClassName assertion, which checks if an element has the given class name. This assertion is generic, and only checks that the object defines a string property className and that one of its space separated values matches the provided string.

The `element` object is a simple stub object. At this point there's no need to use a real DOM element, because all we want to check is that some property was assigned.

The test fails, and Listing 15.8 assigns the class name to pass it.

Listing 15.8 Adding the class

```
function setView(element) {
  element.className = "js-chat";
}
```

At this point you might worry about a few things. Should we really be overriding the class name like that? Should the class name not be configurable? Remember: You ain't gonna need it! At this point, we have no use case demonstrating the need to use an element that already has class names or the need to use another class name than "js-chat." Once we have, we can jot down a few tests to document those requirements, and *then* we can implement them. Right now we don't need them, and they'll just be slowing us down.

15.2.1.3 Adding an Event Listener

Next we will add an event listener to the form's "submit" event. To do this, we will use the `tddjs.dom.addEventHandler` interface we wrote in Chapter 10, *Feature Detection.* Testing event handlers is commonly accepted as a challenging task. The main reasons being that triggering user events from script in a cross-browser manner is less than trivial, and tests need a lot of setup, thus they can easily become complex.

Unit testing event handlers in application code, when done right, is in fact trivial. Attaching event handlers through an abstraction such as `tddjs.dom.addEventHandler` means that all we need to assert is that this method is called correctly. By stubbing it, we gain access to the arguments passed to it, which means that we can manually call the handler to test the behavior of the event handler (in another dedicated test case). Tests that rely heavily on event data, such as mouse coordinates, neighbouring elements, and less tangible data may require complex setup, but such setup can be hidden behind, e.g., a fake event implementation for use in tests.

I'm not saying that you should not test event handlers end-to-end, but I am saying that the application unit test suite is unlikely the right place to do so. First, one would hope that whatever library is being used to add event listeners has its own comprehensive test suite, meaning that in your tests you should be able to trust it. Second, if your application has acceptance tests, or some kind of in-browser

integration tests, those are good places to test end-to-end functionality, including
DOM event handlers. We will return briefly to this topic in Chapter 17, *Writing
Good Unit Tests.*

As there is no need to add an actual DOM event listener while testing, we can
simply stub `addEventHandler` in the tests. Listing 15.9 shows the first test.

Listing 15.9 Expect the element's submit event to be handled

```
"test should handle submit event": function () {
  var controller = Object.create(userController);
  var element = {};
  var dom = tddjs.namespace("dom");
  dom.addEventHandler = stubFn();

  controller.setView(element);

  assert(dom.addEventHandler.called);
  assertSame(element, dom.addEventHandler.args[0]);
  assertEquals("submit", dom.addEventHandler.args[1]);
  assertFunction(dom.addEventHandler.args[2]);
}
```

As we have not yet included `addEventHandler` as a dependency, we use the
`namespace` method to retrieve or define the `dom` namespace before stubbing the
`addEventHandler` method. The test fails, and Listing 15.10 adds the method
call to pass it.

Listing 15.10 Adding a submit event handler

```
var dom = tddjs.namespace("dom");

function setView(element) {
  element.className = "js-chat";
  dom.addEventHandler(element, "submit", function () {});
}
```

Once again, we use the `namespace` method to avoid trouble. Using local
aliases to reduce typing and speed up identifier resolution is useful, but also causes
objects to be cached before we use them. Because the source files are loaded first,
the `tddjs.dom` object is not available when we assign it to the local `dom` variable.
However, by the time the test triggers the call to `dom.addEventHandler`, the
test has filled in the blanks. Using the `namespace` method means both files refer
to the same object without us having to worry about which one loaded first.

Running the test produces some disappointing results. The test passes, but unfortunately the previous test now breaks, as there is no `addEventHandler` method around at the point of running it. We can fix this and the duplicated test code by elevating some common code into a `setUp` method, as Listing 15.11 shows.

Listing 15.11 Extracting code into `setUp`

```
/* ... */
var dom = tddjs.namespace("dom");
/* ... */

TestCase("UserFormControllerSetViewTest", {
  setUp: function () {
    this.controller = Object.create(userController);
    this.element = {};
    dom.addEventHandler = stubFn();
  },

  "test should add js-chat class": function () {
    this.controller.setView(this.element);

    assertClassName("js-chat", this.element);
  },

  "test should handle submit event": function () {
    this.controller.setView(this.element);

    assert(dom.addEventHandler.called);
    assertSame(this.element, dom.addEventHandler.args[0]);
    assertEquals("submit", dom.addEventHandler.args[1]);
    assertFunction(dom.addEventHandler.args[2]);
  }
});
```

Even though both tests use `setView` in the same way, we keep it out of `setUp`, because this call is not part of the setup, rather it is the *exercise* step of the test. Refactoring the test got the tests back on track, and they now both pass.

For the next test, we need to verify that the event handler is bound to the controller object. To achieve this we need `stubFn` to record the value of `this` at call time. Listing 15.12 shows the updated function.

Listing 15.12 Recording `this` in `stubFn`

```
function stubFn(returnValue) {
  var fn = function () {
    fn.called = true;
    fn.args = arguments;
    fn.thisValue = this;
    return returnValue;
  };

  fn.called = false;

  return fn;
}
```

The next test, seen in Listing 15.13, uses the improved `stubFn` to assert that the event handler is the controller's `handleSubmit` method, readily bound to the controller object.

Listing 15.13 Expecting the event handler to be `handleSubmit` bound to controller

```
"test should handle event with bound handleSubmit":
function () {
  var stub = this.controller.handleSubmit = stubFn();

  this.controller.setView(this.element);
  dom.addEventHandler.args[2]();

  assert(stub.called);
  assertSame(this.controller, stub.thisValue);
}
```

This test shows another reason for not elevating the `setView` call to the `setUp` method; here we need additional setup before calling it, to be sure the method uses the stubbed `handleSubmit` method—not the original one, which would fail our test indefinitely. Listing 15.14 updates the call to pass the test. Note that the implementation requires the `bind` implementation from Chapter 6, *Applied Functions and Closures,* in `lib/function.js`.

Listing 15.14 Binding `handleSubmit` as event handler

```
function setView(element) {
  element.className = "js-chat";
  var handler = this.handleSubmit.bind(this);
  dom.addEventHandler(element, "submit", handler);
}
```

We now pass the current test but again fail previous tests. The reason is that the controller does not actually define a `handleSubmit` method; thus, any test that does not stub it fails. The fix is easy enough; define the method on the controller. Listing 15.15 to the rescue.

Listing 15.15 Adding an empty `handleSubmit` method

```
/* ... */

function handleSubmit(event) {
}

tddjs.namespace("chat").userFormController = {
  setView: setView,
  handleSubmit: handleSubmit
};
```

That's the happy path for `setView`. It should also do basic error checking, at the very least verify that it receives an argument. I'll leave doing so as an exercise.

15.2.2 Handling the Submit Event

When the user submits the form, the handler should grab the value from the form's first `input` element whose type is `text`, assign it to the model's `currentUser` property, and then remove the "js-chat" class name, signifying end of life for the user component. Last, but not least, the handler needs to abort the event's default action to avoid the browser actually posting the form.

15.2.2.1 Aborting the Default Action

We'll start with that last requirement; the event's default action should be prevented. In standards compliant browsers, this is done by calling the `preventDefault` method on the event object as Listing 15.16 shows. Internet Explorer does not support this method, and rather requires the event handler to return false. However, as you might remember, `addEventHandler` from Chapter 10, *Feature Detection,* takes care of some basic event normalization to smooth things over for us.

Listing 15.16 Expecting the event's `preventDefault` method to be called

```
TestCase("UserFormControllerHandleSubmitTest", {
  "test should prevent event default action": function () {
    var controller = Object.create(userController);
    var event = { preventDefault: stubFn() };

    controller.handleSubmit(event);

    assert(event.preventDefault.called);
  }
});
```

Again we put our trust in a stubbed function. Passing this test requires a single line of added code, as Listing 15.17 shows.

Listing 15.17 Preventing the default action

```
function handleSubmit(event) {
  event.preventDefault();
}
```

Now that the test passes, we can start worrying about duplicating setup between the two test cases. As usual, we'll simply extract the setup to a local function that both test cases can share, as Listing 15.18 shows.

Listing 15.18 Sharing setup

```
function userFormControllerSetUp() {
  this.controller = Object.create(userController);
  this.element = {};
  dom.addEventHandler = stubFn();
}

TestCase("UserFormControllerSetViewTest", {
  setUp: userFormControllerSetUp,

  /* ... */
});

TestCase("UserFormControllerHandleSubmitTest", {
  setUp: userFormControllerSetUp,

  "test should prevent event default action": function () {
    var event = { preventDefault: stubFn() };
```

```
        this.controller.handleSubmit(event);

        assert(event.preventDefault.called);
    }
});
```

15.2.2.2 Embedding HTML in Tests

Next up is verifying that the model is updated with the username as entered in
an input element. How will we provide an input element in the test? Basically
we have two choices; continue stubbing, e.g., by giving the stub element a stub
`getElementsByTagName` method, which returns a stub `input` element, or
embed some markup in the test.

Although the former approach works and allows us to completely control both
direct and indirect inputs to the method under test, it increases the risk of stubs
not matching reality, and for anything other than trivial cases requires us to write a
whole lot of stubs. Embedding some markup in the test will keep the tests closer
to the production environment, and at the same time requires less manual stubbing. Additionally, by adding the user form inside the test case, the test case better
documents how to use the controller.

JsTestDriver provides two ways to include HTML in a test; in-memory elements
and elements added to the document. Listing 15.19 shows a test that creates some
HTML that is not attached to the document.

Listing 15.19 Embedding HTML in a JsTestDriver test

```
"test should embed HTML": function () {
  /*:DOC element = <div></div> */

  assertEquals("div", this.element.tagName.toLowerCase());
}
```

As you can see, the name before the equals sign names the property JsTestDriver
should assign the resulting DOM element to. It's important to note that the right
side of the equals sign needs to nest elements inside a single root element. It can
contain an arbitrarily complex structure, but there can only be one root node. The
other way to include HTML in tests is by appending to the document, as Listing
15.20 illustrates.

Listing 15.20 Appending elements to the document

```
"test should append HTML to document": function () {
  /*:DOC += <div id="myDiv"></div> */
  var div = document.getElementById("myDiv");

  assertEquals("div", div.tagName.toLowerCase());
}
```

For the most part, not appending to the document is both slightly faster and more convenient, because JsTestDriver automatically assigns it to a property on the test case. Unless we need to pick up elements globally (e.g., by selecting them from the document) or need elements to render, there usually is no gain in appending the elements to the document.

15.2.2.3 Getting the Username

Returning to the controller, the problem at hand is expecting `handleSubmit` to pick up what the user entered in the form's first text input field and using it as the username. To do this, we'll first remove the element stub we've been using so far, and use an actual form instead. Listing 15.21 shows the updated `setUp`.

Listing 15.21 Embedding a user form in `setUp`

```
function userFormControllerSetUp() {
  /*:DOC element = <form>
     <fieldset>
       <label for="username">Username</label>
       <input type="text" name="username" id="username">
       <input type="submit" value="Enter">
     </fieldset>
   </form> */

  this.controller = Object.create(userController);
  dom.addEventHandler = stubFn();
}
```

Running the test confirms that we're still in the green. With an actual form in place, we can add the test that expects `handleSubmit` to read the input field, as seen in Listing 15.22.

Listing 15.22 Expecting `handleSubmit` to read username from field

```
"test should set model.currentUser": function () {
  var model = {};
```

```
    var event = { preventDefault: stubFn() };
    var input = this.element.getElementsByTagName("input")[0];
    input.value = "cjno";
    this.controller.setModel(model);
    this.controller.setView(this.element);

    this.controller.handleSubmit(event);

    assertEquals("cjno", model.currentUser);
}
```

The test adds a stub model object with the so far non-existent `setModel` method. The fact that the method is missing causes the test to fail, so Listing 15.23 adds the method.

Listing 15.23 Adding `setModel`

```
/* ... */

function setModel(model) {
  this.model = model;
}

tddjs.namespace("chat").userFormController = {
  setView: setView,
  setModel: setModel,
  handleSubmit: handleSubmit
};
```

One could argue that a simple setter such as this is superfluous, but providing `setView` and `setModel` methods makes the interface consistent and predictable. When ECMAScript 5 becomes widely supported, we can do one better by using native setters, which untangles the explicit method calls.

Next up, we need to make the `handleSubmit` method actually pick up the current value of the input field. Listing 15.24 fills in the blanks.

Listing 15.24 Picking up the username

```
function handleSubmit(event) {
  event.preventDefault();

  var input = this.view.getElementsByTagName("input")[0];
  this.model.currentUser = input.value;
}
```

Still no luck. To make matters worse, adding that line actually failed the previous test as well, because it didn't set a view. We can fix that by checking that the view is set before asking it for elements, as Listing 15.25 does.

Listing 15.25 Checking that `this.view` is available

```
function handleSubmit(event) {
  event.preventDefault();

  if (this.view) {
    var input = this.view.getElementsByTagName("input")[0];
    this.model.currentUser = input.value;
  }
}
```

That gets the previous test back to green, but the current test still fails. It turns out that `setView` doesn't actually, well, set the view. Listing 15.26 fixes `setView`.

Listing 15.26 Storing a reference to the view

```
function setView(element) {
  /* ... */
  this.view = element;
}
```

And with that, all tests pass. We can now tend to the test case, which currently duplicates some effort. Both of the tests create a stubbed event object, which can and should be elevated to `setUp`. Listing 15.27 shows the updated `setUp`.

Listing 15.27 Stubbing event in `setUp`

```
function userFormControllerSetUp() {
  /* ... */

  this.event = { preventDefault: stubFn() };
}
```

15.2.2.4   Notifying Observers of the User

Once the user has been set, the controller should notify any observers. Listing 15.28 tests this by observing the event, handling the event and asserting that the observer was called.

Listing 15.28 Expecting `handleSubmit` to notify observers

```
"test should notify observers of username": function () {
  var input = this.element.getElementsByTagName("input")[0];
  input.value = "Bullrog";
  this.controller.setModel({});
  this.controller.setView(this.element);
  var observer = stubFn();

  this.controller.observe("user", observer);
  this.controller.handleSubmit(this.event);

  assert(observer.called);
  assertEquals("Bullrog", observer.args[0]);
}
```

That test should trigger all kinds of duplication alarms. Don't worry, we'll get on fixing it shortly. As expected, the test fails because the controller has no observe method. To fix this, we can extend the controller with `tddjs.util.observable`. For this to work we need to fetch the `observable` implementation from Chapter 11, *The Observer Pattern,* in `lib/observable.js`. Furthermore, because `lib/tdd.js` always needs to load before any of the other modules, we must also update `jsTestDriver.conf`, as Listing 15.29 shows.

Listing 15.29 Updated jsTestDriver.conf

```
server: http://localhost:4224

load:
  - lib/tdd.js
  - lib/*.js
  - src/*.js
  - test/*.js
```

Plumbing aside, we can now update the controller implementation, as seen in Listing 15.30.

Listing 15.30 Making `userFormController` observable

```
(function () {
  var dom = tddjs.namespace("dom");
  var util = tddjs.util;
  var chat = tddjs.namespace("chat");

  /* ... */
```

```
   chat.userFormController = tddjs.extend({}, util.observable);
   chat.userFormController.setView = setView;
   chat.userFormController.setModel = setModel;
   chat.userFormController.handleSubmit = handleSubmit;
}());
```

With the controller now observable, we can make it notify its observers for the "user" event, as Listing 15.31 shows.

Listing 15.31 Notifying "user" observers

```
function handleSubmit(event) {
  event.preventDefault();

  if (this.view) {
    var input = this.view.getElementsByTagName("input")[0];
    this.model.currentUser = input.value;
    this.notify("user", input.value);
  }
}
```

The tests pass. However, the two last tests share an awful lot in common, and to keep duplication at bay we will elevate some common setup code. Listing 15.32 shows the updated test case.

Listing 15.32 Elevating shared test setup

```
TestCase("UserFormControllerHandleSubmitTest", {
  setUp: function () {
    userFormControllerSetUp.call(this);
    this.input =
      this.element.getElementsByTagName("input")[0];
    this.model = {};
    this.controller.setModel(this.model);
    this.controller.setView(this.element);
  },

  /* ... */
});
```

The previous test case doesn't really need any of the new setup, and in fact some of it would interfere with its tests. To still be able to use the shared setup, we add a setup specific to the test that calls the shared setup with the test case as this and then adds more setup code.

15.2.2.5 Removing the Added Class

The final requirement for the user form controller is removing the "js-chat" class name once a user is successfully set. Listing 15.33 shows the initial test.

Listing 15.33 Expecting the class to be removed upon completion

```
"test should remove class when successful": function () {
  this.input.value = "Sharuhachi";

  this.controller.handleSubmit(this.event);

  assertEquals("", this.element.className);
}
```

To pass the test, we simply reset the class name if a user name was found. Listing 15.34 shows the updated `handleSubmit`.

Listing 15.34 Resetting the view's class

```
function handleSubmit(event) {
  event.preventDefault();

  if (this.view) {
    var input = this.view.getElementsByTagName("input")[0];
    var userName = input.value;
    this.view.className = "";
    this.model.currentUser = userName;
    this.notify("user", userName);
  }
}
```

15.2.2.6 Rejecting Empty Usernames

If the user submits the form without entering a username, the chat client will fail upon trying to post messages, because the server won't allow empty user names. In other words, allowing an empty username from the user form controller will cause an error in completely unrelated parts of the code, which could be fairly hard to debug. Listing 15.35 expects the controller not to set an empty username.

Listing 15.35 Expecting `handleSubmit` not to notify with empty username

```
"test should not notify observers of empty username":
function () {
  var observer = stubFn();
```

```
  this.controller.observe("user", observer);

  this.controller.handleSubmit(this.event);

  assertFalse(observer.called);
}
```

Passing this test requires a check on the value of the input field, as seen in Listing 15.36.

Listing 15.36 Disallowing empty usernames

```
function handleSubmit(event) {
  event.preventDefault();

  if (this.view) {
    var input = this.view.getElementsByTagName("input")[0];
    var userName = input.value;

    if (!userName) {
      return;
    }

    /* ... */
  }
}
```

The method also should not remove the "js-chat" class name if the username was empty. The method clearly could benefit from notifying the user of the error as well. As an exercise, I encourage you to add tests for and implement these additional cases.

15.2.3 Feature Tests

With that, the user form controller is complete enough to provide the happy path. It clearly could do with more resilient error handling and I strongly encourage you to pick up doing so as exercises. One final touch we will add to the controller before moving on is a set of feature tests to decide if the controller can be supported.

To add proper feature tests we need the actual event implementation as a dependency, because the controller will require its existence at define time. Save the addEventHandler implementation from Chapter 10, *Feature Detection,* in lib/event.js. Listing 15.37 shows the controller including feature tests.

Listing 15.37 Feature tests for `userFormController`

```
(function () {
  if (typeof tddjs == "undefined" ||
      typeof document == "undefined") {
    return;
  }

  var dom = tddjs.dom;
  var util = tddjs.util;
  var chat = tddjs.namespace("chat");

  if (!dom || !dom.addEventHandler || !util ||
      !util.observable || !Object.create ||
      !document.getElementsByTagName ||
      !Function.prototype.bind) {
    return;
  }

  /* ... */
}());
```

Note that because the tests aren't storing a reference to `addEventHandler` before stubbing and restoring it in `tearDown` as we did before, we are effectively overwriting it for the entire test suite. In this particular case this isn't a problem, because none of the tests will register actual DOM event handlers.

When you have added the above feature tests, you need to have the event utilities from Chapter 10, *Feature Detection,* in `tdd.js` for the tests to pass, because the controller will not be defined if its dependencies are not available.

15.3 Using the Client with the Node.js Backend

Having successfully completed one of three client components, we will add some plumbing to the "chapp" Node application from Chapter 14, *Server-Side JavaScript with Node.js,* to have it serve the client. As a low-level runtime, Node does not have a concept of serving static files through its http server module. Doing so requires matching the request's URL to a file on disk and streaming it to the client. Implementing this is well outside the scope of this chapter, so instead we will use a module by Felix Geisendörfer called node-paperboy.[2] A version guaranteed to

---

2. http://github.com/felixge/node-paperboy

work with the code in the book can be downloaded from the book's website.[3] Place it in chapp's `deps` directory.

Listing 15.38 loads the module in chapp's `lib/server.js`. It's set up to serve files from the `public` directory, e.g., http://localhost:8000/index.html will attempt to serve `public/index.html`.

Listing 15.38 Adding static file serving to chapp's server

```
/* ... */
var paperboy = require("node-paperboy");

module.exports = http.createServer(function (req, res) {
  if (url.parse(req.url).pathname == "/comet") {
    /* ... */
  } else {
    var delivery = paperboy.deliver("public", req, res);

    delivery.otherwise(function () {
      res.writeHead(404, { "Content-Type": "text/html" });
      res.write("<h1>Nothing to see here, move along</h1>");
      res.close();
    });
  }
});
```

The `otherwise` callback is triggered if no file is found in `public` matching the requested URL. In that case we serve up a really tiny 404 page. To serve up the chat client, create `public/js`, and copy over the following files:

- tdd.js
- observable.js
- function.js
- object.js
- user_form_controller.js

Save Listing 15.39 in `public/index.html`.

Listing 15.39 The client HTML

```
<!DOCTYPE html PUBLIC "-//W3C//DTD HTML 4.01//EN"
          "http://www.w3.org/TR/html4/strict.dtd">
```

---

3. http://tddjs.com

```html
<html lang="en">
  <head>
    <meta http-equiv="content-type"
          content="text/html; charset=utf-8">
    <title>Chapp JavaScript Chat</title>
    <link type="text/css" rel="stylesheet"
          media="screen, projection" href="css/chapp.css">
  </head>
  <body>
    <h1>Chapp JavaScript Chat</h1>
    <form id="userForm">
      <fieldset>
        <label for="name">Name:</label>
        <input type="text" name="name" id="name"
               autocomplete="off">
        <input type="submit" value="Join">
      </fieldset>
    </form>
    <script type="text/javascript"
            src="js/function.js"></script>
    <script type="text/javascript"
            src="js/object.js"></script>
    <script type="text/javascript" src="js/tdd.js"></script>
    <script type="text/javascript"
            src="js/observable.js"></script>
    <script type="text/javascript"
            src="js/user_form_controller.js"></script>
    <script type="text/javascript"
            src="js/chat_client.js"></script>
  </body>
</html>
```

Save the *very* simple stylesheet in Listing 15.40 in `public/css/chapp.css`.

Listing 15.40 The initial CSS file

```css
form { display: none; }
.js-chat { display: block; }
```

Finally, save the bootstrapping script in Listing 15.41 in `public/js/chat_client.js`.

Listing 15.41 The initial bootstrap script

```javascript
(function () {
  if (typeof tddjs == "undefined" ||
      typeof document == "undefined" ||
      !document.getElementById || !Object.create ||
```

```
    !tddjs.namespace("chat").userFormController) {
  alert("Browser is not supported");
  return;
}

var chat = tddjs.chat;
var model = {};
var userForm = document.getElementById("userForm");
var userController =
  Object.create(chat.userFormController);
userController.setModel(model);
userController.setView(userForm);

userController.observe("user", function (user) {
  alert("Welcome, " + user);
});
}());
```

Now start the server and bring up http://localhost:8000/ in your browser of choice. You should be presented with an unstyled form. Upon submitting it, the browser should alert you with a greeting and hide the form. It's not much, but it's working code, and having a working testbed for the client means we can easily take new components for a spin as they are completed.

15.4 The Message List

The message list will consist of a definition list, in which messages are represented by a dt element containing the user and a dd element containing the message. The controller will observe the model's "message" channel to receive messages, and will build DOM elements and inject them into the view. As with the user form controller, it will add the "js-chat" class to the view when it is set.

15.4.1 Setting the Model

For this controller, we will start by adding the model object. In contrast to the user form controller, the message list will need to do more than simply assign the model.

15.4.1.1 Defining the Controller and Method

Listing 15.42 shows the initial test case that asserts that the controller exists. Save it in test/message-list-controller-test.js.

Listing 15.42 Expecting `messageListController` to be an object

```
(function () {
  var listController = tddjs.chat.messageListController;

  TestCase("MessageListControllerTest", {
    "test should be object": function () {
      assertObject(listController);
    }
  });
}());
```

To pass the test, create `lib/message_list_controller.js` and save it with the contents of Listing 15.43.

Listing 15.43 Defining `messageListController`

```
(function () {
  var chat = tddjs.namespace("chat");
  chat.messageListController = {};
}());
```

Next, we expect the controller to have a `setModel` method, as seen in Listing 15.44.

Listing 15.44 Expecting `setModel` to be a function

```
"test should have setModel method": function () {
  assertFunction(listController.setModel);
}
```

Listing 15.45 adds an empty method.

Listing 15.45 Adding an empty `setModel`

```
function setModel(model) {}

chat.messageListController = {
  setModel: setModel
};
```

15.4.1.2 Subscribing to Messages

`setModel` needs to observe the model's "message" channel. Remember, in production, the model object will be a `cometClient` that streams messages from the server. Listing 15.46 expects `observe` to be called.

Listing 15.46 Expecting `setModel` to observe the "message" channel

```
TestCase("MessageListControllerSetModelTest", {
  "test should observe model's message channel":
  function () {
    var controller = Object.create(listController);
    var model = { observe: stubFn() };

    controller.setModel(model);

    assert(model.observe.called);
    assertEquals("message", model.observe.args[0]);
    assertFunction(model.observe.args[1]);
  }
});
```

The test fails, and Listing 15.47 helps passing it by making the call to `observe`.

Listing 15.47 Calling `observe`

```
function setModel(model) {
  model.observe("message", function () {});
}
```

Next, we'll expect the handler to be a bound `addMessage` method, much like we did with the DOM event handler in the user form controller. Listing 15.48 shows the test.

Listing 15.48 Expecting a bound `addMessage` as "message" handler

```
TestCase("MessageListControllerSetModelTest", {
  setUp: function () {
    this.controller = Object.create(listController);
    this.model = { observe: stubFn() };
  },

  /* ... */

  "test should observe with bound addMessage": function () {
    var stub = this.controller.addMessage = stubFn();

    this.controller.setModel(this.model);
    this.model.observe.args[1]();

    assert(stub.called);
```

```
      assertSame(this.controller, stub.thisValue);
    }
});
```

I jumped the gun slightly on this one, immediately recognizing that a setUp was required to avoid duplicating the test setup code. The test should look eerily familiar because it basically mimics the test we wrote to verify that userFormController observed the submit event with a bound handleSubmit method.

Listing 15.49 adds the correct handler to model.observe. What are your expectations as to the result of running the tests?

Listing 15.49 Observing the "message" channel with a bound method

```
function setModel(model) {
  model.observe("message", this.addMessage.bind(this));
}
```

If you expected the test to pass, but the previous test to fail, then you're absolutely right. As before, we need to add the method we're binding to the controller, to keep tests that aren't stubbing it from failing. Listing 15.50 adds the method.

Listing 15.50 Adding an empty addMessage

```
/* ... */
function addMessage(message) {}

chat.messageListController = {
  setModel: setModel,
  addMessage: addMessage
};
```

Before we can move on to test the addMessage method, we need to add a view, because addMessage's main task is to build DOM elements to inject into it. As before, we're turning a blind eye to everything but the happy path. What happens if someone calls setModel without an object? Or with an object that does not support observe? Write a few tests, and update the implementation as you find necessary.

15.4.2 Setting the View

With the experience we gained while developing the user form controller, we will use DOM elements in place of fake objects right from the start while developing setView for the list controller. Listing 15.51 verifies that the method adds the "js-chat" class to the view element.

Listing 15.51 Expecting `setView` to set the element's class

```
function messageListControllerSetUp() {
  /*:DOC element = <dl></dl> */

  this.controller = Object.create(listController);
  this.model = { observe: stubFn() };
}

TestCase("MessageListControllerSetModelTest", {
  setUp: messageListControllerSetUp,
  /* ... */
});

TestCase("MessageListControllerSetViewTest", {
  setUp: messageListControllerSetUp,

  "test should set class to js-chat": function () {
    this.controller.setView(this.element);

    assertClassName("js-chat", this.element);
  }
});
```

We've danced the extract setup dance enough times now that hopefully the
above listing should not be too frightening. Even though parts of the TDD process
do become predictable after awhile, it's important to stick to the rhythm. No matter
how obvious some feature may seem, we should be extremely careful about adding it
until we can prove we really need it. Remember, You Ain't Gonna Need It. Keeping
to the rhythm ensures neither production code nor tests are any more complicated
than what they need to be.

The test fails because the `setView` method does not exist. Listing 15.52 adds
it and passes the test in one fell swoop.

Listing 15.52 Adding a compliant `setView` method

```
function setView(element) {
  element.className = "js-chat";
}

chat.messageListController = {
  setModel: setModel,
  setView: setView,
  addMessage: addMessage
};
```

That's it for now. We'll need the method to actually store the view as well, but preferably without poking at its implementation. Also, currently there is no need to store it, at least not until we need to use it in another context.

15.4.3 Adding Messages

Onwards to the heart and soul of the controller; receiving messages, building DOM elements for them, and injecting them into the view. The first thing we will test for is that a dt element containing the user prefixed with an "@" is added to the definition list, as Listing 15.53 shows.

Listing 15.53 Expecting the user to be injected into the DOM in a dt element

```
TestCase("MessageListControllerAddMessageTest", {
  setUp: messageListControllerSetUp,

  "test should add dt element with @user": function () {
    this.controller.setModel(this.model);
    this.controller.setView(this.element);

    this.controller.addMessage({
      user: "Eric",
      message: "We are trapper keeper"
    });

    var dts = this.element.getElementsByTagName("dt");
    assertEquals(1, dts.length);
    assertEquals("@Eric", dts[0].innerHTML);
  }
});
```

The test adds a message and then expects the definition list to have gained a dt element. To pass the test we need to build an element and append it to the view, as Listing 15.54 shows.

Listing 15.54 Adding the user to the list

```
function addMessage(message) {
  var user = document.createElement("dt");
  user.innerHTML = "@" + message.user;
  this.view.appendChild(user);
}
```

Boom! Test fails; this.view is undefined. There we go, a documented need for the view to be kept in a property. Listing 15.55 fixes setView to store a reference to the element.

Listing 15.55 Storing a reference to the view element

```
function setView(element) {
  element.className = "js-chat";
  this.view = element;
}
```

With a reference to the view in place, all the tests pass. That leaves the message, which should be added to the DOM as well. Listing 15.56 shows the test.

Listing 15.56 Expecting the message to be added to the DOM

```
TestCase("MessageListControllerAddMessageTest", {
  setUp: function () {
    messageListControllerSetUp.call(this);
    this.controller.setModel(this.model);
    this.controller.setView(this.element);
  },

  /* ... */

  "test should add dd element with message": function () {
    this.controller.addMessage({
      user: "Theodore",
      message: "We are one"
    });

    var dds = this.element.getElementsByTagName("dd");
    assertEquals(1, dds.length);
    assertEquals("We are one", dds[0].innerHTML);
  }
});
```

Again, some test setup code was immediately elevated to the `setUp` method, to keep the goal of the test obvious. To pass this test, we basically just need to repeat the three lines from before, changing the text content and tag name. Listing 15.57 has the lowdown.

Listing 15.57 Adding the message as a `dd` element

```
function addMessage(message) {
  /* ... */
  var msg = document.createElement("dd");
  msg.innerHTML = message.message;
  this.view.appendChild(msg);
}
```

The server currently does not filter messages in any way. To avoid users effortlessly hijacking the chat client, we will add one test that expects any messages including HTML to be escaped, as seen in Listing 15.58.

Listing 15.58 Expecting basic cross site scripting protection

```
"test should escape HTML in messages": function () {
  this.controller.addMessage({
    user: "Dr. Evil",
    message: "<script>window.alert('p4wned!');</script>"
  });

  var expected = "&lt;script>window.alert('p4wned!');" +
                 "&lt;/script>";
  var dd = this.element.getElementsByTagName("dd")[1];
  assertEquals(expected, dd.innerHTML);
}
```

The test fails; no one is stopping Dr. Evil from having his way with the chat client. Listing 15.59 adds basic protection against script injection.

Listing 15.59 Adding basic XSS protection

```
function addMessage(message) {
  /* ... */
  msg.innerHTML = message.message.replace(/</g, "&lt;");
  this.view.appendChild(msg);
}
```

15.4.4 Repeated Messages From Same User

Before we get going on the message form controller, we will add one more test. If we receive multiple messages in a row from the same user, we will expect the controller to not repeat the user. In other words, if two consecutive messages originate from the same user, we will not add a second dt element. Listing 15.60 tests for this feature by adding two messages and expecting only one dt element.

Listing 15.60 Expecting controller not to repeat dt elements

```
"test should not repeat same user dt's": function () {
  this.controller.addMessage({
    user: "Kyle",
    message: "One-two-three not it!"
  });
```

```
  this.controller.addMessage({ user:"Kyle", message:":)" });

  var dts = this.element.getElementsByTagName("dt");
  var dds = this.element.getElementsByTagName("dd");
  assertEquals(1, dts.length);
  assertEquals(2, dds.length);
}
```

Unsurprisingly, the test fails. To pass it, we need the controller to keep track of the previous user. This can be done by simply keeping a property with the last seen user. Listing 15.61 shows the updated `addMessage` method.

Listing 15.61 Keeping track of the previous user

```
function addMessage(message) {
  if (this.prevUser != message.user) {
    var user = document.createElement("dt");
    user.innerHTML = "@" + message.user;
    this.view.appendChild(user);
    this.prevUser = message.user;
  }

  /* ... */
}
```

Note that non-existent properties resolve to `undefined`, which will never be equal to the current user, meaning that we don't need to initialize the property. The first time a message is received, the `prevUser` property will not match the user, so a `dt` is added. From here on, only messages from new users will cause another `dt` element to be created and appended.

Also note that node lists, as those returned by `getElementsByTagName` are live objects, meaning that they always reflect the current state of the DOM. As we are now accessing both the collection of `dt` and `dd` elements from both tests, we could fetch those lists in `setUp` as well to avoid duplicating them. I'll leave updating the tests as an exercise.

Another exercise is to highlight any message directed at the current user, by marking the `dd` element with a class name. Remember, the current user is available through `this.model.currentUser`, and "directed at" is defined as "message starts with @user:". Good luck!

15.4.5 Feature Tests

The message list controller can only work correctly if it is run in an environment with basic DOM support. Listing 15.62 shows the controller with its required feature tests.

Listing 15.62 Feature tests for `messageListController`

```
(function () {
  if (typeof tddjs == "undefined" ||
      typeof document == "undefined" ||
      !document.createElement) {
    return;
  }

  var element = document.createElement("dl");

  if (!element.appendChild ||
      typeof element.innerHTML != "string") {
    return;
  }

  element = null;
  /* ... */
}());
```

15.4.6 Trying it Out

As the controller is now functional, we will update chapp to initialize it once the user has entered his name. First, we need a few new dependencies. Copy the following files from Chapter 13, *Streaming Data with Ajax and Comet,* into `public/js`:

- json2.js
- url_params.js
- ajax.js
- request.js
- poller.js
- comet_client.js

Also copy over the `message-list-controller.js` file, and finally add `script` elements to the `index.html` below the previous includes in the order listed above. Make sure the `js/chat-client.js` file stays included last.

Add an empty `dl` element to `index.html` and assign it `id="messages"`.
Then update the `chat-client.js` file as seen in Listing 15.63.

Listing 15.63 Updated bootstrap script

```
(function () {
  if (typeof tddjs == "undefined" ||
      typeof document == "undefined") {
    return;
  }

  var c = tddjs.namespace("chat");

  if (!document.getElementById || !tddjs ||
      !c.userFormController || !c.messageListController) {
    alert("Browser is not supported");
    return;
  }

  var model = Object.create(tddjs.ajax.cometClient);
  model.url = "/comet";

  /* ... */

  userController.observe("user", function (user) {
    var messages = document.getElementById("messages");
    var messagesController =
        Object.create(c.messageListController);
    messagesController.setModel(model);
    messagesController.setView(messages);

    model.connect();
  });
}());
```

Start the server again, and repeat the exercise from Listing 14.27 in Chapter 14,
Server-Side JavaScript with Node.js. After posting a message using `curl`, it should
immediately appear in your browser. If you post enough messages, you'll notice that
the document eventually gains a scroll and that messages appear below the fold.
That clearly isn't very helpful, so we'll make a note of it and get right on it as we
add some finishing touches toward the end of the chapter.

15.5 The Message Form

The message form allows users to post messages. The steps required to test and implement it are going to be very similar to the user form controller we created previously: it needs a form element as its view; it will handle the form's submit event through its `handleSubmit` method; and finally it will publish the message as an event on the model object, which passes it to the server.

15.5.1 Setting up the Test

The first thing we need to do is to set up the test case and expect the controller object to exist. Listing 15.64 shows the initial test case.

Listing 15.64 Setting up the `messageFormController` test case

```
(function () {
  var messageController = tddjs.chat.messageFormController;

  TestCase("FormControllerTestCase", {
    "test should be object": function () {
      assertObject(messageController);
    }
  });
}());
```

Running the test prompts us to define the object with a big fat red "F." Listing 15.65 does the grunt work.

Listing 15.65 Defining the message form controller

```
(function () {
  var chat = tddjs.namespace("chat");
  chat.messageFormController = {};
}());
```

15.5.2 Setting the View

Just like the user form controller, this controller needs to add the "js-chat" class name to its view and observe the "submit" event with the `handleSubmit` method bound to the controller. In fact, setting the view for the message form controller should work exactly like the one we previously wrote. We'll try to be slightly smarter than to simply repeat the entire process; it seems obvious that the two *form* controllers should share parts of their implementation.

15.5.2.1 Refactoring: Extracting the Common Parts

We will take a small detour by refactoring the user form controller. We will extract a `formController` object from which both of the controllers can inherit. Step one is adding the new object, as Listing 15.66 shows. Save it in `src/form_controller.js`.

Listing 15.66 Extracting a form controller

```
(function () {
  if (typeof tddjs == "undefined") {
    return;
  }

  var dom = tddjs.dom;
  var chat = tddjs.namespace("chat");

  if (!dom || !dom.addEventHandler ||
      !Function.prototype.bind) {
    return;
  }

  function setView(element) {
    element.className = "js-chat";
    var handler = this.handleSubmit.bind(this);
    dom.addEventHandler(element, "submit", handler);
    this.view = element;
  }

  chat.formController = {
    setView: setView
  };
}());
```

To build this file, I simply copied the entire user form controller and stripped out anything not related to setting the view. At this point, you're probably wondering "where are the tests?". It's a valid question. However, we are not adding or modifying behavior, we're merely moving around parts of the implementation. The existing tests should suffice in telling us if the refactoring is successful—at least for the documented/tested behavior, which is the only behavior we're concerned about at this point.

Step two is making the user form controller use the new generic controller. We can achieve this by popping it in as the form controller's prototype object, as seen in Listing 15.67.

Listing 15.67 Changing `userFormController`'s ancestry

```
chat.userFormController = tddjs.extend(
  Object.create(chat.formController),
  util.observable
);
```

Running the tests confirms that this change does not interfere with the existing behavior of the user form controller. Next up, we remove `userFormController`'s own `setView` implementation. The expectation is that it should now inherit this method from `formController` thus the tests should still pass. Running them confirms that they do.

Before the refactoring can be considered done, we should change the tests as well. The tests we originally wrote for the user form controller's `setView` should now be updated to test `formController` directly. To make sure the user form controller still works, we can replace the original test case with a single test that verifies that it inherits the `setView` method. Although keeping the original tests better documents `userFormController`, duplicating them comes with a maintenance cost. I'll leave fixing the test case as an exercise.

15.5.2.2 Setting `messageFormController`'s View

Having extracted the `formController`, we can add a test for `messageFormController` expecting it to inherit the `setView` method, as Listing 15.68 shows.

Listing 15.68 Expecting `messageFormController` to inherit `setView`

```
(function () {
  var messageController = tddjs.chat.messageFormController;
  var formController = tddjs.chat.formController;

  TestCase("FormControllerTestCase", {
    /* ... */
    "test should inherit setView from formController":
    function () {
      assertSame(messageController.setView,
                 formController.setView);
    }
  });
}());
```

Passing the test is achieved by changing the definition of the controller, as seen in Listing 15.69.

Listing 15.69 Inheriting from `formController`

```
chat.messageFormController =
  Object.create(chat.formController);
```

15.5.3 Publishing Messages

When the user submits the form, the controller should publish a message to the model object. To test this we can stub the model's `notify` method, call `handle-Submit`, and expect the stub to be called. Unfortunately, the controller does not yet have a `setModel` method. To fix this, we will move the method from `user-FormController` to `formController`. Listing 15.70 shows the updated form controller.

Listing 15.70 Moving `setModel`

```
/* ... */

function setModel(model) {
  this.model = model;
}

chat.formController = {
  setView: setView,
  setModel: setModel
};
```

Having copied it over, we can remove it from `userFormController`. To verify that we didn't break anything, we simply run the tests, which should be all green. To our infinite satisfaction, they are.

There is no `setModel` related test to write for `messageFormController` that can be expected to fail, thus we won't do that. We're TDD-ing, we want progress, and progress comes from failing tests.

A test that can push us forward is one that expects the controller to have a `handleSubmit` method, which can be seen in Listing 15.71.

Listing 15.71 Expecting the controller to have a `handleSubmit` method

```
"test should have handleSubmit method": function () {
  assertFunction(messageController.handleSubmit);
}
```

Listing 15.72 passes the test by adding an empty function.

Listing 15.72 Adding an empty function

```
function handleSubmit(event) {}

chat.messageFormController =
  Object.create(chat.formController);
chat.messageFormController.handleSubmit = handleSubmit;
```

With the method in place we can start testing for its behavior. Listing 15.73 shows a test that expects it to publish a message event on the model.

Listing 15.73 Expecting the controller to publish a message event

```
TestCase("FormControllerHandleSubmitTest", {
  "test should publish message": function () {
    var controller = Object.create(messageController);
    var model = { notify: stubFn() };

    controller.setModel(model);
    controller.handleSubmit();

    assert(model.notify.called);
    assertEquals("message", model.notify.args[0]);
    assertObject(model.notify.args[1]);
  }
});
```

Listing 15.74 adds the method call to pass the test.

Listing 15.74 Calling `publish`

```
function handleSubmit(event) {
  this.model.notify("message", {});
}
```

Tests are all passing. Next up, Listing 15.75 expects the published object to include the `currentUser` as its `user` property.

Listing 15.75 Expecting `currentUser` as `user`

```
TestCase("FormControllerHandleSubmitTest", {
  setUp: function () {
    this.controller = Object.create(messageController);
    this.model = { notify: stubFn() };
    this.controller.setModel(this.model);
  },
```

```
/* ... */

"test should publish message from current user":
function () {
  this.model.currentUser = "cjno";

  this.controller.handleSubmit();

  assertEquals("cjno", this.model.notify.args[1].user);
  }
});
```

Once again, we extracted common setup code to the `setUp` method while adding the test. Passing the test is accomplished by Listing 15.76.

Listing 15.76 Including the current user in the published message

```
function handleSubmit(event) {
  this.model.notify("message", {
    user: this.model.currentUser
  });
}
```

The final piece of the puzzle is including the message. The message should be grabbed from the message form, which means that the test will need to embed some markup. Listing 15.77 shows the test.

Listing 15.77 Expecting the published message to originate from the form

```
TestCase("FormControllerHandleSubmitTest", {
  setUp: function () {
    /*:DOC element = <form>
        <fieldset>
          <input type="text" name="message" id="message">
          <input type="submit" value="Send">
        </fieldset>
      </form> */

    /* ... */
    this.controller.setView(this.element);
  },

  /* ... */

  "test should publish message from form": function () {
    var el = this.element.getElementsByTagName("input")[0];
```

```
    el.value = "What are you doing?";

    this.controller.handleSubmit();

    var actual = this.model.notify.args[1].message;
    assertEquals("What are you doing?", actual);
  }
});
```

To pass this test we need to grab the first input element and pass its current value as the message. Listing 15.78 shows the required update to `handleSubmit`.

Listing 15.78 Grabbing the message

```
function handleSubmit(event) {
  var input = this.view.getElementsByTagName("input")[0];

  this.model.notify("message", {
    user: this.model.currentUser,
    message: input.value
  });
}
```

The tests now pass, which means that the chat client should be operable in a real setting. As before, we haven't implemented much error handling for the form, and I will leave doing so as an exercise. In fact, there are several tasks for you to practice TDD building on this exercise:

- Form should prevent the default action of submitting it to the server
- Form should not send empty messages
- Add missing error handling to all the methods
- Emit an event (e.g. using `observable`) from the message once a form is posted. Observe it to display a loader gif, and emit a corresponding event from the message list controller when the same message is displayed to remove the loading indicator.

I'm sure you can think of even more.

15.5.4 Feature Tests

Because most of the functionality is taken care of by the generic form controller, there isn't much to feature test. The only direct dependencies are `tddjs`, formController and getElementsByTagName. Listing 15.79 shows the feature tests.

Listing 15.79 Feature testing messageFormController

```
if (typeof tddjs == "undefined" ||
    typeof document == "undefined") {
  return;
}

var chat = tddjs.namespace("chat");

if (!chat.formController ||
    !document.getElementsByTagName) {
  return;
}

/* ... */
```

15.6 The Final Chat Client

As all the controllers are complete, we can now piece together the entire chat client and take it for a real spin. Listing 15.80 adds the message form to the HTML document.

Listing 15.80 Adding the message form to index.html

```
<!-- ... -->
<dl id="messages"></dl>
<form id="messageForm">
  <fieldset>
    <input type="text" name="message" id="message"
           autocomplete="off">
  </fieldset>
</form>
<!-- ... -->
```

Copy over message_form_controller.js along with form_controller.js and the updated user_form_controller.js and add script elements to index.html to include them. Then update the bootstrap script, as seen in Listing 15.81.

Listing 15.81 Final bootstrapping script

```
/* ... */

userController.observe("user", function (user) {
  /* ... */

  var mForm = document.getElementById("messageForm");
  var messageFormController =
      Object.create(c.messageFormController);
  messageFormController.setModel(model);
  messageFormController.setView(mForm);

  model.connect();
});
</script>
```

Firing up the client in a browser should now present you with a fully functional, if not particularly feature rich, chat client, implemented entirely using TDD and JavaScript, both server and client side. If you experience trouble posting messages, make sure you completed `messageFormController` by making its `handle-Submit` method abort the default event action.

15.6.1 Finishing Touches

To get a feeling of how the chat application behaves, try inviting a friend to join you over the local network. Alternatively, if you're alone, fire up another browser, or even just another tab in your current browser. There are currently no cookies involved, so running two sessions from different tabs in the same browser is entirely doable.

15.6.1.1 Styling the Application

An unstyled webpage is a somewhat bleak face for the chat application. To make it just a tad bit nicer to rest our eyes on, we will add some CSS. I am no designer, so don't get your hopes up, but updating `css/chapp.css` with the contents of Listing 15.82 will at least give the client rounded corners, box shadow, and some light grays.

Listing 15.82 "Design" for the chat client

```
html { background: #f0f0f0; }
form, dl { display: none; }
.js-chat { display: block; }
```

```
body {
    background: #fff;
    border: 1px solid #333;
    border-radius: 12px;
    -moz-border-radius: 12px;
    -webkit-border-radius: 12px;
    box-shadow: 2px 2px 30px #666;
    -moz-box-shadow: 2px 2px 30px #666;
    -webkit-box-shadow: 2px 2px 30px #666;
    height: 450px;
    margin: 20px auto;
    padding: 0 20px;
    width: 600px;
}

form, fieldset {
    border: none;
    margin: 0;
    padding: 0;
}

#messageForm input {
    padding: 3px;
    width: 592px;
}

#messages {
    height: 300px;
    overflow: auto;
}
```

15.6.1.2 Fixing the Scrolling

As we noted earlier, the client eventually gains a scroll and adds messages below the fold. With the updated stylesheet, the scroll is moved to the definition list that contains the messages. In order to keep the message form visible, we put a restraint on its height. Because we're more interested in new messages popping in, we will tweak the message list controller to make sure the definition list is always scrolled all the way to the bottom.

We can scroll the list to the bottom by setting the scrollTop property to its maximum value. However, we don't need to determine this value exactly; all we need to do is set it to some value equal to or greater than the max value, and the browser will scroll the element as far as possible. The scrollHeight of an element seems like a good fit; its value is the entire height of the element's contents, which will obviously always be greater than the greatest possible scrollTop. Listing 15.83 shows the test.

Listing 15.83 Expecting the message list controller to scroll its view down

```
TestCase("MessageListControllerAddMessageTest", {
  /* ... */

  "test should scroll element down": function () {
    var element = {
      appendChild: stubFn(),
      scrollHeight: 1900
    };

    this.controller.setView(element);
    this.controller.addMessage({ user:"me",message:"Hey" });

    assertEquals(1900, element.scrollTop);
  }
});
```

This test uses a stubbed element rather than the actual element available in the test. In a test such as this, we need complete control over the input and output to verify its correct behavior. We cannot stub an element's scrollTop property setter; neither can we easily determine that its value was set correctly, because it depends on the rendered height and requires styles to be added to make the element scroll on overflow to begin with. To pass the test we assign the value of scrollHeight to scrollTop as seen in Listing 15.84.

Listing 15.84 Scrolling the message list down on each new message

```
function addMessage(message) {
  /* ... */

  this.view.scrollTop = this.view.scrollHeight;
}
```

15.6.1.3 Clearing the Input Field

When a user has posted her message, it is unlikely that they would like to start the next message with the text from the previous one. Thus, the message form controller should clear the input field once the message is posted. Listing 15.85 shows the test.

Listing 15.85 Expecting the message form to clear message

```
"test should clear form after publish": function () {
  var el = this.element.getElementsByTagName("input")[0];
  el.value = "NP: A vision of misery";

  this.controller.handleSubmit(this.event);

  assertEquals("", el.value);
}
```

Ideally, we would not clear the form until we know for sure the message was sent. Unfortunately, the `cometClient` does not support adding a success callback at this point, so the best we can do is clearing it immediately after having sent it and hope for the best. The proper fix would include adding a third options argument to `cometClient` and wait for success. Listing 15.86 shows the message form controller's updated `handleSubmit`.

Listing 15.86 Clearing the message after publishing it

```
function handleSubmit(event) {
  /* ... */

  input.value = "";
}
```

It would also be nice if the message form gave focus to the input field immediately upon initializing it. I will leave doing so as an exercise.

15.6.2 Notes on Deployment

Copy over the message form and message list controllers to chapp's `public` directory and reload your browser. The application should now be slightly smoother to use.

Simply copying files to deploy them is cumbersome and error prone. Additionally, serving the application with 15 individual script files is not optimal for performance. If you installed Ruby and RubyGems to use the `jstestdriver` and `jsautotest` tools in Chapter 3, *Tools of the Trade,* then you have a JavaScript and CSS concatenator and minifier at your fingertips. Listing 15.87 shows the three required commands to install Juicer, which will conveniently package your scripts for deployment.

Listing 15.87 Installing Juicer and YUI Compressor

```
$ gem install juicer
$ juicer install yui_compressor
```

Run from the root of the Node.js application, the command in Listing 15.88 will produce a single file, `chat.min.js`, containing the entire client-side application.

Listing 15.88 Using Juicer to compress files

```
juicer merge -s -f -o public/js/chat.min.js \
  public/js/function.js \
  public/js/object.js \
  public/js/tdd.js \
  public/js/observable.js \
  public/js/form_controller.js \
  public/js/user_form_controller.js \
  public/js/json2.js \
  public/js/url_params.js \
  public/js/ajax.js \
  public/js/request.js \
  public/js/poller.js \
  public/js/comet_client.js \
  public/js/message_list_controller.js \
  public/js/message_form_controller.js \
  public/js/chat_client.js
```

The final result is a 14kB JavaScript file containing a fully operational chat room. Served with gzip compression, the total download should be about 5kB.

Juicer is also able to find dependencies declared inside script files, meaning that we can jot down each file's dependencies inside comments in them and then simply run "juicer merge chat.js" to produce the complete file, including the dependencies. More information on Juicer is available from the book's website.[4]

15.7 Summary

In this chapter we have been able to pull together a lot of the code developed throughout this book to create a fully functional, entirely JavaScript based browser-based chat application. And we did it all using test-driven development, right from the very start.

---

4. http://tddjs.com

The key aspect of this chapter has been unit testing DOM manipulation, and structuring the outermost application layer in a sensible way. As we've discussed numerous times already, well factored software easily lends itself to unit testing, and the GUI—the DOM—is no exception to this rule.

By employing the Model View Presenter/Passive View pattern, we were able to identify reusable components in the view and implement the chat client in a modular way, resulting in very loosely coupled modules that were easy to test in isolation. Developing these components using TDD was straightforward because each distinct unit had a well-defined responsibility. Dividing a hard problem into several smaller problems is a lot more manageable than trying to solve it all in one go.

An interesting aspect about a pattern such as Model View Presenter is that there are numerous ways to apply it to the problem domain of client-side JavaScript. For instance, in many cases a portion of the DOM will represent the model because JavaScript widgets frequently manipulate the data already found on the page.

The chat client was the final test-driven example, and we have reached the end of Part III, *Real-World Test-Driven Development in JavaScript*. In the final part of the book we'll draw some lessons from the past five chapters as we dive deeper into stubbing and mocking, and finally identify some guidelines for writing good unit tests.

Part IV

Testing Patterns

Mocking and Stubbing

16

While using test-driven development to develop five sample projects, we've become intimately familiar with the `stubFn` function. We have used it as a tool to both inspect interaction between objects, as well as isolating interfaces under test. But what exactly is a stub? We are about to find out as we dive a little deeper into the topic of using *test doubles,* objects that look like the real thing but really are bleak impersonations used to simplify tests.

In this chapter we will look at the general theory of using test doubles, and get to know a few common types of test doubles a little better. Because we have already used stubs extensively in tests throughout Part III, *Real-World Test-Driven Development in JavaScript,* we will relate the discussion to previous examples. We will also look at a more capable stubbing and mocking library and see how such a thing can be used in place of `stubFn` and other homegrown helpers to simplify some of the tests we have written so far.

16.1 An Overview of Test Doubles

A test double is an object that supports the same API, or at least the parts of it relevant to a given test, as the real thing, but does not necessarily behave the same way. Test doubles are used to both isolate interfaces and make tests more convenient; making tests faster, avoiding calls to inconvenient methods, or spying on method calls in place of assertions on direct or indirect output.

The terminology used in this chapter is mostly adapted from Gerard Meszaros book "xUnit Test Patterns," [7] slightly adjusted to the world of JavaScript. In addition to the names and definitions of different types of test doubles, I will use "system under test" to describe the code being tested.

16.1.1 Stunt Doubles

Gerard Meszaros compares test doubles to Hollywood's stunt doubles. Some movie scenes require dangerous stunts, physically demanding feats or other behavior that the leading actor is either not willing or able to perform. In such cases, a stunt double is hired to do the job. The stunt double need not be an accomplished actor, he simply needs to be able to catch on fire or fall off a cliff without being mortally wounded; and he needs to *look somewhat like the leading actor,* at least from a distance.

Test doubles are just like stunt doubles. They take on the job when it's inconvenient to use the leading star (production code); all we require from them is that the audience (system under test) cannot tell it apart from the real deal.

16.1.2 Fake Object

The stubs we've been using aggressively throughout the example projects in Part III, *Real-World Test-Driven Development in JavaScript,* are one form of test doubles. They appear to behave like real objects, but their actions are pre-programmed to force a certain path through the system under test. Additionally, they record data about their interaction with other objects, available in the test's verification stage.

Another kind of test double is the *fake object.* A fake object provides the same functionality as the object it replaces and can be seen as an alternative implementation, only its implementation is considerably simpler. For example, when working with Node.js the file system can easily become inconvenient from a testing perspective. Constantly accessing it can make tests slower, and keeping a lot of test data on disk requires cleanup. We can alleviate these problems by implementing an in-memory file system that supports the same API as Node's fs module and use this in tests.

Fakes differ from stubs in that stubs are usually created and injected into the system from individual tests on a per-need basis. Fakes are more comprehensive replacements, and are usually injected into the system as a whole before running any tests. Tests are usually completely unaware of the fakes because they behave just like the objects they mirror, only significantly simplified. In the Node.js file system example we can imagine a complete implementation of the fs module as an in-memory file system. The test setup can then make sure to place the fake implementation ahead of the built-in one on the load path. Neither individual tests nor production code will be aware that `require("fs")` actually loads a simplified in-memory file system.

16.1.3 Dummy Object

A dummy object, as its name suggests, is usually just an empty object or function. When testing functions that expect several parameters, we are often only concerned with one of them at a time. If the function we're testing throws errors for missing or wrongly typed arguments, we can pass it a dummy to "shut it up" while we focus on behavior not related to the argument in question.

As an example, consider the test in Listing 16.1 from Chapter 15, *TDD and DOM Manipulation: The Chat Client*. The test verifies that the message list controller sets the element's `scrollTop` equal to the value of its `scrollHeight`. However, the method also appends a new DOM element to the view element, and throws an exception if it does not have an `appendChild` method. For the purpose of this test we use a dummy to pass the test on `appendChild` to get to the behavior we want to test.

Listing 16.1 Using a dummy function

```
"test should scroll element down": function () {
  var element = {
    appendChild: stubFn(),
    scrollHeight: 1900
  };

  this.controller.setView(element);
  this.controller.addMessage({ user:"me",message:"Hey" });

  assertEquals(1900, element.scrollTop);
}
```

16.2 Test Verification

Unit tests have four stages; **setup**, often divided between a shared `setUp` method and test specific configuration of objects; **exercise**, in which we call the function(s) to test; **verification**, in which we assert that the result of the exercise stage coincides with our expectations; and finally **tear down**, which never happens inside a test, but rather in a dedicated and shared `tearDown` method.

Before we get into the nitty-gritty of stubs, mocks, and the difference between them, we will explore our options at the verification stage. As we will see shortly, verification strategy is a central issue when making the choice between stubs and mocks.

16.2.1 State Verification

Many of the tests in Part III, *Real-World Test-Driven Development in JavaScript,* determine success by asserting that certain objects have a specific state after some function was called. As an example, consider Listing 16.2 from Chapter 15, *TDD and DOM Manipulation: The Chat Client,* which expects the user form controller to set the `currentUser` property of the model object. It passes a dummy model object to the controller, and then inspects the object's `currentUser` object to verify its behavior.

Listing 16.2 Inspecting an object's state to verify test

```
"test should set model.currentUser": function () {
  var model = {};
  var event = { preventDefault: stubFn() };
  var input = this.element.getElementsByTagName("input")[0];
  input.value = "cjno";
  this.controller.setModel(model);
  this.controller.setView(this.element);

  this.controller.handleSubmit(event);

  assertEquals("cjno", model.currentUser);
}
```

The fact that the last line inspects a property of an object passed to the system under test to verify its success is called *state verification*. State verification leads to intuitive tests that clearly describe the outcome of using some part of the system. In this case, if the input field contains a username when the controller handles a submit event, we expect it to transfer this username to the model object's `currentUser` property. The test does not say anything about how this should happen, thus it is completely detached from the implementation of `handleSubmit`.

16.2.2 Behavior Verification

In many cases, testing the direct output of a test is not as simple as in Listing 16.2. For instance, keeping with the chat client example, the message form controller is in charge of publishing messages from the client to the server through the model object. Because there is no server in the tests, we cannot simply ask it for the message we expected it to receive. To test this, we used a stub, as seen in Listing 16.3. Rather than inspecting some object's state to verify its results, this test stubs the model's `publish` method and then proceeds by asserting that it was called.

Listing 16.3 Inspecting a function's behavior to verify test

```
"test should publish message": function () {
  var controller = Object.create(messageController);
  var model = { notify: stubFn() };

  controller.setModel(model);
  controller.handleSubmit();

  assert(model.notify.called);
  assertEquals("message", model.notify.args[0]);
  assertObject(model.notify.args[1]);
}
```

This test contrasts with the previous one that used state verification. It does not check whether the message was stored somewhere, instead it uses *behavior verification*; it verifies that the model's `publish` method was called with the correct arguments. Having already tested the Comet client to be used in production, we know that the message will be handled correctly if `publish` is called this way.

16.2.3 Implications of Verification Strategy

The chosen verification strategy directly influences how a test reads, which is obvious from looking at the two tests above. Less clear is the fact that the verification strategy also influences production code, as well as its relationship to the tests.

Behavior verification taps into the system's implementation by expecting certain function calls to take place. On the other hand, state verification is a mere observation on the (direct or indirect) input/output relationship. This means that using behavior verification extensively couples the test code tighter to the system, which in turn limits our ability to change its implementation, e.g., through refactoring, without also having to change the tests.

16.3 Stubs

Stubs are test doubles with pre-programmed behavior. They may return a specific value, regardless of received arguments, or throw an exception. Because stubs are used in place of real objects and functions, they are also used as a measure to avoid bumping into inconvenient interfaces.

16.3.1 Stubbing to Avoid Inconvenient Interfaces

Listing 16.4 shows the previous chat client message list controller test again. It uses a stub in place of a DOM element to verify that the message list controller scrolls the element all the way down after appending DOM elements to it.

Listing 16.4 Using a stub to avoid the DOM

```
"test should scroll element down": function () {
  var element = {
    appendChild: stubFn(),
    scrollHeight: 1900
  };

  this.controller.setView(element);
  this.controller.addMessage({ user:"me",message:"Hey" });

  assertEquals(1900, element.scrollTop);
}
```

As noted earlier, the test uses a stub `appendChild`. Furthermore, it specifies a `scrollHeight` with a known value, allowing us to verify that the `scrollTop` property was assigned this value. By using a stub we avoid having to render the element and we avoid calculating the actual `scrollTop` value, thus making the test faster and avoiding possible cross browser issues related to the rendering of the element.

16.3.2 Stubbing to Force Certain Code Paths

Stubs are frequently used to manipulate the system under test to take a specific path, allowing us to verify a single aspect in isolation. For instance, in Chapter 12, *Abstracting Browser Differences: Ajax,* we wrote the test in Listing 16.5 to verify that local requests are considered successful if they have an HTTP status of "0."

Listing 16.5 Expecting success for local requests

```
"test should call success handler for local requests":
function () {
  this.xhr.readyState = 4;
  this.xhr.status = 0;
  var success = stubFn();
  tddjs.isLocal = stubFn(true);

  ajax.get("file.html", { success: success });
```

```
        this.xhr.onreadystatechange();

        assert(success.called);
}
```

By pre-programming `tddjs.isLocal` to always return `true`, we force the request interface through the path that handles local requests. Gerard Meszaros calls these kinds of stubs *Responders*, and they are commonly used to test the happy path through a system.

16.3.3 Stubbing to Cause Trouble

Similar to the responder, a *Saboteur* is a stub that behaves strangely by returning unexpected values or even throwing exceptions. Injecting such a stub into the system allows us to test how well it deals with uncooperative objects and unexpected behavior.

Listing 16.6 shows a test from Chapter 11, *The Observer Pattern,* in which a saboteur is used to verify that all observers are notified even when some of them throw exceptions.

Listing 16.6 Using a saboteur to ensure all observers are notified

```
"test should notify all even when some fail": function () {
  var observable = new tddjs.util.Observable();
  var observer1 = function () { throw new Error("Oops"); };
  var observer2 = function () { observer2.called = true; };

  observable.addObserver(observer1);
  observable.addObserver(observer2);
  observable.notifyObservers();

  assertTrue(observer2.called);
}
```

The saboteur is a useful tool when bulletproofing interfaces intended for a wide audience. They can also be used to mimic a lot of strange behavior in certain browsers, helping us write code that survives even the fiercest host objects.

16.4 Test Spies

Test spies are objects and functions that record information about their usage throughout the system under test. They are useful when determining a function's success is not easily accomplished by inspecting its return value or changes to the state of objects with which it interacts. You may recognize that the stubs in Part III, *Real-World Test-Driven Development in JavaScript,* have frequently been used this way; in fact, test spies are usually implemented as recording stubs.

16.4.1 Testing Indirect Inputs

The `request` interface we built in Chapter 12, *Abstracting Browser Differences: Ajax,* provides many examples of using test spies to verify a test. The interface was built to provide a higher level abstraction over the `XMLHttpRequest` object, and as such its success is mainly defined by its ability to correctly map calls to the underlying object. Listing 16.7 shows a test that verifies that requesting a URL causes the `XMLHttpRequest` object's `send` method to be called.

Listing 16.7 Using a test spy to verify that a method is called on an indirect input

```
TestCase("GetRequestTest", {
  setUp: function () {
    this.ajaxCreate = ajax.create;
    this.xhr = Object.create(fakeXMLHttpRequest);
    ajax.create = stubFn(this.xhr);
  },

  /* ... */

  "test should call send": function () {
    ajax.get("/url");

    assert(this.xhr.send.called);
  }
});
```

The `setUp` pre-programs `ajax.create` to return a `fakeXMLHttp Request` instance, which is assigned to the test for behavior verification. The object returned from `ajax.create` is an *indirect input* to the `ajax.request` method. Stubs or mocks are usually the only way to test the effects of an indirect input on the system under test.

16.4.2 Inspecting Details about a Call

A test spy need not restrict itself to recording whether or not a function was called. It can record any kind of data about its use. The `stubFn` helper used throughout most of Part III, *Real-World Test-Driven Development in JavaScript,* also recorded the value of `this` and the received arguments. As we'll see in Section 16.5, *Using a Stub Library,* the spy can be even smarter, recording `this` and `arguments` for each call and providing a retrieval interface to access the recorded data.

Listing 16.8 shows a test from Chapter 15, *TDD and DOM Manipulation: The Chat Client,* that verifies that the message list controller's `addMessage` method was bound to the controller when registered as an event handler.

Listing 16.8 Using a test spy to verify the `this` binding of an event handler

```
"test should observe with bound addMessage": function () {
  var stub = this.controller.addMessage = stubFn();

  this.controller.setModel(this.model);
  this.model.observe.args[1]();

  assert(stub.called);
  assertSame(this.controller, stub.thisValue);
}
```

16.5 Using a Stub Library

In Chapter 11, *The Observer Pattern,* we used a `called` flag and inline functions to verify that the `observable` interface notified observers when its `notify` method was called. Even though we didn't use specific terminology to describe the pattern in that chapter, we now recognize these functions as test spies.

Because JavaScript's functions are such powerful beasts, we can go a long way without a dedicated stubbing library. However, as we realized in Chapter 12, *Abstracting Browser Differences: Ajax,* declaring the flag and function quickly becomes repetitious, especially when using stubs and spies extensively. Even with the simple `stubFn` helper, we recognized that stubbing global interfaces, such as the `ajax.create` method, came with the burden of adding `setUp` and `tearDown` methods to ensure that the original interfaces were restored after the tests completed.

Motivated by our voracious urge to remove duplication in any form, we will see how using a stubbing library can help reduce the pain of manual stubbing. The library we will be using is called "Sinon"[1] and can be downloaded from the book's website.[2]

---

1. In Greek mythology, Sinon was a spy and a liar who talked the Trojans into accepting the Trojan horse
2. http://tddjs.com

16.5.1 Creating a Stub Function

Creating a stub function using Sinon is very similar to our trusty old `stubFn`.
Listing 16.9 shows a test from the `observable` test case, updated to use `sinon.`
`stub`.

Listing 16.9 Using Sinon to create simple function stubs

```
"test should call all observers": function () {
  var observable = Object.create(tddjs.util.observable);
  var observer1 = sinon.stub();
  var observer2 = sinon.stub();

  observable.addObserver(observer1);
  observable.addObserver(observer2);
  observable.notifyObservers();

  assertTrue(observer1.called);
  assertTrue(observer2.called);
}
```

The only noticeable difference in this example is the way the stubs are created.
Rather than the original inline function that set a property on the function itself, we
now have a simple call to `sinon.stub`.

16.5.2 Stubbing a Method

Throwaway stubs are simple enough to create inline, and don't necessarily warrant
the use of an external library. Stubbing global methods, however, is a bit more
hassle because we must make sure to restore the original method after running the
test. Listing 16.10 shows an extract of the `setUp` and `tearDown` methods of the
Comet client test case along with a test using the `stubFn` method on the global
`ajax.poll`.

Listing 16.10 Spying manually

```
TestCase("CometClientConnectTest", {
  setUp: function () {
    this.client = Object.create(ajax.cometClient);
    this.ajaxPoll = ajax.poll;
  },

  tearDown: function () {
    ajax.poll = this.ajaxPoll;
  },
```

```
  "test connect should start polling": function () {
    this.client.url = "/my/url";
    ajax.poll = stubFn({});

    this.client.connect();

    assert(ajax.poll.called);
    assertEquals("/my/url", ajax.poll.args[0]);
  }
});
```

Listing 16.11 shows the same listing using Sinon to handle stubs. Notice that we still need the `tearDown`, but less manual juggling of the interfaces is required.

Listing 16.11 Using Sinon to handle stubs

```
TestCase("CometClientConnectTest", {
  setUp: function () {
    this.client = Object.create(ajax.cometClient);
  },

  tearDown: function () {
    ajax.poll.restore();
  },

  "test connect should start polling": function () {
    this.client.url = "/my/url";
    sinon.stub(ajax, "poll").returns({});

    this.client.connect();

    assert(ajax.poll.calledWith("/my/url"));
  }
});
```

In addition to simplifying the stub management business, Sinon provides a more fine-grained retrieval interface, resulting in tests that read better. But there is more; Sinon provides a sandbox feature that automatically manages and restores stubs. Listing 16.12 shows an example.

Listing 16.12 Automatically managing stubs with Sinon

```
"test connect should start polling":
sinon.test(function (stub) {
  this.client.url = "/my/url";
```

```
  stub(ajax, "poll").returns({});

  this.client.connect();

  assert(ajax.poll.calledWith("/my/url"));
})
```

By wrapping the test function in a `sinon.test` call and using the `stub` method that is passed to it, stubs are strictly local and are automatically restored upon the test's completion, even if the test throws exceptions. When using this feature we can throw out all the stub related logic in both the `setUp` and `tearDown` methods.

When you have a lot of tests that need this kind of clean up you can also wrap the entire test case object in a call to `sinon.testCase`, which is the same as wrapping every test function in a call to `sinon.test`. Listing 16.13 shows an example.

Listing 16.13 Automatically restoring stubs after each test

```
TestCase("CometClientConnectTest", sinon.testCase({
  setUp: function (stub) {
    /* ... */
    stub(ajax, "poll").returns({});
  },

  "test connect should start polling": function () {
    this.client.connect();

    assert(ajax.poll.calledWith(this.client.url));
  },

  "test should not connect if connected": function () {
    this.client.connect();
    this.client.connect();

    assert(ajax.poll.calledOnce);
  },

  /* ... */
}));
```

16.5.3 Built-in Behavior Verification

Sinon comes with a few assertions that can be used for clearer behavior verification. The problem with the assert in Listing 16.12 is that the resulting error message in case of test failure will be "expected true but was false," which isn't very helpful. By using Sinon's asserts, the error message will instead look something like "expected poll to be called once but was called 0 times." Listing 16.14 shows the test updated to use `assertCalledWith`.

Listing 16.14 Using tailored asserts for behavior verification

```
"test connect should start polling": function () {
  this.client.url = "/my/url";
  stub(ajax, "poll").returns({});

  this.client.connect();

  sinon.assert.calledWith(ajax.poll, "/my/url");
}
```

Sinon is a stand alone library, and does not require JsTestDriver. The reason this works "out of the box" with JsTestDriver is that Sinon uses the same definition of failure, which is throwing an `AssertError`. To use the asserts with another testing framework, simply set the type of exception to throw on failure by overriding the `sinon.failException` string. If your testing framework of choice does not fail by throwing an exception, override the `sinon.fail` method to do the right thing.

To sugar things up even more, Sinon can inject its assertions into another object, allowing them to live side-by-side with the testing framework's assertions. JsTest-Driver uses global assertions. Listing 16.15 shows the necessary code for completely seamless integration.

Listing 16.15 Mixing Sinon's assertions with the default JsTestDriver ones

```
// Typically done in a global helper to share among
// test cases
sinon.assert.expose(this, true, false);

TestCase("CometClientConnectTest", {
  /* ... */

  "test connect should start polling": sinon.test(function (
    stub) {
    this.client.url = "/my/url";
    stub(ajax, "poll").returns({});
```

```
    this.client.connect();

    assertCalledWith(ajax.poll, "/my/url");
  })
});
```

sinon.assert.expose takes three arguments: the target object to inject assertions into; whether or not assertions should be prefixed (i.e., true results in "target.assertCalled"; false results in "target.called"); and finally whether or not fail and failException should also be injected.

16.5.4 Stubbing and Node.js

Sinon exposes a CommonJS module, which means that it can also be used in a CommonJS compliant runtime, such as Node.js. Listing 16.16 shows a test from Chapter 14, *Server-Side JavaScript with Node.js,* in which we stub the getMessagesSince test to return a promise object.

Listing 16.16 Stubbing in Node.js

```
var sinon = require("sinon");

/* ... */
testCase(exports, "chatRoom.waitForMessagesSince", {
  /* ... */

  "should yield existing messages":
  sinon.test(function (test, stub) {
    var promise = new Promise();
    promise.resolve([{ id: 43 }]);
    stub(this.room, "getMessagesSince").returns(promise);

    this.room.waitForMessagesSince(42).then(function (m) {
      test.same([{ id: 43 }], m);
      test.done();
    });
  },

  /* ... */
});
```

Note that Sinon takes care not to override the test object that Nodeunit passes to the test. The stub function is passed after any arguments passed to the function when it is called by the test runner.

16.6 Mocks

Mocks have been mentioned many times throughout the book, but never explained or used. The reason is that manually creating mocks is not as easy as manually creating stubs and spies. Like stubs, mocks are objects with pre-programmed behavior. Additionally, a mock has pre-programmed expectations and built-in behavior verification. Using mocks turns the test upside-down; first we state the expectations, then we exercise the system. Finally we verify that all the mock's expectations were met. Listing 16.17 shows an example using with the "start polling" test.

Listing 16.17 Mocking `ajax.poll`

```
"test connect should start polling": function () {
  this.client.url = "/my/url";
  var mock = sinon.mock(ajax)
  mock.expects("poll").withArgs("/my/url").returns({});

  this.client.connect();

  mock.verify();
}
```

This test states its success criteria upfront. It does so by creating a mock for the `ajax` object, and adding an expectation on it. It expects the `poll` method to be called exactly once, with the URL as argument. In contrast to the stubs we've used so far, mocks fail early. If the `poll` method is called a second time, it immediately throws an `ExpectationError`, failing the test.

16.6.1 Restoring Mocked Methods

The mocks can be undone just like the stubs, by calling `restore` on the mocked method. Additionally, calling `verify` implicitly restores the mocked method. However, if the test throws an exception before the call to `verify`, we might end up leaking the mock into another test, causing a ripple effect.

Sinon's sandbox feature can mitigate the problem for mocks just as much as it does for stubs. When wrapping the test method in a `sinon.test` call, it will receive a `mock` method as its second parameter, suitable for safe mocking. After the test finishes, Sinon not only restores all stubs and mocks, it also conveniently verifies all mocks, meaning that the above test could be written like Listing 16.18.

Listing 16.18 Verifying mocks automatically

```
"test connect should start polling":
sinon.test(function (stub, mock) {
  var url = this.client.url = "/my/url";
  mock(ajax).expects("poll").withArgs(url).returns({});

  this.client.connect();
})
```

The mock once again expects exactly one call—no more, no less. These three lines replace the original four-line test along with both the `setUp` and `tearDown` methods. Less code means less chance of bugs, less code to maintain, and less code to read and understand. However, that alone does not necessarily mean you should prefer mocks to stubs, or even use fakes at all.

16.6.2 Anonymous Mocks

Mocks, like stubs, can be simple anonymous functions to pass into the system. All mocks, including anonymous ones, support the same interface as stubs to pre-program them to return specific values or throw exceptions. Additionally, using Sinon's sandbox, they can be automatically verified, allowing for really short and concise tests.

Listing 16.19 revisits the `observable` test from Listing 16.6, this time using mocks to create anonymous mock functions, one of which is set up to throw an exception. As did the previous mocks, the anonymous mocks expect exactly one call.

Listing 16.19 Using mocks to verify observable's `notify`

```
"test observers should be notified even when some fail":
sinon.test(function(stub, mock) {
  var observable = Object.create(tddjs.util.observable);
  observable.addObserver(mock().throwsException());
  observable.addObserver(mock());

  observable.notifyObservers();
})
```

Because `sinon.test` keeps record of all stubs and mocks, and automatically verifies mocks, this test does not need local references to the two mock functions.

16.6.3 Multiple Expectations

Using mocks, we can form complex expectations by expecting several calls, some or all with differing arguments and this values. The expectation returned by expects can be tuned by calling methods such as withArgs as seen above; withExactArgs, which does not allow excessive arguments; as well as never, once, twice, and the more generic atLeast, atMost, and exactly methods, which tune the number of expected calls.

Listing 16.20 shows one of the original Comet client tests, which expects the connect method not to be called once the client is connected.

Listing 16.20 Expecting connect not to be called a second time

```
"test should not connect if connected": function () {
  this.client.url = "/my/url";
  ajax.poll = stubFn({});
  this.client.connect();
  ajax.poll = stubFn({});

  this.client.connect();

  assertFalse(ajax.poll.called);
}
```

Using Sinon mocks, we can rewrite this test in two ways. The default expectation on mocks is that they will be called one time, and one time only. Never calling them, or calling them two times causes an ExpectationError, failing the test. Even though one call is the default expectation, we can make it explicit, as seen in Listing 16.21.

Listing 16.21 Explicitly expecting one call

```
"test should not connect if connected":
sinon.test(function (stub, mock) {
  this.client.url = "/my/url";
  mock(ajax).expects("poll").once().returns({});
  this.client.connect();
  this.client.connect();
})
```

Notice how the this value retains its implicit binding to the test case, even as a callback to sinon.test. The second way to write this test using mocks, which mirrors the original test more closely, can be seen in Listing 16.22.

Listing 16.22 Using the `never` method

```
"test should not connect if connected":
sinon.test(function (stub, mock) {
  this.client.url = "/my/url";
  stub(ajax, "poll").returns({});
  this.client.connect();
  mock(ajax).expects("poll").never();
  this.client.connect();
})
```

The test looks different, but behaves exactly like the previous one; if the `poll` method is called a second time, it will immediately throw an exception that fails the test. The only difference between these two tests is the resulting exception message in case they fail. Using `once` to expect only call will probably yield an error message closer to the intended result than first stubbing the method and then mocking it with the `never` modifier.

16.6.4 Expectations on the `this` Value

Mocks are capable of any kind of inspection possible with test spies. In fact, mocks use test spies internally to record information about calls to them. Listing 16.23 shows one of the tests from the chat client's user form controller. It expects the controller's `handleSubmit` method bound to it as the submit event handler.

Listing 16.23 Expecting the event handler to be bound to the controller

```
"test should handle event with bound handleSubmit":
sinon.test(function (stub, mock) {
  var controller = this.controller;
  stub(dom, "addEventHandler");
  mock(controller).expects("handleSubmit").on(controller);
  controller.setView(this.element);

  dom.addEventHandler.getCall(0).args[2]();
})
```

This test shows how to use the test spy's retrieval interface to get the first call to the `dom.addEventHandler` method, and then accessing its `args` array, which contains the received arguments.

16.7 Mocks or Stubs?

The comparison of stubs and mocks raises the question, stubs or mocks? Unfortunately, there is no answer, other than "it depends." Stubs are more versatile; they can be used simply to silence dependencies, fill in for not-yet-implemented interfaces, force a certain path through the system, and more. Stubs also support both state verification and behavior verification. Mocks can be used in most scenarios as well, but only support behavior verification.

Although mocks can also be used to silence dependencies, doing so is somewhat unpractical because we must take care to set up the expectations to account for the minimum amount of possible calls, for example by using `expectation.atLeast(0)`.

Wrapping tests in `sinon.test` and using mocks definitely yields the fewest lines of test code. When using stubs, assertions are required, something the implicit mock verification deals away with. However, as assertions go away, tests may also end up less clear and intent revealing.

The upfront expectations used by mocks break the convention that the verification stage is always carried out last. When mocks are involved, we need to scan the entire test for verification code. The problem can be mitigated by keeping mock expectations at the top of the test, but there is still a possibility that further verification is carried out in assertions in the bottom of the test.

Although the choice between stubs and mocks is mainly one of personal preference and project convention, there are cases in which you definitely should not use mocks. Because mocks implicitly perform behavior verification that can break the test—both during the test and after—mocks should never be casually used to fake interfaces that are not the focus of a given test.

As an example of unsuitable use of mocks, consider Listing 16.24, which shows an excerpt of the chat client's form controller `handleSubmit` test case. The `setUp` creates an inline model object whose `publish` method is a stub. Not all tests interact with this object, but it is required by the controller, which is why it's fed to the controller in the `setUp` method.

Listing 16.24 A stub that should not be made into a mock

```
setUp: function () {
  /* ... */
  this.controller = Object.create(messageController);
  this.model = { publish: stubFn() };
  this.controller.setModel(this.model);
  /* ... */
```

```
},

"test should prevent event default action": function () {
  this.controller.handleSubmit(this.event);

  assert(this.event.preventDefault.called);
}
```

Assuming we fell completely in love with mocks, we might have gone and mocked that model object rather than stubbing it. Doing so means that any test may fail as a result of unexpected interaction with the model object—even the tests that focus on something entirely different, such as the event object's `preventDefault` method being called. Mocks should be treated with the same respect as assertions; don't add ones that test things you already know, and don't add ones that don't support the goal of the test.

In the case of using a top-down approach to implement, e.g., the user interface before dependencies such as model objects, both mocks and stubs are good choices. In this case tests will have to rely on behavior verification alone in any case, meaning that stubs lose their advantage of supporting less implementation-specific state verification. In the general sense, however, mocks always rely on behavior verification; thus, they are inherently more implementation specific.

16.8 Summary

In this chapter we have taken a deep dive into the concept of *test doubles*, focusing mainly on *stubs*, *spies* and, *mocks*. Although we have used stubs and spies frequently throughout Part III, *Real-World Test-Driven Development in JavaScript,* looking at them from a wider angle has allowed us to coin some common usage patterns and describe them using established terminology.

Having gotten through all of five sample projects without one, we investigated the effects of using a stubbing and mocking library in tests. The manual approach is easy to employ in JavaScript, and will take you far. Still, using a dedicated library can reduce the stubbing and mocking related scaffolding, which leads to leaner tests and less repetition. Removing manual stubbing logic in favor of a well tested library also reduces chances of bugs in tests.

In light of Sinon, the stubbing and mocking library, mocks were finally presented. Mocks are stubs pre-programmed with expectations that translate into behavior verification. Mocks fail early, by throwing an exception immediately upon receiving an unexpected call.

Closing off the chapter, we discussed mocks versus stubs, wherein we concluded that stubs are generally more versatile and should be used for isolation purposes that don't directly support the goal of the test. Apart from those cases, the choice between stubs and mocks for behavior verification largely is one of personal preference.

In the next, and last chapter, Chapter 17, *Writing Good Unit Tests,* we will extract and review some testing patterns and best practices from our previous sample projects.

Writing Good Unit Tests 17

Unit tests can be an incredible asset. When writing tests as part of the test-driven development cycle, tests help form the design of production code, provide us with an indication of progress, and help us scope down and only implement what we really need. When writing tests after the fact, they help form a suite of regression tests and a security net in which we can comfortably refactor code. However, simply adding unit tests to a project will not magically fix it. Bad tests not only provide little value, they can do actual damage to productivity and the ability to evolve the code base.

Writing good tests is a craft. Even if you already are a skilled programmer, you will find that getting good at writing tests takes time and practice. Throughout the example projects in Part III, *Real-World Test-Driven Development in JavaScript,* we have written a lot of tests, done a fair amount of refactoring, and gotten comfortable with test-driven development. In this final chapter we will identify some guidelines for writing quality tests. As you practice and improve your tests, you can build on this list, adding your own insights.

By the end of this chapter you will be able to better understand some of the choices we made throughout Part III, *Real-World Test-Driven Development in JavaScript,* as well as pinpoint problems that could have been solved in a better way.

17.1 Improving Readability

Writing tests that can be trusted, are easy to maintain, and clearly state their intent takes practice. If you have coded along with the examples in Part III, *Real-World Test-Driven Development in JavaScript,* you should already have some basic training doing this, and possibly even have started to develop a nose for good tests.

Readability is a key aspect of a good unit test. If a test is hard to read it is likely to be misunderstood. This can lead to unfortunate modifications of either tests or production code, causing the quality of both to drop over time. A good test suite effectively documents the code under test, and provides a simple overview of what the code can be expected to do and how it can be used.

17.1.1 Name Tests Clearly to Reveal Intent

The name of a test should clearly and unambiguously state what the purpose of the test is. A good name makes it easier to understand what a test is trying to achieve, thus it has more value as unit level documentation and it lessens the chance of someone changing the test without properly understanding what it's supposed to verify. A good name also shows up in the test runner's report when it fails, pinpointing the exact source of error.

When working with TDD, the test name is the very first time you put a feature down in code. Writing the requirement out in words may help us mentally prepare for the feature we are about to add. If you find it hard to clearly state what the test is supposed to do, then it is likely you have not properly recognized the goal of the test, and it is unlikely that jumping straight to writing test code will result in any kind of quality unit test, or production code for that matter.

17.1.1.1 Focus on Scannability

Good test names make test cases easy to scan. Scanning a test case with well-named tests should give us a good high-level understanding of what the module being tested does and how it is expected to behave in response to given input. It can also help us understand what kinds of cases are not accounted for, which can be useful when encountering trouble using a library in a specific way.

Although naming is one of those things in which personal preference does have a play in what is "clear," I've found the following rules of thumb to be of good help.

- JavaScript property identifiers can be arbitrary strings. Use this powerful feature to name tests with short sentences using spaces, no underscores or camelCasedTestNames.
- Using the word "should" underpins the test as a behavior specification.

- Keep names as short as possible without sacrificing clarity.

- Group-related tests in separate test cases and indicate the relation in the test case name, thus avoiding the same prefix in a large number of tests.

- Never state what code is expected to do using the word "and;" doing so indicates the test is not specific enough, i.e., it is likely trying to test more than one aspect of the target method.

- Focus on the *what* and *why*, not the *how*.

17.1.1.2 Breaking Free of Technical Limitations

All of the tests in Part III, *Real-World Test-Driven Development in JavaScript,* were written using libraries that consider any method whose name starts with "test" to be a test. This leaves room for adding other properties on the test case that are not run as tests. In the interest of using libraries without modification, we have rolled with this, ending up with a bunch of tests with names starting with "test should," which is a bit of a smell.

Because we can easily add helper functions in a closure surrounding the test case, there really is no need for the test case to reserve space for helper methods (i.e., function properties whose names do not start with the obligatory "test"). By considering *any* function-valued property a test, test cases could allow more flexibility in the naming of tests. Luckily, wrapping, e.g., JsTestDriver's `TestCase` function to do just that is simple. Listing 17.1 shows an enhanced test case function. It works just like the original, only all functions except `setUp` and `tearDown` are considered tests.

Listing 17.1 Enhancing JsTestDriver's test case function

```javascript
function testCaseEnhanced(name, tests) {
  var testMethods = {};
  var property;

  for (var testName in tests) {
    property = tests[testName];

    if (typeof property == "function" &&
      !/^(setUp|tearDown)$/.test(testName)) {
      testName = "test " + testName;
    }

    testMethods[testName] = property;
  }

  return TestCase(name, testMethods);
}
```

The function simply loops all the properties of the test object, prepends function property identifiers with "test," and delegates to the original `TestCase`. Listing 17.2, shows a test originally from Chapter 12, *Abstracting Browser Differences: Ajax,* using the enhanced test case.

Listing 17.2 Using the enhanced test case to improve test name clarity

```
testCaseEnhanced("RequestTest", {
  /* ... */

  "should obtain an XMLHttpRequest object": function () {
    ajax.get("/url");

    assert(ajax.create.called);
  }

  /* ... */
});
```

17.1.2 Structure Tests in Setup, Exercise, and Verify Blocks

White space can be used to underline the inherent setup/exercise/verify structure of tests. Listing 17.3, originally from Chapter 15, *TDD and DOM Manipulation: The Chat Client,* shows a test for the user form controller that expects the `handle-Submit` method to notify observers of the submitted user name. Notice how blank lines separate each of the setup/exercise/verify phases of the test.

Listing 17.3 Formatting tests with blank lines to improve readability

```
"test should notify observers of username": function () {
  var input = this.element.getElementsByTagName("input")[0];
  input.value = "Bullrog";
  this.controller.setModel({});
  this.controller.setView(this.element);
  var observer = stubFn();

  this.controller.observe("user", observer);
  this.controller.handleSubmit(this.event);

  assert(observer.called);
  assertEquals("Bullrog", observer.args[0]);
}
```

Physically separating setup, exercise, and verification makes it dead simple to see what setup is required and how to exercise the given behavior, as well as identifying the success criteria.

17.1.3 Use Higher-Level Abstractions to Keep Tests Simple

Unit tests should always target a single behavior, nothing more. Usually this correlates with a single assertion per test, but some behaviors are more complex to verify, thus requiring more assertions. Whenever we find ourselves repeating the same set of two or three assertions, we should consider introducing higher-level abstractions to keep tests short and clear.

17.1.3.1 Custom Assertions: Behavior Verification

Custom assertions are one way to abstract away compound verification. The most glaring example of this from Part III, *Real-World Test-Driven Development in JavaScript,* is the behavior verification of the stubs. Listing 17.4 shows a slightly modified test for the Comet client that expects the client's observers to be notified when the `dispatch` method is called.

Listing 17.4 Expecting observers to be notified

```
"test dispatch should notify observers": function () {
  var client = Object.create(ajax.cometClient);
  client.observers = { notify: stubFn() };

  client.dispatch({ someEvent: [{ id: 1234 }] });

  var args = client.observers.notify.args;
  assert(client.observers.notify.called);
  assertEquals("someEvent", args[0]);
  assertEquals({ id: 1234 }, args[1]);
}
```

Using the Sinon stubbing library introduced in Chapter 16, *Mocking and Stubbing,* we can verify the test using Sinon's higher-level `assertCalledWith` method instead, which makes the test more clearly state its intent, as seen in Listing 17.5.

Listing 17.5 Expecting observers to be notified

```
"test dispatch should notify observers":
sinon.test(function (stub) {
  var client = Object.create(ajax.cometClient);
  var observers = client.observers;
  stub(observers, "notify");

  client.dispatch({ custom: [{ id:1234 }] });

  assertCalledWith(observers.notify, "custom", { id:1234 });
})
```

17.1.3.2 Domain Specific Test Helpers

Another example of repeated patterns from Part III, *Real-World Test-Driven Development in JavaScript*, that could be simplified by a higher-level abstraction is testing of event handlers. Given that the chat client uses the custom `dom.addEventHandler` method in conjunction with `Function.prototype.bind` to bind event handlers, we could extract the scaffolding needed to test this into something like Listing 17.6.

Listing 17.6 Testing event handlers using a higher-level abstraction

```
"test should handle submit event with bound handleSubmit":
function () {
  expectMethodBoundAsEventHandler(
    this.controller, "handleSubmit", "submit", function () {
      this.controller.setView(this.element);
    }.bind(this)
  );
}
```

This simple test replaces two original tests from the user form controller's test case, and the imaginary helper method abstracts away some of the cruft related to stubbing the handler method and `addEventHandler`, as well as obtaining a reference to the handler function passed to it to verify that it is called with the object as `this`.

When introducing domain and/or project specific test helpers such as this, we can also test them to make sure they work as expected, and then use them throughout the project, reducing the amount of scaffolding test code considerably.

17.1.4 Reduce Duplication, Not Clarity

As with production code, we should actively remove duplication from tests to keep them apt for change. If we decide to change the way we create objects of a given type, it is preferable if that doesn't force us to change the creation of an object in 30 tests, unless all those tests specifically target the object creation.

However, there is a fine line to walk when reducing duplication in tests—if we do it too aggressively, we may end up removing important communication from a test. A good way to check if you have slimmed down a test too much is to extract it from its test case along with the name of the test case; is it still clear what behavior the test is describing? If it is not, e.g., because properties are not self-explanatory, or the state of the system is not clear, then we have taken away too much.

Listing 17.7 shows a test from the chat client's message-list controller. The test does not include code to create a controller instance, but still manages to clearly state that setting the view with `setView` causes the element set as view to have its class name set to "js-chat."

Listing 17.7 Reading a test in isolation

```
TestCase("MessageListControllerSetViewTest", {
  /* ... */

  "test should set class to js-chat": function () {
    this.controller.setView(this.element);

    assertClassName("js-chat", this.element);
  }
});
```

Notice how this test also uses the `assertClassName` assertion, which can be considered a high-level assertion.

To avoid repeating too much code throughout Part III, *Real-World Test-Driven Development in JavaScript,* I may have sinned against this guideline a few times. Listing 17.8 shows a test from the same test case that expects `addMessage` to create new DOM elements and append them to the view.

Listing 17.8 Possibly too aggressively DRYed test

```
"test should add dd element with message": function () {
  this.controller.addMessage({
    user: "Theodore",
    message: "We are one"
  });
```

```
var dds = this.element.getElementsByTagName("dd");
assertEquals(1, dds.length);
assertEquals("We are one", dds[0].innerHTML);
}
```

Although this test clearly states what happens when the addMessage method is called, it may not be immediately clear that this.element is associated with the controller by having been set through setView. Making the situation worse, we did not write a test that describes the fact that without first calling setView with a DOM element, the addMessage method is not able to do anything useful—a fact that is not visible from the test in question either.

We could improve the readability of the test by referring to the element as this.controller.view instead, but keeping the setView call inside the test probably yields the best readability. What other changes would you suggest to improve this test's readability in stand-alone mode?

17.2 Tests as Behavior Specification

When writing unit tests as part of test-driven development, we automatically treat tests as a specification mechanism—each test defines a distinct requirement and lays out the next goal to reach. Although we might want to occasionally pick up speed by introducing more code than "the smallest possible amount of test necessary to fail the test," doing so inside one and the same test rarely is the best choice.

17.2.1 Test One Behavior at a Time

Any given unit test should focus clearly on one specific behavior in the system. In most cases this can be directly related to the number of asserts, or if using mocks, expectations. Tests are allowed to have more than a single assert, but only when all the asserts logically test the same behavior. Listing 17.9 revisits a previous example of a test that uses three assertions to verify one behavior—that calling dispatch on the Comet client causes the observer to be notified of the right event and with the right data.

Listing 17.9 Verifying one behavior with three asserts

```
"test dispatch should notify observers": function () {
  var client = Object.create(ajax.cometClient);
  client.observers = { notify: stubFn() };
```

```
client.dispatch({ someEvent: [{ id: 1234 }] });

var args = client.observers.notify.args;
assert(client.observers.notify.called);
assertEquals("someEvent", args[0]);
assertEquals({ id: 1234 }, args[1]);
}
```

Testing only a single behavior in any given test means that when it fails, the source of failure will be obvious. This is a huge benefit because following this guideline will completely eradicate the need of a debugger to test the innards of a method. This single behavior focus also helps make the tests easier to understand.

17.2.2 Test Each Behavior Only Once

Re-testing behaviors already covered in existing tests adds no value to the specification of the system, neither does it help find bugs. It does, however, add to the maintenance burden. Testing the same behavior in more than one test means more tests to update whenever we want to change the behavior, and it means more tests will fail for the exact same reason, reducing the test case's ability to pinpoint erroneous behavior.

The most common source of duplicated verification comes from negligence; while testing each aspect of a method in dedicated tests, it is easy to inadvertently introduce an overlap between tests if we don't pay close attention. Another possible reason for re-testing verified behavior is lack of trust. If we trust our tests, there is no reason to question a previous test's validity by repeating an assertion.

Listing 17.10 shows a test from Chapter 13, *Streaming Data with Ajax and Comet,* in which we expect the `cometClient` not to start polling a second time if `connect` has already been called once. Notice how the test simply assumes that the first call works as expected. The behavior of the first call is covered by other tests, and there is no need to assert that `ajax.poll` *was* called the first time.

Listing 17.10 Assuming `connect` works the first time

```
"test should not connect if connected": function () {
  this.client.url = "/my/url";
  ajax.poll = stubFn({});
  this.client.connect();
  ajax.poll = stubFn({});
```

```
    this.client.connect();

    assertFalse(ajax.poll.called);
}
```

Another less obvious source of re-testing the same behavior is covering browser inconsistencies in the wrong places. If you find yourself testing for DOM-related quirks inside a method whose purpose is not to cover the specific quirk, you need to move the offending code into a dedicated function. This way you can verify that `performBuggyDOMRoutine` handles all the DOM quirkiness properly across browsers, and simply verify that depending interfaces use this method.

17.2.3 Isolate Behavior in Tests

When we test a single behavior at a time, pinpointing the source of error when tests fail is easy. However, discrepancies in indirect inputs may distort the results, causing tests to fail not because the targeted logic is faulty, but because it's dependencies are behaving in unexpected ways. Back in Part I, *Test-Driven Development,* we referred to these kinds of tests as "accidental integration tests." That sure sounds bad, but as we are about to discover, it does not need to be.

17.2.3.1 Isolation by Mocking and Stubbing

One way to completely isolate a unit is to stub or mock all of its dependencies. Some people will tell you this is in fact the *only* way to properly isolate behavior. Throughout Part III, *Real-World Test-Driven Development in JavaScript,* there are lots of examples of tests that stub generously to isolate behavior. Listing 17.11, originally from Chapter 15, *TDD and DOM Manipulation: The Chat Client,* shows a test for the chat client message form controller that stubs all the objects that `handleSubmit` interacts with in order to verify that the message is published through the model object.

Listing 17.11 Stubbing all dependencies

```
TestCase("FormControllerHandleSubmitTest", {
    "test should publish message": function () {
        var controller = Object.create(messageController);
        var model = { notify: stubFn() };

        controller.setModel(model);
        controller.handleSubmit();
```

```
      assert(model.notify.called);
      assertEquals("message", model.notify.args[0]);
      assertObject(model.notify.args[1]);
   }
});
```

Rather than performing state verification on the model object to verify that it received the given message, we stub the `notify` method and use behavior verification to verify that it was called correctly. Tests for the `cometClient` verify that calling the method correctly will make sure the message is correctly sent to the server.

17.2.3.2 Risks Introduced by Mocks and Stubs

In dynamic languages such as JavaScript, there is always a risk associated with test doubles. As an example, consider the test in Listing 17.12, which verifies that the form is not actually submitted when the user submits a message to the chat service.

Listing 17.12 Verifying that the form submit action is aborted

```
"test should prevent event default action": function () {
  this.controller.handleSubmit(this.event);

  assert(this.event.prevenDefault.called);
}
```

Having written this test, we have introduced a new requirement for the system under test. After confirming that it fails, we proceed to write the passing code. Once the test passes, we move on to the next behavior. Upon testing the resulting code in a browser, we will be shocked to find that the code throws an error when posting a message.

The observant reader will already have noticed the problem; we accidentally misspelled `preventDefault`, leaving out the first "t." Because the stub is in no way associated with a real exemplar of the kind of object we are faking, we have no safety net catching these kinds of errors for us. Languages like Java solve these kinds of problems with interfaces. Had the event stub been stated to implement the event interface, we would have realized our mistake, as the test would err because the stub did not implement `preventDefault`. Even if it did—e.g., through inheritance—the call to `prevenDefault` from production code would have erred because this method definitely isn't part of the event interface.

Introducing typos in method names may seem like a silly example, but it's a simple illustration of a problem that can take a lot more obscure forms. In the case of the misspelled method name, you probably would notice the mistake either while initially writing it, during the initial run or, while writing it *again* in production code. If the mismatch between the test double and the real object was the wrong order or number of arguments passed to a method, it would not have been as obvious.

While writing the code for the chat server originally covered in Chapter 14, *Server-Side JavaScript with Node.js,* I did in fact make such a mistake. In my initial attempt at the controller's `get` method, I made a mistake while constructing the expected output. As you might remember, the server was supposed to emit JSON responses that would work with the `cometClient`. Because my initial expectations deviated from the actual format used by the client object, the chat server did not work as expected upon finishing it, even though all the tests passed. The change to make it work was a simple one, but ideally we should avoid such mistakes.

This is not to say you shouldn't use stubs and mocks in your tests. They are effective tools, but need to be used with some care and attention. Always make sure to double check that your test doubles properly mirror the real deal. One way to achieve this is to use a real object as a starting point for the stub or mock. For instance, imagine a method like `sinon.stubEverything(target)`, which could be used to create a stub object with stub function properties corresponding to all the methods of the `target` object. This way you take away the chance of using a fake method that doesn't exist in production code.

17.2.3.3 Isolation by Trust

Another way to isolate units is to make sure that any object the unit interacts with can somehow be trusted. Obviously, mocks and stubs can generally be trusted so long as they properly mirror the objects they mimic.

Objects that are already tested can also be trusted. The same *should* be true for any third party library code in use. When dependencies are previously tested and known to work as expected, the chance of failing a test due to uncooperative dependencies is small enough to provide acceptable isolation.

Although such tests can be considered "accidental integration tests," they usually integrate only a small group of objects, and do so in a controlled manner. The up side to using real objects is that we can use state verification, thus loosening the coupling between test code and production code. This gives us more room to refactor the implementation without having to change the tests, thus reducing the maintenance burden of the application as a whole.

17.3 Fighting Bugs in Tests

Developers who are unfamiliar with unit testing often ask "how do you test your tests?" The answer, of course, is that we don't. That does not imply that we do not take measures to reduce defects in tests. The most important way to reduce the chance of bugs in tests is to never implement logic in tests. A unit test should be a simple sequence of assignments and function calls followed by one or more assertions.

Apart from keeping tests stupid, the most important tool to catch erroneous tests is to write and run them before implementing the passing code.

17.3.1 Run Tests before Passing Them

When tests are written before the required production code, they should also be run before passing it. Doing so allows us to verify that the test fails for the expected reasons, thus giving us a chance to catch errors in the test itself.

Failing a test with an articulated expectation as to how and why the test should fail is in fact the most effective means with which we can fight buggy tests. Skipping this point, we might move on to pass the test immediately. As soon as we have started writing production code, we are a lot less likely to discover faulty testing logic and might as well end up passing the test, thus sneaking the wrong behavior into production code without having tests that can tell us as much.

17.3.2 Write Tests First

To be able to run tests before passing them we obviously need to write them first as well. Because this book has given some insight into the test-driven development cycle and how it can apply to JavaScript, the recommendation to write tests first should not come as a surprise.

Writing tests upfront has benefits beyond making it easier to catch faulty tests. Tests first ensure that code is inherently testable. If you have ever attempted to retrofit unit tests onto code that was not originally written with testability in mind, you will appreciate the importance of testable code.

Writing testable code is not useful only to test it. Unit tests are secluded sample uses of production code, and if writing a test for any given behavior is hard, well, then using that particular behavior is hard. If using a small part of the code base requires half an application's worth of setup, then the design might not be optimal. For example, requiring a DOM element and its CSS API in order to transition a color from red to green is a good example of code that is hard to use for the same reasons as why it is hard to test.

Ensuring that code is testable means ensuring it is loosely coupled and well factored, thus flexible and easy to use, both as a whole and in parts. Writing tests upfront as we do in test-driven development builds testability into the code.

17.3.3 Heckle and Break Code

Sometimes a test suite will be all green, yet the production code clearly exhibits defects. The source to these kinds of errors are often found in the integration between moving parts of the application, but sometimes they can be the result of edge cases not catered for, or worse, bugs in tests.

A great way to smoke out errors in tests and generally assess the quality of a test suite, is to intentionally introduce errors in production code and then make sure the tests fail, and for the right reasons. The following "attacks" can prove useful to find deficiencies in tests.

- Flip the value of boolean expressions.
- Remove return values.
- Misspell or null variables and function arguments.
- Introduce off-by-one errors in loops.
- Mutate the value of internal variables.

For each intentional deficiency you introduce, run the tests. If they all pass, you know that you have either stumbled upon untested code or code that simply doesn't do anything. Either capture the bug with a new unit test or remove the offending code, and continue.

17.3.4 Use JsLint

JsLint[1] is a "JavaScript Code Quality Tool." Inspired by lint for C, it detects syntactical errors, bad practices, and generally provides many more warnings than most JavaScript runtimes do today. Syntax errors can cause weird problems in test cases. A misplaced semicolon or comma can cause only some of your tests to run. Making matters worse, the test runner may not be able to warn you about some tests not being run. Using JsLint both on production code and tests alike will help you remove typos and other syntax errors, making sure the tests run as expected.

---

1. http://www.jslint.com/

17.4 Summary

In this final chapter we have reviewed some simple guidelines that can help improve the quality of unit tests. Tests, when done right are a great asset, but bad tests can be worse than no tests because they introduce a significant overhead in maintenance and complicate working with code without providing any real value.

The guidelines presented throughout this chapter were divided into three groups: techniques to improve readability, an important quality of a good unit test; techniques to generate true unit tests that stay at the unit level; and last, techniques that help avoid buggy tests.

By working through the example projects in Part III, *Real-World Test-Driven Development in JavaScript,* and viewing them from a wider angle both in this chapter and the previous, you should have gained a good understanding of what unit testing and test-driven development is—and isn't. Now it is up to you. The only way to get better is to gain as much experience as possible, and I urge you to start practicing immediately. Create your own learning tests, add features to the example projects from the book, or start new projects of your own using TDD. Once you have grown comfortable within the process that is test-driven development, you won't go back—you will become a happier and more productive developer. Good luck!

Bibliography

[1] Martin Fowler. *Refactoring: Improving the Design of Existing Code*. Addison-Wesley, 1999.

[2] Hamlet D'Arcy. Forgotten refactorings. http://hamletdarcy.blogspot.com/2009/06/forgotten-refactorings.html, June 2009.

[3] Kent Beck. *Test-Driven Development By Example*. Addison-Wesley, 2002.

[4] Wikipedia. You ain't gonna need it. http://en.wikipedia.org/wiki/You_ain't_gonna_need_it.

[5] Douglas Crockford. *JavaScript: The Good Parts*. O'Reilly Media, 2008.

[6] Douglas Crockford. Durable objects. http://yuiblog.com/blog/2008/05/24/durable-objects/, May 2008.

[7] Gerard Meszaros. *xUnit Test Patterns: Refactoring Test Code*. Addison-Wesley, 2007.

Index

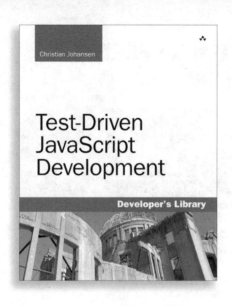

FREE Online Edition

Your purchase of **Test-Driven JavaScript Development** includes access to a free online edition for 45 days through the Safari Books Online subscription service. Nearly every Addison-Wesley Professional book is available online through Safari Books Online, along with more than 5,000 other technical books and videos from publishers such as Cisco Press, Exam Cram, IBM Press, O'Reilly, Prentice Hall, Que, and Sams.

SAFARI BOOKS ONLINE allows you to search for a specific answer, cut and paste code, download chapters, and stay current with emerging technologies.

Activate your FREE Online Edition at
www.informit.com/safarifree

> **STEP 1:** Enter the coupon code: AIMEHBI.

> **STEP 2:** New Safari users, complete the brief registration form.
> Safari subscribers, just log in.

If you have difficulty registering on Safari or accessing the online edition, please e-mail customer-service@safaribooksonline.com